Gender and Food in Transnational East Asias

Gender and Food in Transnational East Asias

Toward a New Dialogue across Boundaries

Edited by
Jooyeon Rhee, Chikako Nagayama,
and Eric Ping Hung Li

LEXINGTON BOOKS
Lanham • Boulder • New York • London

Published by Lexington Books
An imprint of The Rowman & Littlefield Publishing Group, Inc.
4501 Forbes Boulevard, Suite 200, Lanham, Maryland 20706
www.rowman.com

6 Tinworth Street, London SE11 5AL, United Kingdom

Jooyeon Rhee. "Gender Politics in Food Escape: Korean Masculinity in TV Cooking Shows in South Korea," *Journal of Popular Film and Television*, 47:1, 56–64. Taylor & Francis Group, 2019.

Yuko Minowa, Olga Khomenko, and Russell Belk. "Social Change and Gendered Gift-Giving Rituals: A Historical Analysis of Valentine's Day in Japan," *Journal of Macromarketing*, 31:1. SAGE Publications, 2011.

British Library Cataloguing in Publication Information Available

Library of Congress Cataloging-in-Publication Data

Names: Rhee, Jooyeon, editor. | Nagayama, Chikako, 1971- editor. | Li, Eric Ping Hung, 1978- editor.
Title: Gender and food in transnational East Asias : towards a new dialogue across boundaries / edited by Jooyeon Rhee, Chikako Nagayama and Eric Ping Hung Li.
Description: Lanham : Lexington Books, [2021] | Includes bibliographical references and index.
Identifiers: LCCN 2021034357 (print) | LCCN 2021034358 (ebook) | ISBN 9781793623546 (cloth) | ISBN 9781793623553 (epub)
Subjects: LCSH: Food supply—Social aspects—East Asia. | Food consumption—Social aspects—East Asia. | Women—East Asia—Social conditions.
Classification: LCC HD9016.E182 G46 2021 (print) | LCC HD9016.E182 (ebook) | DDC 363.8095—dc23
LC record available at https://lccn.loc.gov/2021034357
LC ebook record available at https://lccn.loc.gov/2021034358

Contents

Acknowledgments

The making of this volume would not have been possible had we not received generous support and encouragement from institutions and many generous souls. The editors are grateful for all the contributors who had faith in this project and shared their finest research with us. We worked together during the extremely challenging time that posed numerous problems on private, communal, and social lives. We thank them for their time, mutual support, encouragement, and collective spirit, all of which were essential in completing the volume. The Asian Studies Program at the Penn State University, Graduate School of Humanities at Nagoya University, and the Faculty of Management at the University of British Columbia—Okanagan campus—were always supportive and intellectually stimulating homes. Special thanks to our professional editors, Nina and Paul, for their professionalism, patience, and expertise that made this edited volume possible. Last, but not least, we would like to express our thankfulness to our families in the United States, Japan, Canada, Korea, the People's Republic of China (PRC), Hong Kong, and Taiwan.

Chapter 7 originally appeared in *The Journal of Popular Film and Television* 47, issue 1 (2019); and chapter 13 is a slightly revised version of an article that originally appeared in the *Journal of Macromarketing* 31, issue 1 (2011). We thank these two journals for permitting us to publish materials in this volume.

This work was supported by the Seed Program for Korean Studies through the Ministry of Education of the Republic of Korea and the Korean Studies Promotion Service of the Academy of Korean Studies (AKS-2020-INC-2230002).

Introduction

Jooyeon Rhee, Chikako Nagayama, and Eric Ping Hung Li

What are the impacts of food on gender dynamics? How do food and culinary practices direct us to new points of view about gender roles and relations in contemporary East Asia and in Asian diaspora communities? How do material and aesthetic representations of food enable us to grapple with multiple sites of gender conflicts in the contexts of nations, neoliberal globalism, and domesticity? How does the study of food widen the intellectual horizon over gender issues and enhance constructive and critical dialogues across multiple disciplines and regions? These are the questions that this volume aimed to tackle back in 2019, shortly before we celebrated the upcoming year. While experiencing the magnitude of the pandemic since then, we felt these questions were increasingly urgent since food and eating, as the most fundamental condition for living, became more precarious than ever before. Direct and indirect experiences of the shortage of food due to the massive unemployment rate and travel bans, increased domestic duties for head cooks in families, the safety of food and health regulations, and so on began to affect our physical and emotional lives tremendously. Government-sanctioned lockdowns, quarantines, and "stay at home" orders made our inquiries about domesticity, belonging, and mobility even more vital and simultaneously urged us to revisit the significance of transnationality under this condition. We and our contributors, who worked in isolation but with a strong sense of collective purpose, have been acutely aware of the importance of studying the relationship between food and gender.

Countries in East Asia (e.g., mainland China, Hong Kong, Japan, Korea, and Taiwan) have been experiencing rapid socioeconomic, cultural, and political changes, all of which greatly influence gender dynamics there. The production and consumption of food encapsulates the changes that affect social positions of women and men and their relationships with their families, the state, and their work; and shape their gender, sexual, ethnic, and national identities. The transnational movement of food and people between East Asia and the rest of the world is also increasingly visible, forming various forces behind the cultural and political constructions of gender politics among and beyond Asian diasporas as well. By critically engaging with history, practices, and representation of food as a constructive window to articulate gender dynamics in the East Asian region, this volume approaches food as a symbolic and material site where gender roles and identities are imagined, performed, and negotiated. It argues that a critical engagement with practices and representations of food from gender perspectives can enhance our understanding of the society and culture of transnational East Asias.

Our use of "transnational East Asias" resonates with the scholarly attempts that have been made in the last two decades to create theoretical and conceptual connections among multiple disciplines and regions in Asian studies in the age of neoliberal globalization that intensifies unequal power relations, especially unequal gender relations. Kuan-Hsing Chen and Chua Beng Huat put forward an intellectual platform, *Inter-Asia Cultural Studies*, to link "together communities in Asia" and "Asia to the global community" (2007, 2). More recently, Tina Chen and Eric Hayot (2015) echo the call for active conversations between Asian and Asian American studies "to approach the aesthetics, history, and culture of Asia from a perspective that undermines the centrality either of European notions of the unparticular universal or of Asian varieties of the un-universalizable particular" (viii). These attempts are a response to the quest to generate new or alternative modes of knowledge production about "Asia" that may be understood as "an emotional signifier to call for regional integration and solidarity" against the backdrop of the neoliberal colonization process (Chen 2010, 213). We are committed to collectively engage in gender studies by deploying theories and histories across disciplinary and regional boundaries to build a bridge between East Asian countries and Asian America by paying attention to movements of thoughts, ideas, materials, and people. However, we are also mindful about the previously constructed colonial structures upon which alternative knowledge productions must be built (Chen 2010). All contributors make succinct connections between the past and present as well as between different regions by identifying and critiquing imperialism, nationalism, and modernization through which the categories and practices of gender and sexuality are reified and continuously transforming in modern East Asia and Asian communities in the United States.

This self-reflective engagement with the transnational also reflects the impact of transnational feminism in gender scholarship, paralleling the so-called Third Wave feminism which questions the monolithic category of "women" in the theorization of social inequality (Grewal and Kaplan 2001;

hooks 2000; Shome 2006). The volume permits a critical exploration of naturalized identities of gender, sexuality, nationality, or ethnicity, while paying close attention to the mechanisms of social mobilization, collectivity, and belonging. In doing so, our chapters also shed light on marginalized people's "complex agency as situated subjects," in aiming at "building resistance and solidarity across borders" (Mohanty 2013, 967). Moreover, this volume contributes to gender scholarship with the following unique features that have been understudied in the fields of gender studies, food studies, and communication/media studies in East Asian contexts.

First, it allows a new way of conceptualizing gender through exploring the interconnectedness between material culture and the symbolic practice of food. This approach addresses a limitation of poststructuralist and postmodern feminism, "flight from nature" (Alaimo 2008, 237), and echoes cultural studies' turn to the materiality and affects of the everyday (Highmore 2010). Second, while gender theories have initially tackled concerns raised by feminist scholars in the West, gender scholarship is now calling for closer attention to intricate ways in which social inequality and identity politics manifest according to local conditions outside the conventional focus. This volume illustrates how the investigation of the relationship between food and gender provides new possibilities to expand our conceptualization of gender. Third, it takes cross-cultural, translocal, and transnational approaches. While each chapter examines the production, distribution, consumption, and representation of food at different locations in East Asia and North America, all chapters are organized under the volume's overall agenda of identifying commonalities and differences between the locations. To carefully avoid overgeneralization and de-historicization, each chapter's systemic theorization of gender and other social relations enables this comparative view. When these regions have been experiencing a dramatically increased level of economic and cultural interactions between them in recent decades, it is crucial to examine the interactions from cross-cultural, translocal, and transnational perspectives. Fourth, this volume is highly interdisciplinary, which aims to reach wider audiences. Contributors draw on sociology, literature, media studies, business anthropology, sexology, and history in their works in this volume. They not only move across multiple disciplines to present refreshing and interesting observations of the relationship between food and gender but also further produce stimulating dialogues for scholars beyond their studies of East Asia and Asian diasporas.

FOOD, BODY, AND EMBODIMENT

Studies of food have witnessed growing diversity in terms of their regional coverage, subject matters, and disciplinary approaches in the English-speaking world. The wealth of the previous and current studies of food in history, sociology, ethnography, literature, visual media, health and security, and gender/sexuality/race not only opened up many possibilities to explore the symbolic and material importance of quotidian, religious, communal, and individual practices of food in human history but also provided useful tools to grapple with pressing social and environmental issues that immediately concern our lives. Recent studies of gendered, racialized, and sexualized notions of Asian food in North America as well as diasporic communities' identity formation through their practices of and relationship with ethnic food in the United States are also noteworthy. Their unpacking of colonial, imperial, and neoliberal food systems, distribution, and consumption underpin the discursive formation of diasporic identities, gender, and racial inequality and discrimination (Ray 2004, 2016; Mannur 2009; Ku, Manalansan IV, and Mannur 2013; Ku 2014; Padoongpatt 2017).

Food allows creative ways to approach gender by shifting conventional focuses in gender studies. The body has been a focal point to articulate the systems of representation and subject formation, through which gendered ways of doing things manifest in society and culture. The politics of the gaze, for example, has been critically examined to grasp gendered positioning in visual culture. As Laura Mulvey's (1975) now canonical work highlights and bell hooks (1992) further complicates, the cinematic gaze differently constructs the dominant and marginalized subject positions along the line of gender and race, while reinforcing the pleasure of looking via the objectification of particular bodies and making others absent from the screen. To challenge this perpetuating inequality in visual politics, filmmaking by women (and women of color) is encouraged (Doane 1981; Trinh 1991; Vanstone 2007), whereas the agency of female film subjects is also explored, and the subject-object binary has been contested (Williams 1991; Swindle 2011). When food enters our research focus, on the other hand, women's active engagement and their roles of both maker and consumer of food come to the fore. But woman's agency is not simply cerebrated here. In our volume, the combined analysis of food and gender invites our attention to the complex ways in which woman's agency is shaped under unique purposes and circumstances—the reinvention of a national identity, war mobilization, maneuverings for survival during the famine, and feminist movements, to name a few.

Socioeconomic and cultural dimensions of the relationship between food and gender have also been prominent in food studies, probing the centrality of gender identity, relations, performance, and representation through food in a North American context (Counihan and Kaplan 1998; Inness 2001; Cairns and Johnston 2015; Parsons 2015; Koch 2019). For systemic cross-cultural comparisons of gender relations in East Asian societies, a substantial number of previous studies have examined women's participation in paid work, hours spent on domestic chores, divorce rates, and cultural manifestation of Confucianism (Tsuya, Bumpass, and Choe 2000; Dommaraju and Jones 2011; Kang, Koo, and Kim 2012). But there has been a growing body of literature that approaches food from a gender perspective in East Asia, examining a historically grounded notion of appetite in China (Farquhar 2002), the hegemonic construction of motherhood in the preparation of lunch boxes for children (Allison 1991), women's food activism (Kimura 2016), gendered representations of food in media (Rhee 2019; Lim and Khiun 2019), and so on. This volume is intended to expand the constructive engagement with the relationship between food and gender by generating a ground for cross-cultural dialogues across disciplinary and regional boundaries.

A NEW DIALOGUE ACROSS BOUNDARIES

In transnational East Asias, food consumption represents not only various local/ethnic cultures but also the changing market landscape that is shaped by global economic systems. Recent food consumption practices reveal multiple effects of "globalization" in terms of the transnational movement of food and regional ingredients across major cities in the world, and in the shared consciousness of food safety, health and environment, and economic inequality. The inseparable nature of food and globalization is witnessed in the increasing variety of food choices and the emerging fusion foods in the East Asian market.

New food choices and brands, consumption rituals, rules, spaces, and consumer identities were introduced to the East Asian markets through market agents and other cultural advocates, popular culture producers, and ambassadors (Ashkenazi and Jacob 2000; Veeck 2000; Watson 1997; Yan 2000). The diversity of food also offers new identity markers and consumption experiences for East Asian consumers (including the East Asian diaspora) to differentiate themselves from their fellow citizens or their foreign counterparts (Augustin-Jean 2002; Wu 2002; Wu and Cheung 2002; Yu 2014). The ongoing reconfiguration of East Asian foodways also redefines gender roles and expectations (Allison 1991; Holden 1997) as well as sexuality and imaginations (Probyn 2000) within and beyond the local geographic boundaries. The commodification of food is also connected to various geopolitical and social movements in East Asias. For instance, the rise of plant-based diets and veganism could be connected with the globalization of foods such as soy (Du Bois, Tan, and Mintz 2008).

While these studies paved an innovative way to study gender and food in each country in East Asia, contributors to this volume employed a variety of theoretical lenses to explore complex issues associated with gender identities, political economy, ethnicization, consumerism, and food production and consumption. Our chapters illustrate the ongoing reconfiguration and representation of gender and foodways among East Asian and diasporic communities. Although gender mainstreaming in policy-making, diversification of gender expressions, and the border crossing of food cultures are in parallel with global trends, each chapter considers their unique manifestations at a local site. The volume reveals that food is not only obtained, cooked, served, and eaten but also displayed, saved, exchanged, and remembered, through which processes actual gender relations and sexualities are constructed and performed.

ORGANIZATION

Part I: Imagination of Culinary Nationalism focuses on culinary imaginations of nations, covering the contentious relationship between the state and citizens in wartime Japan during which time housewives became a scapegoat for food shortages, the state's ideological construction of culinary traditions by gendering food and cooking in contemporary China, and the discursive formation of gastronationalism as shown in popular food films and television in Korea.

Nathan Hopson examines the gendered political economy of Japanese public discourses about food and food waste during the Pacific War years of 1941 to 1945 in "Women, Waste, and War: Food, Gender, and Rationalization in Wartime Japanese Discourse." Kitchen waste, which was generally considered the province of women (housewives especially), was seen as a significant threat to the war effort. Methodologically, Hopson traces how these ideas were translated from laboratories and think tanks into public discourse in *Yomiuri Shinbun*, eventually burdening housewives on Japan's home front while making it easier for military and political leaders to view the war as winnable long after it was lost.

Guojun (Sawyer) He, Dandan Fang, and Jonathan Deschênes discuss how the People's Republic of China (PRC) has been attempting to promote gender equality while simultaneously promoting national food in "A Bite of the Gender Equality Discourse in China: Observations from Food." By viewing the PRC's popular food documentary series, *A Bite of China*, as a state apparatus that promotes gender equality in contemporary China, they closely analyze the content and reception of the series to unravel the relationship between the ideological construction of national Chinese food and gender.

Maria Osetrova explores how the imagination of national food is expressed in gendered terms in the 2000s by examining the popular mass media representation of gastronationalism in "Young Men in Chef Uniforms and

Suffering Mothers in *Hanbok*: Gendered Representation of National Cuisine in the *Sikkaek* Series." Osetrova explains how "Korean national food" was constructed by providing the historical development of royal cuisine traditions and modern cooking practices. Her analysis of the television and film adaptations of the graphic novel (*manhwa*) *Sikkaek* reveals the roots of current gender representation in the public discourse regarding Korean cuisine and—more broadly—the relations between nationalism, national food, and gender.

Part II: Body and Embodiment grapples with the gendered and sexualized female body and female agency by examining cultural expressions and social actions over the literary representation of gendered cannibalism during the Great Leap Forward in China, separatist and exclusive feminist reactions to animal rights and veganism in Korea, and the literary deconstruction of the myth of the male-centered practices of aphrodisiacs in Taiwan.

Shelley W. Chan discusses the problematic relationship between food, gender, and politics in "The Body as Food: Gender, Eating, and Cannibalism in Yan Lianke's *The Four Books*." Chan shows how the narrative of food, both edible and forbidden, and that of eating are not only politically and morally constructed but also articulated in a gender discourse in the Confucian-Communist cultural context. Chan gives a particular emphasis to gendered cannibalism in the setting of the great famine during the Great Leap Forward Campaign to illustrate how women in China are victims of both the masculine state power and fellow citizens who are deeply influenced by traditional patriarchy.

Su Young Choi raises the question as to how Korean women who call themselves vegan feminists identify themselves and strategize their activism in order to characterize the boundary of Korean popular feminism's exclusive politics in "'Veganism Will Rise like Feminism': The Porous Contestation of Intersectional Vegan Feminism against the Exclusive Politics of Korean Popular Feminism." Choi presents a recent debate about the potency and limits of a renewal of feminism since the mid-2010s in South Korea and the conceptual framework of popular feminism. By utilizing qualitative interviewing, textual analysis, and materials from online and offline texts, Choi argues that vegan feminists have contradictory relationships with Korean popular feminism, in which their intersectional criticism is often mixed with an imitation of the separatist or exclusive practices of popular feminism.

In "Embodying Carnal Appetites: Food and Sexuality in Li Ang's *Mandarin Duck Aphrodisiacs*," Chien-wei Pan discusses how Li Ang brings to light multiple meanings of aphrodisiacs by means of her characterization of various women who are gratified by food and sex. Pan argues that Li's work challenges the Chinese Daoist belief of young women as men's symbolic aphrodisiacs by instead presenting women who eat aphrodisiacs and enjoy sex without men. By focusing on female carnal appetites, Pan sees that Li Ang highlights eccentric womanhood in order to transcend the male imaginations of national identities.

Part III: Performance of Masculinity and Femininity sheds light on the manifestation of gender norms and traits in cultural production and everyday life, such as the media performance of effeminate masculinity, by associating men's engagement with cooking and domesticity in Korea; female agency embodied in the practice of domestic femininity through women's active participation in "cook-and-save" cooking practices in Japan; women's self-awareness of physical beauty and active internalization of the discourse of thinness in Taiwan; and the literary configuration of the Cultural Revolution through the depiction of emasculated male intellectuals and empowered women in China.

Jooyeon Rhee's "Gender Politics in Food Escape: Korean Masculinity in TV Cooking Shows in South Korea" examines some of the most popular cooking shows to explore how the image of caring, comforting, and resourceful culinary masculinity in fact reinforces the existing gender norms and hierarchy. TV cooking shows have gained immense popularity in South Korea in the last few years. Rhee shows that male chefs and foodies play a crucial role in providing audiences with a space of domestic comfort in the midst of the intensely competitive and demanding social reality in these TV shows.

Chikako Nagayama's "Neoliberal Women's Agency and Time-Space Management in the Cook-and-Save Method, *Tsukurioki*" offers an illuminating analysis of the relationship between the *joshiryoku* (the female power) discourse and female agency with her examination of the popularity of *tsukurioki* (cook-and-save) books in contemporary Japan. The *tsukurioki* phenomenon in contemporary Japan shows that women turn to practical tools for home cooks to acquire and develop their time and space management, although their unpaid and feminized domestic work is still veiled under the "therapeutic discourse of consumer culture" as promoted in the neoliberal age. Nagayama unpacks the ambivalence of the *tsukurioki* discourse in her provision of the historical dimension of women and cooking in this chapter, with a close examination of the production, consumption, and perception of *tsukurioki* books.

Amélie Keyser-Verreault's "Eating as a Way of Performing Gender: The Intersection of Food, Gender, and Human Capital in Taiwan" seeks to inaugurate a discussion on the relationship between food and the quest for beauty in Taiwan's neoliberal context, focusing on how women use specific ways of eating in their gender performativity. She argues that beauty is a determinant part of women's human capital and that neoliberal subjects must then continually perform important aesthetic labor, including food-related practices, in order to keep their capital attractive.

Gabriel F. Y. Tsang focuses on Zhang Xianliang's reflective novella *Mimosa* (1984) in "(Post-)traumatic Logic of Socialism, Hunger, and Masculinity in Zhang Xianliang's *Mimosa* (1984)," which epitomizes the anti-intellectual history of Mao's China with its fictional record of personal experiences in the early Deng era. Food is a key to accessing the intersection of post-traumatic memories and reimagined gender politics that marked the specific ambivalence of Zhang. An illustration of the representation of food, as a pivotal signifier to determine the power relation between two protagonists during a famine, supports Tsang's argument that the narrative responses to hunger could modify masculinity and empower women beyond socialist regulations and patriarchal conventions.

Part IV: Transnational Practice of Food and Gender examines the intersectionality of consumerism, spatiality, and transnationality in the context of emerging popular culture and the transnational diasporic community in Korea, Japan, and the United States. It interrogates how the transnational movement of food creates new consumer spaces and spatializes consumption patterns of food along the line of gender in Korea, the ways in which Chinese cooking and cookbooks became a site of manifestation of female agency for a Chinese American woman in the Unites States, and how gender roles became a grounding force behind the transformation of the Valentine's Day gift-giving ritual in Japan.

Eric Ping Hung Li, Somin Lee, and Matt M. Husain employ Lefebvre's conception of space to illustrate the interrelationship of gender, food, and space in the context of Korean popular food (K-Food) culture in "Fashioning K-Food: New Gendered Space and Culture in South Korea." They first examine the surge of "K-Food" as a part of the *Hallyu* (or "Korean Wave") culture and as a new trend in the local food culture. They then adopt Lefebvre's framework to showcase the market construction of gendered representations in retail food space. Through the qualitative case studies of food retailers in Korea, the chapter analyzes the complexity, multiplicity, and dynamicity of market-mediated gendered food consumption. They argue that the spatial setting of K-Food not only renews the definitions and standards of "fashion" but also reinforces the gender hierarchy and representations of gender.

In her chapter on the re-presentation of ethnic cuisine in the transnational space, Violetta Ravagnoli explores Grace Chu's contributions to a new identity for Chinese at home and overseas, be it imagined or experienced, in "Grace Chu: Chinese Cooking at the Crossroad of Ethnicization and Emplacement." By analyzing Chu's life, her personal papers, and publications, Ravagnoli stresses the transnational connections behind ethnic cuisines and ultimately shows how Chu's usage of food speaks of her agency as a woman, mother, business enthusiast, and translocal actor.

In their chapter "Social Change and Gendered Gift-Giving Rituals: A Historical Analysis of Valentine's Day in Japan," Yuko Minowa, Olga Khomenko, and Russell Belk discuss the historical transformation of the consumption ritual of Valentine's Day in Japan. They provide a visual and textual analysis of advertisements in print media over the past fifty years. The chapter captures changes in meanings, functions, and the structure of gift-giving rituals corresponding to changes in the national economy, social values, consumer ideology, and gender roles and power relationships in Japanese society. This study supplements the very limited literature on Japanese gift-giving rituals.

In conclusion, this volume places the relationship between food and gender in cross-cultural, cross-regional, and transnational contexts because it aims to identify how global politics, economy, and culture influence gender dynamics in the region; to investigate how regional specificity drives multiple social and cultural actors to maintain or shift the existing gender hierarchy, inequality, and sexual behavior; and to create a collective scholarly channel that can further garner the scholarship of gender and food. The editors and contributors hope that it can be an intellectual platform that further generates constructive and critical ways of doing gender in transnational East Asias by bringing together scholars and students from multiple disciplines and regional interests. This volume will be useful for scholars and students from the fields of anthropology, cultural and media studies, food studies, gender studies, marketing and consumer behavior, sociology, anthropology, urban studies, and diaspora studies. It will also appeal to practitioners, policy-makers, and cultural activists/advocates as well as members of the general public who are interested in learning more about the relationship between gender and food in the transnational East Asian context.

REFERENCES

Alaimo, Stacy. 2008. "Trans-corporeal Feminisms and The Ethical Space of Nature." In *Material Feminisms*, edited by Stacy Alaimo and Susan Hekman, 237–264. Bloomington: Indiana University Press.

Allison, Anne. 1991. "Japanese Mothers and Obentōs: The Lunch-Box as Ideological State Apparatus." *Anthropological Quarterly* 64 (4): 195–208.

Ashkenazi, Michael, and Jeanne Jacob. 2000. *The Essence of Japanese Cuisine: An Essay on Food and Culture*. Philadelphia, PA: University of Pennsylvania Press.

Augustin-Jean, Louis. 2002. "Food Consumption, Food Perception and the Search for a Macanese Identity." In *The Globalization of Chinese Food*, edited by David Y. H. Wu and Sidney C. H. Cheung, 113–130. Honolulu: University of Hawai'i Press.

Cairns, Kate, and Josee Johnston. 2015. *Food and Femininity*. New York: Bloomsbury.

Chen, Kuan-Hsing. 2010. *Asia as Method: Towards Deimperialization*. Durham: Duke University Press.

Chen, Kuan-Hsing, and Chua Beng Huat, eds. 2007. *The Inter-Asia Cultural Studies Reader*. New York: Routledge.

Chen, Tina, and Eric Hayot. 2015. "What Does It Mean to Study Global Asias?" *Verge: Studies in Global Asias* 1 (1): vi–xv.

Counihan, Carole M., and Steven L. Kaplan, eds. 1998. *Food and Gender: Identity and Power*. New York: Routledge.

Doane, Mary Anne. 1981. "Women's Stake: Filming the Female Body." *October* 7: 22–36.

Dommaraju, Premchand, and Gavin Jones. 2011. "Divorce Trends in Asia." *Asian Journal of Social Science* 39: 725–750.

Du Bois, Christine M., Chee-Beng Tan, and Sidney Mintz. 2008. *The World of Soy*. Urbana and Chicago: University of Illinois Press.

Farquhar, Judith. 2002. *Appetites: Food and Sex in Post-Socialist China*. Durham: Duke University Press.

Grewal, Inderpal, and Caren Kaplan. 2001. "Global Identities: Theorizing Transnational Studies of Sexuality." *GLQ: Journal of Lesbian and Gay Studies* 7 (4): 663–679.

Highmore, Ben. 2010. "Bitter After Taste: Affect, Food and Social Aesthetics." In *The Affect Studies Reader*, edited by Melissa Gregg and Gregory J. Seigworth, 118–137. Durham: Duke University Press.

Holden, T. J. M. 1997. "The Overcooked and Underdone: Masculinities in Japanese Food Programming." In *Food and Culture: A Reader (Second Edition)*, edited by Carole Counihan and Penny Van Esterik, 202–220. New York: Routledge.

hooks, bell. 1992. *Black Looks: Race and Representation*. Boston, MA: South End Press.

———. 2000. *Feminism Is for Everybody: Passionate Politics*. Boston, MA: South End Press.

Inness, Sherrie A. 2001. *Kitchen Culture in America: Popular Representations of Food, Gender, and Race*. Philadelphia, PA: University of Pennsylvania Press.

Kang, Myung Koo, and Soo Ah Kim. 2012. "Are Chinese and Korean Families Confucian?: An Interpretive Analysis of Representation in Chinese and Korean Dramas." *Korean Social Sciences Review* 2 (1): 131–150.

Kimura, Aya Hirata. 2016. *Radiation Brain Moms and Citizen Scientists: The Gender Politics of Food Contamination after Fukushima*. Durham: Duke University Press.

Koch, Shelley L. 2019. *Gender and Food: A Critical Look at the Food System*. Lanham, MD: Rowman and Littlefield

Ku, Ji-song. 2014. *Dubious Gastronomy: The Cultural Politics of Eating Asian in the USA*. Honolulu: University of Hawaii Press.

Ku, Ji-song, Martin F. Manalansan IV, and Anita Mannur, eds. 2013. *Eating Asian America*. New York: New York University Press.

Lim, Eunice, and Liew Kai Khiun. 2019. "Her Hunger Knows no Bounds: Female Food Relationships in Korean Dramas." In *Routledge Handbook of Food in Asia*, edited by Cecilia Leong-Salobir, 176–192. New York: Routledge.

Mannur, Anita. 2009. *Culinary Fictions: Food in South Asian Diasporic Culture*. Philadelphia, PA: Temple University Press.

Mohanty, Chandra Talpade. 2013. "Transnational Feminist Crossings: On Neoliberalism and Radical Critique." *Signs* 38 (4): 967–991.

Mulvey, Laura. 1975. "Visual Pleasure and Narrative Cinema." *Screen* 16 (3): 6–18.

Padoongpatt, Mark. 2017. *Flavors of Empire: Food and the Making of Thai America*. Berkeley, CA: University of California Press.

Parsons, Julie M. 2015. *Gender, Class and Food: Families, Bodies and Health*. London, UK: Palgrave.

Probyn, Elspeth. 2000. *Carnal Appetites: Food Sex Identities*. London, UK: Routledge.

Ray, Krishnendu. 2004. *Migrant's Table: Meals and Memories in Bengali-American Households*. Philadelphia, PA: Temple University Press.

———. 2016. *The Ethnic Restaurateur*. New York: Bloomsbury Academic.

Shome, Raka. 2006. "Transnational Feminism and Communication Studies." *The Communication Review* 9 (4): 255–267.

Swindle, Monica. 2011. "Feeling Girl, Girling Feeling: An Examination of 'Girl' as Affect." *Rhizomes* 22. http://www.rhizomes.net/issue22/swindle.html.

Trinh T. Minh-ha. 1991. "Outside In Inside Out." In *When the Moon Waxes Red: Representation, Gender and Cultural Politics*, Edited by Trinh T. Minh-ha, 65–78. New York: Routledge.

Tsuya, Noriko, Larry L. Bumpass, and Minja Kim Choe. 2000. "Gender, Employment and Housework in Japan, Korea and the US." *Review of Population and Social Policy* 9: 195–220.

Vanstone, Gail. 2007. *D is for Daring: The Women Behind Studio D*. Toronto: Sumach Press.

Veeck, Ann. 2000. The Revitalization of the Marketplace: Food Markets of Nanjing. In *The Consumer Revolution in Urban China*, edited by Deborah S. Davis, 107–123. Berkeley, CA: University of California Press.

Watson, James L., ed. 1997. *Golden Arches East: McDonald's in East Asia*. Stanford, CA: Stanford University Press.

Williams, Linda. 1991. "Film Bodies: Gender, Genre, and Excess." *Film Quarterly* 44 (4): 2–13.

Wu, David Y. H. 2002. "Cantonese Cuisine (Yue-cai) in Taiwan and Taiwanese Cuisine (Tai-cai) in Hong Kong." In *The Globalization of Chinese Food*, edited by David Y. H. Wu and Sidney C. H. Cheung, 86–99. Honolulu: University of Hawai'i Press.

Wu, David Y. H., and Sidney C. H. Cheung. 2002. "Introduction: The Globalization of Chinese Food and Cuisine: Markers and Breakers of Cultural Barriers." In *The Globalization of Chinese Food*, edited by David Y. H. Wu and Sidney C. H. Cheung, 1–20. Honolulu: University of Hawai'i Press.

Yan, Yunxiang. 2000. "Of Hamburger and Social Space: Consuming McDonald's in Beijing." In *The Consumer Revolution in Urban China*, edited by Deborah S. Davis, 201–225. Berkeley, CA: University of California Press.

Yu, LiAnne. 2014. *Consumption in China*. Cambridge, UK: Polity Press.

Part I

IMAGINATION OF CULINARY NATIONALISM

Chapter 1

Women, Waste, and War

Food, Gender, and Rationalization in Wartime Japanese Discourse

Nathan Hopson

ABSTRACT

This chapter examines the gendered political economy of Japanese public discourses about food and food waste during the Pacific War years of 1941 to 1945. Kitchen waste, which was generally considered the province of women (housewives especially), was seen as a significant threat to the war effort. Methodologically, I trace how these ideas were translated from laboratories and think tanks into public discourse in *Yomiuri Shinbun*, a representative mainstream newspaper. Scapegoating housewives not only placed an enormous burden on women on Japan's home front but also made it easier for military and political leaders to view the war as winnable long after it was lost.

Introduction

This chapter examines the gendered political economy of Japanese public discourses about food and food waste during the Pacific War years of 1941 to 1945.[1] Functionally, wastefulness was conceived as the opposite of rationalization (*gōrika*), the doctrine of relentless efficiency that had been central to the zeitgeist of cultural and economic modernization since at least the interwar years. Waste was a sign of backwardness and a threat to national security and the war effort. This was particularly true for household and kitchen waste, which were generally considered the province of women, and will be the focus of this chapter. In addition to the gendered politics of space, labor, and progress, I situate kitchen waste within larger questions about food and the national diet. Programs for an ideal wartime diet were predicated not only on the ideal of rational optimization—of both maximizing efficiency and minimizing waste—but also on a central assumption about the wastefulness, ergo backwardness, of women. Japan, in this formulation, was a country of near infinite natural wealth, and the burden of maximizing that natural wealth in the domestic sphere fell firmly upon the shoulders of "the housewife," the imagined center and protagonist of the modern domestic sphere.[2] The resulting syllogism was straightforward (facile), namely, food and many other resource shortages were the fault of women and their failure to reduce waste and raise efficiency for the sake of the nation and its holy war. At times, this misogynist paternalism was only implicit, as in the case of general laments portraying Japan as a staggeringly wasteful country that ignored critical food resources, tossed out edible and nutritious scraps, and literally washed millions of yen worth of nutrition down the drain every year. Nevertheless, the implied subject of this waste was always women—specifically housewives. This effected a double denial. War planners, policy-makers, military brass, and other elites were not forced to face their own failings. In turn, it appears that this contributed to decisions to allow the war to continue even after it was lost. To put it another way, I argue that the basic formula was something like this: *Japan is a nation blessed with untold natural bounty and cursed by the untold profligacy of lazy women.*

Methodologically, I am most concerned with how these discourses were expressed not in the laboratories and think tanks in which they were formulated but rather in the public space of the newspaper, *Yomiuri Shinbun*, in particular. Many books, pamphlets, and screeds were written in wartime Japan on the topic of food and waste, but most were never read by a broad, representative slice of the population. Instead, their influence was filtered down to the public through mass media. In other words, major newspapers are better sources for a *social* history of ideas because they disseminated elite discourses to millions of daily readers and thereby shaped public opinion through framing, agenda setting, and priming (Scheufele and Tewksbury 2007). *Yomiuri Shinbun* is a particularly good source. Under the ownership of former Metropolitan Police bureaucrat and future politician, baseball club owner, and Class A war criminal Matsutarō Shōriki, *Yomiuri* emerged in the 1930s as one of Japan's premier newspapers, with daily circulation growing from just 220,000 in 1930 to over 1.3 million a decade later (Yomiuri Shinbunsha Shashi Hensanshitsu 1955, n.p.).[3] Subsequently, *Yomiuri* emerged as the number one cheerleader for the war. It is within this context that the paper was occasionally critical "of mismanagement and incompetence" in the war effort, both by officials and the public (Shillony 1981, 100). With press freedom in Japan, as elsewhere, severely curtailed during wartime, and with both the market and Shōriki's ideology pushing the paper toward jingoism,

Yomiuri's critiques against state and society never questioned the basic premises of the war.[4] Instead, they exhorted Japan to greater efficiency and less wastefulness in pursuit of victory. If anything, there was a competition between the big broadsheets to be the most patriotic and most prowar paper, and that included public pillorying of impediments to maximum efficiency in the war economy.

In what follows, first, I explore the powerful moral valence which accrued to food and waste in the modern nation-state, with emphasis on Japan. I then sketch out the ubiquitous trope of the housewife in the interwar and wartime years (1918–1945), the expectations of Japanese women in wartime, and the conditions under which they worked on the home front. In the remainder of the chapter, I consider the underlying political and socioeconomic conditions as well as ideologies and assumptions driving discourses on food, waste, and gender in wartime Japan.

The Biopolitics of Food and Waste

Food is fundamental. It is a biological imperative and symbolic medium, entertainment and morality, survival and subjectivity. Food is sine qua non for both individual and society. It is therefore a useful lens through which to examine a tremendously wide range of behavioral, social, economic, political, and other phenomena (Lupton 1996, 1–3; Counihan and Kaplan 2004, 1–5; Belasco 2008, ix). It has also been a primary locus for the practices of disciplining, improving, and mobilizing individual bodies as tools of larger projects of national strengthening that are a salient feature of the modern nation-state. As Alice Weinreb (2017, 3) argued, such state attention to individual bodies reflects not only the rise of modern governmentalities ("the systems of knowledge by which modern states attempt to manage populations") in general and increased attention to projects of visual, spectacular civilization such as hygienic modernity, but also the connection of individual health with national economic and military vitality and a distinctly modern biopolitics, that is, the application of technologies of power to manage and control the lives of citizens, subjects, and so on.[5] The rise of modern biopolitics is especially relevant to concerns about food and waste because the exercise of biopower promises to maximize the efficiency of individuals, families, communities, corporations, and so on, in the service of the state and its ruling elites by apprehending, quantifying, and optimizing "the life forces of populations" (Nadesan 2008, 2–3; see also Rabinow and Rose 2006, 197).

After 1920, the plurality of this work was performed by discourses and practices framed in the language of modern nutrition science. In general, across the industrialized and industrializing world, the nutritional sciences emerged as critical tools for both state and nonstate actors (activists, social reformers, etc.) to document, monitor, and intervene in public health.[6] Efforts to regulate and improve the bodies of subjects and citizens "increasingly connected state power to individual bodies" by the exercise of biopower, that is, the mechanisms of "social and scientific engineering . . . expert administration [and] everyday technologies of the self" through which governments sought to manage the individual body and integrate and strengthen the collective, and—through the disciplinary functions of modern governmentality—to subjectify the populace so that individuals would voluntarily carry out these projects themselves (Weinreb 2017, 3) for both state and nonstate actors. Japan in particular became a world leader in nutrition science, led by its Imperial Government Institute for Nutrition (IGIN), founded in 1920 in response to increasing concern over Japan's "food problems" (*shokuryō mondai*) in the wake of World War I and Japan's 1918 Rice Riots. The IGIN led the charge to rationalize the Japanese diet, realigning it with scientific principles of nutrition (Hopson 2019).

Simultaneously, as principles of Taylorist scientific management and the Progressive Era belief in personal and social perfectibility came to define rationalization as the minimization of waste and maximization of efficiency, waste emerged as an additional site of social cathexis that intersected with both (1) the health and discipline of the individual and national bodies and (2) the connection between resource usage optimization and national strength. As Thomas Hughes (1993, 368) observed, rationalization was generally "associated with [terms such as] *coordination*, *integration*, *stability*, *plan*, *order*, *control*, and *system*. (Emphasis in original)" According to William Tsutsui (1998, 62), in the specific context of interwar and wartime Japan, rationalization was a vaguely defined aspiration to eliminate waste and achieve greater efficiency through modern techniques of measurement and quantification to improve the quality of life. In other words, it was conceptualized similarly to the definition given by contemporary Germany's National Board for Efficiency, that is, "the adoption and employment of all the means of increasing efficiency . . . furnished by technical science and systematic organization."[7] Waste reduction was integral to optimal efficiency, and therefore to rationalization, which was in turn the engine of progress and national strength. As a delectable by-product, rationalization also promised to open the door to a better life for individuals and their families, a selling point that was not lost on the intellectuals and political and economic elites promoting and selling the bright life animated by rationalization. In other words, resource optimization by any name not only promised glory for the state but also held out the possibility to ambitious bourgeois and aspirationally middle-class Japanese—like their counterparts around the world—that they could do more with less and better themselves through modern, scientific living. These visions of rationalization as the methodology of a proper and prosperous modern life had remarkable staying power even in wartime; as Oguma Eiji (2002, 19) has pointed out, discourse often lags behind reality, leaving us with obsolete language (ergo structures of thought) for new situations. And while this framing of rationalization was often and grandiloquently applied to heavy industry, the military, and so on, it was equally at home in the home. There, the subject of rationalization inevitably became women, and especially a particular type, "the housewife."

"The Housewife" and Expectations for Japanese Women

If wartime discourses on dietary optimization and waste reduction assumed as their subject "the housewife," then they also perforce assumed the existence of a broadly shared and understood notion of her identity and role in the home and society as anchor of the domestic sphere and household manager.[8] Prewar Japan's cults of domesticity and productivity, and its modern, middle-class (and middlebrow) consumer culture placed new demands on women—almost always encompassed by this hazy meta-category of "housewife," which centered on married women but was imagined broadly during the interwar years. "Housewife" was the pinnacle of the official teleology that saw married mothers in control of the domestic sphere. This affected Japanese policies on the mobilization of women to support the war effort. Yoshiko Miyake (1991) noted that the state's *ryōsai kenbo* ("good wife, wise mother") ideal had long been in tension with economic incentives to employ young, single, female laborers for the textile and later munitions factories. The role of factory laborer, however, was never intended to be more than a transitional phase on the way to married motherhood in service of the state, and female factory laborers were therefore seen as not fully women. It was not until 1943, therefore, when the hunger of the war industries could no longer be satisfied either by young, unmarried Japanese women or the import of forced Korean and other colonial labor, that Japan reversed course and began recruiting (eventually coercing) married women into wartime industries. As Thomas Havens (1978, 107) pointed out, in fact, "The state was reluctant to conscript workers of either sex," but found it harder to draft women and especially hard to puncture the sanctity of the housewife as feminine ideal. When Japanese politicians, including Prime Minister Tōjō, voiced poetically high-minded concerns about the unique role of women in reproduction and child-rearing, this in fact expressed their desire not to upset the community and family life at the base of society, ergo public morale and support for the war. Until January 1944, when Tōjō changed course and announced the creation of women's "voluntary" labor corps (Joshi Rōdō Teishintai) for aircraft manufacturing and other critical wartime industries, the hegemonic expectation, then, was that adult Japanese women would marry (becoming "housewives") and produce the next generation of soldiers, while simultaneously taking on the additional burdens created by shortages of both goods and male labor. Women were positioned as the keepers of the home front, which made them responsible for much of the daily work of waste reduction and resource management, especially in the kitchen.

The professionalization of housewifery inaugurated by the promulgation of the "good wife, wise mother" ideology in the 1870s as Japan's answer to the Victorian cult of domesticity—and sustained and nurtured in girls' education and the pages of newspapers, books, and women's magazines—demanded increasing art and artifice, knowledge and specialization.[9] While images of the housewife as ideal domestic manager were at least as much prescriptive as descriptive, their aggregate effect was to move the window of expectations. Married women were to be rational, efficient, scientific household and money managers, and the anchor of the new middle-class household (*katei*) that in turn anchored the nation.[10] Expectations for food preparation raised in peacetime by the elevation and professionalization of housewifery died hard in wartime, even in the face of "adversity that stood a half-century of better living on its head" (Havens 1978, 123). By the interwar period at the latest, a new class of educated, literate women were expected to create nutritious, economical meals for their families in order to optimize health and labor outcomes, and there was a growing assumption that home cooking would be not just sustaining, but also delicious and varied. During the first decades of the twentieth century, an expanding circle of skilled and informed housewives—beginning with those educated in women's higher schools and continuing a lifelong journey of self-cultivation—"borrowed on their cultural resources to plan frugal menus," assist in their children's education, and manage the household (Sato 2003, 79). When standards of living were threatened in wartime, many women leveraged these same skills and knowledge in an attempt to keep up at least a semblance of the peacetime good life. On the one hand, the knowledge and skills that so many Japanese women had acquired in previous decades helped them to continue to economize and provide decent food for their families even as conditions deteriorated. As Ishikawa Hiroko et al. (1989, 183) note, it is remarkable that the fundamental difference between the austere meals of the Pacific War and traditional famine foods was not only that wartime home cooking was an admixture of various scientific and pseudoscientific ideas about nutrition and health, but also that women "contrived to somehow make foods that were—to the extent possible—delicious, satisfying, and nutritious" by varying their ingredients and cooking techniques. Echoing this sentiment, Kō Sanae et al. remark that even in the face of worsening wartime food and fuel scarcity, it is notable that "it was considered important to be familiar with many cooking techniques in order to provide better planned, more rational, pleasing food with less ingredients" (Kō, Suga, and Ōtsuki 1991, 103).

And yet, on the other hand, these same housewives were often scapegoated for Japan's food and resource shortage problems. They were often denigrated as ignorant, lazy, and uncreative, unwilling or unable to maintain peacetime standards not because of factors such as unpredictable and deteriorating ration distribution or absolute food scarcity due to planning failures and the loss of incoming food shipments from the colonies, but because of their own personal failings. Functionally, women were tasked with making up for men's failures. Astute readers may note that this was hardly a unique situation, but it was particularly egregious in the case of wartime Japan, where a singularly catastrophic lack of logistical planning left Japan proper's food supply critically vulnerable even before Pearl Harbor. In other words, framing issues with the war effort as primarily questions of disciplining housewives to better manage resources—as opposed to questions of absolute resource scarcity—contributed to making the war seem winnable even when it was not. Shifting the blame for scarcity to working- and middle-class women assuaged elite male (and female) egos, and in doing so delayed realization of the war's futility. The empty optimism and reckless shifting of responsibility by Tsutsui Masayuki, for instance, who worked in Tokyo's metropolitan nutrition section, is emblematic of this longer tendency. Tsutsui (1944) wrote, "The Greater East Asia War has presented major challenges of austerity to the Japanese people on every front, beginning with food. In order to overcome these severe food conditions, I am confident . . . that inventive and creative solutions will appear, facilitating full use and full consumption of foods to eliminate waste and maximize nutrition." While it was no doubt at least partly performative, Tsutsui's delusionally motivated reasoning in May 1944 was also a chilling echo of the incompetence and ill-preparedness that characterized the rhetoric of most Japanese elites vis-à-vis food planning and also laid the burden of reducing the shortage of food on Japan's married women.

Rationing, Distribution, Shortages

As Johnston et al. (1954, 47–49) noted in their seminal study of Japan's wartime food management, Japan had achieved a relatively high level of nominal food security prior to the expansion of war with China in the late 1930s. When the war began, efforts at rationing and control of the domestic food supply were undertaken. However, though there was (nearly) enough rice for peacetime, war quickly upended that precarious balance. Japan's food security was predicated on assumptions that denied the realities of war, such as uninterrupted shipping from the colonies and an unchanging labor force. Japan was heavily dependent on its colonies and overseas conquests in Southeast Asia but could not secure these maritime shipping lanes, making it essential to squeeze maximum efficiency from every grain of rice, that is, to reduce waste at all stages of production, preparation, and consumption. But this was not enough, as hard labor and soldiering increased caloric needs, and resources, labor, facilities, and equipment were diverted and/or destroyed. When Japanese supply convoys began finding their way to the seafloor with more regularity than they did to the metropole's ports, and when the young men who made up the bulk of the agricultural labor force were drafted away to war, food supplies tightened quickly (Unno 2016).[11]

Despite early warning signs, there is little evidence of serious planning for the security of the home islands' food supply. Unno Hiroshi has detailed the ruinous myopia and both personal and systemic failures of food security planning in the months leading up to Pearl Harbor, which are consistent with systemic failures across nearly all aspects of war preparation.[12] With regard to food planning, problems included the prevarication and omission of high-ranking officials such as Planning Board president Suzuki Teiichi and agriculture and forestry minister Ino Hiroya at key junctures; shocking misunderstandings and/or miscalculations of shipping, defense, and manufacturing capabilities; and above all a "tell, don't show" approach to food security that accepted assertions as fact and asked no difficult questions. Food was not the only resource for which Japan faced huge deficits. The army's War Economy Research Office had estimated Japan's industrial capacity at about one-twentieth of the United States. Researchers for the South Manchuria Railway (Mantetsu) likewise reached gloomy conclusions (Unno 2016, 89–114). The Total War Research Institute was especially scathing. Extensive simulations had led to the inescapable conclusion that Japan had no real chance of winning an extended conflict. As with the food security situation, these inconvenient truths were swept under the rug as Japan planned instead for a short, decisive war to bring the Americans to the bargaining table at a disadvantage and permit Japan to negotiate control of its Asian sphere of influence and autarky from the strongest possible military and political situation (Hotta 2013, 164–167). In other words, for both food and resources more generally, the minimal planning undertaken prior to opening a new front with the United States assumed that Japan would quickly secure a bountiful autarkic sphere in East and Southeast Asia. Immediately after Pearl Harbor, the head of Japan's agricultural cooperatives opined that food supplies would improve the longer the war continued (Havens 1978, 117). Such evidence of the lack of both forethought and realism is too copious to cite in detail, but the overarching trend of irrational optimism is neatly summarized in a *Yomiuri* editorial (1942a) demonstrating a complete misapprehension of Japan's precarity:

> The reason that wars in Europe become not just direct and flashy exchanges of bullets and bombs but also barbaric food wars is that, other than the Soviet Union, no country in Europe is food self-sufficient. This is entirely unlike Japan,

> which enjoys a high degree of food self-sufficiency capacity. When the domestic harvest of rice, our major staple, is poor—as it was last year—we can meet annual needs with imports from the colonies (*gaichi*).

The title of Unno's book, *Shokuryō mo daijōbu nari*, is a quote from Suzuki Teiichi at a November 1941 cabinet meeting: "Food is OK, too." For Unno (2016, 51–55, 419), this declaration exemplifies the irresponsibility of Japanese war preparation, especially vis-à-vis food. It was this myopia and self-delusion in policy-making and war planning that foisted the responsibility for waste reduction onto women in the domestic sphere.

Prime Minister Tōjō Hideki, whose cabinet presided over the latter years of the Pacific War, exemplified the self-delusion of elite men who both believed Japan was a land of heaven-sent infinite bounty and saw failures of women's discipline at the core of any problems. Tōjō was known for his "routine of checking the contents of ordinary citizens' household rubbish on his morning strolls . . . as a publicity stunt to make sure that the ration system was working properly and equitably, that there was enough to eat and, moreover, that people were eating well"; and as a panoptic manifestation of state power to discipline the people (women) whose job it was to minimize waste in and from the kitchen (Hotta 2013, 218). "I have long believed it odd that food should ever lack in Japan," mused Tōjō. "For a nation this blessed to be short on food is the result of excessive luxury" (quoted in Marumoto 1944, 280). Fujihara Tatsushi concluded of Tōjō's ignorance and myopia that Japan "never stood a chance in a modern war led by a prime minister so uninformed about food" (Fujihara 2018, 59).

The failure of Japan's razor's edge strategy, which allowed no room for even minor setbacks and deviations, forced the government to ramp up controls at home, especially consumption controls. As critical agricultural resources such as nitrogen for fertilizers, fuel for machinery, and young male laborers were all diverted to military usage, Japan had only limited prospects for increasing production. The Food Management Law of April 1942 created a command economy for agricultural produce, initiating comprehensive government control over food production and distribution and transforming the distribution system into "a bureaucratic hydra" (Havens 1978, 117; see also Piel 2012, 396). It was not enough. As Sheldon Garon (2017, 45) noted, "By 1943, food shortages had become the central aspect of everyday life on the home front."[13] By 1944, imports from Southeast Asia were almost entirely cut off, leaving the Japanese archipelago woefully underfed (Pauer 1999, 93). As the British Hunger Blockade of Germany had been the most effective weapon in World War I, the American starvation of Japan was, according to postwar testimonies by Japanese political, military, and business leaders, "the Allies' most effective tactic in ending the war" (Garon 2017, 51; see also Smethurst 2020).

This had profound effects on the conditions under which Japanese housewives labored on the home front and in the kitchen in particular. Piecemeal rationing was instituted with the outbreak of the Second Sino-Japanese War in 1937. Neighborhood and block associations helped distribute ration cards as part of the distribution system (*haikyū seido*) supervised by national ministries and relevant prefectural and municipal government departments. In 1939, the government stepped up its promotion of communal kitchens and other measures to increase efficiencies of scale; opened "nutritional food distribution centers" (*eiyō shoku haikyūjo*); encouraged victory gardens *à la Japonaise* in schoolyards, factory lots, and parks; and implemented the Rice Milling Regulation Law to minimize waste of Japan's most important staple, as discussed later.[14] That year's Korean rice harvest failure prompted the first rice conservation (*setsumai*) campaign, which included weekly "*setsumai* days" and highlighted the fragility of Japan's maritime-transport-dependent empire-wide food system (Fujisawa 2008, 6; Saitō 2015, 47; Unno 2016, 36–37). Rationing was expanded in April 1940 to include staples such as soy sauce, miso, sugar, beer, oil, and so on. The rationing and distribution system, which began in major cities, spread across Japan, though initially without national standardization for most commodities. "On Christmas Day 1940, the first rice controls were imposed, with particularly inauspicious irony, on the festive rice cakes for the New Year's season" (Havens 1978, 116). Formal, systematic rice rationing began in April 1941 in the metropole's six major cities. By the time Japan launched its assault on the Pacific Fleet in Hawaii, all major and many minor commodities were rationed and subjected to a distribution system. Soon after, even "rice" was being adulterated with all manner of substitutes, including "wheat, barley, soybeans, poor-quality rice and maize" (Pauer 1999, 93). By late 1942, the rice ration was already "rice" in name only for some Japanese, and the situation was only deteriorating. The following year, as much as one-fifth of the total rice ration was substitutes (far more in cities), and the ration in Tokyo had already fallen below the 300 grams per person per day to which people were entitled. "National-strategy rice cooking" (*kokusakudaki*), various porridges (*kayu*, etc.), and other techniques and dishes that extended rice by increasing its cooked volume with additional water amounted to ineffective flailing at best (Fujisawa 2008).

Women, Waste, and War: The Kitchen as Battlefield, 1937–1945

During the peak years of Japan's long war, Japanese women, like their counterparts in the other belligerent nations, were encouraged and cajoled to consider the kitchen as their own battlefield and waste as their own enemy. In this respect, Japan's version of the *Kampf dem Verderb* (struggle against waste) produced messages quite similar to those in Hitler's Germany (Reagin 2007, 152–157; see also Fujihara 2008, 2016). The increasing totalization of war had been noted in World War I, but with its sequel the conflation and imbrication of home front and battlefront was complete and every decision made in every home was linked directly to patriotism, virtue, and the fate of the nation. This convergence affected all the warring parties, but the similarities between Japanese and German gendered discourses and practices of kitchen and other domestic waste management are striking and worthy of attention. In both countries, waste reduction in the domestic sphere generally and the kitchen in particular was, for all intents and purposes, universally understood by policy-makers and pundits to be the responsibility of women. Housewives in Japan were exhorted to conserve rice, reduce "kitchen waste" (*chūkai*) and fuel consumption, and generally improve the efficiency of food-related labor in order to better sustain the war effort. The category "kitchen waste" in itself placed the onus on women. Editorializing after an August 1942 trash inspection tour in Tokyo by "members of high society" (*orekireki*), one government official excoriated women alone as the source of Tokyo's estimated 750,000 kilogram per day of kitchen waste:

> Amidst mountains of kitchen waste, we found nutritious daikon leaves and whole corn with the husk intact! This means that women's sense of wartime urgency remains insufficient. Whether it is vegetables or small fish, women must make the effort not just to find creative ways to prepare every edible bit, but also to appropriately separate out the inedible parts for use as feed, fertilizer, or fuel. (*Yomiuri Shinbun* 1942c)[15]

The similarities with Tsutsui Masayuki's remarks two years earlier, as well as the explicit gendering of waste, are remarkable.

There is substantial additional evidence that bourgeois and "high society" women internalized these discourses, at least performatively. In turn, their conduct as "social betters" undoubtedly had some effect on women of more modest means, though the extent of this is impossible to quantify. A five-part series in *Yomiuri* (1943b) visiting the homes of prominent men and presenting their "waste-free" wives as paragons of wartime virtue is a prime example. Women's magazine contributor Ueno Shigeko bemoaned women's failure to plan and to curb their own consumption for problems even in peacetime that were accentuated in war. Tsutsumi Misao, wife of politician and businessman Tsutsumi Yasujirō, used kitchen waste and night soil as fertilizer for the family garden, sold what she could of the remainder, and burned the rest as fuel for the bath. To conserve electricity, she continued, the household awoke and slept with the rising and setting of the sun. Miyagi Tamayo, wife of a supreme court justice and a formidable figure in her own right, explained that she kept no trash receptacles in the home in order to force herself to eliminate waste.[16] She described using any waste as fuel to simultaneously heat the bath and cook sweet potatoes, for instance, and concluded, "Is not a wasteless lifestyle one in which the housewife pays close attention to small things and is not careless with things?"

The three main categories of physical kitchen waste were rice, other foods, and fuel. The solutions proposed to these problems of waste also fell mostly into three categories: substitution, supplementation, and transformation. Recycling was promoted in several ways, though not nationally and not as vigorously as in Germany, for instance. For reasons of length, fuel waste and recycling are not discussed in this chapter, but should be explored in future research. This section examines each of the remaining issues, beginning with the consensus definition of waste and the role of housewives in Japan.

Japanese visions of the ideal wartime diet almost unanimously focused on waste reduction and the application of nutrition science principles. Though as discussed later there was something of a content shift in 1943, overall, messaging was consistent regardless of author and source: the central organizing goal of public-directed discourse on the wartime diet was to improve resource usage efficiency (often expressed through its negative corollary, waste reduction), and its protagonist was the housewife. Many authors advanced piecemeal solutions to individual issues, while a smaller number advocated more holistic strategies. One of the latter was Marumoto Shōzō. In the manifesto he titled *Shokuryō sensō* ("Food War"), Marumoto (1944, 186–215), an army accountant and head of the Army-affiliated food think tank Ryōyūkai, laid out a comprehensive and far-reaching vision for domestic waste reduction that included "ten tenets of waste prevention."[17] Though some of his proposals were radical even by the standards of the day, they encapsulate the spirit and substance of the age well. For example, Marumoto's basic thesis about waste was quite similar to that of Kagawa Aya, Japan's most prominent woman nutritionist, founder—with her husband—of an eponymous university (Kagawa College of Nutrition), and a contributor to *Yomiuri*. In *Shokuryō sensō*, Marumoto explained how to reduce waste for rice, produce, fish, seasonings and condiments, cooking fuel, overeating, excessive banqueting, vermin, rot, and parasites. Though, reflecting the desperate realities of 1944 Japan, Marumoto's prescriptions were nitpickier and more labor-intensive than similar writings from even a year or two earlier, overall his prioritization of rice, produce, fish, and fuel neatly encapsulate the larger culture of minimizing waste and optimizing efficiency that permeated the public discourse and everyday life of wartime Japan. Marumoto's insistence that women were to play the key role in affecting these waste reduction measures is likewise representative: "Housewives in particular," he wrote, "must have a new awareness and determination regarding food problems" (1944, 253–254).

Kagawa (1940) had made the same basic argument several years earlier, and without taking ten tenets and over twenty pages:

> The greatest fault of home cooking is peeling vegetables, discarding scraps, removing fish innards, washing rice, allowing pots to boil over, etc. This leaves no germ on the rice, no vitamins or calcium in the fish, few vitamins and minerals in the vegetables. What ends up on the table is just a cadaver. The amount of waste is staggering, from 10–20% to as much as 75%.

Kagawa's admonishment was the consensus view of the nutrition science establishment since at least the 1920 establishment of the IGIN (Imperial Government Institute for Nutrition). Kagawa was echoed two years later, for instance, by Inoue Kaneo (1942b), a prominent nutrition scientist at Tokyo's Institute of Physical and Chemical Research (Riken). In a *Yomiuri* series on proper eating, he warned readers that discarding the eyes, skin, bones, and organs of fish was an inexcusable waste of nutrition because doing so left "only the dregs." This sentiment was echoed more colorfully and with more explicit sexism by the influential military nutritionist Kawashima Shirō (quoted in Torii 2001, 219) in a September 1943 roundtable on "diet for decisive victory" for a prominent women's magazine. "Give a madman a knife and at worst one or two people get hurt," he complained. "But give a woman a knife and she'll lop off the tails, peel off the skins, rip out the bones, and cut out the organs."

Substitution and Supplementation

Because of its symbolic and practical importance, rice was treated separately from other foods in discourses on the ideal diet and waste reduction. Rice presented additional specific issues——polishing and washing——beyond the three major wartime food and nutrition conservation strategies such as substitution and supplementation, discussed below. The former problem was officially solved early on with regulatory measures. Beginning in earnest with the November 1939 Rice Milling Regulation Law, white rice was targeted by government campaigns for massive waste reduction. The law responded to the escalating war in China and the poor harvests in both Japan and Korea that year, but also constituted the final settlement of often rancorous debates in the interwar nutrition science community about the proper degree and type of rice milling to minimize waste and maximize nutrition. White rice was seen as the most diabolical bugbear in the struggle against waste. The law designated 70 percent polished rice (*shichibuzuki mai*) as "standard rice," compromising between the taste of white rice, the nutritional wastefulness of polishing, and the expense and technical difficulties of *haigamai*, that is, rice with the bran removed and germ intact, which had been advocated for by the

Ryōyūkai, among others (Hagiwara 1985; Bay 2012, 128–151). However, as the rice ration shifted to less milled rice and finally to brown rice from 1943, many households began hand-milling rice in empty sake bottles. Marumoto (1944, 189–190) spoke for Japanese officialdom when he declared himself speechless at this waste of time, labor, and nutrition, but there is no indication that this uncharacteristic ineloquence had any effect on the practice.

The practice of washing rice before cooking was even more intractable, because there was no easy regulatory or legislative solution. The matter was essentially in the hands of the Japanese women who did the bulk of the rice preparation, and it was at housewives that the rancor of pundits and policy-makers was directed. Kagawa's sharp warnings above typify the response by experts to the nearly universal practice. This was nothing new. Rice washing had been a bugbear for Japan's nutrition establishment for decades by this point. The IGIN and its head, Saiki Tadasu, had made numerous attempts to calculate and publicize the nutrition literally washed down the drain nationwide. One 1929 estimate asserted that roughly 16 percent of protein and 43 percent of fats, nearly three-quarters of minerals, and 100 percent of vitamins were lost to washing—the equivalent of ¥360 million annually (*Jiji Shinpō* 1929; Hopson 2019, 17).[18] Somewhat surprisingly, given the importance accorded this issue by nutritionists—though it does appear several times (Inoue 1942a; Tsutsui M. 1944)—the issue of washing was not central to the anti-waste message in *Yomiuri* during wartime. Perhaps this is because the no-washing mantra was already decades old. Regardless, it was definitely a staple of more wonky or specialized publications, which generally pushed the message that washing was irrational and unpatriotic, a symbol of the selfishness and wastefulness that threatened to undermine the empire (Inoue 1944, 2–3; Marumoto 1944, 186).

Rice was also targeted for *consumption* reduction, mostly through *setsumai*. While men also consumed rice, of course, women were once again targeted for *setsumai* messaging. "No word," observed Saitō Minako (2015, 55), "adorned the pages of wartime women's magazines more often than *setsumai*." Unlike sugar and other "luxury" items, however, rice conserved was rice that had to be replaced. This is why *setsumai* campaigning focused largely on substitution and supplementation. The doctrine of food substitution (*daiyō shoku*) was grounded in the American "New Nutrition," which envisioned foods as quantifiable, interchangeable nutrition delivery media (Levenstein 1993, 9, 92; 1996). It had been the dominant ideological project of the Japanese nutrition establishment in the 1920s (Hopson 2019). In wartime Japan, substitution was comprehensive. It was also alchemy. Nutritional equivalencies trumped custom and taste, and a frenzy of shuffling and innovation ensued. Daikon and squash leaves—uneaten in better times—did double duty as leafy vegetables themselves and as waste reduction measures. Carrot leaves and sweet potato peels enjoyed newly elevated status as sources of nutrition. Beans and fish and insects and more than 7.5 million songbirds a year stood in for meat, while used tea leaves morphed into vegetables (Marumoto 1944, 191; Johnston, Hosada, and Kusumi 1954, 83, 125–126; W. M. Tsutsui 2003, 302; Saitō 2015, 151).

With regard to rice substitutes in particular, in addition to steamed breads of all sorts, porridges (*kayu*), soups with noodles and dumplings, and other mélanges dominated the menu, diluting or eliminating rice, soaking up all sorts of otherwise discarded ingredients, and allowing creative caloric and nutritional supplementation. Especially in the early years of the war, *Yomiuri* ambitiously promoted various porridges, including peanut and vegetable congee (*Yomiuri Shinbun* 1940b) and a chestnut congee from Manchuria introduced by Mishima Kaiun (1940), better known as the creator of the yogurty, lactobacillus-based Calpis beverage. In contrast, after initial skepticism (*Yomiuri Shinbun* 1940c), both sweet and white potatoes took center stage after the war situation became dire in 1943 as perhaps the most ubiquitous of late wartime substitutes. Potatoes were part of the conversation about improving the diet and eliminating waste from early in wartime. As one *Yomiuri* article that included sweet potato leaves and vines in the category of wild forage makes clear, the burden of making do was clearly on housewives. Japan's number one botanist, Makino Tomitarō (1942), wrote, "Depending on women's cooking skills, just about any wild forage can be eaten," including sweet potato foliage. Post-1943 think pieces promising "fundamental solutions to the food problem" constantly returned to potatoes (Katō 1944). Recipes in *Yomiuri* and other late wartime publications mention potatoes with startling frequency, as do survivors' recollections, sometimes for better, sometimes for worse (Tadokoro 1944; *Yomiuri Shinbun* 1945; Hiraoka 1969, 152; Tohara 1969, 105). Kanagawa Prefecture's (1944) guide to a "victory diet" is particularly bleak. Its "tips and tricks for a wartime diet" contain four consecutive sections on potatoes as well as recipes for such novel delicacies as potato and sardine patties scattered throughout.[19]

Transformation

In addition to potatoes, another keystone of rice substitution was "flour," or to be more precise, "powder" (Rath 2015, 150). In pursuit of what Marumoto (1919) had called "relentless omnivorism," officialdom and the commentariat recommended transforming anything and everything into flour or meal and remixing these powders into either ersatz substitutes for peacetime favorites or novel concoctions engineered with nutrition and fuel, labor, and time saving in mind. Just about anything that could be was powdered or pulverized. Acorn flour, "potato flour, sweet potato flour, maize flour, seaweed flour, fishmeal," and soymeal—lumped together as "flour-based foods" (*funshoku*)—played an increasingly important role especially as a substitute for "granular foods" (*ryūshoku*), that is, whole rice and other grains such as millet and barley (Kawahara 1969, 216; Marumoto 1944, 109; Tohara 1969, 104).[20] Recipes for soups with wheat-flour–based dumplings (*suiton*) made frequent appearances on the pages of *Yomiuri*, especially in the Women's section (1940a; 1943c). One recipe (1942b) for a lunch soup called for dumplings made with 30 grams flour, 5 grams julienned and sautéed carrot, and 10 grams sakura shrimp with 50 grams daikon, 10 grams daikon leaves, and 30 grams carrot. This was to be served with rice and 30 grams of pickled daikon (*takuan*). Root vegetables and pickles were highly prized for their shelf life; they did not go to waste.

The role of powder went beyond increased consumption of wheat-flour noodles and dumplings or steamed breads in place of rice. Soymeal, for instance, was recommended as a meat substitute. "In peacetime," Saitō Minako (2015, 97) wrote of its dubious gastronomic virtues, soymeal "was sausage filler at best. Putting aside 'economy and nutrition,' the taste was pretty iffy (*ayashii*)." But substitution never put aside "economy and nutrition," and taste was at best a secondary consideration, as Marumoto (1944, 109–110) pithily argued:

> The purpose of food should not be to please the eye, excite the nose, nor titillate the tongue. We must eat with our heads, not our eyes. We must [believe] in nutrition and respect food as the method to strengthen the body.

Similarly, Saiki Tadasu had long recommended substituting a mix of miso and powdered dried sardines (*niboshi*) for jam to spread on bread (Saiki 1922, 196; see also Hopson 2019, 20). This was, he assured the public, eminently rational. Jam was wasteful emptiness, sardines a nearly perfect food.

Perhaps the archetypal wartime "flour-based food" was *kōa pan* ("Rising Asia Bread"). Not only was it promoted in popular media as nutritious and patriotic rice conservation, but *kōa pan* exemplified the turn to *funshoku* as a way to combine rice conservation with substitution and waste elimination. Barak Kushner (2012, 187) observed that "the name [was] a play on words that suggested Japan's efforts to raise Asia up from backwardness," but the real joke may be that the bread did not rise much at all; like all recommended wartime breads, it was leavened with baking powder rather than yeast and steamed rather than baked to save time and fuel. Even before war with the United States, *Yomiuri* readers were protesting the disappearance of white bread. As "K" from Shibuya wrote (*Yomiuri Shinbun* 1941):

> It is a fine thing that donuts and choux are to be banned in the coming days in order to diminish breadlines. However, I was shocked to read that flavored

> breads had increased to take their place. What we fervently desire is neither donuts nor flavored breads, it is white bread!

In any event, Saitō (2015, 57) is correct that *kōa pan* was conceived "with no thought spared for taste." A 1940 issue of *Fujin no tomo* ("Woman's Friend"), one of Japan's most popular and influential women's magazines, introduced this novel abomination as a patriotic way to "conserve rice and rationalize national nutrition." The recipe called for flour, soymeal, baking powder, salt, powdered seaweed, fishmeal, "substitute vegetables," and even a bit of sugar—which would soon become unavailable. The accompanying illustration incongruously included butter, but it is difficult to imagine that anyone was fooled (Saitō 2015, 56). Even those who were must soon have been disabused of such illusions as rationing was formalized and the food situation deteriorated with rapidity. Most importantly, the recipe in *Fujin no tomo* is a chaotic mix of ingredients that thinkers like Marumoto must have appreciated for its utter, bare bones dedication to waste reduction and nutrition profile optimization.

Concluding Remarks

Bruce F. Johnston et al.'s (1954, 3) seminal postwar history of Japanese wartime food policy echoed Herbert Hoover's famous World War I mantra, "Food will win the war," in its opening line, "Food is a weapon of war." As with most things in wartime Japan, it was a weapon in short supply, jingoistic protests notwithstanding. Food preparation—already overwhelmingly accepted as the burden of women before the war—was imbued with terrible urgency. Japan's modern cult of productivity had encouraged women to better themselves and their families through "lifestyle improvement," "rationalization," and the acquisition and application of specialized knowledge about food and household management. War made these tasks national emergencies, but as I have shown it also led to the scapegoating of women for critical resource shortages on the home front. It was far more comforting for military and civilian elites—and undoubtedly no small percentage of the public—to shift blame for the declining quality and quantity of food to "irrational" and "backward" housewives rather than to face hard questions about the failures of war planning.

NOTES

1. I deploy the term "political economy" in the sense defined by Takeda Hiroko (2005, 5), that is, to demarcate "a web of political, economic and even social

interactions across the public and private sphere, seeking, producing and reproducing power in a contested process of interaction."

2. "Housewife" is the accepted translation for *shufu*. Herein, however, I subsume a larger lexicon that includes such terms as *katei no fujin* ("women of the home"), *katei no shufu* ("housewives of the home"), and even most instances of *fujin* ("women") because during the interwar and war years the term *shokugyō fujin* ("working women") was often used to distinguish wage-earning (married) women from their household manager sistren.

3. From the outset, Shōriki's *Yomiuri* cozied up to and supported conservative politicians and policies and its editorial policy was "in line with readers' mood," that is, pandering to an imagined political commonsense center and thereby serving as a reasonable barometer of public sentiment (Kase 2011, 44–51).

4. The newspaper industry was restructured in 1940 to 1942. As with other industries, consolidation was a prominent feature; the state wiped out about 700 daily newspapers—and thousands of magazines—in its efforts to "eliminate opposition, improve positive control over content, and conserve resources" (Kasza 1993, 299). By the close of 1941, the press operated under multiple censorship statutes and with direct oversight from the Home Ministry and the Cabinet Information Board (CIB) propagandists. The industry was also constrained by an ostensibly voluntary Newspaper League (Shinbun Renmei) established in May of that year—and renamed the Newspaper Association (Shinbunkai) in November 1942. Gregory Kasza (1993, 199 fn 17) argues that the association system was so effective that legal controls were hardly needed. Ben-Ami Shillony (1981, 93) is more to the point: "The wartime government expected the newspapers to demonstrate loyalty by exercising their own self-control, but it did not fully trust them." The Newspaper League system increased the degree to which the CIB could—and did—exert direct, specific pressure on the paper "of every type of article, from current events to fiction," including both censorship and orders to publish CIB propaganda.

5. On hygienic modernity and discourses of civilization, see Laporte (2000), Rogaski (2004), Henry (2005, 2014, chapter 4), Kushner (2011, 34–35).

6. Broadly, the modern nutritional sciences (herein shorthanded, "nutrition science") coalesced out of physiology, chemistry, medicine, biology, and so on, in the nineteenth century as a separate field of inquiry ("nutrition as a discipline of science") toward a "scientific, calculated understanding of food" (Coveney 2006, xii, 159; see also Todhunter 1959; Bammi 1981).

7. Tsutsui (1998, 63) also notes that by 1930, a hybrid German American–influenced, protean concept of rationalization as "the application of science to industry and the industrial structure, 'science' in this case connoting objectivity, the utmost efficiency, and the ascendance of 'fact' over tradition," was deeply embedded in Japanese business culture and had made inroads beyond the business and political communities.

8. On the "birth" and professionalization of the modern housewife as household manager, and especially as an ideal archetype in the interwar years, see Ishii and Jarkey (2002), Maxson (2020).

9. "By the mid-1920s the elements of a 'mass' society," Barbara Hamill Sato (2003, 7, 79) wrote, "revolutionized women's status, and in the process destroyed

the traditional family, the operational site of the Meiji Civil Code and its ideological apparatus, the 'good wife and wise mother' ideology." However, of the "three new types of urban women" who are the focus of her work, the "modern girl" and "professional working woman" were more the deviant avant-garde of womanhood rather than the commonsense mainstream, represented more by the housewife—though as Sato points out, images and expectations for her were changing, too.

10. My use of middlebrow here indexes the similarity between the Japanese middle-class culture of self-cultivation (*shūyō* or *kyōyō*) and American middlebrow culture, both of which became dominant (consumer-)cultural trends in the interwar years (Rubin 1992; Klein 2003, 64–65; Tipton 2009, 98). On the terms *shūyō* and *kyōyō*, Barbara Hamill Sato's (2003, 200, endnote 3) explanation is succinct and useful. On the Japanese cult of domesticity and "cult of productivity," see Nolte and Hastings (1991), Tipton (2004, 150). On the middle-class *katei* in modernizing imperial Japan, see Sand (2003, 25–29).

11. The same point has been made by Daniel Yergin (2014, 333), who wrote, "In devising their military strategy, the Japanese had assumed that the rich resources—the oil, the other raw materials, the food supplies—of the Southern Zone could be welded securely to the economy and needs of the barren Home Islands. . . . That strategy was a gamble, the success of which depended . . . absolutely, on the integrity of Japan's own shipping system." The gamble, as Yergin concludes, did not pay off.

12. Sarah Kovner's (2020) work documenting, among other things, Japan's lack of preparation for Allied POWs is only the latest in a long line of works on this topic.

13. Even Havens's (1978, 118) far rosier narrative admits that "material austerities grew much worse in early 1943." Hardship was not limited to food, of course; baths had become a luxury almost as soon as the Pacific War began, and by 1943 even soap was hard to come by.

14. Nutritional food distribution centers primarily distributed prepared meals to factories and offices "in the name of improving labor efficiency and corporate rationalization" (Namimatsu 2017, 45).

15. Tokyo's daily food waste total continued to rise despite these admonishments and a waste separation program begun in 1942 (Yagi, Ōsawa, and Yamamoto 2013, 148–149), reaching 862,500 kilograms in February 1943 (*Yomiuri Shinbun* 1943a).

16. Tamayo was Japan's first juvenile probation officer, and after Japan's defeat was one of the first women elected to the upper house of the Diet.

17. In 1925, Marumoto, previously first army accountant and recently returned from a five-year stint teaching about diet and nutrition in Korea, Tianjin, and Qingdao, joined Ryōyūkai. He was later elevated to major general.

18. More conservative estimates ranged between a fourth-and-a-half of this shocking figure (Dai Nippon Fujinkai 1944, 21; Marumoto 1944, 186), but the message was the same.

19. Perhaps the grimmest of the book's suggestions was an illustrated guide to recycling lint as a charcoal substitute to conserve fuel (Kanagawa-ken Shokuryō Eidan 1944, 66).

20. While *funshoku* had been an increasing part of the reality of daily life in wartime Japan, it was not until 1944 that the term began to dominate discourse in print

media such as the newspapers—and not always positively (Tadokoro 1944; *Yomiuri Shinbun* 1944a; *Yomiuri Shinbun* 1944b). On postwar flour-based food promotion (*funshoku shōrei*), see Hopson (2020a, 2020b).

REFERENCES

Bammi, Vivek. 1981. "Nutrition, the Historian, and Public Policy: A Case Study of U.S. Nutrition Policy in the 20th Century." *Journal of Social History* 14 (4): 627–648.

Bay, Alexander R. 2012. *Beriberi in Modern Japan: The Making of a National Disease*. University of Rochester Press.

Belasco, Warren James. 2008. *Food: The Key Concepts*. Oxford, New York: Berg.

Counihan, Carole, and Steven L. Kaplan, eds. 2004. *Food and Gender: Identity and Power*. London: Routledge.

Coveney, John. 2006. *Food, Morals and Meaning*. Hoboken: Taylor & Francis Ltd.

Dai Nippon Fujinkai. 1944. *Kessen shokuseikatsu kufūshū*. Dai Nippon Fujinkai sōsho 7. Kokumin Tosho Kankōkai.

Fujihara Tatsushi. 2008. "Daidokoro no nachizumu: Ba ni umekomeraeru shufutachi." In *Shoku no kyōdōtai: Dōin kara rentai e*, 71–118. Kyoto: Nakanishiya.

———. 2016. *Nachisu no kitchin: "Taberu koto" no kankyōshi (Küchengeschichten: Essen-Kochen-Nationalsozialismus)*. Kyōwakoku.

———. 2018. *Kyūshoku no rekishi*. Tokyo: Iwanami Shoten.

Fujisawa Yoshitomo. 2008. "Senchū, sengo no shokuryō, eiyō mondai." *Shōwa no kurashi kenkyū*, no. 6 (March): 5–17.

Garon, Sheldon. 2017. "The Home Front and Food Insecurity in Wartime Japan: A Transnational Perspective." In *The Consumer on the Home Front: Second World War Civilian Consumption in Comparative Perspective*, edited by Hartmut Berghoff, Jan Logemann, and Felix Romer, 29–53. Oxford, New York: Oxford University Press.

Hagiwara Hiromichi. 1985. *Eiyō to shokuyō no keifu: Shushoku ronsō kara kenkō shokuhin made*. San Rōdo.

Havens, Thomas R. H. 1978. *Valley of Darkness: The Japanese People and World War Two*. New York: Norton.

Henry, Todd A. 2005. "Sanitizing Empire: Japanese Articulations of Korean Otherness and the Construction of Early Colonial Seoul, 1905-1919." *The Journal of Asian Studies* 64 (3): 639–675.

———. 2014. *Assimilating Seoul: Japanese Rule and the Politics of Public Space in Colonial Korea, 1910-1945*. University of California Press.

Hiraoka Minetarō. 1969. "Haikyū shokuhin nikki." In *Sensōchū no kurashi no kiroku*, edited by Kurashi no Techōsha, 149–156. Kurashi no Techōsha.

Hopson, Nathan. 2019. "Nutrition as National Defense: Japan's Imperial Government Institute for Nutrition, 1920-1940." *Journal of Japanese Studies* 45 (1): 1–29.

———. 2020a. "Eiyō shidōsha (kitchin kā): Amerika nōsanbutsu to sengo Nihon no shokuseikatsu hensen." *JunCture*, 2020-03-26, no. 11: 30–45. https://doi.org/10.18999/juncture.11.30.

———. 2020b. "Ingrained Habits: The 'Kitchen Cars' and the Transformation of Postwar Japanese Diet and Identity." *Food, Culture & Society*, November, 1–19. https://doi.org/10.1080/15528014.2020.1806637.

Hotta, Eri. 2013. *Japan 1941: Countdown to Infamy*. New York: Alfred A. Knopf.

Hughes, Thomas Parke. 1993. *Networks of Power: Electrification in Western Society, 1880-1930*. Softshell Books. Baltimore, MD: John Hopkins University Press.

Inoue Kaneo. 1942a. "Senji eiyō dokuhon 4: Okome wa amari toguna, Rikagaku Kenkyūjo Inoue Kaneo (rensai)." *Yomiuri Shinbun*, March 3, 1942, sec. Kenkō.

———. 1942b. "Iwashi wa atama ga daiji." *Yomiuri Shinbun*, March 13, 1942, sec. Shoku.

———. 1944. *Kessenka no shokuseikatsu*. Kokumin Tosho Kankōkai.

Ishii, Kazumi, and Nerida Jarkey. 2002. "The Housewife Is Born: The Establishment of the Notion and Identity of the Shufu in Modern Japan." *Japanese Studies* 22 (1): 35–47. https://doi.org/10.1080/103713902201436732.

Ishikawa, Hiroko, Hiroko Ichige, and Ayako Ehara. 1989. *Shokuseikatsu to bunka: shoku no ayumi*. Edited by Hiroko Ishikawa. Kōgaku Shuppan.

Jiji Shinpō. 1929. "3600-man en o arainagasu kome togi no songai," June 7, 1929.

Johnston, Bruce F., Mosaburo Hosada, and Yoshio Kusumi. 1954. *Japanese Food Management in World War II*. Stanford University Press.

Kagawa Aya. 1940. "Shokuseikatsu no kaizen." *Yomiuri Shinbun*, December 10, 1940, sec. Shoku.

Kanagawa-ken Shokuryō Eidan, ed. 1944. *Kessen shokuseikatsu kufūshū*. Kanagawa-ken Shokuryō Eidan.

Kase Kazutoshi. 2011. "Shinbunsha no shihon tokusei to sharon: Rōdō kumiai hōan no hyōron o jirei to shite." In *Senkanki Nihon no shinbun sangyō: Keiei jijō to sharon o chūshin ni*, edited by Kase Kazutoshi, 41–58. Tōkyō Daigaku Shakai Kagaku Kenkyūjo. https://jww.iss.u-tokyo.ac.jp/publishments/issrs/issrs/pdf/issrs_48.pdf.

Kasza, Gregory James. 1993. *The State and the Mass Media in Japan, 1918-1945*. University of California Press.

Katō Kanji. 1944. "Shokuryō mondai no konponsaku 1-4: Uchihara Kungenjochō Katō Kanji." *Yomiuri Shinbun*, February 4–15, 1944.

Kawahara Toshie. 1969. "Nigeru." In *Sensōchū no kurashi no kiroku*, edited by Kurashi no Techōsha, 216–217. Kurashi no Techōsha.

Klein, Christina. 2003. *Cold War Orientalism: Asia in the Middlebrow Imagination, 1945-1961*. Berkeley: University of California Press.

Kō Sanae, Suga Yoshie, and Ōtsuki Shin'ichirō. 1991. "Senjika ni okeru shoku seikatsu: Shōwa 19-nen hakkō bō fujin zasshi ni miru chōri, kondate men kara no kentō." *Chūgoku Tanki Daigaku kiyō* 22 (June): 99–109.

Kovner, Sarah. 2020. *Prisoners of the Empire: Inside Japanese POW Camps*. Cambridge, MA: Harvard University Press.

Kushner, Barak. 2011. "Going for the Gold: Health and Sports in Japan's Quest for Modernity." In *The East Asian Olympiads, 1934–2008: Building Bodies and Nations in Japan, Korea, and China*, edited by William Tsutsui and Michael Baskett, 34–48. Leiden: Global Oriental.

———. 2012. *Slurp! A Social and Culinary History of Ramen, Japan's Favorite Noodle Soup*. Leiden, Boston: Global Oriental.

Laporte, Dominique. 2000. *History of Shit*. Translated by Nadia Benabid and Rodolphe el-Khoury. MIT Press.

Levenstein, Harvey A. 1993. *Paradox of Plenty: A Social History of Eating in Modern America*. New York: Oxford University Press.

———. 1996. "The Politics of Nutrition in North America." *Neuroscience & Biobehavioral Reviews* 20 (1): 75–78.

Lupton, Deborah. 1996. *Food, the Body, and the Self*. London: Sage Publications.

Makino Tomitarō. 1942. "Zassō wa shokuryō yobigun (jō): chōri shidai de oishiku taberareru." *Yomiuri Shinbun*, October 8, 1942.

Marumoto Shōzō. 1919. "Tetteiteki zasshokushugi." *Shokuryō hyōron* 4 (9): 39–42.

———. 1944. *Shokuryō sensō*. Shintaishūsha.

Maxson Hillary. 2020. "Kakeibo to gendai Nihon no katei ryōri no seiritsu." Translated by Nathan Hopson. *JunCture*, no. 11 (March): 46–57. https://doi.org/10.18999/juncture.11.46.

Mishima Kaiun. 1940. "Daiyō shoku ni kuri-gayu: Yasukute bimi de shōka mo yoku eiyō ni tomu." *Yomiuri Shinbun*, January 14, 1940.

Miyake, Yoshiko. 1991. "Doubling Expectations: Motherhood and Women's Factory Work Under State Management in Japan in the 1930s and 1940s." In *Recreating Japanese Women, 1600-1945*, edited by Gail Lee Bernstein, 267–295. University of California Press. https://doi.org/10.1525/9780520910188-015.

Nadesan, Majia Holmer. 2008. *Governmentality, Biopower, and Everyday Life*. New York: Routledge.

Namimatsu Nobuhisa. 2017. "Eiyōgaku no keisei to Saiki Tadasu." *Acta humanistica et scientifica Universitatis Sangio Kyotiensis*, no. 50 (March): 25–53.

Nolte, Sharon H., and Sally Ann Hastings. 1991. "The Meiji State's Policy Toward Women, 1890-1910." In *Recreating Japanese Women, 1600-1945*, edited by Gail Bernstein, 151–174. University of California Press.

Oguma Eiji. 2002. *"Minshu" to "aikoku": Sengo Nihon no nashonarizumu to kōkyōsei*. Shin'yōsha.

Pauer, Erich. 1999. "A New Order for Japanese Society: Planned Economy, Neighbourhood Associations and Food Distribution in Japanese Cities in the Second World War." In *Japan's War Economy*, edited by Erich Pauer, 85–105. London, New York: Routledge.

Piel, L. Halliday. 2012. "Food Rationing and Children's Self-Reliance in Japan, 1942-1952." *Journal of the History of Childhood and Youth* 5 (3): 393–418.

Rabinow, Paul, and Nikolas Rose. 2006. "Biopower Today." *BioSocieties* 1 (2): 195–217. https://doi.org/10.1017/S1745855206040014.

Rath, Eric C. 2015. "The Invention of Local Food." In *The Globalization of Asian Cuisines: Transnational Networks and Culinary Contact Zones*, edited by James Farrer, 145–164. New York: Palgrave Macmillan US. https://doi.org/10.1057/9781137514080_8.

Reagin, Nancy Ruth. 2007. *Sweeping the German Nation: Domesticity and National Identity in Germany, 1870-1945*. New York: Cambridge University Press.

Rogaski, Ruth. 2004. *Hygienic Modernity: Meanings of Health and Disease in Treaty-Port China*. University of California Press.

Rubin, Joan Shelley. 1992. *The Making of Middlebrow Culture*. University of North Carolina Press.

Saiki Tadasu. 1922. "Keizai eiyō hō no hanashi." In *Eiyō ryōri kōshūroku*, edited by Asahi Shinbunsha, 175–199. Tokyo Asahi Shinbunsha.

Saitō Minako. 2015. *Senka no reshipi: Taiheiyō Sensōka no shoku o shiru*. Iwanami gendai bunko. Shakai 291. Tokyo: Iwanami Shoten.

Sand, Jordan. 2003. *House and Home in Modern Japan: Architecture, Domestic Space, and Bourgeois Culture, 1880-1930*. Harvard University Asia Center.

Sato, Barbara Hamill. 2003. *The New Japanese Woman: Modernity, Media, and Women in Interwar Japan*. Duke University Press.

Scheufele, Dietram A., and David Tewksbury. 2007. "Framing, Agenda Setting, and Priming: The Evolution of Three Media Effects Models." *Journal of Communication* 57 (1): 9–20.

Shillony, Ben-Ami. 1981. *Politics and Culture in Wartime Japan*. Oxford: Clarendon Press.

Smethurst, Richard J. 2020. "Planning for War: Elite Staff Officers in the Imperial Japanese Army and the Road to World War II." *Asia-Pacific Journal: Japan Focus* 18 (21 (3)). https://apjjf.org/2020/21/Smethurst.html.

Tadokoro Tetsutarō. 1944. "Nameshi to funshoku to kyōdō suiji." *Yomiuri Shinbun*, June 28, 1944.

Takeda, Hiroko. 2005. *The Political Economy of Reproduction in Japan: Between Nation-State and Everyday Life*. London, New York: Routledge.

Tipton, Elise K. 2004. "Japanese Women and the 'Cult of Productivity.'" In *Women Workers in Industrialising Asia*, edited by Amarjit Kaur, 149–172. London: Palgrave Macmillan UK.

———. 2009. "How to Manage a Household: Creating Middle Class Housewives in Modern Japan." *Japanese Studies* 29 (1): 95–110. https://doi.org/10.1080/10371390902780555.

Todhunter, Elizabeth Neige. 1959. "The Story of Nutrition." *Food, The Yearbook of Agriculture*, 7–22.

Tohara Teruko. 1969. "Kaisui no okayu." In *Sensōchū no kurashi no kiroku*, edited by Kurashi no Techōsha, 104–105. Kurashi no Techōsha.

Torii Toshiko. 2001. "*Fujin kōron* no shoku kanren kiji ni miru sensō." In *Sensō to josei zasshi: 1931-1945*, edited by Kindai Josei Bunkashi Kenkyūkai, 208–224. Domesu Shuppan.

Tsutsui Masayuki. 1944. "Kanso seikatsu no shihyō (12): Muda naku taberu." *Yomiuri Shinbun*, May 6, 1944.

Tsutsui, William M. 1998. *Manufacturing Ideology: Scientific Management in Twentieth-Century Japan*. Princeton University Press.

———. 2003. "Landscapes in the Dark Valley: Toward an Environmental History of Wartime Japan." *Environmental History* 8 (2): 294–311. https://doi.org/10.2307/3985713.

Unno, Hiroshi. 2016. *Shokuryō mo daijōbu nari: Kaisen, shūsen no ketsudan to shokuryō*. Nōrin Tōkei Shuppan.

Weinreb, Alice Autumn. 2017. *Modern Hungers: Food and Power in Twentieth-Century Germany*. New York: Oxford University Press.

Yagi Yoshio, Ōsawa Masaaki, and Yamamoto Kōhei. 2013. "Ajia shokoku tō e no Nihon no 3Rtaiken no iten sokushin ni kansuru kenkyū." K22036. Kankyōshō. https://www.env.go.jp/policy/kenkyu/suishin/kadai/syuryo_report/pdf/K22036-1.pdf.

Yergin, Daniel. 2014. *The Prize: The Epic Quest for Oil, Money & Power*. New York: Free Press.

Yomiuri Shinbun. 1940a. "Nani ga yoi ka, isshū ikkai no setsumai ni: Shushoku wa mugimeshi deshō, imoiride eiyō mo jūbun," May 9, 1940.

———. 1940b. "Doredake ga hitsuyō ka: Eiyō in taru daiyōshoku, takaku tsuku no wa imorui desu," November 28, 1940.

———. 1941. "Shoku pan ka ajitsuke pan ka," March 21, 1941, sec. Dokusha no me.

———. 1942a. "Shasetsu: Kokumin eiyō taisaku e no kanshin," January 31, 1942.

———. 1942. "Asu no kondate," March 3, 1942.

———. 1942b. "'Koko ni muda ari': Orekireki no gomi shigen tansaku," August 15, 1942.

———. 1943. "Sutezu ni kanzen ryōri: Shi ga 'shokuhin muda nashi undō' noridashi," February 14, 1943.

———. 1943a. "'Muda nashi katei' o iku," March 2–9, 1943.

———. 1943b. "'Suiton' in 'nagashi-yaki': haikyū no komugiko de setsumai ryōri," July 9, 1943.

———. 1944a. "Komugiko no jōzu na tsukaikata: Aku made shushoku daiyō to shite chōri," June 28, 1944.

———. 1944b. "Shasetsu: Funshoku no senji futekikakusei," September 4, 1944.

———. 1945. "Kotoshi no shokuseikatsu, Shimada Nōshō ni kiku: Te wa utsu 'hara ippai,' mazu shōtoshi e imo tokuhai," January 1, 1945.

Yomiuri Shinbunsha Shashi Hensanshitsu. 1955. *Yomiuri Shinbun hachijūnenshi*. Yomiuri Shinbunsha.

Chapter 2

A Bite of the Gender Equality Discourse in China

Observations from Food

Guojun (Sawyer) He, Dandan Fang, and Jonathan Deschênes

ABSTRACT

Given the important role of food in China, this chapter seeks to investigate how the modern Chinese government has sought to diffuse gender equality into the society through food. We anchor our probe in the analysis of the first season of the popular food documentary, *A Bite of China*. We first briefly introduce how modern China has evolved to become a society wherein gender equality is officially promoted. Drawing upon Foucault's (1980) theory of governmentality, we consider the evolution of gender in/equality as a sociopolitical process triggered and shaped by different regimes and their political and economic motives deriving from governance needs. Accordingly, we theorize the Chinese government's production of the documentary as a governmentality effort in encoding its gender equality agenda to people's daily dealings with food. Such an effort functions to transform food into an apparatus of impelling gender equality, that is, a sociocultural template visualizing and illuminating a guidance for gender-equal conduct in the society through performing everyday cooking activities in designated ways exemplified in the documentary.

INTRODUCTION

Given the indispensable role that food plays in all political, sociohistorical, sociocultural, and socioeconomic arenas, taking the lens of food to understand societies is neither arbitrary nor casual (Allison 1991). In cultural anthropological research, food has been widely considered as a crucial carrier of sociocultural meanings that reflect the evolving development of societies (Carrington 2008; Mintz 1986). In this strand of literature, the process of purchasing, preparing, cooking, and consuming food is thought to be an ideal ground to observe gender/power negotiation (Counihan and Esterik 2012) in both domestic and sociocultural realms.

In the domestic realm, family members of both genders are found to negotiate their power by playing decisive roles in different activities relevant to food resource acquisition, processing, and allocation (Carrington 2008; Clark 2013). For instance, females have the power to decide their own and family meals (Weismantel 1989, 100), since they typically perform routine grocery shopping and serve as families' nutrition "gatekeepers" (Counihan 2008). Males, acting as financial backbones of their families, indirectly balance females' power by budgeting their shopping (Counihan 2008), by taking charge of purchasing heavy-lifting yet essential goods (e.g., staple, oil, salt) for an entire household and carrying them home (Flynn 1999), and by suggesting to females how to prepare family meals (Starrels 1994).

In the sociocultural realm in Western societies, food mirrors people's gender/power negotiations. For instance, in Clark's (2013) study of an American punk community, meat is perceived as a symbol of patriarchal social hierarchies that are established and enforced by mainstream society. To subvert patriarchy and compromise the power of mainstream society, punk community members, regardless of their genders, proactively perform as vegetarians. Taking a macro perspective in the American context, Swenson's (2009) study shows how public opinion on cooking reflects the rising social status of women. Prior to the 2010s, in the masculinism-dominant American society, cooking was mainly presented in popular culture (e.g., in magazines and TV shows) as a routine chore duty impairing males' manhood and thus exclusively left to women. Shaped by the constantly evolving feminism, cooking in the 2010s has been gradually reframed by the media as a masculine performance, "a professional, public challenge rather than a domestic chore" (Swenson 2009, 151). Accordingly, cooking is perceived by the public as a career enabling men to showcase manhood in societies—that is, to show how men are physically more capable of long working hours and labor-intensive tasks than women (Scholes 2011).

In the Asian context, although the intersection of food and power negotiations received scant attention, food has played important roles in those countries. For instance, in China, over 5,000 years of history, Chinese consumers have been developing various ways to name, collect, cook, decorate, serve, and eat food according to different geographical conditions and natural characteristics across the nation, making food a collection of unique cultural symbols that manifest ordinary people's understandings and hopes of good lives (Zhai 1993). Commercially, today's Chinese food market is projected to reach US$1,310,816 million in 2021, with a 4.8 percent increase annually.[1] Culturally, millions of active food vloggers across different platforms in China are enthusiastically sharing their experiences of seeking, prepping, cooking, and eating delicacies with an enormous number of their followers (Xinhua Net 2020).

In the Chinese context, the scholarly discussion on gender/power mainly comes from two perspectives. One revolves around consumer researchers' observation of how consumers express their gender identities through consuming and appropriating goods—ranging from fashion products to automobiles and household items—and how marketers infuse gender stereotypes in their design, production, and promotion of these goods (Gao 2008; Grau and Zotos 2016). The other focuses on calling for the state to address gender inequality issues that exist in the sociocultural and socioeconomic fields, especially at workplaces, job markets, and educational institutions across the country (Angeloff and Lieber 2012; Cooke 2001; Huang and Lowry 2015). Nevertheless, gender equality in China has barely been examined through the lens of food. Since the People's Republic of China (PRC) was founded in 1949, the concept of gender equality has been officially established by the Chinese Communist Party (CCP) (Ji et al. 2017). Given the important role of food in China, this chapter seeks to investigate the CCP's promotion of gender equality in the food context, probing the CCP's efforts in using food to carry out its gender equality agenda.

This chapter first offers a brief historical account on how modern China has evolved to become a society wherein gender equality is officially promoted. We unfold this evolution by following a Foucauldian account and considering gender in/equality as a discourse, which is broadly defined as "a social boundary defining what can be said and what cannot be said" (Crowley 2009, 341) and usually derives from sociocultural and political institutions (e.g., media outlets and state apparatuses) that communicate agendas consisting of ideas, attitudes, courses of action, beliefs, and practices to social actors (Foucault 1969/1972). This allows us to better appreciate the evolution of gender in/equality as a sociopolitical process triggered and shaped by different regimes and their political and economic motives deriving from governance needs. Next, to further understand how the modern Chinese government seeks to diffuse gender equality into the society through food, we present our research design surrounding *A Bite of China*, a food docuseries produced by the predominant state-owned Chinese television network, China Central Television, between 2012 and 2018. A multiple-phase inductive coding method, useful for processing qualitative data (Strauss and Corbin 1990), is employed as the analytical tool to identify how gender equality is woven into the food documentary. Subsequently, drawing upon Foucault's (1980) theory of governmentality, we discuss and theorize our interpretation of the CCP's production of *A Bite of China* as a governmentality effort in encoding its gender equality agenda to people's daily dealings with food. Such an effort functions to transform food into an apparatus of impelling gender equality, that is, a sociocultural template visualizing and illuminating a guidance for gender-equal conduct in the society through performing everyday cooking activities in designated ways exemplified in the documentary.

The Changing Face of the Gender in/Equality Discourse in China

Sociohistorically and socioculturally, China has long been a masculine and patriarchal society due to its Confucianist roots (Chan 2000). Originating from the Spring and Autumn period (771–476 BC), Confucianism put a great emphasis on establishing social orders by forming a strict system of social hierarchy (Condon 1977). It celebrated the monarch, ranked it at the top of the hierarchy, and sought to educate people to be loyal (i.e., Zhong) and obedient to the ruling monarch (Hunsaker 2016). For this reason, with only a few noticeable exceptions,[2] nearly all Chinese feudal regimes until the Qing Dynasty (1644–1912) were in favor of Confucianism (Huang and Lowry 2015; Ruskola 1994), positioning it as their predominant sociocultural ideology to help build, rationalize, and sustain monarchical power and rulings (Phillips 2014).

Although the Confucianist social hierarchy was constituted by a number of constructs such as age, social status, ranks and occupations in bureaucracies, and social and domestic roles (Condon 1977), its basic unit was family (Furth 1988), where the gender inequality discourse emerged. In family settings, male members were endowed with superiority and authority by Confucianists' advocation of females' natural inferiority and obedience to males (Shu and Zhu 2012). For instance, the "Three Obediences" (daughters obey fathers, wives obey husbands, and widows obey adult sons) and "Four Virtues" (acknowledging men's superiority and women's inferiority, being reticent, keeping herself clean and tidy, and being proactive in doing chores) were firmly established as codes of conduct for females in the domestic sphere (Ruskola 1994). Accordingly, male family members were viewed as authorities in families and meant to be looked after by their female counterparts. Thus, social roles were gendered in families, forging the concept of "nan zhu wai nv zhu nei," which means that men (husbands) go out and earn money while women (wives) stay at home and manage housework.

The end of the nineteenth century and the beginning of the twentieth century marked an important turning point of gender inequality. A feminist movement emerged around the end of the Sino-Japanese war (1894–1895), leading to a strong focus on women's rights that stimulated a campaign to establish widespread education for young women and to end the cruel practice of foot-binding (Lee 1995). Consequently, various cultural figures began advocating for female rights (e.g., *The Women's Bell* [Nüjie zhong] authored by Jin Tianhe emerged as the first Chinese feminist manifesto [Zhang 2020]) and argued that women should be allowed to adopt the male role in society (Chen 1928).

The feminist movement was accelerated with the end of the Qing Dynasty. In 1911 a local uprising in Chengdu, in the Sichuan province, orchestrated by gentry, officials, religious leaders, and commoners, spread across the country within months, and ultimately led to the demise of China's last imperial dynasty and the birth of the Republic of China (Zheng 2018). During this fast-paced revolution, many women found themselves joining the army. While men were fighting to achieve liberation from the imperial past, women fought a parallel war for their rights (Edwards and Zhou 2011). This period saw the emergence of various feminine organizations, such as the Female Alliance, the Militant Women's Society, and the Women's Organization for Peace (Lee 1995). Following the anti-imperialist May Fourth Movement that deployed in 1919, the feminist agenda was supported by intellectuals previously exposed to Western ideas and societies promoting "equality between women and men [. . .] educational opportunities for women, labor force participation of women" (Li 2000, 31). As Li (2000) further explained, however, this movement mostly affected a small group of urban and elite women, but not their countryside counterparts that represented the vast majority of the female population. It was only after the establishment of the CCP in 1921 that gender equality for the majority began.

In 1949, under the leadership of the CCP and Mao Zedong (hereafter "Mao"), the PRC was officially established, moving the country into the Mao's era (1949–1976). To divorce the new Communist China from the feudalist and capitalist one (Barmé 1996; Jin, Manning, and Chu 2006), the party endeavored to carry out two agendas. Politically, the party sought to establish a new sociopolitical order based on Marxist-Leninism and Maoism (Leese 2013), rendering the Maoist China to have a place neither for the Confucianist gender inequality discourse nor for advocates of gender equality that was found in the Chinese feminist manifesto (Jin, Manning, and Chu 2006). Socioeconomically, as Mao was eager to defeat Western capitalist and imperialist countries (e.g., the United Kingdom and the United States), the party strived to enlarge the labor market to boost the national economy (Riskin 1987). Since the Confucianist gender inequality expelled women from extrafamilial activities, it became unfit for Mao's economic agenda. In this background, the Maoist gender egalitarianism surfaced to erase male/

female gender differences in people's lives, so that the masses of both genders could be effectively mobilized to carry out Mao's agendas of maximizing productivity in agricultural and steel industries (Huang and Lowry 2015; Ji et al. 2017; Pimentel 2006). This led to dramatic changes in people's economic, productive, and domestic lives especially in the People's Commune Movement between 1958 and 1983. Specifically, the state used production teams as the basic unit to form communes to substitute townships nationwide (Zweig 1983). To generate a large number of laborers needed by the agricultural and industrial sectors (Tatli, Ozturk, and Woo 2017), the state directed the communal leaders to free women from chores (Bowen et al. 2007) by transforming some domestic and private activities into collective and public events. Private and domestic cooking, for instance, was banned and replaced by communal dining known as *Daguofan* (Dikötter 2010)—that is, collective meals prepared and served by a small number of workers to all communal members. Women with few domestic duties were encouraged to dress in the Mao suit, the specific outfit that was originally designed in gray or dark blue for and worn by men (see figure 2.1)[3] (Thompson and Tian 2008). The Mao suits on women effectively occluded their female physical characteristics and made them look like men, thus hindering them from expressing individuality (Angeloff and Lieber 2012; Huang and Lowry 2015). Coupled with Mao's argument that women "hold up half of the sky," the genderless outfits

Figure 2.1 Mao Suit (Also Known as the Mao-Style Sun Yat-Sen Suit). *Source*: "Explore the Evolution of People's Outfits over the Past Seven Decades Since the Inception of People's Republic of China," SOHU.com.

portrayed women as "iron girls" who were as strong and capable as men to engage in all productive, sociopolitical, and socioeconomic activities (Huang and Lowry 2015; Jin, Manning, and Chu 2006). This paved the way for factories and production teams to assign identical labor-intensive workloads to all workers (Jin, Manning, and Chu 2006) without considering the significant physical differences between men and women (Heyward, Johannes-Ellis, and Romer 1986; Sell, Hone, and Pound 2012).

Mao's era ended upon his death in 1976. From then, the new CCP administration chaired by Deng Xiaoping endeavored to overwrite Maoism, especially in the economy. In 1978, Deng's administration coined the Open Door Policy, marking the launch of the Chinese Economy Reform that sought to substitute the Maoist agenda amid planned economy for Deng's market economy (Lampton 2014). In academic publications and mass media outlets, Chinese intellectuals began discussing barriers to economic growth. They attributed the disappointing economic performance to the Maoist egalitarianism: it denounced individuality and ignored individual contributions, thus demotivating individual workers in all productivities (Jing 2016; Pimentel 2006; Zhang 1996). Intellectuals also attributed the unsatisfactory progress with addressing gender inequality to the low level of national economic development (Pimentel 2006). Intellectuals' criticism provided Deng's administration with theoretical grounds to rationalize its market economy turn, and to remove the planned economy in the name of tackling the Maoist egalitarianism to revive the national economy (Pimentel 2006; Zhang 1996). Hence, promoting gender equality became a key sociocultural and socioeconomic agenda.

From the 1980s onward, the state continued mobilizing intellectuals to study Chinese gender issues in aspects such as domestic and market activities, marriage, education attainment, job/labor markets, wages, and property ownership (Pimentel 2006; Shu and Zhu 2012; Tatli, Ozturk, and Woo 2017). From the 2000s onward, intellectuals' outputs afforded the state to steer different political, judicial, and administrative apparatuses to introduce dozens of new regulations and laws[4] that aimed to identify, sanction, and alleviate gender inequality conducts remaining in domestic, educational, social, and commercial realms (Cooke 2001; Shu and Zhu 2012).

To ensure that the gender equality agenda was efficiently diffused to and associated with people's everyday lives, since the early 2000s, the state has mobilized mass media outlets (e.g., newspapers, magazines, and online blogs) to portray the domestic sphere as the frontline of resolving gender inequality. Mostly in the text-based format, these media outlets featured articles acknowledging and exemplifying the status quo of gender inequality in domestic chore allocation. These articles idolized Chinese men taking care of all chores and their families as moral exemplars,[5] encouraging

Chinese men to take equal or more responsibility in chores to allow women to make meaningful lives according to their personal interests (The Paper 2020).

Overall, the evolution of the gender in/equality discourse in China is seen as a sociocultural and historical process originally rooted in a philosophical system that became largely shaped by different Chinese regimes. Especially after its birth, the CCP mobilized a number of state apparatuses and mass media outlets to align the discourse to its changing sociopolitical and socio-economic agendas. In the alignment efforts, different administrations seem to have shared the focus on the familial chore duties. However, scholarly investigation into the modern Chinese government's efforts in using food to impel the up-to-date gender equality agenda is scant. People's dealings with food, such as food preparation, cooking, decorating, serving, and eating, are among the most essential chores fueling all human activities and among the most ideal vehicles mirroring gender in/equality as one of manifestations of gender/power negotiations (Mintz and Du Bois 2002). Accordingly, we concentrate on probing the intersection of food and gender equality by unveiling the CCP's efforts in blending food with its current gender equality agenda in a state-produced visual media source, which is better elaborated in the next section below.

Research Design

This chapter draws data from a popular three-season Chinese food documentary TV series *A Bite of China* (hereafter "the documentary") for two reasons. First, the documentary was produced between 2012 and 2018 by the China Central Television (hereafter "CCTV"), a predominant national television network that is directly owned and operated by the state. Since its inception in 1958, CCTV has covered more than 1.18 billion Chinese people and served as the party's major source for shaping ideologies and public opinion.[6] In social science research, CCTV and its products (e.g., TV series, official news broadcasts appearing on its website and social media accounts) have been commonly treated as valuable data sources to study the CCP-advocated social, political, economic, and cultural agendas (Brady 2017; Chan 2000), and to interpret the party's approaches of presenting its reflections on the country's past and present, and its vision for the society (Müller 2013). Therefore, this documentary is an appropriate data source affording our investigation.

Since its launch in 2012, the documentary has drawn substantial attention from Chinese and overseas foodies, who were proactive in watching and discussing it in online communities (Kunze 2018) to better understand Chinese food culture (Yang 2015). We concentrate our analysis on the first season which sets the tone for the presentation of the subsequent two seasons and focuses on

Chinese ordinary people's lives and stories to showcase a variety of familial, commercial, and traditional foods, their histories, and their processing methods. In this season, stories following two lines/themes are included: those themed by food, aiming to introduce diverse Chinese cuisines; and those themed by individuals, seeking to reveal the nuanced food culture and dynamics of interpersonal relationships among both genders behind their dealings with food.

We collected the episodes (seven episodes of around forty-nine minutes each with English dubbing) from YouTube.[7] While telling 55 stories of individuals or families surrounding different foods, this season introduces approximately 155 kinds of foods deriving from over 60 geographical locations across China (see table 2.1). We focused on all visual, oral, and textual information: 26,446 words were transcribed from the voice-over (hereafter VO, also known as off-camera commentary aiming to provide additional or supportive information about narratives [Kozloff 1989]). Seventy pages of field notes were also taken while watching the episodes.

In data analysis, to probe how the gender equality agenda is infused into the documentary, we followed an inductive data analysis method consisting of open, selective, and theoretical coding (Strauss and Corbin 1990). In open coding, we went through all VO transcripts and watched all seven episodes of the documentary several times to develop a wealth of codes. A total of ninety-one codes were generated, representing a wide range of meanings and symbols that are relevant to the CCP's gender equality agenda. In selective coding, which seeks to identify causal relations among individual codes generated in the open coding, we organized all ninety-one codes into thirty-one code categories standing for different causes and contexts wherein people are shown handling food. We ended our data analysis upon theoretical coding, which serves to synchronize individual code categories into core categories representing the central phenomenon of the study. The theoretical coding led to the emergence of three main approaches representing the CCP's efforts in forging the discourse of gender equality through demonstrating people's handling of food.

A Reading of *A Bite of China*: Blending Gender Equality into Food

Throughout our analysis, we have uncovered that the discourse of gender equality is blended into ordinary Chinese people's dealings with food through three approaches. The first approach creates countermemories of gender inequality in China. The second uses commercial contexts to form a renewed image of in-power modern Chinese women. The third utilizes both familial and extrafamilial contexts to make gender equality a fait accompli performed in people's daily handlings of food.

Table 2.1 An Overview of Season 1 of *A Bite of China*

Episode	*Title*	*Dish*	*Region*
Episode 1 (49′12″)	The Gift from Nature	16 dishes, such as deep-fried lotus root sandwich, grilled *matsutake*, stewed spareribs with lotus root, Nuodeng ham fried rice, stewed bamboo shoots, etc.	Shangri-la, Yunnan; Suichang County, Zhejiang; Liuzhou, Guangxi; Dali, Yunnan; Jiayu County, Hubei; Chagan Lake, Jilin; Sanya, Hainan
Episode 2 (49′07″)	The Story of Staple Food	16 dishes, such as Jiaxing meat sticky rice dumpling, Qishan noodles with minced pork, Lanzhou beef lamian, beef chow fun, Longevity Noodles, etc.	Xiangfen, Shanxi; Suide County, Shaanxi; Kuche, Xinjiang; Liping, Guizhou; Guangzhou, Guangdong; Xi′an, Shaanxi; Lanzhou, Gansu; Qishan, Shaanxi; Jiaxing, Zhejiang; Jiaxing, Zhejiang; Ningbo, Zhejiang; Beijing
Episode 3 (49′10″)	Inspiration for Transformation	5 dishes, including tofu, quark, milk tea, Shaoxing wine, soy sauce.	Jianshui, Yunnan; Shiping, Yunnan; Shou County, Anhui; Xilingol League, Inner Mongolia; Shaoxing, Zhejiang
Episode 4 (49′59″)	The Flavor of Time	6 dishes, including Pao cai, Chinese sausage, Wo Hing preserved meats, cured fish, preserved pork, Jinhua ham, and shrimp paste.	Yanbian Prefecture, Jilin; Hong Kong; Xiangxi Prefecture, Hunan; Jinhua, Zhejiang
Episode 5 (50′58″)	The Secret of Kitchen	4 dishes, including Qiguo ji (Yunnan steamed chicken soup), Baozi, braised sea cucumber, and West Lake fish in vinegar gravy.	Kunming, Yunnan; Yangzhou, Jiangsu; Hangzhou, Zhejiang; Shunde, Guangdong; Shandong
Episode 6 (49′11″)	The Equilibrium of Tastes	15 dishes, such as spring onion flatbread, cured spare ribs, *mapo doufu*, spicy hot pot, steamed fish, Chenpi duck, sweet and sour pork ribs, smoked duck, seaweed egg drop soup, seaweed fish ball pot, etc.	Shantou, Guangdong; Wuxi, Jiangsu; Macau; Zhenjiang, Jiangsu; Sichuan; Chongqing; Guangzhou, Guangdong
Episode 7 (49′14″)	Our Fields	8 dishes, such as fish in sour soup, Saipangxie, crab-roe tang bao, tofu with crab yolk, red braised pork belly with taro, fried pumpkin flowers, etc.	Zhangzidao, Liaoning; Jingjiang, Jiangsu; Xinghua, Jiangsu; Shigatse, Tibet; Beijing

Source: CCTV, "*A Bite of China*—Season 1."

The Use of Food to Create Countermemories of Gender Inequality

Countermemories are usually produced by mass media outlets, which apply rhetorical strategies to shape public opinions about certain sociocultural events that happened in the past (Thompson and Tian 2008). In our study, we notice that the documentary strives to create the countermemories of the gender inequality history that has been largely influenced by Confucianism and Maoism by establishing food processing as a genderless collective conduct, and spotlighting food handlings performed in a gender-equal but not egalitarian fashion.

The establishment of food processing as a genderless collective conduct begins with the emphasis that the VO puts on the long history of a wide range of individual regional food and its crucial role in sustaining the development of local societies. Yellow buns (Ep.2), for instance, are characterized as a popular staple food in northern Shaanxi made of millet that people have planted for over 8,000 years. The initial emphasis on the long history of millet then allows the documentary to attribute the thousands of years' development and prosperity of Shaanxi to the food, as it has served as the major staple food crop feeding the locals for centuries. Next, the documentary begins coupling the VO with imageries to present the respect and enthusiasm of both food makers and consumers for traditionally made food as a legacy of regional food culture. Food makers are portrayed as respecting and maintaining traditional methods of food-making that were developed by their ancestors. In the story of yellow buns, an ancient stone mill is shown being powered by a donkey (Ep.2) while the VO explains that modern Shaanxi locals prefer applying the ancient collective wisdom to make the most authentic yellow buns. Correspondingly, consumers are shown as being passionate about these traditionally made foods. The stall selling yellow buns is seen being packed by people on the street while the VO addresses these people as a collective concept, local consumers, who have been passionate for these buns for thousands of years. In this way, consumers' enduring enthusiasm for food serves to signal recognition and celebration of food makers' efforts in using food-processing methods of collective wisdom to make genuine local delicacies.

Taken together, food and food processing are no longer associated with individuals' personal lives. Instead, food is made more a collective concept symbolizing its regions of origin and legacy than an individual concept associated with private consumer goods. Food processing is made more a collective conduct practicing region-specific ancient wisdom than a personal conduct performed by local individuals. Although geographical locations are considered as vessels accommodating and manifesting individuals' gender/power negotiations (Mills 2007), they do not necessarily come with gendered images. Therefore, establishing food as a collective concept representing regional legacy and food culture contributes to diluting public memory about the female-stereotyped dealings with food in premodern Chinese history.

The overwriting of the Maoist gender egalitarianism and people's memory of the historical image of "iron girls" emerge from scenes visualizing food handlings as activities performed by both genders according to their natural physiological differences. Take the story about Jianshui Stinky Tofu Ball (Ep.3), a snack local to Jianshui for about 200 years, for example. Using a shoulder pole, Yao, the protagonist, carries dozens of kilograms of Tofu Balls and walks for forty minutes to sell them in town. Meanwhile, his wife takes charge of the less labor-intensive but still indispensable part of work. She works beside the Daban Well, an ancient water source that their ancestors' lives depended on for centuries, and uses traditional wrapping and fermentation methods to hand make Tofu Balls with genuine flavors. In the story about sea cucumbers and abalones (Ep.7), male professional divers spend hours every day diving to the seafloor close to Zhangzi Island, Dalian, and harvesting the seafood, while female professional chefs work in hotels transforming the seafood into luxury dishes. Unlike advocates of the Maoist gender egalitarianism, these scenes illustrate food-handling practices as events that are made possible by the close collaborations between men and women, who take different, yet balanced, roles according to their physical constraints. Accordingly, the Maoist advocate of gender egalitarianism in the past is masked by people's gender-balanced dealings with food today.

To summarize, by focusing on demonstrating people's dealings with food today, the documentary invokes a regionalism-oriented method to shift the public attention to food and cooking away from their originally gendered historical context, and make food, its processing, methods, and food culture become genderless outcomes of following collective wisdom. Meanwhile, the purposeful demonstration of males performing much more physically demanding tasks than females allows the documentary to undermine public memory about the Maoist gender egalitarianism implemented by the state six decades ago.

The Use of Non/Commercial Contexts to Empower Modern Chinese Women

Since the 1940s, the CCP has used mass media outlets to establish individuals with distinctive contributions to certain sectors/professions as models and promote them to the society (Zhai 1993), aiming to call for the population to align views, values, and conduct to these models (Zhang 2000). This approach is also found in the documentary: leading female culinary masters in commercial cooking are featured to dismiss the gendered stereotypes of females as domestic laborers and cooks and males as dominant participants in extrafamilial events. This can be best exemplified by Zhou Saiqun's story presented in Ep.5.

Zhou's story is constructed in both commercial and noncommercial settings. Beginning with the commercial setting, Zhou's story unfolds through the VO remarking on the gender-bending culinary art industry: "Female cooks are rarely seen in China. . . . Female chefs who cook hot dishes in restaurants are even more rare" (Ep.5, 32'18"). Following this, Zhou is introduced as a noticeable exception: she is a famous female professional chef with over thirty years of experience and an instructor in culinary arts of Hunan cuisine at the Xindongfang Cuisine Education, a leading Chinese culinary school. Scenes of Zhou's professional life in the culinary school are zoomed in. In the classroom, Zhou, in a professional chef uniform, is standing in front of her students, mostly males, and demonstrating fundamental culinary skills such as cutting, chopping, frying, food plating, and presentation. Simultaneously, students are seen paying full attention to her demonstration. Later, Zhou is shown assigning different culinary tasks to her students, and walking around to supervise them, correct their mishandlings, and evaluate their performances. All students are shown respectfully listening to and following Zhou's guidance to improve their skills. Clearly, Zhou's image is readily different from the Confucianist view of gender roles that women as the inferior gender should obey men as educators in mastering knowledge and skills. As an advanced professional chef and master of culinary knowledge and skills, Zhou symbolizes a woman holding the power as an educator in commercial settings. She delivers knowledge and skills, creating and implementing discipline in her own way. Thus, Zhou's story constructed in commercial settings weakens the historical gender stereotype of male superiority and builds up the gender image of empowered modern women.

Notably, Zhou's image of an empowered modern woman may lead to interpretations of female superiority that contradict the gender equality discourse. This potential contradiction is addressed by the second part of Zhou's story constructed in the noncommercial context. This part begins with a scene of Zhou in her home kitchen assisting her daughter, Yang, who is cooking a family dinner. As the VO explains, although Zhou and Zhou's mother are both professional chefs, Yang is not a skilled cook but a professional makeup artist working at a local television station. Following this are two scenes: one shows Yang skillfully putting makeup on television celebrities at her workplace, and the other shows Yang cooking in the kitchen, accompanied by Zhou and Zhou's mother. In the latter scene, both Zhou and Zhou's mother serve as Yang's assistants, guiding her to properly cut vegetables and safely load raw fish into an oil-boiling pan to fry. These two scenes suggest Yang's lack of cooking skills as a result of her focus on her makeup artist career, thus symbolizing the changing social value about the historical stereotype of females as domestic chore laborers mentioned earlier. For the new generation of Chinese women represented by Yang, mastering cooking is neither a social nor a familial expectation. Instead, women's immature domestic cooking is tolerable and understandable, especially if it is the result of their pursuit of extrafamilial careers.

When the dinner is served, Zhou, smiling, sits closely with her mother and Yang. As the VO explains, "Zhou won't evaluate her daughter's amateur practice with her professional taste buds, for the Chinese, dishes for the family need no unique skills" (Ep.5, 31'30"). Yang keeps observing her mother's facial reaction to the dinner and says, "I don't think you are excited" (Ep.5, 31'45"). Zhou keeps smiling and eating without speaking. Taken together, these noncommercial scenes function to counterbalance Zhou's women-in-power image established in the commercial context. Unlike in culinary classrooms, Zhou at her family table is portrayed as a typical Chinese woman, namely a loving, accommodating, encouraging, and supportive mother, rather than a serious, rigorous, demanding, and authoritative culinary instructor.

The Use of Extra/Familial Contexts to Exemplify Gender-Equal Conduct

As mentioned earlier, gender in/equality as a discourse is shaped by the changing sociocultural and sociopolitical agendas advocated by a state. Due to its fluidity and contextuality, gender in/equality largely remains what Wiemer-Hastings and Xu (2005) called "abstract concepts" that are "characterised by their links to external concepts rather than by intrinsic properties" (Wiemer-Hastings and Xu 2005, 721). However, abstract concepts, for instance, a political slogan of "promoting the gender equality agenda,"[8] would reduce people's comprehension efficiency, making them reluctant to know more (Wiemer-Hastings and Xu 2005). To make a concept easily understood and translated into actions by the public (Wiemer-Hastings and Xu 2005), it must be concrete, namely linked to "an object, along with its attributes, parts and functions, actions performed on or with the object, and relations to other objects" (Wiemer-Hastings and Xu 2005, 732). In the delicacy documentary, associated with people's dealings with food in both familial and extrafamilial contexts, gender equality becomes a concrete concept performed by Chinese people on a daily basis, making food handling a de facto gender-equal conduct in modern China.

A good example of using the familial context to concretize gender equality is Bai Bo's family story of making *Jiaozi* (i.e., dumplings, Ep.2). The story starts with the VO explaining Bai Bo's concept of family derives from watching his grandmother making *Jiaozi*, one of the most highly ritualized foods in China that is meant to be made for and shared with family members on special occasions such as the Spring Festival (Zhao, Wang, and Wang 2015). As Bai explains, "When I was small, I remembered my grandmother making *Jiaozi* with diverse stuffing. When I saw *Jiaozi* being boiled in the pot, I found it a busy and joyful thing. It represents family and reunion" (Ep.2, 45'55"). The grandmother's *Jiaozi*-making image in Bai's childhood memory sketches a typical female stereotype of domestic cooks and servers in the past, thus making gender inequality a concept associated with concrete contents.

Bai's story continues with the scenes shifting to the *Jiaozi* making of his present family. Bai's father is mincing meat with a Chinese kitchen knife, while his mother is preparing vegetable ingredients intended to mix with minced meat to make *Jiaozi* stuffing. Later, Bai's wife, parents, and mother-in-law are seen sitting around a table and wrapping stuffing into ready-made *Jiaozi* flour skin to make the crescent-shaped *Jiaozi*. Through these imageries, *Jiaozi* making is transformed from a once-gendered cooking task conducted solely by Bai's grandmother to a current family activity performed conjointly by both genders.

To further concretize gender equality, *Jiaozi* making as a gender-equal conduct is generalized to represent general domestic cooking as de facto gender-equal activities in all Chinese families. As the VO stresses, "When a lot of food has been put on the production lines for manufacturing, the Chinese people, who cherish the concept of family the most in the world, repeat the same things, every year, at their homes" (Ep.2, 46'11"). Subsequently, with a close-up of Bai's parents making *Jiaozi*, a monologue from Bai is added to suggest that collaborations between both genders in domestic cooking are valuable and should be preserved:

> The concept of family in Chinese people's value is to be passed on from generation to generation. When I inherited it from my parents, I would pass on it to my kids. These *Jiaozi* are like seeds planted in their souls. No matter where they go, how far they go, they can always remember the delicacies that their parents made for them. (Ep.2, 46'35")

Since *Jiaozi* making in Bai's current family is constructed as a gender-equal conduct, Zhou's monologue with an emphasis on passing the *Jiaozi*-making tradition to future generations thus implies the vision of performing gender equality through cooking for the future Chinese society.

Going beyond the familial context, the documentary also uses the extra-familial context to articulate that performing gender equality through a wide range of food-handling–related events leads to social and economic prosperity. Take the booming market of *matsutake*, for example (Ep.1). Its development is attributed to close collaborations between male and female individuals from Shangri-La, Yunnan. Unlike the historical stereotype of Chinese women remaining at home for chore duties, modern women, such as Zhuoma, the heroine in the *matsutake* story, and her daughter contribute to the development of the *matsutake* market by acting as *matsutake* collectors working in the Shangri-La mountains. Their hard work is recognized by modern Chinese men, who are seen as generous *matsutake* dealers paying Zhuoma a fair price. The export market value of *matsutake* is maximized by collaborations between factory workers of both genders, who immediately start cleaning, slicing, and packing as soon as *matsutake* is delivered by dealers, and ship it to Japan within twelve hours after harvest. Similarly, Guizhou's provincial intangible cultural heritage, the Long Table Banquet (Ep.7), is also shown as a result of efforts made by locals of both genders and different age groups from Xiayao Village. Every year, modern Xiayao locals work together to prepare dishes and arrange tables and chairs, so that all residents can sit along the tables face-to-face, enjoying food and liquor in a long street.

Situating the association of people's food handlings with gender equality and cross-gender collaborations in both familial and extrafamilial contexts, the documentary transforms gender equality from an abstract concept that is akin to a political slogan to a concrete one that involves food and its processing. This transformation contributes to providing the population with a template exemplifying and visualizing gender-equal conduct in action. Accordingly, the context of food enables the documentary to illuminate a guidance for practicing gender equality in China, that is, having people of both genders to conjointly deal with food on a daily basis.

Discussion

In this study, we sought to explore the intersection of food and gender equality, an understudied research arena in the Chinese context. We anchored our probe in the analysis of the first season of the popular food documentary, *A Bite of China*. By focusing on the documentary's textual and visual contents narrated in food and food handling, we identified three approaches that function to embed the state-advocated gender equality agenda into the context of food. By establishing food as a genderless collective concept that is produced by both males and females according to their sex-based differences in physiology, the documentary occludes the Confucianist stereotype of women as inferior domestic cooks and the Maoist advocation of females as iron girls. When conveyed to the public by the documentary, this approach dilutes the public memories about the gender inequality and egalitarian discourses installed in Chinese history. By spotlighting female commercial chefs, the documentary portrays a new image of modern Chinese women, who have power and skills to deliver knowledge while playing the role of loving mothers. By exemplifying people's dealings with food in familial/extrafamilial contexts as events made possible by close and harmonious collaborations between both genders, the documentary presents today's handling of food as a template of gender-equal conduct in daily life.

In general, the use of food to impel state-advocated agendas revealed in our research parallels Allison's (1991) study of the intersection between school kids' lunch boxes and the stereotype of Japanese females as carers of kids and laborers of chores. In Allison's (1991) work, the educational system, popular culinary magazines, and schoolteachers work conjointly to form the institutional power molding Japanese mothers into the well-established gender inequality discourse, which emphasizes the stereotype of women as domestic cooks and family care providers. Lunch boxes thus become carriers helping sustain the state-advocated female stereotype. Our analysis extends Allison's (1991) work by underlining the gender-equality discourse in the making, that is, the CCP's use of food and propagandic apparatus to rewrite the discourse of gender inequality and egalitarianism, the once-prevailing sociocultural and political agendas. To better conceptualize our research analysis, we invoke the Foucauldian concept of governmentality.

Governmentality concerns states' strategic exercise of power to control a population not by relying on punitive and repressive forces (Giesler and Veresiu 2014). Instead, governmentality seeks to control ways that members of a population foster their lives (Collier 2009) by forging "the conduct of conduct" (Foucault 1982, 220)—that is, "a form of activity aiming to shape, guide or affect the conduct of some person or persons" (Gordon 1991, 2). The operation of governmentality relies on the use of an apparatus, which includes any individuals, institutions, materials, and symbolic resources serving to "capture, orient, determine, intercept, model, control, or secure the gestures, behaviours, opinions, or discourses of living beings" (Agamben 2009, 14). As Foucault (1980, 194) addresses, "I understand by the term 'apparatus' a sort of . . . formation which has as its major function at a given historical moment that of responding to an urgent need. The apparatus thus has a dominant strategic function." Accordingly, apparatuses are strategic tools helping the state construct its sociocultural and political agendas as guidance on the conduct of a population.

In our research context, the production of the documentary can be theorized as a governmentality practice of appropriating popular culture to impel sociocultural and political agendas advocated by the state, which is visualized in figure 2.2. The identification of contradictions represented on the far left side of the model indicates the beginning of the governmentality efforts, in which the state identifies contradictions between the current agendas (e.g., gender equality) it seeks to impel and the previous sociopolitical discourses (e.g., Confucianism and gender egalitarianism) that were prevailing and widely accepted by the society but contradictory to today's agendas. As governmentality is characterized by its limited reliance on the use of repressive and disciplinary power (Giesler and Veresiu 2014), such identification enables the state to impel its agendas by seeking to mobilize propagandic apparatuses (e.g., CCTV) to address contradictions remaining in the popular culture.

Next, the identification and formation of discursive fields represented in the middle of the model articulates state-mobilized propagandic apparatuses' efforts in shaping public opinions on the contradictory discourses. Since governmentality aims to shape people's ways of fostering lives (Collier 2009), it urges propagandic apparatuses to firstly identify specific goods (e.g., food) deriving from a popular culture (e.g., the food culture) that is a part of people's routine life in the present and from the contradictory discourse (e.g., gender inequality) originated from in the past. The propagandic apparatuses then work on constructing a discursive field consisting of stories about people's dealings with these goods in the public culture according to the state's current agendas (e.g., gender equality). Since people's dealings with these goods (e.g., as genderless collective activities; today's women as culinary authorities) occlude or override the contradictory discourse, goods they are handling are thus transformed into apparatuses generating countermemories useful for shaping public opinions on the contradictory discourse.

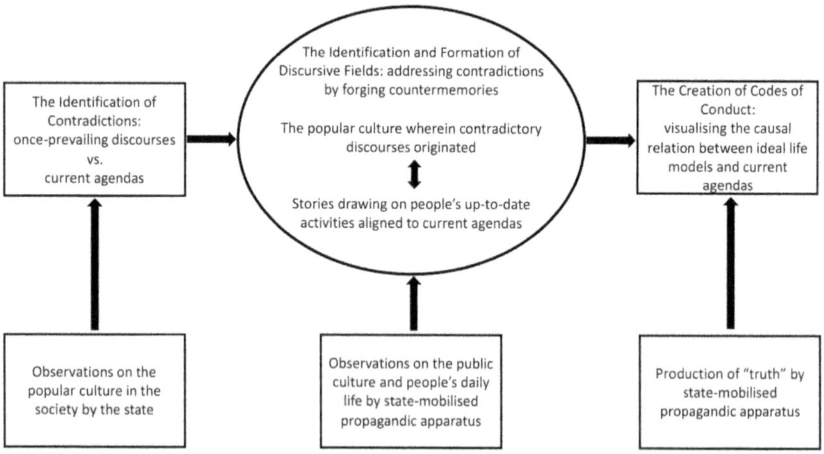

Figure 2.2 The Governmentality Practice of Appropriating Popular Culture to Impel State-Advocated Agendas. *Source*: Created by Authors.

Finally, the creation of codes of conduct represented on the far-right side of the model illuminates the efforts in making people's practice of the state-advocated agendas a pathway to ideal life models valued and cherished by a society. To accomplish this, propagandic apparatuses provoke storytelling methods to visualize a causal relation between people's fostering of their lives guided by the agendas, the prosperity, and the harmony of socioeconomic and familial activities. Such causal relation functions to present state agendas as the guidance on living in ideal life models, thus making agendas resemble "truth"—that is, "the ensemble of rules according to which the true and the false are separated and specific effects of power attached to the true" (Foucault 1980, 132). Since ideal life models are rather seductive to people, "truth"-like state agendas are made effective in inducing and convincing people to submit to and behave in designated ways (Lorenzini 2015). As such, the state's promotion of sociocultural and political agendas becomes a governmentality practice wherein the involved goods, like food in this chapter, help the state to have "government in the name of truth" (Gordon 1991, 8) and thus serve as the apparatus of truth.

NOTES

1. "Consumer Markets/Food/China," Statista, accessed February 5, 2021, https://www.statista.com/outlook/40060000/117/food/china.

2. However, regimes established by ordinary people's rebellions and uprisings did not always select Confucianism as their official ideology. These rebellions and uprisings included, for example, the Chen Sheng and Wu Guang Uprising against the Qin regime in 209 BC, and the Taiping Rebellion in 1851, which led to the establishment of the Christian-Shenic regime, the Taiping Heavenly Kingdom (1851–1864).

3. "Explore the Evolution of People's Outfits Over the Past Seven Decades Since the Inception of People's Republic of China," SOHU.com, August 27, 2019, https://www.sohu.com/a/336579986_120215769.

4. For a full review on laws and legal bills introduced to China to promote gender equality since 1950, see Angeloff and Lieber (2012) and Ji et al. (2017).

5. "Love Her, Never Leave Her, and Miracles Would Come," *People's Daily*, February 5, 2021, https://mp.weixin.qq.com/s/LpmHluG1Df0lTpwh8BauXw. In this article, the state praises Zhang, a thirty-two-year-old ordinary man, who devoted more than ten years of his life to taking care of his then-girlfriend, now-wife, who was in a severe coma caused by health issues: on a daily basis, Zhang cleaned the apartment, took care of his wife's personal hygiene, cooked for and fed her, and massaged her atrophied muscles. With his decade-long enduring endeavors, Zhang eventually brought her back to health and they started a happy family. As the article exemplifies, "It is Zhang's enduring efforts that create miracles one after another. When unexpected and miserable things happen in young couples' lives, 'not giving up our

lives' is not always the choice that everyone would make. . . . [Notably], Zhang's persistence and perseverance eventually reward him with great happiness."

6. "The Introduction to the China Central Television," CCTV, accessed February 7, 2021, https://www.cctv.com/profile/intro.html.

7. CCTV纪录 (CCTV Documentary), "A Bite of China 01 Gift of Nature (HD)," April 9, 2014, YouTube Video, 49:12, https://www.youtube.com/watch?v=AizamOIZijs&list=PLEmk2mJtZJ7FIVleraLI2t9xhqYVkiWqU&ab_channel=CCTV%E7%BA%AA%E5%BD%95.

8. "Promote Gender Equality and the Global Development of Women Causes," *People's Daily*, October 3, 2020, http://world.people.com.cn/n1/2020/1003/c1002-31882710.html.

REFERENCES

Agamben, Giorgio. 2009. *"What is an Apparatus?" and Other Essays*. Stanford, CA: Stanford University Press.

Allison, Anne. 1991. "Japanese Mothers and Obentōs: The Lunch-box as Ideological State Apparatus." *Anthropological Quarterly*: 195–208.

Angeloff, Tania, and Marylène Lieber. 2012. "Equality, Did You Say? Chinese Feminism After 30 Years of Reforms." *China Perspectives* (4): 17–24.

Barmé, Geremie. 1996. *Shades of Mao: The Posthumous Cult of the Great Leader*. New York: ME Sharpe.

Bowen, Chieh-Chen, Yan Wu, Chi-en Hwang, and Robert F. Scherer. 2007. "Holding Up Half of the Sky? Attitudes Toward Women as Managers in the People's Republic of China." *The International Journal of Human Resource Management* 18 (2): 268–283.

Brady, Anne-Marie. 2017. "Guiding Hand: The Role of the CCP Central Propaganda Department in the Current Era." In *Critical Readings on the Communist Party of China (4 Vols. Set)*, 752–772. Leiden: Brill.

Carrington, Christopher. 2008. "Feeding Lesbigay Families." In *Food and Culture: A Reader*, edited by Carole Counihan and Penny Van Esterik, 259–286. London and New York: Routledge.

CCTV. 2012. "A Bite of China—Season 1." https://tv.cctv.com/2017/01/19/VIDAtIyRXSWBaJGZ1itGdZFE170119.shtml.

Chan, Sin Yee. 2000. "Gender and Relationship Roles in the Analects and the Mencius." *Asian Philosophy* 10 (2): 115–132.

Chen Dongyuan. 1928. *Chinese Women's Life History*. Shanghai: The Commercial Press.

Clark, Dylan. 2013. "The Raw and the Rotten: Punk Cuisine." In *Food and Culture: A Reader*, edited by Carole Counihan and Penny Van Esterik, 231–242. London and New York: Routledge.

Collier, Stephen J. 2009. "Topologies of Power: Foucault's Analysis of Political Government Beyond 'Governmentality.'" *Theory, Culture & Society* 26 (6): 78–108.

Condon, John. 1977. *Interpersonal Communication*. New York: Macmillan.
Cooke, Fang Lee. 2001. Equal Opportunity? The Role of Legislation and Public Policies in Women's Employment in China. *Women in Management Review* 16 (7): 334–348.
Counihan, Carole. 2008. Mexicanas' Food Voice and Differential Consciousness in the San Luis Valley of Colorado. *Food and Culture: A Reader* 2: 354–368.
Counihan, Carole, and Penny Van Esterik, eds. 2012. *Food and Culture: A Reader*. London and New York: Routledge.
Crowley, Úna. 2009. "Genealogy Method." In *International Encyclopedia of Human Geography*, vol. 4, edited by R. Kitchin and N. Thrift, 341–344. Oxford: Elsevier.
Dikötter, Frank. 2010. *Mao's Great Famine: The History of China's Most Devastating Catastrophe, 1958–62*. New York: Walker & Company.
Edwards, Louise, and Lili Zhou. 2011. Gender and the "Virtue of Violence": Creating a New Vision of Political Engagement Through the 1911 Revolution." *Frontiers of History in China* 6 (4): 485–504.
Flynn, Karen Coen. 1999. "Food, Gender, and Survival among Street Adults in Mwanza, Tanzania." *Food and Foodways* 8 (3): 175–201.
Foucault, Michel. 1969/1972. *The Archaeology of Knowledge*. Translated by A. M. Sheridan Smith. New York: Pantheon Books.
———. 1980. *Power/Knowledge: Selected Interviews and Other Writings, 1972–1977*. New York: Vintage.
———. 1982. "The Subject and Power." In *Michel Foucault: Beyond Structuralism and Hermeneutics*, edited by Dreyfus Hubert and Paul Rabinow, 208–228. Brighton: Harvester Press.
Furth, Charlotte. 1988. Androgynous Males and Deficient Females: Biology and Gender Boundaries in Sixteenth-and Seventeenth-century China. *Late Imperial China* 9 (2): 1–31.
Gao, Zhihong. 2008. "Gender Discrimination in Chinese Recruitment Advertisements: A Content Analysis." *Journal of Asia-Pacific Business* 9 (4): 395–418.
Gordon, Collin. 1991. "Governmental Rationality: An Introduction." In *The Foucault Effect: Studies in Governmentality*, Edited by Burchell, Graham, Colin Gordon, and Peter Miller. 1–52. Hemel Hempstead: Harvester Wheatsheaf.
Giesler, Markus, and Ela Veresiu. 2014. Creating the Responsible Consumer: Moralistic Governance Regimes and Consumer Subjectivity. *Journal of Consumer Research* 41 (3): 840-857.
Grau, Stacy Landreth, and Yorgos C. Zotos. 2016. "Gender Stereotypes in Advertising: A Review of Current Research." *International Journal of Advertising* 35 (5): 761–770.
Heyward, Vivian H., Sandra M. Johannes-Ellis, and Jacki F. Romer. 1986. "Gender Differences in Strength." *Research Quarterly for Exercise and Sport* 57 (2): 154–159.
Huang, Ying, and Dennis T. Lowry. 2015. "Toward Better Gender Equality? Portrayals of Advertising Models' Occupational Status in Chinese Magazines." *Journal of International Consumer Marketing* 27 (1): 69–83.

Hunsaker, William D. 2016. "Spiritual Leadership and Organizational Citizenship Behavior: Relationship with Confucian Values." *Journal of Management, Spirituality & Religion* 13 (3): 206–225.

Ji, Yingchun, Xiaogang Wu, Shengwei Sun, and Guangye He. 2017. "Unequal Care, Unequal Work: Toward a More Comprehensive Understanding of Gender Inequality in Post-reform Urban China." *Sex Roles* 77 (11): 765–778.

Jin, Yihong, Kimberley Ens Manning, and Lianyun Chu. 2006. "Rethinking the 'Iron Girls': Gender and Labour During the Chinese Cultural Revolution." *Gender & History* 18 (3): 613–634.

Jing, Hongxia. 2016. "A Review on the Workpoints System in the Period of Collective Economy." *China Economist* 7: 41–42.

Kozloff, Sarah. 1989. *Invisible Storytellers: Voice-over Narration in American Fiction Film*. Berkeley, CA: University of California Press.

Kunze, Rui. 2018. Tasting a Good Life: Narratives and Counter-Narratives of Happiness in the Documentary A Bite of China 2 (2014). *China Perspectives* (2018/1–2): 45–53.

Lampton, David M. 2014. *Following the Leader: Ruling China, from Deng Xiaoping to Xi Jinping*. Berkeley, CA: University of California Press.

Lee, Wong Yin. 1995. "Women's Education in Traditional and Modern China." *Women's History Review* 4 (3): 345–367.

Leese, Daniel. 2013. *Mao Cult: Rhetoric and Ritual in China's Cultural Revolution*. Cambridge, UK: Cambridge University Press.

Li, Yuhui. 2000. "Women's Movement and Change of Women's Status in China." *Journal of International Women's Studies* 1 (1): 30–40.

Lorenzini, Daniele. 2015. "What is a 'Regime of Truth'?" *Le Foucauldian* 1 (1): 1.

Mills, Sara. 2007. "Geography, Gender and Power." *Space, Knowledge and Power: Foucault and Geography*: 49–51.

Mintz, Sidney Wilfred. 1986. *Sweetness and Power: The Place of Sugar in Modern History*. Harmondsworth: Penguin.

Mintz, Sidney W., and Christine M. Du Bois. 2002. "The Anthropology of Food and Eating." *Annual Review of Anthropology* 31 (1): 99–119.

Müller, Gotelind. 2013. *Documentary, World History, and National Power in the PRC: Global Rise in Chinese Eyes*. London and New York: Routledge.

Phillips, Andrew. 2014. "Civilising Missions and the Rise of International Hierarchies in Early Modern Asia." *Millennium* 42 (3): 697–717.

Pimentel, Ellen Efron. 2006. "Gender Ideology, Household Behavior, and Backlash in Urban China." *Journal of Family Issues* 27 (3): 341–365.

Riskin, Carl. 1987. *China's Political Economy: The Quest for Development Since 1949*. Oxford [Oxfordshire] and New York: Oxford University Press.

Ruskola, Teemu. 1994. "Law, Sexual Morality, and Gender Equality in Qing and Communist China." *The Yale Law Journal* 103 (8): 2531–2565.

Scholes, Lucy. 2011. "A Slave to the Stove? The TV Celebrity Chef Abandons the Kitchen: Lifestyle TV, Domesticity and Gender." *Critical Quarterly* 53 (3): 44–59.

Sell, Aaron, Liana S. E. Hone, and Nicholas Pound. 2012. "The Importance of Physical Strength to Human Males." *Human Nature* 23 (1): 30–44.

Shu, Xiaoling, and Yifei Zhu. 2012. "Uneven Transitions: Period- and Cohort-related Changes in Gender Attitudes in China, 1995–2007." *Social Science Research* 41 (5): 1100–1115.

Starrels, Marjorie E. 1994. "Husbands' Involvement in Female Gender-typed Household Chores." *Sex Roles* 31 (7–8): 473–491.

Strauss, Anselm, and Juliet Corbin. 1990. *Basics of Qualitative Research*. Newbury Park, CA: Sage Publications.

Swenson, Rebecca. 2009. "Domestic Divo? Televised Treatments of Masculinity, Femininity and Food." *Critical Studies in Media Communication* 26 (1): 36–53.

Tatli, Ahu, Mustafa Bilgehan Ozturk, and Hong Seng Woo. 2017. "Individualization and Marketization of Responsibility for Gender Equality: The Case of Female Managers in China." *Human Resource Management* 56 (3): 407–430.

The Paper. 2020. "Does the Housework Done by Women Have Economic Value? Attention to Women." November 17. https://www.thepaper.cn/newsDetail_forward_10031554.

Thompson, Craig, and Kelly Tian. 2008. "Reconstructing the South: How Commercial Myths Compete for Identity Value Through the Ideological Shaping of Popular Memories and Countermemories." *Journal of Consumer Research* 34 (5): 595–613.

Weismantel, Mary J. 1989. *Food, Gender, and Poverty in the Ecuadorian Andes*. Philadelphia: University of Pennsylvania Press.

Wiemer-Hastings, Katja, and Xu Xu. 2005. "Content Differences for Abstract and Concrete Concepts." *Cognitive Science* 29 (5): 719–736.

Xinhua Net. 2020. "Li Ziqi: Vlogger Who Amazes the World with China's Countryside Life." March 3. http://en.people.cn/n3/2020/0503/c90000-9686626.html.

Yang, Fan. 2015. "A Bite of China: Food, Media, and the Televisual Negotiation of National Difference." *Quarterly Review of Film and Video* 32 (5): 409–425.

Zhai, Qiang. 1993. "Transplanting the Chinese Model: Chinese Military Advisers and the First Vietnam War, 1950–1954." *The Journal of Military History* 57 (4): 689.

Zhang, Mei. 2000. Official Role Models and Unofficial Responses: Problems of Model Emulation in Post-Mao China. *Chinese Perspectives in Rhetoric and Communication* (1): 67.

Zhang, Wei-Wei. 1996. *Ideology and Economic Reform Under Deng Xiaoping, 1978–1993*. London and New York: Routledge.

Zhang, Yun. 2020. *Engendering the Woman Question: Men, Women, and Writing in China's Early Periodical Press*. Leiden: Brill.

Zhao, Rongguang, Gangliu Wang, and Aimee Yiran Wang. 2015. *A History of Food Culture in China*. New York: World Scientific.

Zheng, Xiaowei. 2018. *The Politics of Rights and the 1911 Revolution in China*. Stanford, CA: Stanford University Press.

Zweig, David. 1983. "Opposition to Change in Rural China: The System of Responsibility and People's Communes." *Asian Survey* 23 (7): 879–900.

Chapter 3

Young Men in Chef Uniforms and Suffering Mothers in *Hanbok*

Gendered Representation of National Cuisine in the Sikkaek *Series*

Maria Osetrova

ABSTRACT

This chapter discusses the relations between nationalism, national cuisine, and gender, and the way these relations are manifested in mass media based on an analysis of the *Sikkaek* series (a graphic novel written by Hur Young Man, its two film adaptations, and a same-titled TV drama). Building on the idea of gastronationalism—which claims that a nation can be understood by its foodways—the chapter demonstrates that the intensification of this type of cultural nationalism in Korea with its peak in the late 2000s led to the revision of the image and gender identity of those representing the national food, with male figures beginning to gain more authority. The chapter argues that though the four *Sikkaek* versions have different authors, media formats, and production teams, all applied the same dichotomous structure of gender roles to authenticate national foodways: a "strong" figure of a male professional chef as a defender of Korean cuisine and a "weak" figure of a mother as the embodiment of a Korean tragic past. The chapter concludes that such a gendered imagination of the national foodways enhances the gender inequality in the domain of national dietary practices and does not fully correspond with reality.

INTRODUCTION

The perception of national food traditions in Korea has been changing dramatically since the end of the nineteenth century. By the turn of the millennium, this perception took the form of what the specialists call "culinary nationalism" (Ferguson 2010; Cwiertka 2014, 365) or "gastronationalism" (DeSoucey 2010, Osetrova 2016), meaning the assumption that a nation can be understood and explained by the means of national foodways. Such discourse has penetrated the domain of Korean mass culture, resulting in a flood of TV programs, films, shows, advertisements, and other media content showing Korean food as an outstanding cultural asset of the nation that not only reflects national palates but also symbolizes traditional customs, values, aesthetics, philosophy, and a traditional way of life. Together with the elevated status of Korean cuisine in the public opinion and its linkage with new symbolic meanings, the general image of the person best suited to present Korean national foodways has also changed. Unlike the 1980s and early 1990s when national food was introduced in the mass media mainly by female cooks (Rhee 2019, 56), in the 2010s male professional chefs started to gain more authority in this sphere (Kim 2015, 112–115). The end of the 1990s and the 2000s became the time when the conditions for this shift were formed.

As Anne McClintock has pointed out, all nationalisms are gendered as "no nationalism in the world has granted women and men the same privileged access to the resources of the nation-state" (McClintock 1991, 105). In the case of gastronationalism, one such resource is the national food culture, so it is interesting to analyze how this type of cultural nationalism sees the gender roles regarding national food, especially with a country's national culinary tradition becoming a part of its international image and an instrument of soft power used by the state to strengthen the country's global identity and ascendance.

Korean gastronationalism was a product of its time and historical conditions. Its genesis and evolution were shaped first, by the developmental nationalism of the 1970s (Yoon 2007, 18–20); second, by the global-local tensions taking place in the domain of Korean national foodways since the late 1980s due to the influence of dietary globalization (Nelson 2000; Pemberton 2001); and finally, from the late 1990s, by the cultural expansion known as *Hallyu* or the Korean Wave. The first success story of *Hallyu* related to Korean cuisine was the TV drama *Dae Jang Geum* (The Jewel of the Palace, 2003), which featured Chosŏn royal culinary traditions. The unprecedented popularity of the drama in Asia and later in other parts of the world demonstrated the enormous potential of Korean food as an ambassador of Korea's national brand and a tool of its promotion. That was one of the reasons why *hansik* (Korean food) became a trendy subject in Korean popular culture and media products in the 2000s. The most representative case among them was the *Sikkaek* series, which includes the original graphic novel drawn by Hur Young Man from 2002 to 2010, two film adaptations of the graphic novel (*Sikkaek: Le Grand Chef*, 2007, and *Sikkaek: Kimchi Battle*, 2009), and a TV drama adaptation (2008).

This chapter aims to explore how the imagination of national food was performed in gendered terms in the 2000s by examining the representation of gastronationalism in mass media. To do this, the example of the *Sikkaek* series will be scrutinized. The analysis will seek to understand the roots of current gender representation in the public discourse regarding Korean cuisine and—more broadly—the relations between nationalism, national food, and gender.

Who Is *Sikkaek*?

There is no direct translation of the Korean word *sikkaek* (食客) in English. In a broad descriptive sense, it means "a guest who comes to eat," though such a definition misses many other nuanced meanings of the word, such as glutton (an excessively greedy eater), heavy eater (a person who eats a lot), and foodie (someone who has a particular interest in food). In the graphic novel the protagonist defines *sikkaek* as "a person who knows taste well" (Hur 2003, vol. 1, 33), similar to the Western notion of *gourmet*, which is translated into Korean by other words such as *misikka* or *siktorakka*, or just expressed in Korean pronunciation as *guomei*. Mainly due to Hur Young Man's graphic novel, the notion of *sikkaek* in contemporary South Korea and the Korean language has changed significantly, from a relatively negative connotation of a "sponger," "freeloader," or "parasite" to a positive and modern one—"gourmet." Due to this transformation, the word *sikkaek* today is widespread in the language and has become a popular name for restaurants and other food-related enterprises.

The titles of the first and second movies in the *Sikkaek* series are translated for Western audiences as *Le Grand Chef*, while the title of the TV drama in English is *Gourmet*. Interestingly enough, in both cases the French origin words were chosen. Such a choice can be interpreted as an intention of the filmmakers to invoke associations with French cuisine for the audience, thus creating the image of Korean food as prestigious and sophisticated. It can also be explained by the fact that French cuisine is globally recognized as one of the world's best and this fact is well-known in Korea. That is why when the *hansik* globalization campaign was launched in 2008, one of its goals was openly proclaimed as making Korean cuisine "enter the top-five of the best cuisines in the world," with the other four being French, Italian, Japanese, and Chinese.[1]

All the characters in *Sikkaek*, regardless of their role and significance in the text (a food vendor, a food columnist, restaurant owners, their staff and customers, cooks, farmers, and fishermen), can in a sense be called *sikkaek*. Every issue revolves around a specific food that the characters travel far to find, fight for, research, rescue, or learn to cook and ultimately eat. The root of their adventurous activities is always Korean food. However, the main *sikkaek* of the series is male—the protagonist of the story, a food vendor named Sŏngch'an.

Four Versions of the *Sikkaek* Series

Sikkaek was originally created by famous Korean cartoonist Hur Young Man who published the first issue of his graphic novel (*manhwa*) in September 2002 in the *Dong-a Ilbo* (*Dong-a Newspaper*). In 2008 he switched the publication venue to *Qook* online magazine where he continued publishing the comics until 2010. Simultaneously, the cartoon was published in comic book format (twenty-seven volumes in total) by Kimyŏngsa publishing house (Hur 2003–2010). The novel eventually consisted of 135 issues, each devoted to a particular Korean food product or dish. Hur is one of the most established *manhwa* artists of today's Korea and his *Sikkaek* was quite influential at the time: since 2003 several million copies of the comic have been sold in Korea and in 2004 it received the Korean Cartoon Grand Prize and the Grand Prize at the Bucheon International cartoon festival.[2] Furthermore, the comic book was included on a list of recommended reading for middle and high school students by the Korean teachers' association *Ch'aekttase*.[3]

Due to the phenomenal popularity of the *manhwa* it was first made into a movie, *Sikkaek: Le Grand Chef*, in 2007 (directed by Jeon Yung Su). It was later made into a twenty-four-episode television drama (shown on the SBS channel from June 18 to September 9, 2008), and finally a sequel movie, *Sikkaek: Kimchi Battle*, in 2009 (directed by Baek Dong Hun). All four versions have the same title, several common main characters, and plotlines, and they all talk about the deep connection between Korean food, culture, and history. However, in spite of these similarities they cannot be considered just screen versions of the comics.

First, the scenarios in the TV drama and especially the movies differ greatly. While *Sikkaek: Le Grand Chef* and the TV drama were created based on some issues of the *manhwa*, the scenario of *Sikkaek: Kimchi Battle* was almost entirely rewritten, retaining only some characters and minor details. Hur himself often mentioned in his interviews that he never interfered in the moviemaking process since he sees it as a totally independent work.[4] What is more, the four versions of *Sikkaek* differ not only in terms of script writers, production teams, and media formats, but—most importantly—in the messages they transmit to the public. The graphic novel primarily concentrates on introducing indigenous ingredients of various Korean regional food, their places of origin, and local eating customs. It is full of nostalgia toward the good old times when food was prepared manually, slowly, and with natural ingredients, without the use of industrial technologies. It stands for the diversity of national tastes and against the standardization of Korean cuisine. By contrast, the plot of the TV drama and the movies put in the center the connection between national food and national identity, presenting Korean cuisine as a homogeneous entity.

For the aforementioned reasons, *Sikkaek* cannot be analyzed just as the work of one particular author, but as a multilayered cultural phenomenon of the 2000s that was shaped under social and ideological influences in Korea. These conditions were primed by the general rethinking of the cultural significance of Korean national cuisine that originated in the 1980s and continued throughout the 1990s, as well as by the intensification of *Hallyu*, and by the proliferation in Korean society of the idea that national food can stimulate Korean exports and contribute to the global image of the country. The most striking innovation of the 2000s in the sphere of national food was the active promotion of Korean food among non-Korean consumers. These ideas were already circulating in the public discourse, and the makers of the *Sikkaek* movies and TV drama were expecting a positive response toward and interest in their products (Jeon 2011). Also, it is important to point out that while the *Sikkaek* comics initially targeted domestic readers, its cinematic versions took the foreign audience into consideration as well. Gendered representation of the national food in the series also correlates with these processes.

Representation of Gender Roles in *Sikkaek* and Their Symbolic Meanings

All four *Sikkaek* versions tell the story of a food vendor named Sŏngch'an who travels around Korea in search of the best food to buy and sell. On the road, he meets various people engaged in the production, distribution, preparation, and consumption of Korean foodstuff and through this experience he comprehends the connection between Korean food, national history, his personal family history, and Koreanness. At the same time, in many of the comic's issues and in all of the film and drama adaptations, Sŏngch'an is put in circumstances where he has to defend the authentic taste of Korean cuisine and essence of Korean food culture against those who try to appropriate them. In the first movie he tries to prove that he deserves the knife of the last Chosŏn royal chef (*taeryŏng suksu*) who had refused to serve the Japanese invaders and in protest used the knife to cut off his hand. By claiming the right to become the heir of the last royal chef, Sŏngch'an puts himself in the position of the guardian of not only national palates but national honor and memory as well. In the TV drama Sŏngch'an competes with his stepbrother Pongju to become the head of a renowned restaurant of royal cuisine. Pongju eventually loses the competition because he prefers modern cooking techniques and business methods while Sŏngch'an's adherence to traditional patterns brings him victory. In the second movie Sŏngch'an is challenged by his stepsister Changŭn who intends to shut down the restaurant that their family has run for years. Changŭn is a famous fusion chef who had left Korea long before to get trained in Japan. The story revolves around their shared childhood and memories of their mother figure and her food. In the last round of the contest the siblings have to make the best kimchi that represents the taste of Korea and a "mother's taste." Paradoxically, they make the same product, and though Changŭn actually wins, the real victory is on Sŏngch'an's side since he is the only one who understands kimchi as an embodiment of their mother's soul.

Sŏngch'an has a girlfriend—a journalist named Chinsu who often accompanies him on his trips. The choice of the main characters' names is not random. Put together in one word they make a Korean idiomatic expression, *chinsusŏngch'an*, that can be translated as "sumptuous feast." On the one hand, such wordplay can be interpreted as the author's idea of harmonious coexistence of the feminine and masculine elements in the national food narrative. On the other hand, the main hero is still a male who is always presented as an expert in food while his female partner is subordinate to him and does not know much about cooking. Such a gender hierarchy can be observed in the first movie and in the TV drama in particular. The viewers see various professional chefs who cook in restaurant kitchens (in many cases, restaurants of *kungjung ŭmsik* [royal cuisine], which is considered to be the most sophisticated and symbolically rich part of Korean traditional foodways). These chefs are all male, while females are in secondary positions—assistants, waitresses, cleaners, beginners in cooking, observers, and reporters of male culinary successes.

The kitchen of the royal cuisine restaurant Unamjŏng—one of the main story locations for the graphic novel, the first movie, and the TV drama—is shown as a man's world with its strict hierarchy and almost army-like discipline. Apprentices who fail to perform their work properly are punished physically. There is a prevailing atmosphere of fierce competition and orientation for the best results among chefs. Most of them see mastering the art of cooking as their main life goal, sacrificing other important aspects like family or romantic relationships, social ties, and leisure. In the first movie the teenager Sŏngch'an, while studying at Unamjŏng, learns to make traditional fermented sauces that are considered to be the backbone of Korean flavor. When he stores his jar for the long process of fermentation, he writes a personal vow on the back of the jar's lid: "Become the best!" This scene is intended to show the boy's sincerity and full dedication to mastering Korean cuisine from his very early years. But male chefs in *Sikkaek* are not only highly qualified and dedicated professionals in cooking but also possess knowledge about food—technological, nutritional, historical, and cultural. While selling his goods Sŏngch'an explains to his female clientele the nutritional and medicinal effect of every food item, advising on when it is best to consume them. The buyers are delighted with such a competent vendor and even jokingly call him *paksa* (a holder of an academic degree).

There is only one female character who is presented as a food expert in all *Sikkaek* stories—a mother. But mothers cook at home for the family, thus revealing the following dualism: males are professionals and cook for money in specialized public spaces, while females have no professional background in gastronomy and cook for free in home kitchens for family members. Professional male chefs often cook exquisite delicacies; mothers cook simple but emotionally loaded dishes that remind their eaters of childhood and a mother's love and care as expressed through her food. However, this is not to say that mothers are placed lower than professional male chefs in the gender hierarchy of *Sikkaek*. The image of the mother is very important for the whole series and it is closely connected to the theme of national food. In fact, the graphic novel starts with the epigraph "For all of us, mother's food will always be remembered as the best taste ever" (Hur 2003, vol. 1, 1). In the first movie Sŏngch'an says, "The most delicious food in the world coincides with the number of mothers." The figure of the mother in this context is presented not only as a person who gives birth—in other words, gives life—but also as a person who feeds, which can also be understood as giving life. Hur writes, "The food and mother resemble each other. This is the origin of our life and our eternal longing; at least it is like this for Koreans" (Hur 2003, vol. 1, 77). The series finishes with the same idea: in the twenty-seventh volume of the novel an elderly chef, one of Sŏngch'an's mentors, states, "Food is mother" (Hur 2010, vol. 27, 166). Chinsu concludes, "Food creates feelings and translates deep emotions. It makes people crave for it. Indeed, food is mother!" (211).

A mother's love toward her child is not expressed directly, because directness is not considered appropriate in Korean traditional culture. It is rather expressed implicitly with acts such as feeding. There are numerous examples in the *Sikkaek* series of a grown man recollecting his early years and thinking of his mother through food-related images or even smells. For example, the very first issue of the graphic novel is titled, very typically, "Mother's rice." It tells the story of a Korean American called James who was adopted by an American family at the age of four and who returns to Korea in his twenties to look for his biological parents. James knows neither their names nor their exact home address; the only memory from his Korean childhood is the taste of his mother's rice, which she gave him before leaving. However, this seemingly unreliable clue proves to be an effective search tool in Korea (Hur 2003, vol. 1, 14–73). In the first movie a similar example is the story of the charcoal maker, his mother, and sweet potatoes; in the second movie, the story of a bushranger, his mother, and crab meat.

The topic of mothers and motherhood is the point where several themes intersect that are important for understanding the connection between national food and national identity. These are childhood and food memories, nostalgia (for youth years and for the good old times, for the old/"traditional" Korea), history (individual history, family history, and Korean modern history), childhood traumas, hardships of the past, and tragic historic events. For example, the second story from the graphic novel titled "Dried Yellow Corvina in Red Pepper Paste" describes the hero arriving in his native village of Haenam, in Chŏllado Province, during *ch'usŏk*. While staying with his parents Sŏngch'an decides to visit the house of his neighbor, an old woman. While helping her with gardening, he remembers his school days when his family was poor and he could not take proper lunches to school. This upset him greatly and to cheer him up the old woman secretly treated him to delicious dried yellow corvina in a red pepper paste. Since that time, Sŏngch'an has had a special affection toward the dish and the woman. These good relations, traditionally considered a very important part of life in rural society, proved to be the foundation of Sŏngch'an's character, and once again the national food and a mother-like figure are central to it (Hur 2003, vol. 1, 78–97).

The theme of mothers or mother-like figures, family, and childhood represented through the national food images can be broadened out to the theme of the motherland, where every Korean is related to each other not only by blood but also through common eating patterns. In this regard, the taste of mother's food can be interpreted as a taste of the motherland that constitutes one's national identity. This strong gastronationalistic message is expressed in *Sikkaek* through female (mother) imagery. But it is essential to emphasize here that not any mother fits the criteria—the image of the mother used here has a certain type: it is always a woman of a low social and educational background with a difficult life story. This woman endures endless life trials and has to work hard to earn her living. This prevents her from paying enough attention to and taking proper care of her children, and she fully realizes this conflict and suffers because of it. As a rule, the conflict ends tragically—the mother and her child have to part, bringing heavy trauma to both. Such an image of a mother unambiguously correlates with the image of twentieth-century Korea, with its turbulent past of colonial oppression, civil war, afterwar devastation, poverty, and the difficulties of industrialization. Thus, traumas of childhood parallel traumas of Korean history that find reflection in every version of *Sikkaek.*

One example that articulates this parallel of personal and historical trauma is the Korea-Japan confrontation. Though not all the Japanese characters in the series are depicted negatively, Japan as a national entity is presented there as an aggressive and dangerous Other, starting from colonizers that deprive Korea of its sovereignty and moving to modern businessmen who intend to steal Korean products and food technologies and sell them under Japanese brands. A curious detail: in the *Sikkaek* TV drama, characters with negative traits (including Koreans) meet to discuss their treacherous plans in restaurants serving Japanese cuisine. Such a framework demonstrates that protecting the national cuisine from Japanese attacks is equivalent to defending national dignity and cultural independence. This role is assigned in *Sikkaek* to male professional chefs who deserve admiration and respect while females (mothers) are shown as victims of the historic circumstances who deserve sorrow and empathy.

The Korea-Japan confrontation theme, as well as gendered representation of the national food in *Sikkaek* in general, is also reflected strongly in the second movie although the male-female dichotomy there has a slightly different configuration. First, one of the two main characters is a professional female chef (Changŭn) who competes with her male counterpart and stepbrother (Sŏngch'an). Besides the confrontation between siblings, there are several other female competitors in the cooking contests' scenes, and one of the three kimchi contest jury members is also female. This means that in the second movie women are already included in the sphere of professional gastronomy and are not merely the assistants of male chefs. Second, the story is not set in a royal cuisine restaurant but an ordinary Korean restaurant named Ch'unyanggak. Third, the owner and main cook of the restaurant is a mother. Although Sŏngch'an has a female competitor in this film, the female character appears masculine. Changŭn's behavior and manners are tough, she devotes all her time and energy to her career (there is no romance in her story line), and even her fashion style in the majority of her scenes is more unisex than feminine. Further, she is an antagonist of the story and stands for the powers that have negative connotations in the *Sikkaek* series (prefers foreign food and fusion food—for example, she drinks wine, while Sŏngch'an consumes only Korean alcohol in all the movies; sticks to the modern, over-technological, and over-scientific approach to cooking rather than traditional and manual methods; represents the Japanese line in the story). More importantly, she is in conflict with her mother.

The conflict is rooted in Changŭn's childhood when her mother worked as a restaurant *kisaeng* (Korean courtesan). This had traumatized Changŭn, complicating her relationship with her mother while turning her against authentic

Korean cuisine. Here again we see a mother who suffers due to difficult life circumstances caused by the turbulence of Korean history in the twentieth century. This is another vivid example of how the national food topic is connected to national identity issues through the themes of motherhood, family traumas, and Korea's dramatic recent history. The mother-daughter conflict is resolved when Sŏngch'an explains to his stepsister that their mother loved and cared for Changŭn very much, though she was not able to ensure a happy childhood for her daughter. The symbol of their mother's love and care is her special kimchi recipe, which contains cinnamon to protect Changŭn's weak health. After that Changŭn reconsiders her relationship with her mother and with her mother's (Korean) food, allowing her to come to terms with her past traumas and change her mind about closing their family restaurant. Instead, she reopens it and cooks there herself. At the very end of the movie when the credits start to roll, the viewers see Changŭn and Sŏngch'an, appeased and happy, working amicably in Ch'unyanggak, both in *hanbok*, both using traditional cooking utensils and methods. Therefore, the plot and configuration of the second movie can be interpreted just as an alternative version of the same gender role contraposition as in the first movie and the TV drama, where Korean cuisine is introduced by male professional chefs and suffering mothers, thus depriving other female identities of the chance to present the national foodways.

The Sphere of National Food as a Gendered Space in the Twentieth and Twenty-First Centuries

The picture of Korea's national foodways and the stories around it that the *Sikkaek* series offers to viewers are not entirely a fantasy of their creators. They are rather a mixture of fictional events and characters together with some stories of real people and historic facts. This also applies to the gendered representation of Korean cuisine in the series. Some elements reflect the historic realities of Korea while others are projections of *Sikkaek*'s creators. Therefore, it is interesting to trace which parts have a historic basis, which are imagined, and why.

Alimentation, preparation, and management of food were historically perceived as women's responsibility in Korea (Molony, Theiss, and Choi 2016, 108). In accordance with the traditional views, it was considered inappropriate for noble men not only to cook, but even to approach the kitchen, so if a male member of a noble family needed something in that area he had to ask for help. However, the classic literature concerning the questions of agriculture and food processing in Chosŏn were written by male scholars (e.g., *San'gayorok*, *Suunjappang*, or *Tomundaejak* [Chŏng 2009, 182–199]). The first cookbook authored by a noble female was *Ŭmsik timibang* but it was written in the Korean alphabet *han'gŭl*, which at that time was considered lower in status in comparison to the texts written in classical Chinese. What is more, though the book was created in the sixteenth century, it was only in the latter half of the twentieth century that it was rediscovered by specialists (Yoon 2020). Thus, here we can already see the segregation between food knowledge that was perceived as men's territory and regular cooking and food management that was considered women's job in traditional Korea.

The situation has gradually started to change since the beginning of the twentieth century with the emergence of higher education for women and the establishment of home economics (*kajŏnghak*) departments in universities and colleges, where modern Korean women have started to systematically research the national diet and write about it—in other words, produce and transmit the knowledge to the following generations (Park 2013, 267–293). The first book on Korean cuisine written in the modern period of Korean history was *Chosŏn yori chebŏp* (1913) by female author Pang Shinyŏng, regarded today as "the Bible" of Korean modern cooking books (Chŏng 2009, 223–227).

After the Liberation of Korea from colonial rule, female specialists in home economics and nutritional science continued to research and systemize the knowledge about Korean cooking and eating traditions, but at that time and until the end of the 1960s national foodways were seen in Korean society as a habitual everyday routine not related directly to the sphere of national interests. The first sign that Korean food traditions had started to enter the pantheon of national treasures was Chosŏn royal cuisine being registered in the Korean list of important intangible cultural properties under the number 38 in December 1970. The person who played a key role in that process was a female professor of home economics, Hwang Hyesŏng (1920–2006). She was the one who had actually reintroduced *kungjung ŭmsik* to the Republic of Korea, as after 1910 when Chosŏn was taken over by Japan and the royal court lost its significance, royal cuisine had also been slowly going into the shadows. In 1971 Hwang established the Institute of Royal Cuisine where, together with her daughters, she shared her expertise with home economics students and anyone who was interested in the subject. In 1972 Hwang got the official status of Intangible Cultural Asset Holder that later was passed to her eldest daughter, Han Pokryŏ. In the 1990s Hwang and her family also opened two high-end restaurants of royal cuisine in Seoul (Moon 2010). However, they were visited by a very limited number of VIP guests while general Korean restaurant-goers of that time preferred Japanese restaurants when they were looking to eat out in a way that reflected high status. Nevertheless, until the end of the 1990s Chosŏn royal cuisine as well as Korean cuisine in general was presented in the broad public discourse mainly by female food professionals—home economics professors, nutritional science experts, national diet researchers, and instructors of culinary academies.

The true rediscovery of royal cuisine (or at least its contemporary interpretation) by today's Koreans happened in 2003 after the success of *Dae Jang Geum*, a TV drama that turned the royal cuisine into a nationwide obsession. *Kungjung ŭmsik* became a buzzword in restaurants and other food-related businesses, Chosŏn court delicacies began to be sold in premium food sections of Korean department stores, and Asiana Airlines started serving them to their first-class passengers.[5] The reason that Chosŏn royal cuisine gained more popularity in Korean society in the 2000s than in the 1970s lies in the historical background of the period. Unlike the 1970s, in the 2000s there was a strong social request for national food values that had been formed by a complex of gastronationalistic factors. The first was a sense of anxiety about losing national dietary traditions that had been rising in Korean society since the end of the 1980s and throughout the 1990s as a reaction to the flow of foreign (Western) eating habits into Korea.

The second factor was the "gentrification of national taste," to borrow the term of historian and food anthropologist Katarzyna Cwiertka. As Cwiertka (2004) notes, in the 1980s insufficient food supply completely disappeared as a social problem in South Korea and formerly exclusive types of food were now available to almost everyone. In these circumstances it was not surprising that middle- and upper-class Koreans were ready to embrace the imagery of the refined tradition of royal cuisine as a type of exotic and prestigious food to emphasize their status (Cwiertka 2004).

The third factor was the effect of *Hallyu* that made visible for Koreans the power of *hansik* as an attractive symbol of Korean culture to be promoted among foreign fans. The term *hansik* per se is an invention of the 2000s, when Korean cuisine was included in the "sacred" group of "han" terms like *Han'guk* (Korea), *hanbok* (Korean traditional dress), *hanok* (Korean traditional house), *han'gŭl* (Korean alphabet), *hanji* (Korean rice paper), and several others. Interestingly, before the 2000s there was no word *hansik* with the meaning "Korean food" in Korean dictionaries. In the 1990s and earlier, national cuisine was basically called *han'guk yori* (Osetrova 2016, 36). What is more, in 2011, in accordance with the latest *Hallyu* trends, yet another term for national cuisine was coined: K-Food. The change indicated that national culinary tradition has officially become a *Hallyu* locomotive together with K-pop and K-drama—terms that had appeared earlier.

The fourth factor in the rise of interest toward royal cuisine and national foodways in general (strongly related with the third one) was the proliferation of culinary diplomacy ideas in the world during the early 2000s. Sam Chapple-Sokol, a researcher into the theories and history of culinary diplomacy, defines culinary diplomacy as the use of soft power of cuisine which allows nations with less military, political, or economic strength to put their imprint on the world around them (Chapple-Sokol 2013, 174). Culinary diplomacy proclaimed its official goals as using food and cuisine to create cross-cultural understanding for improving cooperation (Chapple-Sokol 2013, 161) but simultaneously aimed at reaching economic and national-branding benefits as well. The first country to try this method was Thailand, which initiated its culinary diplomacy campaign called "Global Thai" from 2002 to 2003. The campaign's purpose was to increase the number of Thai restaurants in the world, which would add to the Thai economy on the one hand, and on the other, would make new opportunities for cross-cultural interactions as Thai restaurants became unofficial embassies to introduce Thai culture and people to the world (Chapple-Sokol 2013, 174–175). Apparently, the example of Thailand together with *Hallyu*'s successes convinced the Korean government to try their own culinary diplomacy project. In 2008 the authorities announced the launch of the *hansik* globalization program (*hansik segyehwa*) that was designed to make foreign consumers not only try and like Korean food, but make it part of their regular eating habits as a sign of a modern and prestigious lifestyle (Osetrova 2016, 105–125).

All these factors brought changes to the pool of culinary and extra-culinary meanings attached to national foodways and thus caused a revision in the image of the figure presenting Korean cuisine to the general public—domestic and foreign. Such a revision was inevitably mirrored in the mass media.

As I have shown earlier, the cinematic versions of *Sikkaek* actively exploit the theme of *kungjung ŭmsik*. This can be explained by the fact that after the success of *Dae Jang Geum*, royal cuisine was already a familiar and appealing framework for a food-genre movie and thus could attract broader viewership. But at the same time *kungjung ŭmsik* was an appropriate setting to plant the figure of a male professional chef into the national food discourse as the domain of royal cuisine provided the suitable historic background for it.

If we look at Chosŏn royal kitchens from a gendered point of view, we can see a strict scheme of gendered labor. Special court ladies (*chubang sanggung*) were responsible for everyday meals of the king and his family while male cooks (*taeryŏng suksu*) were in charge of royal feasts. Unlike *chubang sanggung* who lived in the palace full-time and, as with all other females of the palace, were considered to be the king's women, *taeryŏng suksu* had the right to live outside and have families of their own. Usually, the *suksu* profession was passed down from father to son (Han'guk minjok munhwa taebaekkwa sajŏn 1991–2002, vol. 13, 332), and this historic fact is repeatedly utilized in the plot of the *manhwa*, the first movie, and the TV drama.

After the colonization of Chosŏn by the Japanese Empire, many *suksu* left the palace and started working in commercial restaurants, or *yojŏng* (Han 2001, 257). Later on, male chefs mainly worked in the kitchens of big hotels in Korea (Han 2001, 261–268). However, after the Liberation it was considered more prestigious for them to specialize in Japanese or Western cuisines rather than Korean cuisine, which had a lower status at that time. That is why until the end of the 1990s and the early 2000s there were not many male chefs to represent Korean cuisine.

As we could see in the previous sections, the notion of *taeryŏng suksu* is widely used in *Sikkaek*. Apparently, it was this series that familiarized the term in contemporary Korean language, as before the 2000s it was known only among specialists on royal cuisine which were very few. There was a *taeryŏng suksu* character in *Dae Jang Geum* too, however, in that drama he was a minor character as the core of the plot was constituted by all-female kitchen intrigues and court power struggles. The need to bring the male figure into the national food discourse in the 2000s was also due to an international (mainly Western) trend of showing the profession of chef as a socially respected male occupation. This can be explained by the neoliberal turn that stressed the significance of well-being and high-end eating-out as a sign of a modern lifestyle (Warde and Martens 2000). However, female professional chefs failed to receive the same recognition even in the West where media showed men as the masters of restaurant kitchens and women mainly as guardians of the domestic cooking space (Druckman 2010). That is why the cinematic version of *Sikkaek* chose to place a male professional chef in the center of its narrative. What is more, in accordance with that trend it was more appropriate to show national foodways through the "strong" image of a male chef rather than the "weak" figure of a suffering mother. Thus, the male (chef) face of Korean food stands for national pride and international attractiveness, while the female (mother) one arouses warm nostalgic feelings and adds sentiment. Such an emotional mixture could contribute to the commercial success of the series as well as help to promote *hansik* globally.

This gendered construction of national cuisine representation can be found not only in media but also in other national food-related initiatives of the 2000s. For instance, the abovementioned *hansik* globalization program launched by the government in 2008 was supported by the first lady Kim Yunok (the spouse of President Lee Myŏngbak) who introduced Korean cuisine at various state and diplomatic events. One of her first actions in this role was a special interview she gave to CNN on October 19, 2009, where she explained to the American audience what Korean food she cooks for her husband and how it keeps him in good shape. In the interview she especially emphasized the idea of *yaksik-tongwŏn*—a traditional Korean conception of Chinese origin claiming that proper food can serve as medicine to the body.[6] Thus, we can see that even on the level of the governmental program the female representation of the national cuisine employs the mother-like image.

The male "faces" of the *hansik* globalization program are professional chefs. One of the most important among them was Edward Kwon (Kwŏn Yŏngmin)—a celebrity Korean chef who got famous thanks to his work in the world's leading hotel restaurants like the Ritz-Carlton in Seoul and San Francisco, Sheraton in Tianjin, or Fairmont in Dubai. However, if we compare him to *Sikkaek* characters, Kwon acted more in Pongju's or Changŭn's style rather than Sŏngch'an's as he firmly advocated for the adaptation of Korean traditional tastes to global standards.[7] Another important contradiction between such a gendered media representation of national food and the social reality is the fact that while female food professionals remain in the shadows in the *Sikkaek* reflection, in real life they still play an active role. Ironically enough, the food scenes director for all three *Sikkaek* cinematic productions was a female professional food specialist, Kim Sujin. There are more examples of this kind: the food scenes consultant for *Dae Jang Geum* was Han Pokryŏ, a daughter of Professor Hwang Hyesŏng, who revived the royal court food tradition for modern Koreans. Han also supervised the South Korean reception at the historic Inter-Korean Summit of 2000. The supervisor of the 2007 Inter-Korean Summit was another renowned *hansik* specialist: Professor Yun Sukcha, a director of the Institute of Traditional Korean Food (*Han'guk chŏnt'ong ŭmsik yŏn'guso*). All these experts are female.

CONCLUSION

Sikkaek as a multilayered cultural phenomenon could only appear in the 2000s when gastronationalistic ideology was at its zenith in Korea. Actually, *Dae Jang Geum* and *Sikkaek* became the first Korean movies of the so-called "food film" genre (in which food plays a starring role and/or where leading characters are cooks and the camera focuses in on food preparation so that it fills the screen [Bower 2004, 5–6]). The *Sikkaek* series absorbed and represented all the perceptions and sentiments about national foodways that had been circulating in the Korean public discourse in those years, such as seeing certain products and eating customs as an epitomization of Korean national character and culture (Han 2000), heavy laudation of traditional cuisine, and contrapositioning Korean food against other countries' culinary traditions, stressing *hansik*'s potential to reinforce Korea's global image. For this reason, *Sikkaek* showed national food in a gentrified manner constructed in a way that could appeal to viewers and fulfill their fantasies and expectations. This explains why the *Sikkaek* filmmakers unintentionally chose the same type of gender roles to represent national foodways: the figure of a male professional chef met global cookery industry trends and looked convincing, ready to advocate for national cuisine on the field of international culinary competition. The female image in its turn expressed in a mother figure manifested the ideas of the motherland and tragic Korean past.

Such an approach to female roles in the domain of national cuisine can be seen not only in *Sikkaek* but also in some other media products of the 2000s and later. For example, gender studies scholar Jooyeon Rhee in her analysis of contemporary Korean TV cooking shows describes the TV program *Han'gugin-ui papsang* (Koreans' dinner table) that features rural *ajummas* (a Korean word for middle-aged women with children, that is, mothers) and their home dietary routine. As Rhee explains, in the program food and cooking are embellished with nostalgia for the traditional kitchen and motherly love. However, these women's femininity is solely defined by their domestic role; they are women with no profession who put family first in their lives. The *ajummas* are fetishized in this program with a national rhetoric but in reality such a representation only reproduces the gender stereotype about domestic cooking as blue-collar or women's work in the name of nostalgia and tradition (Rhee 2019, 56, 59). The same tendency can be observed in *Sikkaek* where there are no professional female chefs on the screen (except for Changŭn, but as it was shown she is presented with a masculine image) and the only female identity with Korean cookery proficiency is a "suffering mother."

The topic of national cuisine was a hot issue in the 2000s, which is why the mass media exploited it actively. Besides *Dae Jang Geum* and *Sikkaek* there were other TV dramas featuring Korean food in their plot. For example, *Chintcha chintcha choahae* (*Love Truly*, MBC, 2006) tells the story of a young provincial girl who is given a chance to become a chef at the presidential residence, or *Sindŭr-ŭi manch'an* (*Feast of the Gods*, MBC, 2012). The show was unofficially called a "female version of *Sikkaek*" because it was about a celebrated restaurant of royal cuisine named *Arirang* where the head chef and all the characters were women. However, these gender-alternative representations of national food themes in media appeared much less successful in viewership. The first *Sikkaek* movie was the most popular in terms of box office results (3,038,868 tickets sold) while the sequel movie *Kimchi Battle* has not reached even a million (460,636 tickets sold).[8] As for drama ratings, the most successful was the *Sikkaek* drama, reaching 25.5 percent of the channel's viewers, while the *Feast of the Gods* reached 20.4 percent and *Love Truly* only 12.3 percent.[9] These numbers indirectly indicate that the media products featuring professional female chefs attracted a smaller audience. As for *Sikkaek*, it should be added that the series did not end in the 2000s but continued to exist in new formats. First, in 2014 Hur Young Man started the sequel *manhwa*, *Sikkaek-2*, and later in 2019 he became the host of the new TV food show *Sikkaek Hur Young Man-ŭi paekpan kihaeng* (can be translated as "A food trip of *sikkaek* Hur Young Man"), featuring a similar gender structure where a male media star travels around the country to taste traditional Korean dishes served to him mainly by humble female cooks that run simple, authentic eateries.

All these prove that mass media not only reflect the imagery that the audience wants to see but also construct it on the basis of the dominant-at-the-moment ideological climate in society. The 2000s witnessed the surge of gastronationalistic rhetoric that was picked up and reworked by mass media and this resulted in the revision of the gendered representation of national foodways. With the status elevation of Korean cuisine, female food specialists failed to find their place in the national food media narrative, giving way to male professional chefs who had been rare guests in that field before the 2000s. The only role left for a female person that stands for authentic Korean taste in the mass media was that of a mother. Therefore, it can be concluded that Korean gastronationalism maintains gender inequality in the realm of national dietary practices and this confirms one of the basic standpoints of the specialists in food and gender (Counihan and Kaplan 1998, 11) who emphasized that gender relations around food mirror the power struggle between genders in general.

NOTES

1. "Campaign starts to globalize Korean food," *The Korea Times*, Oct. 16, 2008, http://www.koreatimes.co.kr/www/news/biz/2008/10/123_32807.html. Accessed Feb. 2, 2021.

2. "Major cartoonist hands over works to museum," *The Korea Herald*, May 22, 2011, http://www.koreaherald.com/view.php?ud=20110522000263. Accessed Feb. 2, 2021.

3. "Chung3, 2kaewŏrŭi chayu (Two months of freedom of middle school third-years)," *Hankyoreh*, Jan. 4, 2011, https://news.naver.com/main/read.nhn?mode=LSD&mid=sec&sid1=001&oid=028&aid=0000039821. Accessed Feb. 3, 2021.

4. "Match'aja sammalli, hŏyŏngman 'sikkaek' 27kwŏn taejangjŏng mamuri [A long way in search for taste, Hur Young Man has finished the last 27th volume of *Sikkaek*]," *Newsis*, May 24, 2010, https://newsis.com/ar_detail/view.html?ar_id=NISX20100524_0005268313&cID=10607&pID=10600. Accessed Feb. 2, 2021.

5. "Asiana offers high quality in-flight meals," *The Korea Times*, Nov. 29, 2007, https://www.koreatimes.co.kr/www/tech/2020/09/129_14612.html. Accessed Feb. 19, 2021.

6. "First lady promotes Korean food via CNN," *The Korea Times*, Oct. 19, 2009, http://www.koreatimes.co.kr/www/news/nation/2009/10/113_53774.html. Accessed Feb. 22, 2021.

7. "Localization key to food globalization," *The Korea Times*, Feb. 26, 2009, http://www.koreatimes.co.kr/www/culture/2019/09/141_40297.html, Accessed Feb. 22, 2021; "Edward Kwon's Quest to Globalize Korean Cuisine," *Koreana* 33 (2): 64–67.

8. The website of the Korean Film Council, https://www.kobis.or.kr/kobis/business/mast/mvie/searchMovieList.do. Accessed March 1, 2021.

9. According to Nielsen Korea (television audience measurement).

REFERENCES

Bower, Anne L. 2004. "Watching Food: The Production of Food, Film, and Values." In *Reel Food: Essays on Food and Film*, edited by Anne L. Bower, 1–13. New York: Routledge.

Chapple-Sokol, Sam. 2013. "Culinary Diplomacy: Breaking Bread to Win Hearts and Minds." *The Hague Journal of Diplomacy* 8: 161–183.

Chŏng, Hyekyŏng. 2009. *Ch'ŏnnyŏn hansik kyŏnmullok* [Millennium records of Korean food]. Seoul: Saenggag-ŭi namu.

Counihan, Carole M., and Steven L. Kaplan, eds. 1998. *Food and Gender: Identity and Power*. Amsterdam: Harwood Academic Publishers.

Cwiertka, Katarzyna J. 2004. "Daejanggeum and the Gentrification of Korean Food Culture." *Korea Foundation Newsletter* 13 (1). http://newsletter.kf.or.kr/english/print.asp?no=471.

———. 2014. "The Global Hansik Campaign and the Commodification of Korean Cuisine." In *The Korean Popular Culture: Reader*, edited by Kyung Hyun Kim and Youngmin Choe, 363–384. Durham: Duke University Press.

DeSoucey, Michaela. 2010. "Gastronationalism: Food Traditions and Authenticity Politics in the European Union." *American Sociological Review* 73 (3): 432–455.

Druckman, Charlotte. 2010. "Why Are There No Great Women Chefs?" *Gastronomica* 10 (1): 24–31.

Ferguson, Priscilla Parkhurst. 2010. "Culinary Nationalism." *Gastronomica* 10 (1): 102–109.

Han, Bokchin. 2001. *Uri saenghal 100-nyŏn—ŭmsik* [A century of our life—food]. Seoul: Hyŏnamsa.

Han, Kyung-Koo. 2000. "Some Foods are Good to Think: Kimchi and the Epitomization of National Character." *Korean Social Science Journal* 27 (1): 221–235.

Han'guk chŏngshin munhwa yŏn'guwŏn (Academy of Korean Studies). 1991–2002. *Han'guk minjok munhwa taebakkwa sajŏn* [Encyclopedia of Korean culture]. Sŏngnam: han'guk chŏngshin munhwa yŏn'guwŏn.

Hur, Young Man. 2003–2010. *Sikkaek*. Vols. 1–27. Paju: Kimyeongsa.

Jeon, Yun Su. 2011. "Sarye yŏn'gu—changp'yŏn kŭngnyŏnghwa <Sikkaek> pŭllaindŭ monit'ŏ sisa kyŏlgwa punsŏk" [Case study—analysis on blind monitoring results of the feature film <Le Grand Chef>]. *Hyŏndae yŏnghwa yŏn'gu* 27 (2): 235–262.

Kim, Soochul. 2015. "1980-nyŏndae ihu han'guk t'ellebijŏn ŭmsik-p'ŭrogŭraem-gwa ŭmsik-munhwa-ŭi kwan'gye-e taehan koch'al <onŭr-ŭi yori>esŏ <naengjanggo-rŭl put'ak'ae>kkaji" [Rethinking television food program and national food culture in South Korea since the 1980s: from <Onŭr-ŭi yori> show to <Naengjanggo-rŭl put'ak'ae>]." *Pangsong munhwa yŏn'gu* 27 (2): 86–112.

McClintock, Anne. 1991. "'No Longer in a Future Heaven': Women and Nationalism in South Africa." *Transition* 5: 104–123.

Molony, Barbara, Janet Theiss, and Hyaeweol Choi. 2016. *Gender in Modern East Asia: An Integrated History*. Boulder, CO: Westview Press.

Moon, Ok Pyo. 2010. "Dining Elegance and Authenticity: Archeology of Royal Court Cuisine in Korea." *Korea Journal* 50 (1): 36–59.

Nelson, Laura. 2000. *Measured Excess: Status, Gender, and Consumer Nationalism in South Korea*. New York: Columbia University Press.

Osetrova, Maria. 2016. "National Food and Gastronationlism in Contemporary Korea." PhD diss., Yonsei University, Republic of Korea.

Park, Kyoung Hee. 2013. "State and Food in South Korea: Moulding the National Diet in Wartime and Beyond." PhD dissertation, Leiden University, the Netherlands.

Pemberton, Robert W. 2001. "Wild-Gathered Foods as Countercurrents to Dietary Globalization in South Korea." In *Asian Food: The Global and the Local*, edited by Katarzyna Cwiertka with Boudewijn Walraven, 76–94. Richmond: Curzon Press.

Rhee, Jooyeon. 2019. "Gender Politics in Food Escape: Korean Masculinity in TV Cooking Shows in South Korea." *Journal of Popular Film and Television* 47 (1): 56–64.

Warde, Alan, and Lydia Martens. 2000. *Eating Out: Social Differentiation, Consumption and Pleasure*. Cambridge, UK, and New York: Cambridge University Press.

Yoon, Hahna. 2020. "The Oldest Cookbook in Korean was Written by a Genius Noblewoman." *Atlas Obscura*, Sept. 3, 2020. https://www.atlasobscura.com/articles/first-korean-cookbook.

Yoon, In-jin. 2007. "Han'guk minjokchuŭi tamnon-ŭi chŏn'gae-wa taeanjŏk minjokchuŭi-ŭi mosaek [The development of South Korea's nationalism discourses and the exploration of alternative of nationalism in a global era]." *Han'guk sahoe* 8 (1): 5–30.

Part II

BODY AND EMBODIMENT

Chapter 4

The Body as Food

Gender, Eating, and Cannibalism in Yan Lianke's The Four Books

Shelley W. Chan

ABSTRACT

This chapter studies *The Four Books*, a banned novel by Yan Lianke, one of the most prominent writers in contemporary China. It focuses on the relationship between food, gender, and politics, which is an important part of the novel, and investigates how the narrative of food, both edible and forbidden, and that of eating are not only politically and morally constructed, but also articulated in a gender discourse in the Confucian-Communist cultural context. It also analyzes the gendered cannibalism in a setting of the great famine during the Great Leap Forward Campaign launched by Mao Zedong in the late 1950s, and examines Chinese manhood exemplified by a major character in the novel. This chapter finds that women in China are victims of both the masculine state power and fellow citizens who are deeply influenced by traditional patriarchy. Mao Zedong's advocacy for Chinese women seemingly improved their political, social, and economic status, yet it was ultimately an attempt to strengthen the collective power rather than an awareness of gender equality. In addition, this chapter discusses how gendered food and the issue of cannibalism in *The Four Books* establish a dialogue with two principal modern Chinese writers, Lu Xun and Mo Yan.

INTRODUCTION

Yan Lianke (1958–) is one of the most controversial writers in mainland China today. Nationally and internationally known, this prolific writer has won numerous important awards at home and abroad, including two consecutive Lu Xun Literary Prizes (1997 and 2001), the Franz Kafka Prize (2014), the Dream of the Red Chamber Award (2016), and the Newman Prize for Chinese Literature (2021), to list just a few. However, he has not been able to publish his books in China for several years. *The Four Books*, one of his most important novels, was set during the Great Leap Forward Campaign launched in the late 1950s during which approximately thirty million people died of starvation. The book was rejected by about two dozen publishers on the mainland before eventually being published in Taiwan and Hong Kong in 2011. By setting the story in the Great Leap Forward Campaign, and especially by writing about the great famine during the campaign and the resulting cannibalism, a common by-product of famines, Yan Lianke stepped in a politically tabooed zone that had rarely been fully delineated by novelists due to its sensitive nature.

A masterpiece of contemporary Chinese literature, *The Four Books* is a powerful yet complicated novel to the extent that no single article can exhaust its importance. What catches the attention of the present writer is exactly the book's complexity, especially in portraying the relationship between food and gender, a topic hardly explored in depth by other writers in China. Throughout the novel, food and eating are heavily invested with gender significance, and the food-related happenings are turned into gender-imprinted activities. Meanwhile, female and male bodies form a victim-victimizer-redeemer relationship. The reactions of the fictional characters to the extreme adversity, in which food is essential for survival, are paradoxically depicted as consistent and inconsistent with the shared assumptions of gender and sexuality in Chinese society. This chapter investigates how the narrative of food, both edible and forbidden, and that of eating are not only politically and morally constructed, but also articulated in a gender discourse in the Confucian-Communist cultural context. While analyzing survival cannibalism in the novel, the chapter also discusses gender-related self-offering cannibalism and an alternative/quasi vampirism, which exemplifies human absurdity driven by extreme political/societal hardship. Furthermore, the chapter sheds light on how gendered food and the issue of cannibalism in *The Four Books* establish a dialogue with two principal modern Chinese writers, Lu Xun (1881–1936), the father of modern Chinese literature, and Mo Yan (1955–), the 2012 recipient of the Nobel Prize in Literature.

The Great Leap Forward: The Masculine State Power over the Female Body

Immediately after the establishment of the People's Republic of China (PRC) in 1949, and especially after its involvement in the Korean War from 1950 to 1953, Mao Zedong (1893–1976), the supreme leader of the Chinese Communist Party (CCP), decided to speed up the construction of new China to catch up with the developed countries in the West. The first Five-Year Plan, introduced in 1953, adopted the Soviet model to build up the economy of the new regime. The second Five-Year Plan from 1958 to 1962 was of great significance. As scholars observed, "The year 1958 began with the Chinese Communist leaders optimistic about their ability to lead the country up the path of rapid economic development and social progress" (MacFarquhar and Fairbank 1987, 293). During this Five-Year Plan, Mao launched a social and economic campaign called Three Red Banners, consisting of the General Line for Socialist Construction, the Great Leap Forward, and the People's Communes. These Three Red Banners set the tone and direction for the socialist construction: under the general line that urged people to exert the utmost effort, strive for the best, and build socialism in a greater, faster, better, and more economical way, speed and collectivism were highly emphasized. Farmers all over the country were organized into People's Communes. "By the end of 1958, virtually the entire rural population of some 500 million was under the control of this new and bizarre form of organization which formed the institutional framework of the Great Leap Forward" (Becker 1996, 104). As a matter of fact, the foundation of the new republic was not solid enough for such a speedy construction. Mao was overambitious, the party he led was overconfident, and their orders did not always prove to be reasonable and logical. To the contrary, the orders they gave more often than not violated the rules of nature, such as setting unrealistically high goals for industrial and agricultural productions. Unfortunately, local officials were competing with one another to cater to the people above and their eagerness for quick success, which led to common practices of false reporting, boastfulness, and exaggeration among local leadership. As discussed by Fairbank:

> Part of China's inheritance was that their state of morale, their loyalty to the center . . . CCP . . . could reassert the old practices of officialism, oriented upward toward seeking their superiors' approval rather than downward to serve the people. When morale was high, local authorities might zealously compete to report how well they had carried out the center's orders. In addition to overoptimistic false reporting, they might coerce the populace to get results. . . . Underlying this situation was another inherited factor, the docility of the Chinese peasantry, who were remarkably inured to following the dictates of authority. . . . The people trusted Chairman Mao. This at once opened the door to utopianism and illusion because the party cadres, drawn increasingly from the upper ranks of the peasantry, were fervently ready to go along, follow the leader, and bring the masses with them. Thus local obedience to the party, plus the personal cult of Mao Zedong, could create mass hysteria. (Fairbank 1992, 368–369)

False science and false promises, plus natural disasters which the CCP has always blamed for their situation, led to a great famine from 1959 to 1962, one of the most serious in human history.[1] It is commonly believed that approximately thirty million people starved to death, but the actual number of deaths remains unknown, like Zhou Xun claims, "The history of the Great Famine in China has long been obscured by official taboos and restricted access to primary sources. Until 1990 very little essential archival material on the subject was available either to historians or to the general public" (Zhou 2012, ix). Cases of cannibalism during the famine were reported.

It is against this background that Yan Lianke writes his phenomenal novel, *The Four Books*, a novel about famine, hunger, and cannibalism intertwined with power and control between men's and women's traditional gender roles. The story of *The Four Books* is about a group of intellectuals who are sent to a labor camp during the Great Leap Forward, namely, the ninety-ninth district, one of the camps in the Re-Ed region alongside the banks of the Yellow River, China's mother river. They receive reeducation through hard labor in the camp because their thoughts are at odds with Mao and the central government. The district is run by a nameless juvenile called the Child, who is controlled by people above him. The characters are nameless as well, being identified with their professions, such as the Author, the Musician, the Scholar, and so on, and they work under extremely harsh physical conditions. In order to motivate these men and women to work hard, the Child establishes an award system, giving red blossoms or stars as rewards to those who do well, with promises that accumulating a certain amount of the rewards will bring them freedom. Under such circumstances, the dark side of human nature is exposed, and human values such as trust, integrity, and ethics are defeated by the strong desire to leave the camp.

An experimental work by Yan Lianke, *The Four Books* has a title that would make the reader associate it with the Confucian classics of the *Analects*, *Mencius*, *The Great Learning*, and the *Doctrine of the Mean*. Nevertheless, the novel is actually structured by a mixture of Yan's own four fictional books: *Heaven's Child*, *Old Course*, *Criminal Records*, and *A New Myth of Sisyphus*. Two of the books are written by the character of the Author who is collecting materials and composing a long novel entitled *Old Course*. Meanwhile, in order to obtain paper, pens, and ink for writing his novel from the Child, and more importantly, in order to please the Child so as to get more rewards, he accepts a secret task that the Child assigns to him: to spy on his fellow detainees by recording and reporting their words and activities. The reports form his second book: *Criminal Records*. The anonymous *Heaven's Child* is written in a biblical style and in the third-person narrative voice describing how the Child runs the camp. Lastly, *A New Myth of Sisyphus*, a philosophical revision of *Myth of Sisyphus*, is a disproportionately short manuscript and is supposedly written by the Scholar. The first three books interweave together to fabricate the story of *The Four Books*, and the short fourth book ends the entire novel. To be precise, the novel has sixteen chapters altogether. While sometimes one chapter contains several segments from one book only, other times one chapter is composed of segments from different books. The very last chapter, that is, Chapter 16, is the entire book of *A New Myth of Sisyphus*.

Chapter 1 of the novel, "Heaven's Child," takes the form of four segments from the book *Heaven's Child*. It tells of the Child returning to the camp from the town where he had received instructions from the higher-ups, and announcing the camp's ten commandments, emphasizing that those who tried to flee would be executed. Similar to local leaders all over China at that time, the Child coerced the detainees to set unrealistically high yielding goals for their agricultural production. Besides assigning the Author to keep watch on his fellow detainees, the Child also encouraged the detainees to spy on one another so as to be rewarded the opportunity to return home.

One of the activities being spied on was the illicit relationship between two detainees, the Scholar, a married man, and the Musician, a single woman. The Technician, the youngest detainee in the reeducation camp, discovered their relationship and wanted to be rewarded with permission to "return home for a month" (Yan 2015, 29). Interestingly, it was food that disclosed their affair. After one day's hard work, the detainees were taking a break and some of them were baking sweet potatoes as snacks. At this point, "the Technician pulled me [the Author] aside behind one of the furnaces and whispered, 'Author, look at this. The Musician is about to give the Scholar the sweet potato she is holding'" (61). After a minute, the Author saw that the Musician "walked over and squatted down directly behind the Scholar, discreetly placing the sweet potato she was holding into his pocket. The scholar . . . retreated to the far end of the area. After making sure no one was around, he hid between a furnace and a wood pile, and began eating" (61–62).

The relationship between food and women has been a much-discussed topic in gender studies. More often than not, women are portrayed as food providers, cooks, and feeders. "Women's bodies have the capacity to manufacture food for their infants which categorises them as feeders, and in western culture women have traditionally borne most of the burden of cooking for and nourishing others" (Sceats 2000, 2). In the abovementioned episode, food supplies are adequate, as it is the beginning of the Great Leap Forward—for working hard to smelt steel, the detainees' district is awarded 25 kilograms of pork and 15 kilograms of beef and mutton. As a result, life is not that hard, and they even feel that the atmosphere in the camp is like celebrating the New Year. In this case, the sweet potato that the Musician gives the Scholar serves not so much as lifesaving food but as a token of love. Nevertheless, this token filled with the woman's affection to the man accidentally reveals her secret to the Technician, which eventually brings the couple in love big trouble while potentially putting the Technician in a favorable position to escape from adversity. Whereas an affair between a man and a woman serves as a public entertainment in ordinary times, this one is politicized, being regarded as a wonderful opportunity to win a reward so as to speed up the process of returning home for a political detainee because "catching a pair of adulterers will earn us at least twenty small blossoms, which can be converted into four medium-sized ones" (Yan 2015, 62).[2] However, the Technician's dream was dashed due to the Author's decision of keeping this opportunity for himself: while he alerted the Scholar to the danger of being discovered and arrested, he reported the affair to the Child at the same time. Later the Scholar and the Musician were caught red-handed and led away in the absence of the Technician. The Author was rewarded with red blossoms, and the district was given food: 7.5 kilograms of pork and 15 kilograms of beef. The incident brought joy to the district: while men and women worked hard on their own duties, they also spent time discussing the adulterous affair, which, together with the extra food, got them excited. Ironically, the adulterous affair disclosed by food not only earns physical food for these political inmates but also provides them with exciting entertainment in their boring and miserable lives. A triangular relationship among food, gender, and politics is thus formed. Politics is translated through food and gender in the following way: the love that the Musician shows to the Scholar is remorselessly consumed by her fellow detainees, who, by consuming it, have been turned into predators at the same time as being prey in this social and political turmoil.

Food has been an important topic of scholarly studies. As David Arnold claims:

> Its importance was felt at all levels of society, both by those who suffered directly for want of basic sustenance and those whose authority, security and profit were threatened as the indirect consequence of death and mass starvation—from the family to the state, from the peasant households of medieval Europe or Imperial China to the colonial empires of the nineteenth century and the international market economy of the present day. Food was, and continues to be, power in a most basic, tangible and inescapable form. . . . Food was not only essential for the maintenance of human life and bodily activity, but was also fundamental to the structures of dominance and dependency that arose out of this most vital of all commodities. Food (and the denial or absence of food that famine entailed) was (and remains even in a relatively secure and secularized society like our own) richly symbolic, a potent and recurrent motif in the semantics of kingship and statecraft, in the language and imagery of religion and culture. (Arnold 1988, 3–4)

Ancient Chinese philosophy regards the appetites for food and sex as part of human nature, and so they are in a juxtaposed dimension, both belonging to basic human instincts. In *The Four Books*, however, food and sex are complicated by power, and converted into a trading relationship. The flaws of the Great Leap Forward Campaign gradually show, and food supplies start to get tight: "There wasn't enough to eat . . . eating only one meal a day, consisting of a two-*liang* black bun and a bowl of cornmeal broth" (Yan 2015, 228).[3] The detainees' faces and legs become swollen from hunger. Finally, a famine is presented to the reader. Food becomes a token of power dictating everything, including human conscience, dignity, and sex, and "signif[ying] something beyond nourishment and pleasure, and a history of the nation . . . eating is chronicled" (Farquhar 2002, 93). David Arnold, who believes that historians should "speculate on famine's wider historical character and meaning," asserts that "in a singular way famine is, or should be, of particular moment to the history-making of our time. . . . Famine opens up to our understanding at least a fragment of the historical experience of subordinate social groups and of their interactions with the state and elites that would otherwise remain lost to us" (Arnold 1988, 2–3). In *The Four Books*, the narrative of food is not only politicized but also moralized and sexualized, opening up the reader's understanding of the experience of Chinese intellectuals at the particular historical moment of the Great Leap Forward Campaign.

The Author continued to spy on the detainees and report to the Child in *Criminal Records*. At first, the Author traded a little grain for every page of the report he had submitted. When the grain supply was reduced, he received a fistful of grain for five pages, and eventually he was only able to get a handful of fried soybeans when he turned in new submissions. His sensitivity was sharpened by hunger, and he made new discoveries in the process of spying: he witnessed the Musician trading her own body for food. It is almost a cliché in feminist criticism that women and the female body are treated as commodities in patriarchal societies. Yet, unfortunately, this is still true even in Communist China in which gender equalities are advocated and celebrated. The communist government has made efforts to break the Confucian tradition of valuing men over women, and Mao's sayings in favor of women have played a rather important role in improving Chinese women's political, social, and economical statuses after 1949.[4] However, the tradition of considering women as the second sex has been so deeply rooted that these efforts certainly have not eradicated the commodification of the female body. When a woman is trapped in an extremely dire situation, a man gets an easy good opportunity to turn the woman's body into a commodity in exchange for his "help" as a provider. In the novel, the Musician is such a woman—the exceptionally poor economic/materialistic conditions caused by the failure of the Great Leap Forward drives her to struggle on the verge of death. To trade her body for food from a male provider becomes the only way out for her. As a result, the Musician sleeps with a male leader of a different district on a regular basis because the man has the power to get food. The following quote discloses how the woman is turned into a nonhuman when the male higher-up uses food to bait her like baiting an animal:

> The man took a fist-sized bag from his waist and lifted it, and then they both disappeared into the empty furnace. . . . The man was on top and panting as he did his thing, like a pig, while the Musician angled her head away from him and stared upward. The object of her gaze was a small hole in the side of the furnace, in which there was a black bun. The bun was about two feet from her face. . . . The man, however, didn't let her eat it, and instead made her focus on the task at hand. The Musician kept staring at the bun, her eyes looking as though they were about to explode. . . . After a brief rest, he reached into his pants pocket and pulled out a steamed bun. . . . He said three words to the Musician: "Pure fine grain." He nudged the Musician's shoulder, and she quickly got out from under the comforter and began crawling forward like a dog, such that he could then enter her from behind. As he did so, she raised her head even higher, staring intently at that steamed bun. (Yan 2015, 255–256)

Indeed, when the woman with limited resources is forced to sell her body to survive the famine, she has not turned herself into a nonhuman. It is the man who not only exploits her body but also takes away her human dignity and dehumanizes her. That the man who has power and a better supply of food becomes the agent of the dehumanization of the woman exemplifies the hierarchical relation between the sexes in general and the complications of food, sex, and politics in the context of the Great Leap Forward Campaign.

A similarly graphic and disturbing scene appears in the novel *Big Breasts and Wide Hips* by Mo Yan: a male cook trades food for sex with a young female rightist;[5] the latter allows the man to put his male organ that is "unaffected by the famine of 1960" into her body while she is trying to grab the steamed bun in the man's hand (Mo 2005, 434). Mo Yan's female character is also reduced to nonhuman: "Like a dog stealing food, she forced herself to tolerate the painful posterior attack as she gobbled down the food, continuing to swallow even when it was gone. . . . The dry bun had gone down hard, stretching her throat, so she thrust out her neck like a duck" (434).

In a time when people were so starved that "women stopped menstruating, and their breasts stuck to their ribs" (Mo 1995, 460),[6] this man's organ was "unaffected by the famine of 1960," as quoted above. The inequality between the sexes and the sexual exploitation of women by men with either political power (like the leader in Yan Lianke's story) or materialistic power (like the cook in Mo Yan's novel) are clearly displayed. The famine actually provided an opportunity for those males who abuse their power to take advantage of women, and this is proved by the comments made by the higher-up in Yan Lianke's novel after having intercourse with the Musician: "Thank God for the famine. That was fucking great!" (Yan 2015, 256). The fact that the two most prominent contemporary Chinese writers wrote about the sexual abuses that Chinese women had experienced discloses the generality of this phenomenon. Gang Yue has pointed out, "Prolonged hunger can reduce humans to helpless creatures" (Yue 1999, 295). Interestingly, the upsetting scenes in both texts contain animal imagery to bring out the notion of dehumanization on both ends: the sexual predators and the victims. We have seen the images of pig, dog, and duck in the above descriptions from both novels. Actually in *Big Breasts and Wide Hips* Mo Yan described the rapist as a male rabbit after mating (Mo 1995, 461).[7] When one scrutinizes both scenes, one can see that the animal images that Yan Lianke uses are culturally harsher and sterner than those used by Mo Yan. In Chinese tradition, pigs and dogs are more often than not used with negative connotations. When somebody is said to be worse than pigs and dogs (*zhugou buru*), it is almost like a curse for a heinous and evil villain lacking the most basic human virtues. Not to mention that the word "dog" used for a woman would easily cause the association with "bitch," an insulting expression for women not only in English but in the Chinese language as well. The use of animal imagery serves to lay bare the double victimization of women: while they suffer from starvation as much as men do during the great famine, their animal instinct for survival drives them to become the target of male sexual exploitation. On the other hand, while the two women become "helpless creatures," the two men are turned into the lowest nonhumans by their own beastly behavior, so low that it is beyond anyone's language ability to describe it. Both male characters in the novels are indeed worse than animals, as no animal would humiliatingly tease its prey like these humans to maximize the satisfaction of its own desire. As Peter Brooks asserts, the body is "at once the subject and object of pleasure, the uncontrollable agent of pain" (Brooks 1993, 1). It is also "the agent and object of desire" (5). In the cases of Yan Lianke's and Mo Yan's stories, the male body is the subject and agent of pleasure and (sexual) desire, while the female body is the object of male sexual desire but the subject and agent of pain and the desire for survival.

The Musician is such a tragic figure under the oppression/consumption of masculine power that the abuse/use of her body does not stop even after her death. Ironically, the exploitation of the Musician does not only come from the direct sexual assaulter but also from her fellow male detainees. The food she obtained by selling her own body no doubt prolonged her life, but at the same time it helped other men. Even in such a difficult time the Musician did not forget her role as a food provider—intentionally for the Scholar, but unintentionally for the Author. The Author returned to the ninety-ninth district after his voyeurism of the consummation in the abandoned furnace and went to the Scholar's dormitory, where he found some fried soybeans that the Musician had hidden there for the Scholar. He stole the food. This happened more than one time. Later the Author told the Scholar what he saw the Musician and the other man doing, and confessed to him: "Whenever the Musician hid some food under your covers for you, I would always steal it and eat it" (Yan 2015, 272). The shocked but magnanimous Scholar later indicated his understanding: "These days, as long as someone manages to avoid starving to death, it doesn't really matter what else they do" (272). A gentleman like the Scholar, who had tried hard to help the Musician with heavy labor work and to collect more rewards to go home, asked the Author this question when he learned that the Musician had gone to see the man again: "When the Musician returns, will she bring *us* something to eat?" (280).[8] After he got the affirmative reply, he made a promise: "As long as she can come back and give *us* half a bowl of soybeans, I plan to divorce my wife and marry the Musician as soon as we have a chance to return home" (280–281).[9] Indeed, famine and hunger show their incomparable and ultimate power. When one faces death in a big famine like this, what matters is how to manage to live on. Other things, like human dignity, fairness, faithfulness, and so on, have to give way to the animal instinct for survival. The common feelings in a romantic relationship, such as jealousy and anger over a partner's unfaithfulness, do not matter. In the above quoted dialogues, when the word "us" is used, the Scholar and the Author are strangely bonded together to form a male league to consume the female body. To believe that granting a marriage to the woman to whom he is indebted is a kind of compensation, the Scholar holds, maybe unconsciously, a male chauvinist mindset, and he probably does not realize that he is doing harm to another woman, his own wife. The ultimate victims are women after all.

The Musician was also seen trying to get food from the Child by offering herself to him without success.[10] Eventually she choked to death:

> She had died while kneeling on that grass and those blankets. . . . Blood was flowing down the inside of her legs. . . . When she died, her mouth was full of soybeans that she had not yet had a chance to swallow, and she was tightly grasping more beans in her hands. . . . She was menstruating when she died. She must have been kneeling in front of that man and ravenously eating fried soybeans. (Yan 2015, 283)

She died bleeding, and bleeding indecently, with her body being invaded and the food that she had traded for with her body causing her death. She died with her body and menstruation blood exposed to the male gaze of the rapist and the voyeur, the Author. The remorseless description of menstruation blood in the scene is powerful in that it further demonstrates what and how women have suffered, and also symbolizes the traditional concept of women being inferior to men, as observed by scholars. Susan Brownell and Jeffrey Wasserstrom assert that "women's blood was considered to be constantly depleted by childbirth and menstruation; moreover, to be ruled by one's blood meant that one was controlled by one's emotion. Thus, physiology was used to justify women's submission to the superior vitality of men" (Brownell and Wasserstrom 2002, 287). Not to mention in traditional Chinese culture, like in many other cultures, menstruation is considered unclean and dangerous. "Imagined as a source of contagion, liable to make crops wither and to offend the gods, it has been associated with female threats to forms of cosmic and social order managed and defended by men" (Brownell and Wasserstrom 2002, 291). The blood was like a scarlet letter symbolizing the humiliation she had suffered and the loss of her dignity as a woman. Indeed the Musician reduces herself to a sexual commodity, yet at the same time she is still acting as the food provider for a man, the Scholar, and unconsciously for a second man, the Author. Being the sign of vitality, the life-nurturing menstruation blood symbolizes her will to not only save her own life but also her lover's. One may argue that the Musician challenges the hierarchical order by sleeping with a leader and also trying to convince the Child to have sex with her. It is true that there is a certain degree of agency in the Musician, which makes her the only person who does not commit cannibalism among the major detainee characters. However, what she aims at is actually the power the men possess, and in her mind the only translation of power is food. What she does is not challenging their authority, as challenge usually suggests subversiveness. The Musician does not intend to subvert the hierarchy but only uses the men with power to meet her needs.

Unfortunately, her body was consumed by a man, the Author, even after her death:

> I took her head and placed it on my leg, letting her long hair flow through my fingers like water. A sense of conjugal warmth seemed to emanate from her dead body and entered through my thigh into my own body. . . . After caressing her face for a while, I hugged her body close to mine, so that her entire upper body was leaning against my legs. In this way, I enjoyed the love of a female corpse. (Yan 2015, 285)

Without doubt, as a woman, the Musician falls victim to the maltreatments of the opposite sex. First of all, she is one of the numerous female sufferers of the nationwide famine launched by Mao and his government, a man of supremacy and the state apparatus representing masculine power. Second, the extreme hunger forces her to trade her body with a man for food. Third, two other men, the Scholar and the Author, are relying on the food she has obtained by scarifying her body as well as her human dignity. Her "role as a consumable" turns herself into an edible woman, to borrow the title of a novel published in 1969 by Margaret Atwood, and the men are eating her body as food to quench their physical and sexual hunger (Sceats 2000, 96). Lastly, even after her death, she is consumed by a man, the Author, who not only steals her food but also uses her dead body to satisfy his sexual desire.

Cannibalism and the Negotiation of Manhood

While the Musician traded her body for food, other people ate weeds, wild roots, bark, leaves, leather shoes and belts, and even white clay. People began to die, and, "in the desperation of their hunger people turn to unfamiliar or forbidden foods" (Arnold 1988, 6)—"People were secretly eating human flesh" (Yan 2015, 244).

Yan Lianke is by no means the first modern Chinese author to write about cannibalism. Lu Xun (1881–1936), the father of modern Chinese literature, is known for writing on the theme of people eating people in his "A Madman's Diary" in 1918, arguably the first vernacular modern Chinese fiction. A piercing criticism of the oppressive Chinese traditional culture, the fiction tells a story of a man who suffers from paranoia and believes that people, including his own family members, are planning to eat him, as when he reads between the lines of the Chinese classics, what he gains is two Chinese characters only: *chiren* (eat people). Mo Yan's novel *The Republic of Wine* is another example of a Chinese writer writing about cannibalism. In the novel, a detective is investigating a case where the leaders of a town named Liquorland are reported to eat braised human babies. Although both Lu Xun and Mo Yan list some cannibalistic cases in Chinese history in their stories, the whole *chiren* motif remains by and large in the metaphorical dimension. Gang Yue's observation on writing about cannibalism is apt on Yan Lianke's *The Four Books* when he asserts, "Cannibalism contains a strong political edge, yet the style of writing cannibalism is tinged with surrealism" (Yue 1999, 21). Unlike Lu Xun and Mo Yan, Yan Lianke's descriptions of cannibalistic behaviors are real but paradoxical. For instance, while most people eat human flesh for survival, some practice cannibalism to end their own lives, as they no longer have the desire to live on but are too weak to kill themselves: two detainees eat the body of "the researcher from the agricultural bureau" so they can gain the strength to hang themselves (Yan 2015, 246). They leave a letter telling their fellow detainees, "If any of you wish to live a few more days, you are welcome to eat our flesh. . . . We are leaving these red blossoms and pentagonal stars for you" (246).

Cannibalism has been divided into different categories, such as endocannibalism, exocannibalism, survival cannibalism, ritual cannibalism, and so on. This case in *The Four Books* hardly falls into any of these categories, as the purpose of the cannibalistic practice is paradoxical. If the two cannibals do not eat their fellow detainee, the Researcher, they will starve to death. However, their reason for eating the Researcher is to enable them to end their lives. If the actions of eating and not eating human flesh lead to the same final destination—death—why do they bother to commit cannibalism? I argue that Yan Lianke uses this paradoxical cannibalistic episode to highlight the hopelessness and helplessness of these intellectuals during a very dark page of modern history in China. They are longing to live on, but are despairing over their miserable reality. Even after gaining some strength by eating their peer, they decide to use the strength to kill themselves. Yet they offer their own corpses to the other detainees to encourage survival cannibalism and leave their prizes to them in the hope that their peers might survive to regain the freedom that they have longed for.

This self-offering cannibalism leads to the examination of two more surreal and creepy episodes: another case of self-offering cannibalism and an alternative/quasi vampirism, all committed by the Author, a very interesting character to exemplify masculine values in Chinese culture.

When the famine had just started, the Author's peer detainees discovered that he was spying on them, and so he was beaten up and humiliated. Moreover, the Author was not able to write his own book anymore as his peers would find the pages he had written and destroy them. As a result, he requested to live alone, away from the group, and promised the Child that he could "produce a field of wheat with ears even larger than ears of corn," so the Child "could then take these ears of wheat to the capital and bestow them as a tribute" (Yan 2015, 184–185). One day the Author accidently cut his finger, and he squeezed blood from his fingertips into the water he would use to water the wheat plants. When he discovered that a couple of wheat sprouts that had water with his blood grew better than the others, he started watering all other wheat plants with bloody water. This continued and became more and more frequent. Later he went so far as to slice his fingers, arms, and legs "so that my blood started pouring onto the roots of the plant" (208).

The formulaic revolutionary propaganda during Mao's time demonizes those who are categorized as class enemies, such as landlords and capitalists, by labeling them bloodsuckers who prey on the working classes. In *The Four Books*, the wheat plants are politicized and personified as bloodsuckers as they become important bargaining chips for the Author. At the same time, the Author, an intellectual, is degraded into someone who trades his blood for food and freedom. The wheat plants grew stronger and bigger, and "the entire area became full of that thick smell of blood and wheat" (209). To further dehumanize the Author, Yan Lianke makes him eat the blood-fed grain, arguably turning him into a vampire who sucks his own blood: "I put the grain in my mouth and chewed it, and my mouth was immediately filled with the taste of wheat and blood" (211). The combination of blood and wheat is echoed by the menstruation blood and soybeans in the death scene of the Musician we have discussed, enhancing the struggling and suffering of people, men and women, during the great famine, a mostly man-made calamity.

As Gang Yue points out, "Cannibalism and hunger are invested with gendered desires as well as thematic concerns and generic attributes" (Yue 1999, 289). The following self-offering cannibalism is a good example to study the male gender in the context of China. As discussed above, the Author witnessed the Musician's death in the furnace, and obtained womanly comfort from her body. Then he "felt it was only right that I bury her in the wasteland behind the compound" (Yan 2015, 285). With much effort, the Author managed to carry her corpse back to the wasteland. He was too weak to bury her, and so he had to head back to their dormitory to eat some fried soybeans. He also meant to collect her relics and notify the Scholar. To his astonishment, among the relics were more than a dozen pages from his own *Criminal Records*, on which the activities of the Musician and the Scholar were recorded. Feeling extremely shocked and ashamed, the Author decided that "I should slice two pieces of flesh from my body—from my thighs—boil them, and present them to the Musician's grave, inviting [that guy] to eat them while I watched. I knew that if I did this, it would bring me a tremendous feeling of relief" (290).[11]

China has a history of *gegu liaoqin*—cutting a piece of flesh from one's own thigh to feed one's ailing parent as an enhancement for the efficacy of medicine, which is mentioned in Lu Xun's "A Madman's Diary," when the paranoid madman imagines he would be eaten by his folks. The earliest recorded offering of one's own flesh to someone else is from a pre-Qin document, and it is between a duke and his subordinate who do not have a biological relationship.[12] Later it was intermingled with the Confucian notion of filial piety, one of the most essential parts of Confucianism. While the subordinate offers his own flesh to the duke to show his loyalty, and children offer their flesh to their parents out of the obligation of filialness, the Author's offering of his own flesh to the Musician and the Scholar who have been victims of his disgraceful behavior can be interpreted as a redemption of his soul distorted by revolutionary hunger.[13] Instead of eating the enemies in the name of class struggle or revolution like the episodes recounted in Zheng Yi's 1993 book, *Scarlet Memorial: Tales of Cannibalism in Modern China*, the Author's cannibalistic behavior belongs to medical cannibalism, but the two pieces of flesh from his own thighs are not for the purpose of healing the eaters but healing himself. The desire for self-healing was so strong that the Author's "mind kept returning to that urgent need to slice off two chunks of [his] own flesh" (Yan 2015, 291). He did it eventually, and cooked the two chunks of his flesh with some salt he had managed to obtain. When the Scholar returned to the dormitory, he saw the "meat" soup and the half bag of fried soybeans and asked: "Did the Musician give you this?" When urged by the Author to eat the food while it was still hot, the Scholar "focused on eating that piece of meat with dark red streaks" (296). The self-healing is effective. Watching the Scholar eating the "meat" soup, the Author felt more and more relieved: "Just as the Scholar was about to finish eating, the pile of spasms running through my body began to subside, as did the shivers down my spine. . . . At this point, I knew that the thorn embedded in my heart had finally been dislodged," and he felt grateful to the Scholar and the Musician, "as though they had helped save me" (297).

As an intellectual who writes books, the Author obviously falls into the category of *wen* in Kam Louie's categorization of *wen-wu* (cultural attainment-martial valor) in his *Theorising Chinese Masculinity: Society and Gender in China*, which, according to him, is "the single most important Chinese paradigm explaining the performance of gendered identities—in particular masculinity" (Louie 2002, 4). Louie believes, "While the ideal masculine image achieves a harmony between *wen* and *wu*, . . . the relationship between the two forces has been one of dynamic opposition as well as harmony" (17). At the same time, he also points out that *wen* has been considered superior to *wu* "right from the beginning of Chinese philosophical thought" (4).

Scholars have shed light on different concepts of Chinese manhood in terms of appellations and the associated standards, notably *zhong* (loyalty) and *yi* (righteousness) that have been considered core values men are supposed to possess. As for *zhong*, according to Bret Hinsch, there are "two types of loyalty: to the state and to one's male peers," and these two types of loyalty are "a major source of dramatic tension" (Hinsch 2013, 123). *Yi*, "the most important term related to Chinese honor," as Hinsch asserts, has key importance "to masculine identity" (33). In *The Four Books*, when the two types of *zhong* are in conflict, or when *zhong* and *yi* do not seem to be compatible, the Author tries to negotiate these two values on his own terms to defend his masculine identity.

Let us analyze the Author with these two core values of *zhong* and *yi*. In the first place, his spying on his peer detainees and snitching to the Child, a symbol of the state apparatus, can be regarded as loyalty to the state, although his motivation is hunger and the desire for freedom. Yet being loyal to the state inevitably results in a disloyalty to his peers when these two parties' interests are in conflict. Being a *wenren* (a *wen* person, an intellectual, a scholar) who should pay attention to self-control and self-cultivation so as to become a good and righteous human being, his sense of guilt is so deep that it can only be compensated by doing something he considers right—"I felt it was only right that I bury her in the wasteland behind the compound"—as quoted earlier. The fact that he carried the Musician's body to the wasteland instead of the room that is used to store dead bodies indicated his intention to keep the whole body and thus the dignity for the dead Musician, as the hungry detainees were found eating corpses in the morgue. After the dramatic cutting and cooking of his own flesh, he felt that his disloyalty to the Musician and the Scholar had finally been balanced, compensated, and corrected by his *yi* behavior: "I felt that I could finally face the world. . . . It was as if I had made amends for those pages from my *Criminal Records*" (Yan 2015, 294).

After he took the Scholar to say farewell to the Musician and let the latter bury her body, the Author took the pages of his *Criminal Records* that he had found in the Musician's belongings and placed them in front of her grave. Then he took "a piece of meat from the pot . . . [and] sliced the meat into strips, which [he] then placed on top of those pages" (300). The meat here, as we have known, is in fact his own flesh. Begging for forgiveness and trying to correct his former shameful behavior with righteousness, the Author offered his own body as sacrifice to the dead Musician, which can also be viewed as payback, with his male body, for the comfort he had stolen from her female body earlier in the furnace.

Scholarship on Chinese masculinity finds that ancient Chinese considered vengeance as a defense of honor, which is of crucial importance to masculine identity: "Early historians recognized vengeance as a major motivation for the behavior of powerful men and made it a stock theme in their writings" (Hinsch 2013, 34). The Author's self-abusive behavior is also a type of vengeance—instead of revenge for the harms done by others, his vengeance is one for himself, for his disloyal/dishonorable other self. This is why when he "saw the two chunks of [his] flesh floating in the water, like an enemy crying out for mercy," he was "[o]verwhelmed by a sense of lightness and exhaustion (after vengeance)" (Yan 2015, 294).[14] Hunger, the desire for freedom, and the attempt to correct the previous mistakes drove the Author into a schizophrenic state. Indeed, he regained peace in his mind, but he may not have realized that he actually committed another immoral deed by turning the Scholar into a cannibal. In fact, the Author himself also drank "some water from the pot in which [he] was cooking the flesh" (294)—he drank his own flesh soup, and so he himself also became a cannibal in a broad sense. Through sharing his flesh, the Author once again bonded with the Scholar to form a male league, but this time the league helped him negotiate and discover/recover his manhood.

CONCLUSION

In 1918, Lu Xun's writing of *chiren* in his short story "A Madman's Diary" metaphorically accused the thousand years of Chinese culture of being oppressive and cruel, offering a new perspective for cultural criticism. In 1992, Mo Yan's story of eating human babies in *The Republic of Wine* inherited Lu Xun's questioning of the Chinese culture and ambiguously extended the criticism to modern society and the ruling party. Besides, Mo Yan's 1996 novel *Big Breasts and Wide Hips* celebrates Chinese women with the female body as the central metaphor. With his mighty and remorseless pen, Yan Lianke responds to Lu Xun and Mo Yan with his *The Four Books* published in 2011, a macabre novel that firms up the tabooed cannibalism during the Maoist regime, enriches the gallery of women's portraits, and expands the response to include a negotiation of Chinese manhood. Interwoven with politically and ethically forbidden topics, Yan's novel illustrates how men and women deal with food, or more precisely, the lack of it, during the great famine caused by the Great Leap Forward Campaign, whose purpose was ironically to speed up socialist construction so people would be materially better off. Carlos Rojas, the translator of *The Four Books* and several other books by Yan Lianke, maintains that

> as Michel Foucault and others have argued, the modern state derives its authority and legitimacy from its biopolitical relationship to its citizens—a relationship that is predicated on the state's ability to nurture life. Embedded within this biopolitical logic, however, is an inverse necropolitical one, in that the state's ability to provide the conditions for nurturing life is inextricably intertwined with its parallel ability to withhold those same conditions. (Rojas 2015, 188)

Obviously, the men and women in *The Four Books* are simply vulnerable and powerless individuals in such a biopolitical situation that their lives do not matter, let alone being nurtured. The body, both the female one and the male one, is severely violated. The relationship between food and gender showcased in the novel makes it clear that women are still the more vulnerable sex despite Mao's claim of them holding up half the sky. When Mao and the CCP encourage Chinese women to step out of their domestic space and participate in the public space—the socialist construction—it is an attempt to strengthen the state power rather than an awareness of gender equality. Women are made equal merely in the composition of the workforce and their contribution to the collective power, but not in the essential mindset of the state leaders, the ordinary people, and even women themselves. Even if they serve as feeders and food providers, their bodies have consistently been eaten at a metaphorical dimension.

NOTES

1. I am indebted to Jasper Becker for the terms "false science and false promises" (Becker 1996, 58).

2. The barter system set by the Child works like this: five small blossoms would be converted into a medium-sized one, five medium-sized blossoms would be converted into a big star, and those who get five big stars would be allowed to go home and return to their work. Besides this, an informant would be awarded one month's home leave.

3. One *liang* is equivalent to 0.05 kilogram.

4. Mao has two household sayings encouraging Chinese women to participate in the socialist construction: "Women can hold up half the sky" and "Time is different. Men and women are equals. What men can do women can also do." The first one is thought to have been said in the early 1960s, but it is hard to find the source. According to Xueping Zhong, "Women can hold up half the sky" "is a Mao-era household phrase that most people have assumed to be a direct quote from Mao Zedong. The interesting truth is that it is actually not clear where and when Mao said or wrote it, and, for that matter, whether or not it was a direct quote." The second saying of Mao is from CCP Committee of Hunan Province, "Fully Bring Out Women's Initiative in the Revolution and Construction," *Hongqi (Red flag)* 10 (1971): 63; quoted from Hongjun Su, "A Feminist Study on Mao Zedong's Theory of Women and the Policy of the Chinese Communist Party toward Women through a Study on the Party Organ Hongqi (1959–88)," *Chinese Historians* 3, no. 2 (1990): 21–35. For the above information, I am indebted to Zhong 2011, 227.

5. "Rightists" refer to citizens who either criticized the government or were in favor of capitalism during the Anti-Rightist Campaign launched by Mao from 1957 to 1959.

6. My translation.

7. This was omitted by the translator.

8. Emphasis mine.

9. Emphasis mine.

10. The Child is a very interesting character who is worthy of another chapter. Unlike other conventionally created patriarchal figures, as a male who possesses power, he refuses the sexual offer from the Musician, so much so that the Musician believes that he is not a normal man, implying his impotency. At the end of the novel, the Child gives food and stars to the detainees so that they can leave, and then nails himself to a cross like Jesus. Here I will not go into detailed analysis of this character, but would like to raise a question about his seeming impotency and his final redemption: Does Yan Lianke suggest that a man can recover his human decency only by losing his masculinity? Moreover, the Child seems to be in the same group of Yan Lianke's redeemed good-man characters, which is also an interesting topic for further research.

11. Here I changed the translation from "inviting everyone to eat" to "inviting that guy to eat." The original Chinese phrase *naren* means "that person," not every person. Here "that guy" refers to the Scholar.

12. The Qin Dynasty dates from 221 to 207 BC.

13. I am indebted to Gang Yue for the term "revolutionary hunger" (Yue 1999, 150).

14. The words "after vengeance" are mine. The original Chinese text has the phrase *fuchou hou*, which translates to "after vengeance" or "after revenge," but it was not translated. Since it is important for my discussion here, I added it back.

REFERENCES

Arnold, David. 1988. *Famine: Social Crisis and Historical Change*. New York: Basil Blackwell.

Becker, Jasper. 1996. *Hungry Ghosts: Mao's Secret Famines*. New York: The Free Press.

Brooks, Peter. 1993. *Body Work: Objects of Desire in Modern Narrative*. Cambridge, MA: Harvard University Press.

Brownell, Susan, and Jeffrey N. Wasserstrom, eds. 2002. *Chinese Femininities/ Chinese Masculinities: A Reader*. Berkeley: University of California Press.

Fairbank, John King. 1992. *China: A New History*. Cambridge, MA: The Belknap Press of Harvard University Press.

Farquhar, Judith. 2002. *Appetites: Food and Sex in Post-socialist China*. Durham: Duke University Press.

Hinsch, Bret. 2013. *Masculinities in Chinese History*. Lanham: Rowman & Littlefield.

Louie, Kam. 2002. *Theorising Chinese Masculinity: Society and Gender in China*. Cambridge, UK: Cambridge University Press.

MacFarquhar, Roderick, and John K. Fairbank, eds. 1987. *The Cambridge History of China*, vol. 14, *The People's Republic, Part I: The Emergence of Revolutionary China, 1949-1965*. New York: Cambridge University Press.

Mo Yan. 1995. *Fengru feitun* [Big Breasts and Wide Hips]. Beijing: Zuojia chubanshe.

———. 2005. *Big Breasts and Wide Hips*. Translated by Howard Goldblatt. London: Methuen Publishing Limited.

Rojas, Calos. 2015. *Homesickness: Culture, Contagion, and National Transformation in Modern China*. Cambridge, MA: Harvard University Press.

Sceats, Sarah. 2000. *Food, Consumption and the Body in Contemporary Women's Fiction*. New York: Cambridge University Press.

Yan Lianke. 2015. *The Four Books*. Translated by Carlos Rojas. New York: Grove Press.

Yue, Gang. 1999. *The Mouth that Begs: Hunger, Cannibalism, and the Politics of Eating in Modern China*. Durham: Duke University Press.

Zhong, Xueping. 2011. "Women Can Hold up Half the Sky." In *Words and Their Stories: Essays on the Language of the Chinese Revolution*, edited by Ban Wang, 227–247. Leiden: Brill.

Zhou, Xun, ed. 2012. *The Great Famine in China, 1958–1962: A Documentary History*. New Haven: Yale University Press.

Chapter 5

"Veganism Will Rise like Feminism"

The Porous Contestation of Intersectional Vegan Feminism against the Exclusive Politics of Korean Popular Feminism

Su Young Choi

ABSTRACT

Vegan feminism is an ideology and social movement that aims to establish equality and justice within a wider web of human/nonhuman interrelations by overcoming anthropocentric and patriarchal society. This study asks how Korean women who call themselves vegan feminists identify themselves and strategize their movement within the political context of South Korea, a region where the recent resurgence of feminist activism has generated intense public discussion about its potentials and limits. Employing the qualitative methods of semi-structured interviews, textual analysis, and participant observation, this study presents how vegan feminists have contradictory relationships with Korean popular feminism, in which their intersectional criticism is often mixed with an imitation of the separatist or exclusive practices of popular feminism. I argue that an analysis of the South Korean vegan feminist activism shows two important implications for scholars of feminist politics and the environment. One is to consider "parity of participation" (Fraser 2009)—social arrangements that enable people to participate as peers in public life—as a significant condition of justice to halt the perpetuation of the exclusive politics of Korean popular feminism. The other is to pay attention to the potential of Korean vegan feminism for social change that cuts across anthropocentric borders and encourages an active response to ecological crisis.

INTRODUCTION

> I reject the proposal that feminists should also become vegans. The reason why I became a feminist was to speak out against discrimination and violence that females experience, not to feel guilty about the problems of animals.

A member of FEMI-POWER PROJECT (FPP hereafter), a student group at the Sookmyung Women's University, made the above declaration in an argumentative poster titled "Does intersectionality claimed by vegan feminism exist?" on a university bulletin board. The Twitter account of FPP also shared a photo of this poster on June 14, 2019, to publicize and reaffirm their position that feminism should pay exclusive attention to the problems of "women," not anything else.[1] FPP's poster was circulated among people who identify themselves as vegan feminists and who criticized this restrictive position. Then one of them created a webpage titled "Misunderstandings about Vegan Feminism"[2] on August 13, 2019. The page contests the viewpoints of FPP that feminism cannot intersect with veganism, and that the oppression and exploitation of animals are unrelated to the gendered power relations of patriarchal society. Intersectionality is "a way of understanding and analyzing the complexity in the world, in people, and in human experiences," and it has served as an analytical tool by which people can grasp and express how multiple intersecting power relations shape the complexity of the world and of themselves (Collins and Bilge 2016, 2) . Thus, intersectional politics confronts the interlocking axes of social division and the mutual construction of different power relations in aiming for social justice or equality. It also appreciates the principle of "relationality," a commitment to developing coalitions or relationships across social divisions based on "a *both/and* frame" rather than "an *either/or* binary thinking" (Collins and Bilge 2016, 27) (Emphasis in original). Given that, the above confrontational episode sheds light on the essentialist and exclusive inclination of young Korean feminists who antagonize intersectional politics under the motto of "feminism of women, by women, for women," and their tension with a subgroup like "vegan feminists" who aspire to diverge from such a bounded imagination of what feminism can and should do.

Vegan feminists in South Korea are a community of people who participate in a range of critical inquiry and practice that seeks justice and equality for nonhumans and women, and they consider this commitment to end speciesism and sexism in all forms a central part of their identity. Also, they tend to share an affiliation to animal rights movements that attempt to create a world in which animals have "moral rights" (Reagan 2003) to live as "sentient beings" (Singer 1977), not as properties or instruments to be exploited or mistreated by humans. Vegan feminism, thus, can be understood as an ideology and social movement that aims to define and establish equality and justice within a wider web of human/nonhuman interrelations by highlighting the significance of overcoming anthropocentric and patriarchal society. Vegan feminism largely shares its viewpoints with previous ecofeminism movements (Gaard 2002; Shiva and Mies 2014) in the sense that both problematize patriarchal society as the common source of oppression and exploitation of nonhumans and women. Still, vegan feminism in South Korea has been informed and affected more directly by the discourses of intersectional feminism and the practices of animal rights activism in the West.

This chapter asks how Korean women who call themselves vegan feminists identify themselves through their words and actions and strategize their movement within the political context of South Korea, a region where the recent resurgence of feminist activism has generated intense public discussions about its potentials and limits. And it presents why and in what processes vegan feminists come to have contradictory relationships with Korean popular feminism, in which their intersectional criticism is often mixed with an imitation of the separatist or exclusive practices of popular feminism. I argue that an analysis of the South Korean vegan feminist activism, including its contradictory relationships with popular feminism, shows two important implications for scholars of feminist politics, food, and the environment. One is to consider the task of achieving "parity of participation" (Fraser 2009)—social arrangements that enable people to participate as peers in public life across economic, cultural, and political domains—as a significant condition of justice to halt the perpetuation of the exclusive and separatist orientation of resurged Korean feminist activism and enable the politics of solidarity (Baik 2019). The other is to pay attention to possibilities and potentials that Korean vegan feminists have opened up toward creating an inclusive and comprehensive vision for social change that cuts across anthropocentric borders and encourages an active response to ecological crisis around the globe.

In what follows, I first present the recent debate about the potency and limitation of "feminism reboot" (Sohn 2017) since 2015 in South Korea, the conceptual framework of popular feminism (Banet-Weiser 2018; Gill 2016; B. Kim 2018), methods of qualitative interviewing and textual analysis, and materials from online and offline texts. I then present a qualitative analysis of the contradictory ways in which intersectional vegan feminism negotiates the boundary of South Korean popular feminism. Lastly, I discuss what this contradiction might mean in understanding the tasks and possibilities of popular feminism and beyond.

A Debate on "Feminism Reboot" in South Korea

Scholars have debated over how to understand *exclusive politics* and *hate-based activism* as the notable tendencies of "feminism reboot" in South Korean feminism (B. Kim 2018). "Feminism reboot" is a term suggested by Sohn (2017) to refer to the resurgence of feminist activism against misogyny and digital sexual violence (e.g., spy cam filming) in South Korea since 2015. Before examining the details of this debate, it is important to note the clear achievements of resurged Korean feminism, such as the creation of a heightened social consciousness and emancipatory solidarity against misogyny, sexual violence, and gender discrimination; the shutdown of the nation's largest porn website, Soranet; the generation of an increased public attention to the structural gender inequalities revealed by the #MeToo movement (N. Lee 2016); and the decriminalization of abortion by a 2019 order of the Constitutional Court of Korea.

While the significance of these achievements was widely recognized, commentators raised concerns with regard to the exclusive politics and hate-based activism of some feminist groups and organizations. In particular, the debate has primarily contested the strong assumption of the essential category of "biological female" as the "fundamental" boundary of solidarity embedded in resurged Korean feminism. This essentialist, separatist, and exclusive biological notion of womanhood has resonated across the South Korean public sphere through controversial cases. For instance, the opposition to the enrollment of a transgender woman at the Sookmyung Women's University in early 2020 led this person to abandon her plan to attend. Another example is found in the visible participation of young feminists in creating negative sentiments against Yemeni refugees who arrived in Jeju in 2018. These feminists, in effect, aligned with right-wing populists' agenda of anti-immigration and ways of essentializing others (e.g., characterizing refugees as foreign criminals and sexual offenders) (Jun 2020).

In this debate, however, some scholars argue that asserting the category of "women" is still a valid and necessary strategy in feminist politics because this assertion as a discursive strategy enables "women" to act as a social collective and as the agents of activism and social change (S. Jeong 2018; R. Kim 2017). When it comes to actual feminist practices and expressions, this idea of asserting the category of "women" has often been connected to a set of separatist efforts in South Korea, as shown in the examples of "women-only" spaces or participation in feminist actions (e.g., street protests, crowdfunding, exhibit events, etc.). S. Jeong (2018) defends this separatist approach to feminist politics as an understandable tactic against the overwhelming realities of sexual violence and misogynistic culture in Korean society. Further, Yoon (2019) highlights that solidarity with other minorities should be pursued only when the agenda for women is explicitly maintained, so as to not compromise the forefront against the oppression of women as the movement's top priority.

The above essentialist emphasis implies that awareness of different kinds of oppression (e.g., speciesism, heteronormativity, racism) and distinguishable positionalities among women, as well as intersectional solidarity with other minorities, are only conditionally encouraged if not entirely rejected. This separatist and exclusive position of South Korean radical feminism has been widespread among female youth from teenagers to those in their thirties. The approach of radical feminism has thus become a visible norm for young women in offering them model practices (e.g., rejecting makeup, dating, sex, marriage, childbirth, etc.) with regards to how to become, act like, and live as a feminist (A. Kim 2019; Kang 2019; Choo 2019).

The choice of using the category of "biological female" as the fundamental boundary of feminist solidarity has been criticized for having negative effects on feminist politics more generally. Thus, for example, Hyomin Lee (2019) attempted to show that "women first" feminism helps to stigmatize or "other" sexual minorities like transgender and queer people, to reproduce hatred toward people who are not classified within the category of "heterosexual women," and to position women as victims who do not have any type of privilege in society. Go (2019) further examined the discourse of "Hyung-ja (honorary man)" in Womad, a cyberfeminist community known as a group of militant and exclusive feminists, to show how members of this community aspire to become neoliberal subjects (e.g., to be economically successful and wealthy women) individually as a solution to the oppression of the patriarchal Korean society. Here, the practice of maintaining the rigid category of "women" is more connected to using feminism as a reduced and instrumentalized survival strategy for a precarious subject in a neoliberal regime rather than as a bridge to act in solidarity. In emphasizing the importance of intersectionality, B. Kim (2018) further suggested that the notion of "woman" in feminist politics should be understood as the political product of a particular historical and cultural context rather than as a static and ahistorical category. From this point of view, the instability caused by perceiving women's internal diversity beyond one essential category is not a weakness that should be suppressed or removed. On the contrary, the complications that arise in acknowledging the diversity of women provide a resource to understand the relationship among different kinds of oppression in a complex socioenvironmental world. Furthermore, in resisting the conventional, heteronormative, and anthropocentric category of "woman," feminists are able to examine their own conditions of privilege in relation to other minorities and nonhuman species, and thus to politicize an oppressive patriarchal society more fundamentally.

On a parallel vein, feminist scholars and critics have paid attention to the conditions under which reignited feminism emerged as an exclusive and separatist movement. Drawing on interviews with women in their twenties and thirties who identified themselves as feminists or feminism supporters, Choo (2019) found that these conditions include an intensified anxiety of being a victim of physical and/or sexual violence; fear of social stigma around being a feminist, especially in regard to losing job opportunities; and lack of social networks or institutional resources (e.g., women's studies courses in a college, student clubs and associations, etc.) in which they could freely express and discuss a feminist agenda. These findings imply that the emotionally terrified, socially isolated, and economically precarious lives of young women in South Korea may lead them to seek solidarity with other women only within an individualized and anonymous online context. Taking a political-economic perspective, B. Kim (2018) argued that the failure of the neoliberal regime and post-authoritarian system in South Korea ignited particular sensibilities among young women. These sensibilities include an autistic and exclusive vision for life, disbelief in one's ability or agency to make positive life changes, and emotional withdrawal from any collective imagination for social transformation. Based on this observation, Choo (2019) proposed that contemporary feminist politics should act to dissolve the exclusive boundaries of resurged feminism by building sociopolitical spaces where women can reduce anxiety, experience being understood, and understand others' experiences and how these other experiences are entwined with their own.

Survival, Political Consumption, and Antagonism to Intersectionality: Key Features of Popular Feminism in South Korea

In the above debate between essentialist and intersectionalist positions of feminist politics, popular feminism has been a key conceptual framework to understand the features of contemporary feminist actions and articulations. Feminist scholarship in North America and Europe has noted that feminism has recently become *popular*. Specifically, feminist expressions and practices have emerged across a networked media landscape and many Western women have openly associated with feminism through consuming popular culture and engaging in social media–based activism. Conceptualizing this phenomenon as "popular feminism," Banet-Weiser (2018) characterized its prominent features as (1) commitment to media visibility and accessibility; (2) focus on individuals' empowerment, self-confidence, and competence; and (3) symbiotic relationship with popular misogyny.

Popular feminism often regards "seeing or purchasing feminism [e.g., buying Dior's 'We Should All Be Feminists' T-shirts] as the act of changing patriarchal structures" (Banet-Weiser 2018, 4). This sensibility resides in the postfeminist legacy of celebrating individual achievement—the economic success of females along with autonomy, resilience, and positivity that entrepreneurial subjects need to survive and thrive—as the ultimate goal of feminism (Gill 2016; Banet-Weiser, Gill, and Rottenberg 2020). Both popular feminism and popular misogyny aim to increase individual capacity for economic accomplishment, view sexism or feminism as a key obstacle to achieving this capacity or a source of psychological injury, and operate within the economy of media visibility, a technological and economic context devoted to the accumulation of views, clicks, and "likes" (Banet-Weiser 2018). In this regard, many critics have found the popular feminism of North America and Western Europe to be a "mainstream" cultural force that tends to confine feminist politics within neoliberal consumer culture, marginalize intersectional feminism, and flatten the meanings and possibilities of feminism in general (Banet-Weiser, Gill, and Rottenberg 2020; Banet-Weiser and Portwood-Stacer 2017; Fischer 2017; Jackson 2020).

In comparison, Korean popular feminism has shown a slightly different picture from the Western one, despite some similarities like the affiliation with social media–based activism (Baer 2016; Jeong and Lee 2018), and the neoliberal tendency to treat economic success as a significant goal of feminism. First off, Korean popular feminism advocates "survival" as women's most urgent need. The motto of survival resonates in feminist discourses as the need to achieve economic stability, physical security, and mental health, based on the dominant sensibility of "victimhood" and "crisis" from widespread precarity and violence against women (Hyomin Lee 2019). In other words, Korean popular feminism is conceived and functions as a means to survive (B. Kim 2018). For instance, investigating the movement of "Tal-corsets (taking off all corsets)" among female youth, A. Kim (2019) found that women "take off their corsets" not only to liberate themselves from pressure over their appearance, but also to have an "equal condition" in competing with their male counterparts. Here, popular feminist practice is meant to prevent the waste of one's scarce resources (e.g., money, time, attention, etc.), and, ultimately, to help participants survive in a highly competitive society fraught with gender discrimination and violence.

The second difference between Western and Korean popular feminism is found in its "political consumption" (Hyunjae Lee 2019) of media along with its explicit focus on "speed" and "number" (e.g., making feminist books into prompt best sellers, making certain hashtags trend on Twitter, or selling out tickets for feminist cultural products like films or lectures). Such a political consumption aims to represent the "collective power" of women on social media and in popular culture by aggregating all resources (e.g., money, attention, skills, talents, number of clicks, views, and replies on social media) that female participants can mobilize. For example, words like *Hwaryŏk* (firepower) and *Ch'onggong* (full-scale attack) are used to refer to feminists' commitment to online demonstrations of their collective voice in a timely manner through intensified consuming activities.

This popular feminist strategy of political consumption has at least two causes: (1) ongoing frustration from the lack of social support and institutional resources in the offline world (Kang 2019); and (2) an ingrained disbelief in the capacity of South Korean society, and South Korean men in particular, to make positive changes voluntarily, which correlates with existential fears of backlash and witch hunts (Choo 2019; B. Kim 2018). These feelings of despair and pessimistic viewpoints may explain popular feminists' obsession with mobilizing resistant power only through women and visualizing this mobilization online as the only political space available to them. Despite some achievements, from media visibility to political consumption of feminist media, J. Kim (2016, 2020) noted that such "politics of speed and number" discourage if not exclude in-depth feminist discussions and internal criticisms, viewing them as blockages in the online "battle" for timely demonstrations of collective power.

The third, and final, difference between Western and Korean popular feminism is the widespread tendency of Korean popular feminists to antagonize proponents of the intersectional approach explicitly and aggressively, rather than avoiding or marginalizing them implicitly or indirectly as is done in Western popular feminism (see the case of how white feminists devalued intersectionality through the oblique tactic of "rejecting the term, not the concept" in Collins and Bilge [2016, 107–109], and the absence of intersectional values in celebrity popular feminism in Jackson [2020]). That is because intersectional feminism is considered to pose a serious threat to the vibrant collectivity of feminism and its limited resources. Specifically, intersectional criticism on the singular understanding of women as biological females has been perceived as an obstacle in popularizing the feminist agenda based on the singular position of women as victims. As popular feminists aspire to achieve social change by mobilizing collective pressure from the quantitative expansion of a unified feminist front under the straightforward feminist agenda, they have not welcomed internal diversity within women, and what intersectional feminism can bring about instead: awareness of various sources of oppression; self-reflection, including on one's own privilege on a certain dimension (e.g., belonging to the human species in the context of animal exploitation); and understanding disparate voices and life experiences. Rather, some popular feminists claim that intersectional feminists unfairly and excessively impose moral demands on women, and that (popular) feminists should be careful not to let such demands derail the priority of the feminist agenda.

The above features of Korean popular feminism have made South Korea a more challenging political space for intersectional feminists to raise their voices. The question then becomes, "How, if at all, do intersectional feminists overcome the exclusive politics of popular feminism in redefining the goals and agenda of that movement?" The present chapter addresses this question through an in-depth examination of the activism of intersectional feminists who came to be known as "vegan feminists" in the contemporary Korean public sphere.

Methods and Materials

Young women in their twenties and thirties are the main demographic characteristic of vegan feminists and the participation of female teenagers in the movement has increased. Vegan feminists have presented themselves as a collective both online and offline to raise consciousness about the realities of animal exploitation and gender discrimination as well as to spread vegan practices. For instance, the "Vegan Feminist Network" organization has had its Facebook page since March 2017 and its participants have attended various offline public events such as public forums (e.g., 2030 Ecofeminism Forum), public marches and protests (e.g., march for animal rights, march for decriminalizing abortion, rally on International Women's Day on March 8, protest against Taeku Ch'imaek [chicken & beer] festival), and festivals (e.g., vegan festival, Seoul queer culture festival). On top of showing their public presence on the streets and in forums, the members of the Vegan Feminist Network regularly meet with each other to have seminars, develop agendas, translate non-Korean vegan feminism materials, prepare for internal public events (e.g., vegan camp), network, and socialize.

On the organizational level, twenty-eight organizations, which participated as plaintiffs in filing a petition with the Constitutional Court on the lack of vegetarian or vegan canteens at public bodies on April 6, 2020, exemplified the types of associations with which Korean vegan feminists align themselves. These organizations include nine vegan-related civic organizations (e.g., Vegans at Jeju, VegeDoctor), seven college vegan clubs (e.g., Veggie Ssukssuk at the University of Seoul), seven animal rights organizations (e.g., Animal Liberation Wave), and five environmental organizations (e.g., Korean Women's Environmental Network, Guardians of Climate) and subunits of political parties (e.g., Youth at Korean Green Party).

Adopting the qualitative methods of semi-structured interviews, textual analysis, and participant observation (Tracy 2013), my analysis relies on a set of interview data, media texts (e.g., podcasts, websites, social media accounts), and field notes taken at various online and offline arenas (e.g., smartphone chat applications, vegan events such as the Vegan Festa and public lectures). I interviewed eighteen participants who identified themselves as vegan feminists to various degrees, including seven college students and two high school students. Interviews and participant observation at offline sites were conducted at vegan cafés or spaces (e.g., the organic culture center) for vegan events in Seoul between June and July 2019. Online participant observation in a vegan "room" located on KakaoTalk, a mobile messaging app for smartphones, has been ongoing since the author joined the room in June 2019. The number of participants in the room was around sixty when the author joined. As of March 2021, there are ninety participants sharing veganism- or feminism-related news, asking for petition participation, and promoting or introducing climate-related content to the members.

The Critical Frontstage of Vegan Feminism along with Animal Rights Advocacy

Korean vegan feminists have responded to the hostility and exclusivity of popular feminists by criticizing what they defined as the rationale for "anti-solidarity" in this movement. As part of this critique, vegan feminists attempted to build alternative online spaces and channels through which participants could articulate who they are, explain their views, and introduce their mission statement to the general South Korean public. These expressions included detailed accounts such as the following, which appears on the webpage entitled "Misunderstandings about vegan feminism" discussed in the introductory section of this chapter:

> I think the claim, that feminism cannot go together with veganism because they are two different movements that have different aims, derives from the dichotomous logic of zero-sum game that refuses to see how the oppression of women and the oppression of animals are both rooted in patriarchal society.[3]

As is apparent from this excerpt, the author explicitly criticizes what she or he considers "zero-sum game" logic. Specifically, the author asks readers to think of patriarchal society at a structural level so as to recognize that carnism, the invisible belief system that conditions people to eat certain animals (Joy 2011), and sexism are intricately entwined (Adams 2015). This perspective is aimed to counter popular feminist views that regard vegan feminists as "competitors" who pose an acute risk to their already limited resources. Here, the notion of "zero-sum game" refers specifically to the idea that one party's gain is another party's loss (as in some scenarios of game theory).

Additionally, some vegan feminists created specialized podcasts with the aim of generating a verbal space where they could discuss various issues and themes of veganism and feminism. Given that a podcast is structured as an episodic audio series that allows creators to incorporate diverse guest voices, this initiative provided vegan feminists with means to share their views with non-vegan feminist audience members, discuss sensitive issues among themselves, and enrich public discussions on relevant issues by adding the voices of vegans and vegan feminists who operate in diverse social, cultural, economic, and political arenas. Thus, for example, Munyŏng,[4] a host of a vegan podcast, explained in an interview how she and the other hosts created an episode entitled "Is Veganism a Moral Corset Imposed on Women?", especially to intervene into the debate among popular and vegan feminists:

> I was upset and disturbed a lot when I heard the comment "Veganism is a moral corset imposed on women. Women are told not to eat meat more easily than men" during a class discussion at my university. I think I was able to became a vegan because I had become a feminist first. Feminism had helped me to see and confront with the oppression women experience, which again opened my eyes to violence and pain that humans put on non-human species on the earth. For me, both veganism and feminism are political choices and commitments to confront injustices and oppression, not the instrumental means to become or present myself as a moral being. When I felt that the intention of vegan feminism was misunderstood, and that exclusive feminists insist on and compete for the position of victimhood, this motivated me to create the episode challenging the idea of seeing veganism only as an unfair request—Don't eat meat—imposed on women.

As this commentary indicates, intersectional vegan feminists have tried to apply feminist approaches in accordance with their political commitment to liberate all living creatures, including nonhumans, from any type of oppression. This application led such activists to reach out to, and to associate themselves with, various other activist groups. Thus, for example, the hosts of the abovementioned vegan podcast have initiated public dialogues with members of the Animal Liberation Wave, a movement organization that acts against speciesism and for the liberation of animals and their rights, as well as with activists concerned with the human rights of sex workers who are regularly ostracized from the mainstream of popular feminism. More generally, the application of intersectional approaches to feminism enabled vegan feminists to develop reflexivity with regard to various perspectives and positionalities of individuals—especially individual women—relative to multiple and complex relations of power.

On a similar vein, Sangmi, one of the core members of the Vegan Feminist Network, a movement organization that seeks to end speciesism and sexism in all forms, said in an interview:

> All women can join our organization. We try to include any person who has experienced womanhood or identified herself as a woman, or been oppressed in relation to passing or not passing as a woman.

The Vegan Feminist Network also collaborated with Move, an animal rights organization, in creating the first vegan camp between February 22 and 24 in 2019. This event was principally open to anyone interested in veganism. About 150 people attended the event, which provided participants with various programs concerning veganism and animal rights activism, as well as with informal opportunities to meet like-minded people and thus to network or socialize. In a similar spirit, the Vegan Feminist Network's Facebook group page has been committed to posting commentaries on various activist issues and concerns, such as vegan feminist opinions about sex toys, information on new books about ecofeminism, calls to participate in public marches for animal rights and the Transgender Day of Remembrance as well as in several vegan festivals, and requests to come together in solidarity with climate action groups such as School Strike 4 Climate. The digitally based cultural production of vegan feminists also provided a basis for more intricate networking among vegan feminists. Here, one could mention the creation of, and participation in, a vegan KakaoTalk messenger group for daily engagement, the recruitment of new participants, and the organization of consciousness-raising street demonstrations.

That said, it is the frontstage of digital media on which the critical consciousness and clear alternatives of vegan feminists combined with animal rights advocacy are seamlessly and coherently presented. Still, an examination of participants' emotions, attitudes, and practices at the movement's backstage reveals a more complex and ambivalent set of relationships with the agenda and activities of popular feminism, to which I turn next.

The "Success" of Popular Feminism as a Role Model at the Backstage

The intersectional contestation of popular feminism became much less effective once vegan feminists began to adopt its methods and models as part of their own movement-building efforts. Indeed, vegan feminism shares many commonalities with South Korean popular feminism in practice if not in principle. Similar to popular feminism's usage of "women-only" spaces and forms of participation, vegan feminists promote separatist forms of engagement despite their explicit deconstruction of the category of "women" and the continued inclusion of LGBTQ community members. For example, one finds that the Vegan Feminist Network restricts membership to persons who identify themselves as "women" with the assumption that one's gender identity is essential for the understanding of vegan feminist principles and practices. Aside from some exceptional cases, it appears that both popular and vegan feminists tend to dismiss the possibility of "feminist men" or "male allies."

Additionally, vegan feminists do not refrain from applying separatist and exclusive approaches in negotiating new relationships and alliances as part of their activist and social practices. Thus, for example, vegan feminists are often ready to cut new interpersonal and political ties that emerge in both online and offline spaces if the other parties to the relationship express disagreement with the values and activities of intersectional vegan feminism. That is apparent from the following excerpts, where Chuhŭi and Sangsŏn describe their efforts to restrict communication only to like-minded people who adhere to vegan feminist principles:

> I feel comfortable the most when I communicate with other vegan feminists. Feminists often exclude transgender people, which I cannot agree with. Many [male] vegans show sexist attitudes towards women, which I cannot stand, either. This is why I just like hanging out with other vegan feminists. This is also why I recently got out of Vegan Soul—a vegan group based on KakaoTalk, an instant messaging application—when many people [who identified] as feminists were against transgender people. I also withdrew myself from another online vegan community when I was disgusted to hear its male organizer say to other male participants, "If you become a vegan, you can date many women."

> How did I create the current vegan KakaoTalk group? I got inspired by my friend [a vegan feminist]. She complained to me about a vegan KakaoTalk group she had joined and found that group tolerating misogynistic comments she cannot tolerate. I told her at that time, "Why would you put up with that? Get out of there. Let's make another group." That was how.

In trying to account for the recurrent choice of meeting and interacting with people who already share their convictions and attitudes, many of my vegan feminist interviewees expressed a pessimistic view that Korean society, and Korean men in particular, will resist all positive change. This interpretation is very similar to that of Korean popular feminists as discussed in the previous section. In practice, vegan feminists believe that the only realistic line of action would be to enlighten women, particularly feminists, to become vegans and thus to join the vegan activist effort of challenging the anthropocentric power relations through which society reproduces violence against animals. In other words, vegan feminism's realistic mission as a social movement is to build and expand a political community whose membership is primarily based on one identity: vegan feminist women.

In addition to this identity-based, separatist, and essentialist approach to movement building, intersectional vegan feminists share the activist strategy of political consumption with their popular counterparts. As popular feminism often regards "seeing or purchasing feminism as the act of changing patriarchal structures" (Banet-Weiser 2018, 4), vegan feminists' main method of social change is to change consumption patterns, especially with regard to eating—the most basic and fundamental practice of all people in all places and times. Based on this, movement participants hope to flood social media and the field of popular culture with vegan representations and artifacts, and thereby raise awareness and increase their numbers in the general population. Many vegan feminists are thus proud to experience the rise of feminism in the contemporary public conversation. The recognizable public presence of popular feminism gives vegan feminists a hopeful vision, a reliable reference, and clear evidence that they can endure any hardship in their journey toward a minority vegan feminist lifestyle. In the following excerpt, Hyeyŏn, an illustrator and book author, expresses this position:

> How vegans have received backlash from society and how they have been portrayed as oversensitive kill-joys are very similar to how feminists have been treated in this society. Nevertheless, feminism has been successful so far. I used to participate in a feminist book club and film club. Now I see emerging vegan book clubs and documentary watching clubs. The change is so rapid. That's why I believe veganism will rise like feminism.

As apparent from this excerpt, as well as from other interview data, the majority of participants in any vegan-related gathering, meeting, or group are women (about 80 to 90 percent), especially women in the age range of early twenties to late thirties. Additionally, feminists constitute a large portion of movement participants as well. Many vegan feminists indicate that they self-identified as feminists prior to becoming vegan, and that this later transformation was informed by their feminist mindset and convictions. Popular feminism thus appears to provide vegan feminists with a social, cultural, and political model of "success" that they can take and apply in their own movement-building and public-awareness–raising endeavors. In this situation, vegan feminism appears to undergo a process of mimetic isomorphism (DiMaggio and Powell 1983) whereby its structures and practices become more and more similar to those of the dominant popular feminism. This isomorphism is likely to impede, significantly, the original goals of South Korean intersectional feminists to challenge the exclusive, separatist, and essentialist politics of popular feminism and create an inclusive and expansive movement that contests the multiple relations of power in patriarchal society.

Common Front against Anti-Feminism and Misogyny

In attempting to explain why vegan feminists have modeled their movement after the exclusive and separatist example of popular feminism, it is important to recognize that both communities needed to defend their participants from backlashes of popular misogyny and reactionary anti-feminism in South Korea—hence the explicit theme of "survivalism" among popular feminists discussed earlier. Indeed, many of my vegan feminist interviewees recalled vivid and traumatic memories of being attacked by vegan haters, both individually and collectively, in online spaces such as personal or group social media accounts (e.g., Twitter, Instagram, and Facebook), and the reply sections of vegan content in various online outlets such as news portals, webtoons, and podcast platforms. These online attacks included series of malicious mocking verbal responses; posting of dozens of meat images; and the exposure of vegan feminists' individual identities in public spaces such as Namuwiki, which is widely recognized as South Korea's most popular wiki platform. In the following excerpt, Sangmi, a member of the Vegan Feminist Network, recalls the shocking experience of finding herself as the target of such a hostile attack right after the first public appearance of her group at a vegan festival in the capital city of Seoul in October 2017:

> Participating in a vegan festival was our first "activity" after making our organization. Also, we were a small group of twenty people then. However, our presence in that vegan festival was immediately known to male-dominated online communities such as Ilpë [a famous far-right, misogynistic community website known to aggressively reproduce a gender-discriminatory discourse]. From the next day of the vegan festival, we got an influx of malicious comments on our Facebook group page to the extent I had to shut down my phone due to constant alerts, like thirty times per hour. After three or four days, feminists also joined and criticized us, saying "I'm a feminist and I must say women's human rights are much more urgent than animal rights," or "Why do you guys interfere with feminism by imposing animal rights upon it?" The number of views for the post of our Facebook page was up to 100,000 when we had only 300 followers. Such a hostile attack was so shocking and overwhelming to us.

As apparent from the following commentary by Minchi, a vegan feminist and a college student, public attacks on vegan feminists were not limited to digital media and online platforms:

> Honestly, I am afraid of proceeding with my vegan activism on my college campus as its social, cultural, and political environments are too barren or harsh to receive vegan feminism positively. I belong to the college of social sciences and I sense very cynical or hateful responses towards veganism or feminism if

> not getting direct curses. This is why I felt so liberated, happy, and joyous when I participated in the vegan camp and met people who shared the same values with me and had a chance to learn from each other.

On top of such public online and offline backlashes, many vegan feminists recount ongoing experiences of conflict and tension with intimate family members and friends that emerged directly from their stated adoption of a vegan lifestyle. Thus, many interviewees testified about severing social ties with close friends who refused to accept their choice of a vegan diet, as well as the need to distance themselves from parents and grandparents who disregarded their moral convictions and insisted on forcing them to eat meat to be "healthy." Such distressing experiences are described to have led these women to hide their vegan identities, especially in the workplace and other environments characterized by social anonymity. With this practice, they have attempted to create and manage a public impression of themselves as "normal" and avoid the potential stereotype of a "strange minority." In this way, they in effect negotiated the dichotomous public experience of being either invisible or over-visible common to many minority groups across the globe.

On the formal and institutional level of South Korea's sociopolitical culture, environmental discourse and consciousness have little resonance or effect, and are therefore unlikely to lead to policy-making and legislation. For example, the support rate of the Korean Green Party in the election of members for the National Assembly in 2020 was 0.21 percent. This poor result, along with the rapidly increasing greenhouse gas emissions and coal-fired power plant exports per capita, is correlated with the international perception of South Korea as one of the world's leading "climate villains" (Mathiesen 2016). In this situation, vegan feminists cannot afford to expect any substantial institutional support (e.g., the provision of resources or inclusion in influential social networks) for their consciousness-raising activities concerning the voicelessness of animals and the more-than-human world more generally.

To the extent that vegan feminists need to ready themselves for possible backlash and attacks on a regular basis, and given their multilayered experiences of interpersonal and sociopolitical marginalization, these women can best restore a political sense of agency through separatist practices of exclusion, that is, by cutting off and distancing themselves from potential supporters who do not already understand and agree with their agenda. To do otherwise would be to expose one's fragile vegan self to emotionally draining experiences of frustration and fear, as well as exposing the group's few safe spaces to antagonism and abuse. A case in point that I observed was the choice of group members to move into a new KakaoTalk chat room in response to the infiltration of a single individual who attacked the participants. That is, group participants chose to distance themselves from the attacker rather than engaging with him in any dialogical way albeit their obvious advantage in numbers.

As J. Kim (2018) and others have observed, the production and distribution of misogynistic discourses have become a major way to establish and affirm hegemonic group solidarity among South Korean men. This emergent and ongoing trend is another factor that leads vegan feminists to rely on the success of popular feminism as a major source of inspiration. It should therefore come as little surprise that these women choose to maintain a gap between their words and deeds, that is, a gap between their explicit intersectional critiques of popular feminism and their implicit adoption of this movement's community-building practices. One can therefore conclude that as long as vegan feminists need to defend themselves against the extreme misogyny of popular masculine discourses, the similarity between popular and intersectional vegan feminism will persist, if not grow.

CONCLUSION

This chapter has traced the ways in which Korean intersectional vegan feminists identify themselves and navigate their activism under the exclusive political constraints of Korean popular feminism. Based on this exploration, the chapter has shown that vegan feminism has had a contradictory relationship with its popular counterpart to the extent that its intersectional criticism, with an emphasis on the principle of relationality, ends up reproducing the separatist practices of interpersonal, social, and political exclusion.

To explain this puzzling feature of contemporary South Korean vegan feminism, the chapter has conducted an in-depth analysis of some vegan feminists' critical voices and consciousness. In so doing, the chapter explicated participants' moral principles, sentiments, and beliefs on the one hand, and their largely unintended adoption of separatist, essentialist, and exclusive movement-building practices on the other. The hegemonic status of popular feminism as a replicable role model and a successful example for young feminist individuals and groups has been reinforced by the harsh conditions of public censure and persecution led by the discourses and practices of popular misogyny. Under this condition, vegan feminists often have resorted to separatism as a condition for their movement's existence, regardless of their intersectional convictions that encourage commitment to develop coalitions or relationships across social divisions.

The result of the analysis indicates that "an autistic and exclusive vision for life" and "emotional withdrawal from any collective imagination for social transformation," which B. Kim (2018) suggested as noticeable sensibilities among young Korean women, are sustained to some extent even in the scenes of intersectional politics that rose to transcend the limits of popular feminism. Given that, I highlight the urgent task of achieving "parity of participation" (Fraser 2009)—social arrangements that enable people to participate as peers in public life across economic, cultural, and political domains—as a significant condition of justice to halt the perpetuation of the exclusive and separatist orientation of resurged Korean feminist activism and enable the politics of solidarity (Baik 2019). The separatist approach of feminist politics can be relaxed and mitigated mainly within social and political contexts where young women can be safe, welcomed, appreciated, encouraged, and recognized as peers who participate in public life without feeling a need to create a separate and safe zone. In that regard, I agree with the suggestion of Choo (2019) to build sociopolitical spaces and secure institutional resources for the inclusion and encouragement of feminist voices and their collective efforts, which will be a basis for a more inclusive and comprehensive feminist politics.

Enabling societal conditions that release feminists—and women in general—from their existential need to defend themselves against misogynistic threats and social exclusion is connected to the other consideration I suggest for scholars of feminist politics, food, and the environment. It is to pay attention to the possibilities and potentials that Korean vegan feminists have opened up toward social change that cuts across anthropocentric borders and encourages an active response to environmental crisis. Vegan feminists in South Korea have initiated a dialogue about this ecological vision that not only goes beyond the discourses of victimhood and exclusive solidarity promoted by popular feminists but also contributes to the expansive agency of feminist politics in intervening into the anthropocentric and patriarchal relations of power that eternalize the ecological crises of the earth.

NOTES

1. https://twitter.com/femipower_P/status/1139419443405021186.
2. https://veganstudies.github.io/2019/08/13/on-vegan-feminism.html.
3. All of the quotes in this chapter were translated by the author.
4. All the names appearing in this chapter are pseudonyms.

REFERENCES

Adams, Carol. 2015. *The Sexual Politics of Meat: A Feminist-Vegetarian Critical Theory*. Anniversary edition. New York, NY: Bloomsbury Academic.

Baer, Hester. 2016. "Redoing Feminism: Digital Activism, Body Politics, and Neoliberalism." *Feminist Media Studies* 16 (1): 17–34. DOI: 10.1080/14680777.2015.1093070.

Baik, Mi-Youn. 2019. "The Transition of Feminist Politics after the Korean #MeToo Movement: Toward 'Politics of Solidarity.'" *The Korean Review of Political Thought* 25 (2): 68–92. In Korean.

Banet-Weiser, Sarah. 2018. *Empowered: Popular Feminism and Popular Misogyny*. Durham, NC: Duke University Press.

Banet-Weiser, Sarah, Rosalind Gill, and Catherine Rottenberg. 2020. "Postfeminism, Popular Feminism and Neoliberal Feminism? Sarah Banet-Weiser, Rosalind Gill and Catherine Rottenberg in Conversation." *Feminist Theory* 21 (1): 3–24. DOI: 10.1177/1464700119842555.

Banet-Weiser, Sarah, and Portwood Stacer, Laura. 2017. "The Traffic in Feminism: An Introduction to the Commentary and Criticism on Popular Feminism." *Feminist Media Studies* 17 (5): 884–888. DOI: 10.1080/14680777.2017.1350517.

Choo, Jihyun. 2019. "Feminisms: The Expression of Social Transformation, Risk, and Communication." *Women's Studies Review* 36 (1): 59–91. In Korean.

Collins, Patricia, and Bilge, Sirma. 2016. *Intersectionality (Key Concepts)*. 1st edition. Cambridge, UK: Polity.

DiMaggio, Paul, and Powell, Walter. 1983. "The Iron Cage Revisited: Institutional Isomorphism and Collective Rationality in Organizational Fields." *American Sociological Review* 48 (2): 147–160. DOI: https://doi.org/10.2307/2095101.

Fischer, Mia. 2017. "Trans Responses to Adichie: Challenging Cis Privilege in Popular Feminism." *Feminist Media Studies* 17 (5): 896–899. DOI: 10.1080/14680777.2017.1350520.

Fraser, Nancy. 2009. *Scales of Justice: Reimagining Political Space in a Globalizing World*. New York, NY: Columbia University Press.

Gaard, Claire. 2002. "Vegetarian Ecofeminism: A Review Essay." *Frontiers: A Journal of Women Studies* 23 (3): 117–146.

Gill, Rosalind. 2016. "Post-Postfeminism? New Feminist Visibilities in Postfeminist Times." *Feminist Media Studies* 16 (4): 610–630. DOI: 10.1080/14680777.2016.1193293.

Go, Eunhae. 2019. "Discourse Analysis on Honorary-Men ('Hyung-Ja') Discourse of Website <Womad>." *Media, Gender, & Culture* 34 (4): 53–97. In Korean.

Jackson, Sue. 2020. "'A Very Basic View of Feminism': Feminist Girls and Meanings of (Celebrity) Feminism." *Feminist Media Studies*. DOI: 10.1080/14680777.2020.1762236.

Jeong, Euisol, and Lee, Jieun. 2018. "We Take the Red Pill, We Confront the DickTrix: Online Feminist Activism and the Augmentation of Gendered Realities in South Korea." *Feminist Media Studies* 18 (4): 705–717. DOI: 10.1080/14680777.2018.1447354.

Jeong, Seung-Hwa. 2018. "Saving Radical Feminism from Hating Queer: A Thought about Solidarity between Feminism and LGBTQ Activism." *Cultural Science* 95: 50–73. In Korean.

Joy, Melanie. 2011. *Why We Love Dogs, Eat Pigs, and Wear Cows: An Introduction to Carnism*. Reprint edition. Newburyport, MA: Red Wheel.

Jun, Euy Ryung. 2020. "'Accidental Solidarity in the Essentialization of the Other': The Gendered Politics of Ban Damunhwa and Anti-Refugee Sentiments in South Korea Economy and Society." *Economy and Society* 125: 360–401.

Kang, Yewon. 2019. "Study of Popularization of Feminism and Becoming a Teenage Feminist in the Digital Era." MA Thesis, Ewha Womans University.

Kim, Aera. 2019. "The Movement of 'Tal-Corsets' (taking off all corsets), #getreadywithme: Popular Feminism in the Digital Economy." *Journal of Korean Women's Studies* 35 (3): 43–78. In Korean.

Kim, Bo-Myung. 2018. Feminism Revival and the Politics of Survival. *Economy and Society* 118 (Summer): 101–137. In Korean

Kim, Jin-Sook. 2018. "Misogyny for Male Solidarity: Online Hate Discourse Against Women in South Korea." In *Mediating Misogyny: Gender, Technology, and Harassment*, edited by J. Vickery and T. Everbach, 151–169. London: Palgrave Macmillan.

Kim, Joohee. 2016. "The Feminism of Speed and the Politics of Inertia." *Literature and Society* 29 (4): 19–34. In Korean.

———. 2020. "For the Radicalization of Popular Feminism." *Journal of Korean Women's Studies* 36 (2): 187–193. In Korean.

Kim, Ri-Na. 2017. "The Megalians Project of the Category of Women and the Solidarities: The Important Thing is Not Who but Our Plan." *Journal of Korean Women's Studies* 33 (3): 109–140. In Korean.

Lee, Hyomin. 2019. "Radical Reconstruction of Feminist Politics: Focusing on the Critical Analysis of 'TERF' in South Korea." *Media, Gender, & Culture* 34 (3): 159–253. In Korean.

Lee, Hyunjae. 2019. "Gender Justice and 'Breaking the Glass Ceiling' in the Neoliberal Era: A Proposal of Critical Feminism as a Transformative Remedy." *Gender and Culture* 12 (2): 43–73. In Korean.

Lee, Na-Young. 2016. "Misogyny, Gender Discrimination, and Feminism: A Feminist Project of Social Justice Surrounding the Gangnam Station 10th Exit." *Culture and Society* 22: 147–186.

Mathiesen, K. 2016. "South Korea Leads List of 2016 Climate Villains." *Climate Home News*. https://www.climatechangenews.com/2016/11/04/south_korea_climate_villains.

Regan, Tom. 2003. *Animal Rights, Human Wrongs: An Introduction to Moral Philosophy*. Lanham, MD: Rowman & Littlefield Publishers.

Shiva, Vandana, and Maria Mies. 2014. *Ecofeminism (Critique Influence Change)*. London, UK: Zed Books.

Singer, Peter. 1977. *Animal Liberation: A New Ethics for our Treatment of Animals*. Later Printing edition. New York, NY: Avon Books.

Sohn, Hee Jeong. 2017. *Feminism Reboot*. Seoul: Woodpencilbooks. In Korean.

Tracy, Sarah. 2013. *Qualitative Research Methods: Collecting Evidence, Crafting Analysis, Communicating Impact*. Hoboken, NJ: Wiley-Blackwell.

Yoon, Ji-Yeong. 2019. "The Feminism Upheaval: The Point of Conflict in Feminisms as the Site of the New Thought." *Culture and Society* 27 (1): 7–75. In Korean.

Chapter 6

Embodying Carnal Appetites

Food and Sexuality in Li Ang's Mandarin Duck Aphrodisiacs

Chien-wei Pan

ABSTRACT

In *Mandarin Duck Aphrodisiacs* (*Yuanyang chunshan*, 2007), the prominent Taiwanese writer Li Ang presents eight stories about sensual dining enjoyment, in which different female characters demonstrate their unusual appetites for food and sex. As the Chinese Daoists put it (van Gulik 2003, 49), young women were regarded as men's symbolic aphrodisiacs, in that it was thought that men could enhance their sexual performance by incessantly copulating with women. To challenge such a belief, Li Ang boldly suggests that women who eat aphrodisiacs enjoy sex without men.

In this chapter, I study how Li Ang brings to light multiple meanings of aphrodisiacs by means of her characterization of various women who are gratified by food and sex. I argue that by focusing on female carnal appetites, Li Ang highlights eccentric womanhood in order to transcend male imaginations of national identities. Furthermore, what constitutes the idea of aphrodisiacs lies in how food, be it ordinary or unusual, arouses diners' carnal desires for which Li Ang accentuates different bodily senses. By revealing men's anxiety to maintain sexual potency and how they become weak after consuming aphrodisiacs, Li Ang also hints at the identity crisis in general and a notion of corporeal nationalism in particular in contemporary Taiwan.

INTRODUCTION

Due to her interest in portraying sex and human bodies, Li Ang (1952–) is perhaps one of the most controversial writers in the Chinese-speaking world. Born in Lugang, an old town in Zhanghua County, Li Ang revealed her literary talent when she began her writing career. She quickly gained literary fame after shocking her readers with *The Butcher's Wife* (*Shafu*, 1983), in which a desperate woman murders her husband in the same way that he would have slaughtered and dismembered his pigs. On publishing *All Sticks Are Welcome in the Censer of Beigang* (*Beigang xianglu renren cha*, 1997), Li Ang was accused of slandering the female politician Chen Wenqian (1958–) by alluding to her lascivious private life—when Lin Lizhi, the female protagonist, who mesmerizes others with her curvy figure, ascertains her power by sleeping with different men. In Li Ang's other works such as *Dark Night* (*Anye*, 1985), *The Lost Garden: A Novel* (*Miyuan*, 1991), and *Male Sleeping Beauty* (*Shui meinan*, 2017), for example, the female protagonists are not always depicted as sexual victims when they are curious about sexual activities. For Li Ang, it is essential to enhance the visibility of women whose presences have been shadowed (or ignored) in patriarchal society. The images of women, therefore, memorably come to the fore with their extraordinary attributes, most of which are associated with sex and sexuality.

This chapter analyzes Li Ang's feminist perspective by studying *Mandarin Duck Aphrodisiacs* (*Yuanyang chunshan*, 2007), focusing on the interconnection between erotic dishes and female sexuality. More specifically, I argue that Li Ang relies on the portrayal of food to constitute a notion of corporeality/carnality to shed new light on women's sexual desires. Traditionally, unlike men who are known for their intellectual talents, women have been associated with their corporeal bodies. However, feminist/queer theorists such as Judith Butler and Elizabeth Grosz attempt to revisit such soul/body dichotomies in order to redefine contemporary feminism. For Butler (1993), "to invoke matter is to invoke a sedimented history of sexual hierarchy and sexual erasures which should surely be an object of feminist inquiry" (22). Besides that, in working to unveil such sexual hierarchy by investigating misogynist thoughts, Grosz (1994) finds that "women are somehow more biological, more corporeal, and more natural than men" (14). Although I refer to Grosz's idea of corporeal feminism, which theorizes the body "outside patriarchal and racial categories" (Grosz 1994, 15), I do not intend to initiate another feminist debate in the following discussions. Rather, I aim to reappraise Li Ang's feminist thinking when she shows her obsession with narrating women's corporeal bodies.

As the first novel in Taiwan that specifically deals with food and sex, *Mandarin Duck Aphrodisiacs* is presented as an alternative literary feast, comprised of four parts: (1) the beginning, (2) the middle, (3) entremets, and (4) the end, each of which contains two stories. In her text, Li Ang regales the readers with eight interrelated stories, each using names related to food: "Civet and Pangolin" (*Guozili yu chuanshanjia*), "Curry Rice" (*Gali fan*), "Beef Noodles" (*Niurou mian*), "Pearl Milk Tea" (*Zhenzhu naicha*), "Aphrodisiacs" (*Chun shan*), "The National Banquets" (*Guoyan*), "Menu Dégustation," and "Vegetarian Diets" (*Su zhai*). Read together, the eight different stories epitomize a Taiwanese hybrid food spectacle from the late Qing period to the contemporary era.

Despite the eight interrelated stories, the narrative structure of the novel is underpinned by two main story lines revolving around characters' food memories. First, the female protagonist Wang Qifang reminisces about various dishes she ate from childhood to adulthood. In addition, some women (such as her mother, cousin, and a female assistant) with whom Wang lives and others (such as two fictional women, called A and B, and Soong Mei-ling who appear in Wang's imagination) also partake in constructing collective food memories. In other words, instead of staying home and cooking meals for men, women in the text are known for their interest in eating sensual and exotic dishes. Second, the father and other male characters share collective memories of eating unique dishes (including aphrodisiacs) while women seem to disappear in most of the dining scenes. Although intersecting and intermixing the food memories of both sexes, Li Ang concentrates on women's appetites because of which they willingly travel around the world in search of various cuisines. In this regard, Li Ang seems to offer an alternative history of female food consumption that departs from the male-centric food spectacle.

Concerning the current scholarly analysis of *Mandarin Duck Aphrodisiacs*, two major interpretative frameworks parallel the two kinds of memory accounts mentioned earlier. First, critics acknowledge that the father plays a pivotal role in constructing the daughter's food knowledge. Liu Liangya (2015), for instance, notices the father's revisional accounts whenever he recalls the time of the Japanese Occupational Period and the Kuomintang (KMT) regime, the likes of which prevalently appear in literary accounts published in the post-martial law era (464). Further, for Dai Huaxuan (2017), the father's funeral at the end of the story signals the major transition of Li Ang's writing style—concerning how Li Ang maintains the old tropes, such as women and sex—and opens new avenues for her future works (97–130). Nevertheless, by concentrating on the paternal figure in the text, neither Liu and Dai can adequately explain the women's unusual appetites.

In terms of the second feature, critics focus on how the female characters' anomalous appetites, by eating and drinking like men, weaken their phallocentric imagination of the aphrodisiacs. Hong Shanhui (2012) suggests that the representations of food and sex pertain to Li Ang's objective to reappraise the patriarchal understanding of power (301). In a similar feminist line of inquiry, Qiu Zixiu (2012) contends that Li Ang aims to transcend the "archaic" and "parochial" cultural stereotype regarding the diverse types of food (5). My following analysis of the novel may align with the feminist reading endorsed by Hong and Qiu, but what differentiates my investigation from theirs is my emphasis on the notion of female bodies, or more specifically, the implications of carnality.

The book title, *Mandarin Duck Aphrodisiacs*, already gives some clues to Li Ang's endeavor to rediscover women's bodies in the male historical/literary tradition. The word "aphrodisiacs" is reminiscent of another book, *Aphrodite: A Memoir of the Senses* (*Afrodita*, 1998), by Isabel Allende (1942–) who believes that even ordinary edible ingredients with associations of human reproductive organs can arouse the eaters' sexual desire. Moreover, the concept of the mandarin duck may recall the Mandarin Duck and Butterfly School of popular literature in the 1910s and 1920s that has been criticized for being so sentimental as to be feminine. By juxtaposing both the "mandarin duck" and the "aphrodisiacs" in the title, Li Ang hints at her intention to add Chinese elements to sensuous dishes.

My main purpose in this chapter is to unravel how Li Ang intermingles her two favorite themes, bodies and food, to reinvigorate the notion of female sexuality, a realm in which she has been indulging ever since beginning her writing career. Li Ang's interest pertains to feminists' insistence on intervening in the politics of the everyday: regarding the imbrication of food, body, and sex, critic Elspeth Probyn (2000) suggests we examine the minute details of life "at a gut level" and "draw out the tangibility of power, its textures and flavours" (7). Moreover, Deborah Lupton (1996) astutely points out that "philosophy is masculine and disembodied; food and eating are feminine and always embodied" (3). As Carole M. Counihan (1999) puts it, "Eating and intercourse both involve passage across body boundaries of external substances that are then incorporated into the body" (9). That is, food and sex are two overlapping metaphors that become concrete when the body, as the boundary or the agency, rejects or accepts them.

To explicate how Li Ang brings to light the unusual female bodies, I divide my analysis into three parts. First, I present the process of how aphrodisiacs are veiled as ordinary food by investigating the father's memory, which is replete with bittersweet memories of being colonized by the Japanese and the Chinese nationalists. Second, I examine the so-called aphrodisiacs, paying attention to how women unfold their carnal desires. What constitutes the aphrodisiacs—from the ordinary dish to erotic food—involves different bodily senses. Third, I focus on the connection between women and Taiwan by investigating how Li Ang constructs a notion of modern womanhood.

Finally, by scrutinizing the dishes that are associated with diseases and death, I dwell on methods that women have to use to maintain their femininity and sexuality—that is, by ending the male potency myth.

The Father's Secret Dishes

As a girl, Wang Qifang had two kinds of childhood, both of which are intimately connected with food. The first, as with many girls, is related to sweets, such as colorful candies or regional desserts. However, it is the second kind that I want to explore in this section, which is during the days when she stays with her father who enjoys consuming the wild animals that allegedly enhance men's sexual performance. Dishes that contain the meat of wild creatures are regarded as aphrodisiacs—due to how vibrant and ferocious these animals are—and are unsuitable for children. Yet Wang, the apple of her father's eye, has a chance to sample the unique dishes. In addition, by listening to her father's reminiscences, she learns about his unusual dining experiences during visits to countries such as Japan and mainland China. Why does her father offer aphrodisiacs to his daughter at an age when she is supposed to solely enjoy simple sweets like other girls?

The father's aphrodisiacs and the relevant memories of food become relics of how Taiwan was over the course of the twentieth century, namely, from a wartime colonial state to a postwar renegade province. Food thus becomes, in Katarzyna J. Cwiertka's words, an "index" that enables us to peek at what people usually ate in the concurrent period (Cwiertka 2013, 4). In the socio-historical context constructed by fictional food accounts, I also suggest that we observe the implications of interpersonal intimacy when the father shares food with his daughter. That is, it is painful for the father to reminisce about what happened in wartime and postwar Taiwan, but by disclosing some concurrent stories about cooking and eating it allows him to tell his daughter the social secrets which are oftentimes isolated from the collective memories.

It is crucial to decipher why the father refrains from telling his daughter the actual historical events but relies instead on recounting his memories of food. As Wang Qifang recalls, "My father did not want to learn Japanese, the official language of the Japanese colonizers. But neither could he speak Mandarin, the official language of the Han race" (Li 2007, 38). Wang's father does not accept his Chinese identity when he is arrested by the Chinese Nationalist Army after the February 28 Incident. In daily life, the father tends to communicate with his children in Hokkien (*fu lao hua*), the regional dialect spoken in coastal regions such as Fujian (Li 2007, 20). That is, Wang's father reveals his Taiwanese identity, one that is neither Japanese nor Chinese, through his daily use of his regional dialect. To complicate the issue of the father's national identity, Li Ang invites us to dwell on the food that he consumed daily in three interrelated stories: "Civet and Pangolin," "Curry Rice," and "Beef Noodles." Sequentially, the three stories correlate with the historical development of Taiwan from the Japanese colonization to the KMT regime.

In "Civet and Pangolin," numerous air-raid shelters are shown in Lucheng, a fictional town rife with a sense of gloom. As the narrator reveals, there are "caves" in ruins where one can find a single shoe, a broken Japanese clog, an umbrella with a hole, some battered clothes, and the bodies of dead animals (Li 2007, 13). In contrast to these deserted caves, a comparatively furnished one exists in the backyard of Wang Qifang's residence despite the fact that it is no longer being used as a shelter. Capon Arhat (*yanji luohan*), a male worker who castrates roosters for a living, usually brings various wild animals to Wang Qifang's father. For fear of terrifying other family members, the two men usually kill these animals in the shelter, turning it into an animal slaughterhouse. However, without witnessing how these animals are killed, Wang Qifang only sees the animals' body parts as food ingredients being simmered inside a cooking pot.

Eating wild animals supposedly strengthens the male eaters' masculinity. What the men want, after killing the animals in the air-raid shelter, is to acquire the animals' "unique vitality," embodied in the form of the meat (Fiddes 1991, 67). That is why ecofeminist Carol J. Adams (1990), while exploring the idea of meat consumption, argues that "meat is a symbol for what is not seen but is always there—patriarchal control of animals" (16), and she even succinctly states that "people with power have always eaten meat" (26). Wang Qifang does not know whether her male family members become more powerful after eating the wild animals, but she can vividly recall that she has eaten dishes containing Chinese softshell turtles (Trionychidae, or *bie*), masked palm civets, pangolins, and other animals that have been ingredients in dishes.

In contrast to the above "wild" eating scenes, in "Curry Rice," Li Ang demonstrates a civilized way of eating when food is served in modern restaurants. The dish "curry rice" is related to Wang's father who, along with other Taiwanese friends, used to entertain a Japanese writer in an extravagantly furnished railway restaurant in colonial Taipei. According to the father's recollection, the Japanese writer, after his fellow diners had ordered the dishes they desired, would finally (and humbly) order a plate of curry and rice to mollify his homesickness. However, the Japanese writer's reason to order last turned out to be courteous: "Curry rice is inexpensive, and if I order curry rice first, other people will not order high-priced dishes out of politeness, thus causing trouble for other guests and the host" (Li 2007, 35). The Japanese writer's decision is not groundless regarding how the narrator describes the uniqueness of the restaurant: The exterior of the building is intentionally decorated with red bricks, revealing a sense of elegance. And inside the restaurant, there are utensils made in the UK, and interior decorations are imported from other foreign countries. Furthermore, Wang's father and his friends usually have oxtail soup, steak, and crème brûlée, all of which, in these men's minds, are ostensibly Western (Li 2007, 55–56).

The Japanese writer's thoughtfulness in ordering the curry dish is not simply out of courtesy when he, as a colonizer, visits the colonial capital. The narrator hints at the fact that Japan became a modern nation during the Meiji period and that Taiwan was rapidly modernized owing to Japanese colonization (Li 2007, 57). Alongside the concept of colonial modernity, curry, *korokke* (croquettes), and *tonkatsu* (breaded pork cutlets) were three Western dishes that the Meiji people frequently consumed (Takashi 2000, 68). As an outsider, the Japanese writer tries to ease his food nostalgia when he has the chance to have curry, which is implicitly related to Western modernization in his homeland, that is, Japan. Without realizing the writer's homesickness, Wang's father discloses his admiration of his decorum in the restaurant, even though he negates his Japanese identity when he refuses to learn Japanese.

A different kind of restaurant, namely, the modern Chinese restaurant, is inserted into the foodscape when Li Ang aims to complicate the idea of refined methods of food consumption. According to Wang's father, he usually came to Taipei with his brother to dine at the famous Penglai Isle Restaurant (*Penglai dao jiujia*), where they could eat fusion dishes that combined different regional flavors from places such as Fujian, Guangdong, and Sichuan. These dishes are called *jiujia cai*, literally meaning that diners usually have the company of courtesans. To put it differently, Wang's father also considers *jiujia cai* as a kind of *waisheng cai*, indicating that these dishes originate from the mainland when Taiwan was still one of the provinces. However, as the father recalls, with the growing population of Chinese people who relocated to Taiwan with the KMT government, the transplanted mainlanders insisted on their original way of eating and did not accept the fusion of different regional dishes (Li 2007, 48). Hence, an implied antagonism occurs when diners begin to define the notion of authentic Chinese dishes.

In "Beef Noodles," the dining scene moves to a prison where detainees sentenced to death awaited execution. The horrific prison scene pertains to the memory of the White Terror when the KMT government imposed martial law in 1949. An anonymous prisoner is captured because of his dissident political viewpoints—his embracing the idea of Taiwan independence, a crime meriting the death penalty before the lifting of martial law in 1987. Financed by his family members, the prisoner has the chance to have a bowl of beef noodles once or twice a week. Out of sympathy and kinship, the prisoner wants to buy the man incarcerated in the opposite cell a bowl of beef noodles. However, he fails in his mission when his fellow prisoner is executed without warning the following day. One may wonder why the jail, part of the KMT's state apparatus, offers the wealthier prisoner beef noodles in particular. As the narrator finally reveals, beef noodles were invented in Taiwan, a fact which shocks the prisoner who believed they had been invented in mainland China.

The symbol of beef was usually used as an indicator to identify those who had recently moved to Taiwan (*waishengren*) because local Taiwanese people (*benshengren*) relied on cattle for fieldwork and rarely ate beef. The unnamed prisoner, captured because of his Taiwanese consciousness, had believed that beef noodles were invented in China and that the government officials punished the prisoners by feeding them a Chinese dish. However, after realizing that beef noodles were invented in Taiwan, the prisoner discloses his bewilderment and loses faith in his support for Taiwan independence.

The above three stories, associated with the father's memory, lead us to revisit the alternative memories of Japan and China through the prism of food. That is, men in the stories reveal their Japanese and hybrid Taiwanese identities by exhibiting what they eat in different scenarios. However, the father finds it difficult to tell a linear and complete story: what he presents are accounts concerning dishes such as wild animals, curry, and beef noodles, all of which disclose a sense of bewilderment toward what actually happened in the past. Seen in this vein, the father also alludes to his identity crisis in that he cannot define who he really is when he is accompanied by his daughter.

It is noteworthy that the dishes mentioned in the three short stories, except for wild animals, are regular dishes that people consume daily, quite different from the common image of what an aphrodisiac should be. That is, food and sex are two distinct matters in the father's memory; sex and sexuality should be kept hidden in his daily life. Yet when Li Ang attempts to discover women's sexual consciousness, food and sex are interdependent. The notion of female sexuality will be quickly elucidated in the following section.

Aphrodisiacs and Sexual Fantasies

As an adult, Wang Qifang finally realizes that the wild animals that her father consumed were aphrodisiacs, and this realization shatters her memory of childhood, which is sugarcoated by the experiences of consuming sweets. It seems that the burden of the historical memories—men cannot clearly disclose their national identities—explains why they usually reminisce about the past discursively in the same way that they secretly consume wild animals while hiding out from other family members. For these men, eating aphrodisiacs indicates that they can enhance (or at least maintain) their potency, but how do their female sexual partners evaluate their performances? What about women who eat the same dishes—can they also be sexually aroused? Answers to these questions, I contend, are closely connected with the physical bodies in regards to Li Ang's presentation of the characters' sexualities.

In "Aphrodisiacs," Li Ang focuses on the issues of erotic dishes specifically for women by revealing the origins, contents, and functions of several edible ingredients that can raise women's sexual desire. There are some hints of how women can benefit from consuming aphrodisiacs. For instance, without knowing the function of erotic dishes, while consuming the meat of wild animals, Wang Qifang only feels that "the whole body (at least the upper body) is aroused by the sweet smell of the meat" (Li 2007, 29). Here, the differentiation between the upper body and the lower body brings to mind the sociocultural meanings of different bodily senses. According to David Howes (2003), "Sight and hearing were traditionally linked with intellectual activity and civilized behaviour . . . while taste, touch, and smell were associated with animality, . . . —in short, 'primitive'—senses" (4). In particular, Li Ang relies primarily on the "primitive" senses—smell, taste, touch—while demonstrating the efficacy of eating aphrodisiacs.

To begin with, several erotic dishes are allegedly derived from mainland China, supposedly a homeland of ancient sexual knowledge. As the narrator hints, "The ancient ethnic group that originated from northern China believed in the idea of 'you are what you eat' and made efforts for full execution" (Li 2007, 135). The idea of becoming what you eat explains why aphrodisiacs must contain the parts of different animals. When men want bigger penises, for instance, they can eat the penises of animals such as mules, bulls, tigers, deer, and rhinoceroses, which are bigger and more potent than those of men (Li 2007, 136). In addition to the wild animals mentioned earlier, the variegated (and mostly dismembered) animals' body parts confirm the Chinese men's obsession with eating animals to improve their physical prowess.

In his seminal book *Sexual Life in Ancient China*, R. H. van Gulik (2003) illustrates ancient sexual practices from the Zhou to the Ming dynasties. Many of the sexual practices seem peculiar by modern standards, for example, men absorbing their semen during sexual intercourse following Daoist practices (van Gulik 2003, 317). The studies of sexual beliefs have been considered by others, such as Frank Dikötter (1995), Judith Farquhar (2002), and Huang Kewu (2016), who have examined various sexual practices and discourses from Qing to post-socialist China. More specifically, Chinese men have been accustomed to adopting variegated ways to improve their sexual performance. By alluding to these ancient sexual practices in China, Li Ang intentionally shows how sexual knowledge is frequently practiced (or misused) in Taiwanese society. Nevertheless, it is the continuation and discontinuation of Chinese sexual knowledge that enlivens the images of various aphrodisiacs in Taiwan.

Eating is not the only method that can improve men's sexual performance when having sex with women—especially virgins. The so-called Daoist sexual practices (*fang zhong shu*) rely on the sexual union of men and women that maintains the balance of yin and yang, two opposite forces that constitute the whole universe. Therefore, men are advised to have sex with many women (the yin) to improve their male bodies (the yang) for the sake of potency enhancement, or for the motto "Borrow feminine force to strengthen men's physical health" (*cai yin bu yang*). Furthermore, by the same logic, women in Li Ang's writing become the best ingredients to regain men's potency, because "the female bodies . . . are the most effective aphrodisiacs" (Li 2007, 139). It is essential to know how men absorb the essence of the female body because the process is both phallocentric and gruesome. During sexual intercourse, the man who regards the woman as his aphrodisiac will

> slowly, repeatedly and straightforwardly conquer the vagina with his penis, and he gradually depletes the energy of the female body, resulting in the situation that the woman becomes lifeless, withers, and finally dies. (Li 2007, 139)

The emaciated female bodies disclose Li Ang's worries that women, along with animals, are exploited to complete the grotesque imagination of male potency. But how can women resist men's incessant sexual intrusions in the hope of absorbing their energy (the yin)? To highlight men's misuse of female bodies, Li Ang spotlights the swollen vaginas of females who can be considered victims when men constantly have sex with them. The narrator uses the analogy of eating to explain why the women, with swollen vaginas, should stop having sex because "the swollenness represents a kind of fullness" and it also means that "eating again will revert the situation into an unpleasant one: the vagina [like a mouth] will throw up and turn out the lips" (Li 2007, 141). Hence, a sense of feminist awakening arises when women with swollen vaginas cease to have sex with men.

Instead of being men's aphrodisiacs, Li Ang encourages women to actively explore other sexual activities, say, having a threesome—rather than sexual intercourse that involves only one man and one woman. The increased number of sexual partners—from one-on-one sex to a threesome—conforms to Anthony Giddens's observation that "almost everyone is thus addicted to sex in any case" (Giddens 1992, 77). However, it is interesting how Li Ang uses the analogy of food to explain the procedure of a ménage à trois: there being one man and two women (A and B), who, after finishing a luxurious dinner, want to enjoy a threesome. The woman A, out of curiosity, has the chance to see the woman B's vulva, which may look like "a small petal," "a small shell," "a small butterfly," "a small snail," or "a nine-headed abalone" (Li 2007, 145). The abalone resembles the vulva because "the center is slightly raised, surrounded by a dark and wrinkled skirt, and it looks exactly like the vulva" (Li 2007, 146). By ignoring the man in the threesome, the woman A curiously fingers the vagina of woman B, and witnesses female ejaculation. By touching the fluids that woman B squirts, woman A recalls the time she also felt such greasy liquids while cleaning oysters. A comment from the narrator explains this: "They can be aphrodisiacs for each other" (Li 2007, 148). That is, by not only seeing but also touching the female genitals, women—used to being aphrodisiacs for the exclusive use of men—reveal how they can be sexually attracted by other women.

Despite the sensuous details of the human threesome, the scene of female masturbation suddenly inserted into the sexual spectacle discloses Li Ang's idea of female sexual autonomy. Without the help of others, women can fulfill their sexual desires by using the same hands they use to prepare daily meals. What these independent women receive, by masturbation, are the feelings of "warmness, comfort, fullness, peacefulness, joy, and unbounded perfection" (Li 2007, 158). By witnessing how satiated the woman becomes, the narrator thus raises the question: "Then, should she need aphrodisiacs? What should she have the aphrodisiacs for?" (Li 2007, 159).

By highlighting the anatomical differences between women's erogenous zones and men's penises, Luce Irigaray (1985) pertinently explains women's sexual contentment when they touch themselves. A "woman 'touches herself' all the time," Irigaray writes, "and moreover, no one can forbid her to do so, for her genitals are formed of two lips in continuous contact" (24). This is why Irigaray proposes that the ideal sex for women should not be the single kind of sex that is easily associated with the symbol of the penis on which women must depend.

Although illuminating women's autoeroticism via the examples of food and sexual intercourse at the same time, Li Ang actually brings to the fore women's need for both love and sex. One possible clue can be found at the end of the story, when the narrator explains that women like Wang Qifang and the women A and B will only contact their lovers after three or four days when they feel the need for love and sex (Li 2007, 163). In other words, Li Ang disagrees with the stereotypical understanding that "women want love, men want sex" (Giddens 1992, 66), and by unfolding women's sexual fantasies, she demonstrates that women can satisfy both needs as long as they begin to explore their lower body parts that have been falsely reserved for men. Without being treated as men's aphrodisiacs, women can still fulfill their carnal desires and reveal a sense of sexual autonomy.

Women and the Nation

Contrary to the above sexual fantasies, I am going to investigate how food conceptualizes modern womanhood and sheds new light on the idea of a feminized nation. Various dishes in this section are interwoven with female figures—the entire body per se. To be more specific, when women's fragmented body parts are associated with desires, the whole bodies, as metaphors, signify their connection with the bigger entity, say, the nation. Of course, a feminized nation is not solely a Taiwanese invention since there are several other personifications, such as Britannia, Marianne, and Columbia, all of whom are the ideal embodiments of feminized nationhood. But unlike the above imaginings of nations, Taiwan, allegorized as a woman, is known for her unusual appetites in that she is willing to consume numerous kinds of foreign cuisines.

In addition to the female protagonist Wang Qifang, various women come to the fore in "Pearl Milk Tea" and "The National Banquets" when Li Ang proffers different qualities of modern womanhood. The story of "Pearl Milk Tea" centers on the unusual life of Qianhui, the cousin and playmate of Wang Qifang. Instead of being the docile daughter of the owner of the famous local bakery, Qianhui wishes to marry a man whom she loves rather than the one of whom her parents approve. She falls in love with a travel agent, Wuxiong, who is not an ideal son-in-law due to his lack of proper education and his lewd job that involves socialization with pimps and prostitutes. In spite of the disapproval of the family, Qianhui still marries Wuxiong, but their happy marriage ends when he dies in a plane crash. As a widow, Qianhui only dresses in black and thus earns the name "Black Rose" (*Hei meigui*). Yet the color of black is uncannily associated with the drink, pearl milk tea, which Qianhui allegedly invents: people believe that Qianhui, due to her knowledge of making pastries, invented the globally known beverage, and the drink always appears wherever there are Taiwanese people (Li 2007, 122).

A cup of pearl milk tea, as a metaphor, denotes the notion of the modern womanhood that Li Ang aims to bring to light by telling the story of a popular drink. To be more specific, Qianhui's modern female consciousness—financial independence and transnational mobility—is illustrated through the symbol of the tea. Besides, Qianhui becomes wealthier than the local male aristocrats when she receives insurance benefits after her husband's tragic death and inherits the stocks of the family business. In terms of mobility, she is obsessed with traveling around the world, visiting lesser-known countries like Eritrea, Montenegro, Bosnia, and Cape Verde, thus widening her worldview (Li 2007, 123). Furthermore, Qianhui is accustomed to drinking champagne—and only the oldest and most expensive ones for which she willingly travels abroad, making herself famous at different hotels. The notion of female independence, regarding the assets and the ability to travel around the world, is the first type of woman that Li Ang alludes to while employing the female image to represent Taiwan.

In "The National Banquets," Li Ang hints at the second type of woman who has to attend different sociopolitical events to represent Taiwan. This time, Li Ang refers to the anecdotes of the former president Chiang Kai-shek and his wife Soong Mei-ling. The narrator states, "The ruler's wife or the so-called first lady, being both majestic and affectionate, running the orphanages, garnering the skill of Chinese painting, and owning both talent and virtue, does not eat with the president" (Li 2007, 165–166). The first lady, owing to her Western upbringing, declares in English that "besides her Chinese face, she is a westerner in every way" (Li 2007, 167). Takc breakfast for example—she is accustomed to a Western diet and usually has a cup of fresh juice, sunny-side up eggs, bacon, sausages, toast, and a cup of coffee. However, the president, known for his resolve in wanting to save China after witnessing small fish swimming upstream when he was little (Li 2007, 165), only eats a bowl of congee with some fermented bean curd and pickles (Li 2007, 168). Hence, it is discernible that each simply eats different food.

Despite their dietary differences, both the president and the first lady have to attend national banquets where they entertain foreign guests with authentic Chinese cuisines since the Chiang regime proudly claims that the Republic of China is the real China. The feast, therefore, is tainted with the mysterious ambience of people trying to decipher the ingredients of the dishes that are given arcane names to create a sense of auspiciousness. For example, when there is the dish "Flying Dragons and Dancing Phoenix" (*long fei feng wu*), people may come up with the idea that it must contain snakes, noting the similarities they share with dragons (Li 2007, 171). However, for the sake of the foreign guests, the menus are bilingual, and through the English names of the dishes people can immediately comprehend the content of each dish:

五福臨門錦繡盤	Assorted Cold Dish
錦上添花慶圍爐	Shark's Fin Soup
龍飛鳳舞迎新春	Sautéed Lobster with Diced Chicken
和氣生財大好市	Braised Dried Oysters with Seaweed
代代平安好福氣	Stewed Tofu Skins with Stuffing
牛轉乾坤行大運	Stewed Beef Tendons
年年有餘滿華堂	Sweet and Sour Fish with Lotus Seeds
長命百歲富貴菜	Mustard Greens in Chicken Soup
一團和氣金元寶	Dumplings Stuffed with Fish Meat and Vegetables
年年高昇好彩頭	Chinese New Year Radish Cake
全家團圓樂陶陶	Glutinous Rice Ball Soup
大吉大利慶豐收	Fruits in Season. (Li 2007, 172–173)

The first lady, with a good command of English, is able to recognize the ingredients of each dish. In stark contrast with his wife, the president can only understand the food he eats when he sees it. This is the exact female image—a woman who is elegant and has a good command of at least one foreign language—that Li Ang aims to portray when she inculcates the importance of female autonomy. Although the name of Soong Mei-ling is never mentioned in the story, we can still visualize that the image of Madame Chiang has been woven into the collective memories of the Taiwanese people due to implications such as her Western upbringing, dining preference, and linguistic ability.

However, authentic Chinese dishes are no longer served in the national banquets because the new president advocates the notion of Taiwanese consciousness. The new president insists on incorporating Taiwanese regional dishes and thus irritates the Chiang loyalists, who think that these dishes do not conform to the expected standards and are therefore inappropriate (Li 2007, 186). However, due to the new president's insistence, dishes such as smoked duck (*ya shang*) and marinated pork livers (*dangan*), usually regarded as regional snacks, are now elegantly presented at the national banquets.

Until now, I have not discussed the relevance between the female body and the national banquets, even though I did refer to the first lady and her food preferences. It is necessary to sketch the conventions and transitions of the national banquets because the first lady, the dominating female figure, usually wears a *qipao* to strengthen her Chineseness on these diplomatic occasions. To illuminate the significance of female bodies, Li Ang intentionally inserts another national symbol: "national opera" (*guoju*). The unusual juxtaposition of "national banquet" (*guoyan*) and "national opera" (*guoju*) in one story verifies Li Ang's unconventional literary imagination—eating and acting are equally significant when it comes to representing a particular nation. Before being known as the national opera, the Peking opera had been exclusively performed in the Chinese Armed Forces Cultural Activity Centre (*Guojun wenyi huodong zhongxin*), a place where the army loyal to Chiang could see various performances (Li 2007, 174). Celebrated female characters such as the Tang consort Yang Yuhuan and the Han beauty Wang Zhaojun, though wearing anachronistic dresses in a style of neither the Han nor Tang dynasties, act on the stage to characterize how an individual woman can either save the nation (such as Wang Zhaojun) or lead to the decline of the empire (such as Yang Yuhuan) (Li 2007, 179). To put it differently, the female actors' bodies, wrapped in dresses that exemplify their Chineseness, are keenly associated with the nation.

Nevertheless, the Peking opera is finally elevated as the national opera when the government adopts it as political propaganda. The narrator explains that "to recuperate the deep-rooted Chinese traditional culture, we should revive the national opera" and "Mao Zedong, the gangster of China, is deconstructing the great and ingrained Chinese culture by launching the Cultural Revolution" (Li 2007, 175). Furthermore, across the strait, Jiang Qing (1914–1991), or Madame Mao, is another powerful woman who plays a pivotal role in transforming the traditional opera. A full description of how Madame Mao engages in the process of reforming theater shows how dramas are simplified because of a woman's will:

> In fact, in China, where Peking opera was nurtured, people confidently modified the traditional Chinese dramas that come from the native land. First, it was the renowned Chairman's wife who, during the period of the Cultural Revolution, turned the thousands of traditional *xiqu* into only eight model theaters. After the Reform and Opening began, the officials still substantially changed the traditional dramas. (Li 2007, 184)

Thanks to the modernization of dramas that Madame Mao pioneered, modern decorations such as "Moulin-Rouge-styled feathers," "plastic flowers," and "black tulle" are now legitimately and blatantly attached to the costumes of the actors/actresses (Li 2007, 185). However, unlike Madame Mao who significantly revised the traditional *xiqu*, Madame Chiang in Taiwan does not deliberately turn the national banquet into a Western banquet to pander to her taste. It is the contrast between the two first ladies that Li Ang endeavors to demonstrate while comparing two different national symbols, that is, the national banquet and national opera.

It is worthwhile to examine the closing remarks that appear at the end of Li Ang's work that reveal the Taiwanese consciousness that she alludes to by conjuring up the imaginings of the national opera. This account appears after Wang Qifang reminisces about viewing the Peking opera in Beijing and compares it to the "national opera" of Taiwan:

> [Taiwanese people] use their ways to make full use of the final moment of the great Chinese culture, and they come here to give a full performance. Thence the lights are extinguished and people are scattered. History cannot be repeated, and what can be repeated is not the same appearance. . . . With the gestures that signify the despondency, they no longer perform in the same way! (Li 2007, 191)

Wang Qifang's understanding, read as a national allegory, discloses the notion of national independence when the actors/actresses, with their gestures, take leave from the Chinese tradition. By adopting the symbol of the national opera, the work shows both a continuation and a discontinuation of the traditional culture. On the one hand, traditional Chinese culture is maintained through constantly performing the authentic Peking opera—as the national opera—in Taiwan. On the other hand, when authorities in mainland China aim to remodel the traditional performing arts, they are already creating novel forms of drama during the Cultural Revolution and in subsequent years. The final claim of the passage that they no longer perform in the same way strongly verifies the cultural break between Taiwan and mainland China.

While employing the national symbols—from a cup of pearl milk tea to the distinction between the national banquet and the national opera—Li Ang foregrounds different female figures that are more suitable to represent Taiwan's national imagery. Without being men's aphrodisiacs, as I explored in the previous section, independent women such as Wang Qifang, Qianhui, and Madame Chiang are eager to show their unusual appetites, most of which have been ignored in patriarchal society. In other words, food not only liberates women's restrained sexualities but also empowers them to exhibit their womanhood that is essential for them to deconstruct the myth of enhancing male potency.

Conclusion: Demystifying the Male Potency

To shed new light on food and sexuality, Li Ang finally regales her readers with vegan dishes which are associated with religious abstinence to draw the distinction between aphrodisiacs and meatless meals. The narration of vegetarian diets appears when Wang Qifang's mother decides to have a vegetarian feast, a symbolic act to cleanse her husband's sin of being a glutton. The mother's understanding is based on the Buddhist notion of karma—indeed, her husband has killed a great many animals for the sake of his insatiable appetite. Buddhists, believing in karma, avoid eating animals for fear that they may become them in the afterlife. Yet there is already karma when the father has a stroke, caused by his high-protein and high-fat diet, and is left unable to eat. As Wang Qifang recalls, the father has lain in bed for ten years, seems to have lost the ability to swallow, and keeps the food in his mouth (Li 2007, 228). To help her father swallow food more easily, Wang takes the doctor's advice to use a blender to puree his meals, which look like "the vomit that comes from one who eats but does not fully digest" (Li 2007, 229). Nevertheless, the nauseating descriptions of the pureed food highlight her father's inability to chew, and when he loses the ability to masticate, there is no distinction between food and vomit.

Eventually, the father's death relieves him from eating unappetizing food—and at the same time overrides his wish to enhance his sexual prowess by consuming wild animals. Moreover, the death of the father indeed signifies that Wang Qifang is about to begin a new life of her own: at the end of the funeral, there is a passage that discloses Wang Qifang's bittersweet food experiences with her father:

> And then, in an unstoppable manner, Wang Qifang begins to smile, and the laugh lines are more visible and finally occupy the whole face. But the tears are spilling out of her eyes. (Li 2007, 265)

Instead of mainly mourning for the loss of her father, the female protagonist has both joyful and tearful expressions, revealing an equivocal attitude when she recalls her experiences of eating with her father. Yet it is the cheerful attitude that catches my full attention: Is she happy that her father no longer has to suffer from eating meals that resemble baby food? Or is she happy that she can once again have positive food experiences after his passing? The narrator, of course, leaves the doubtful facial expression unexplained. But we can see the smile, the laugh lines, and the tears, all of which exhibit a moving facial expression and reinforce the notion of corporeality/carnality.

A man with any physical impairment is rarely the ideal type to represent a mighty nation, but this abnormal image becomes quintessential when Li Ang highlights female characters to envision an alternative national imagery of Taiwan. To criticize the problems of a male-dominated nation, she attempts to point out the peril of the male potency imagination. That is, a man's worth lies in the flawless, potent body, but once the body is no longer unbroken, the man's value is thus diminished. In conclusion, it is helpful to decipher the contrast—the father sharing food with the daughter and the funeral of the father at the end. By revealing the sickness and even death of the father, Li Ang seems to put an end to the potency myth, showing instead that the more aphrodisiacs men consume, the sicker they will become.

REFERENCES

Adams, Carol J. 1990. *The Sexual Politics of Meat: A Feminist-Vegetarian Critical Theory*. Cambridge: Polity Press.

Allende, Isabel. 1998. *Aphrodite: A Memoir of the Senses*. Translated by Margaret Sayers Peden. London: Flamingo.

Butler, Judith. 1993. *Bodies that Matter: On the Discursive Limits of "Sex."* New York: Routledge.

Counihan, Carole M. 1999. *The Anthropology of Food and Body: Gender, Meaning, and Power*. New York: Routledge.

Cwiertka, Katarzyna J. 2013. "Introduction." In *Food and War in Mid-Twentieth Century East Asia*, edited by Katarzyna J. Cwiertka, 1–8. Surrey: Ashgate.

Dai Huaxuan. 2017. *Juguangdeng wai: Li Ang xiaoshuo lunji* [Outside the spotlight: on Li Ang's novels]. Taipei: Wan juan lou.

Dikötter, Frank. 1995. *Sex, Culture and Modernity in China: Medical Science and the Construction of Sexual Identities in the Early Republican Period*. Honolulu: University of Hawaii Press.

Farquhar, Judith. 2002. *Appetites: Food and Sex in Post-Socialist China*. Durham, NC: Duke University Press.
Fiddes, Nick. 1991. *Meat: A Natural Symbol*. London: Routledge.
Giddens, Anthony. 1992. *The Transformation of Intimacy: Sexuality, Love and Eroticism in Modern Societies*. Cambridge: Polity Press.
Grosz, Elizabeth. 1994. *Volatile Bodies: Toward a Corporeal Feminism*. Bloomington: Indiana University Press.
Hong Shanhui. 2012. "Toushi yinshi shuxie: Li Ang yuanyang chunshan de shenti, luxing, guozu yu lishi lunshu" [Seeing through food writing: the body, travel, and national/historical discourse in Li Ang's mandarin duck aphrodisiacs]. In *Bu diao de huaji: Li Ang guoji xueshu yantaohui lunwenji* [Floral season without withering: Li Ang's international conference proceeding], edited by Jiang Baochai and Lin Zhenshan, 297–321. Taipei: lianhewenxue.
Howes, David. 2003. *Sensual Relations: Engaging the Senses in Culture and Social Theory*. Ann Arbor: The University of Michigan Press.
Huang Kewu. 2016. *Yan bu xie bu xiao: jindai zhongguo nanxing shijie zhong de xiexue, qingyu yu shenti* [Laughing for the obscene: banter, lust, and body in the modern Chinese male world]. Taipei: Lianjing chuban gongsi.
Irigaray, Luce. 1985. *This Sex Which Is Not One*. Translated by Catherine Porter and Carolyn Burke. Ithaca, NY: Cornell University Press.
Li Ang. 1983. *Shafu* [The butcher's wife]. Taipei: Lianhe baoshe.
———. 1985. Anye [Dark nights]. Taipei: Shibao chuban.
———. 1991. *Miyuan* [The lost garden]. Taipei: Zhuzhe faxing.
———. 1997. *Beigang xianglu renren cha* [All sticks are welcome in the censer of Beigang]. Taipei: Maitain chubanshe.
———. 2007. *Yuanyang chunshan* [Mandarin duck aphrodisiacs]. Taipei: Lianhewenxue.
———. 2017. *Shui mei nan* [The male sleeping beauty]. Taipei: Youlu wenhua.
Liu Liangya. 2015. "Jingqi xiaoshuo dui rizhi shiqi de chongxin jiyi: yi yuanyang chunshan yu shuimian de hangxian zhong de fanjiyi rentong yu hunza weili" [Retrospection of Japanese colonial period in recent novels: antimemory, identification and hybridity in *yuanyang chunshan* and *shuimian de hangxian*]. *Qinghua xuebao* 45 (3): 457–486.
Lupton, Deborah. 1996. *Food, the Body, and the Self*. London: Sage.
Probyn, Elspeth. 2000. *Carnal Appetites: FoodSexIdentities*. London: Routledge.
Qiu Zixiu. 2012. "Cong hauijiu xiangchou dao wuweizazhen: Li Ang yinshi xiaoshuo yuanyang chunshan de kuawenhua pingxi" [From nostalgia to ambivalence: a transcultural critique of Li Ang's mandarin duck aphrodisiacs]. In *Bu diao de huaji: Li Ang guoji xueshu yantaohui lunwenji* [Floral season without withering: Li Ang's international conference proceeding], edited by Jiang Baochai and Zhenshan, 258–296. Taipei: lianhewenxue.
Takashi, Morieda. 2000. "The Unlikely Love Affair with Curry and Rice." *Japan Quarterly* 47 (2): 66–74.
van Gulik, R. H. 2003. *Sexual Life in Ancient China: A Preliminary Survey of Chinese Sex and Society from ca. 1500 B.C. till 1644 A.D.* Leiden: Brill.

Part III

PERFORMANCE OF MASCULINITY AND FEMININITY

Chapter 7

Gender Politics in Food Escape

Korean Masculinity in TV Cooking Shows in South Korea

Jooyeon Rhee

ABSTRACT

TV cooking shows have gained immense popularity in South Korea in the last few years. In these shows, male chefs and foodies play a crucial role in providing audiences with a space of domestic comfort in the midst of the intensely competitive and demanding social reality. This chapter examines some of the most popular cooking shows to explore how the image of caring, comforting, and resourceful culinary masculinity in fact reinforces the existing gender norms and hierarchy.

MEN IN SOUTH KOREAN TV COOKING SHOWS

Often called *mŏkppang*—a combination of "eat" (*mŏktta*) and "broadcasting" (*pangsong*)—TV cooking shows have significantly increased in number over the last decade. The sheer variety of these shows is overwhelming: they can include cooking Korean and foreign dishes, talking about food, introducing high- and low-end restaurants, cooking competitions, and watching others eat food. In this new wave of *mŏkppang*, one noticeable trend is the surge of male chefs and "foodies"[1] rather than the professional female cooks and chefs who dominated TV cooking shows between the 1980s and 2000s. Men play a significant role in promoting cooking in a dominant number of cooking shows today. Unlike conventional cooking shows in the past that focused on the cooking process and nutritional values of food, both professional and nonprofessional male chefs and foodies in these shows emphasize the pleasure of cooking and eating in domestic settings and, by extension, men's attentiveness to domestic affairs.

There are some professional chefs who became famous in South Korean (hereafter Korean) TV cooking shows. Similar to the image of chefs in the West, they appear "overplayed, oversensitive, and controlling" in their kitchens (Hyman 2008, 43). They tend to follow the trend in the cookery industry in the West, where male chefs skillfully brand their images for promoting restaurant businesses and food chains (Ashley et al. 2004, 177). The appearance of successful professional chefs in Korean TV cooking shows signifies more than a transnational flow of the popular image of male chefs in the Western world. It also challenges the conventional notion of cooking as blue-collar work or women's jobs. Men in chef uniforms or aprons present a new possibility to cross gender and class boundaries. It is also noteworthy that male characters in food-related businesses have frequently appeared in Korean TV dramas recently, where they are portrayed to be just as serious, professional, and successful as men with white-collar careers such as lawyers, doctors, stockbrokers, and so on.

However, the number of professional chefs in Korean TV cooking shows is very small, and these are not the kind of chefs audiences are fascinated with. The most famous cooking shows are those where male foodies—actors, singers, comedians, and so on—perform a culinary masculinity quite new to Korean audiences. This chapter defines culinary masculinity as a new model of masculinity mainly represented in media where male chefs and foodies emphasize domesticity through cooking and consuming food. It is quite distinct from hegemonic masculinity in Korea, which is characterized by patriarchal domination over women's bodies, labor, and emotion, and which is normalized and legitimized by social practices and institutional measures.[2]

One explanation of the popularity of these male celebrity chefs and foodies can be found in the projection of their passion to obtain knowledge in food and cooking skills. Men admitting their interest in domestic work in the public space created a refreshing counterpoint, especially when they have long been privileged to remain as "the served" rather than "the servers" of food. Their expression of the desire to learn about cooking for their families is even more dramatic since domestic cooking has not only been dominantly regarded as a women's job in Korea, but is also commonly represented as women's emotional investment in family life. Men's willingness to invest their emotion, energy, and time into cooking may be viewed as a welcome change to a society where many people feel that gender inequality at work and home is alarming. As more women enter job markets and as men's status as providers for their families is being destabilized due to the economic crisis since the late 1990s, the image of middle-class men, both married and single, in media is being transformed from patriarchal and work-centered to emotional, caring, and domestic (Kim and Pyke 2015, 512–513).

The mobilization of men into the kitchen in media, however, fails to address the rigid gender norms in Korea—the place where men spend the shortest time on domestic labor among the OECD countries (Kwak 2015). In these shows, men inform and educate the audiences about food, eating, and lifestyle. Male chefs and foodies present gendered labor as a leisurely activity while failing to recognize women's unpaid daily labor that is essential to family life. And professional male chefs' demonstration of culinary expertise and knowledge, as well as the collaborative workings among male chefs and foodies, convey that the restaurant business is an inherently men's arena. The issue is not their cooking skills but the mediation of male power through media: as in the popular cooking shows in the United States such as those on the Food Network, media explain the isolation of women from the culinary business by presenting men as the fearless masters of the restaurant kitchen while domesticating women in it (Druckman 2010).

The men-focused collective endeavor to promote cooking may be viewed as a response to the increasing social pressure on men to be more attentive to domestic affairs, but the hegemonic gender relations prevail through naturalizing the cooking business as men's work, normalizing women's domestic work, and affirming men's ability to authenticate taste. No matter how effeminate and family-friendly male foodies and chefs appear to be, these shows thoroughly fail to acknowledge the pervasive gender norms and hierarchy in contemporary Korea. This chapter contextualizes the TV cooking shows in their relationship to the current economic and social environment and analyzes some of the most popular shows to problematize the male-dominant representation of food and cooking as a site of gender inequality.

CHIPPAP (HOME-COOKED MEALS) PHENOMENON IN THE AGE OF POST-ECONOMIC CRISIS

Women's cooking for families is predominantly perceived as an act of care and love. And the actual time spent doing the unpaid labor of cooking is not recognized. Family members and the general public view their cooking as an emotional investment for a happy family life. This gendered notion of care has been criticized as a source for women's oppression (DeVault 1991) and recent feminist scholarship challenges the notion by engaging vigorously with the relationship between gender and food (Gillis and Hollows 2009). In the Korean context, food study has been concentrated on food nationalism and health (Osetrova 2016; Chung et al. 2016; Park 2016), and the scholarly exploration of the relationship between gender and food is sparse. Some noticeable pieces on food, health, and gender in the Korean context deal with the gendered consumption of health food, in which men's ill-health is often blamed on their wives' negligence of their duty to attend to their husbands' health (Lee 1996). Married women are often expected to look after their husbands' health not just because of the wellness of the family's economic and social lives but also because doing otherwise would pose a threat to national development, since men are expected to maintain their stamina to be competitive in industrial sectors. In the consumption of health food, for example, the main consumers have been middle-class, middle-aged men, but their wives are largely responsible for purchasing health food and medicine for their husbands (Lee 1996).

Korean people's interest in health and food was enhanced right after the International Monetary Fund (IMF) financial crisis, during which attentiveness to one's body went beyond health; it extended to surgical processes for bodily transformation. In this challenging neoliberal economic environment, one's higher education and fit body were considered signs of diligent self-care that could work favorably for them to obtain social mobility in the form of employment and marriage. It was around this time when the "well-being movement"—a popular imagination of wellness that could be maintained by investing time and money in health and food—popped up everywhere. This well-being movement was enthusiastically followed by both young and old, middle-class and marginalized middle-class people, though the phenomenon was also gendered. Cosmetic surgeries and diets were practiced mostly by women, while men hit the gym to tone their bodies. These practices may indicate how status-conscious Korean people are, performing their status through looks by taking extreme measures such as cosmetic surgeries at times (Elfving-Hwang 2013). In short, people are capitalizing on their bodily image to display their adaptability and competence.

In the post-IMF crisis, Korea has witnessed a number of major challenges such as weakened democracy, the sharp increase of the unemployment rate, and the economic gap between the poor and the rich due to the government's neoliberal economic policies (Lim and Jang 2006). The signs of societal crisis are seen in recent statistics. As of 2014, Korea was ranked very low in the areas of social welfare among OECD member countries, including fertility rate (the lowest among OECD members), political corruption, unbalanced taxation, and so forth (Kwak 2015). The unemployment rate among young people is increasing each year, and had reached 10.2 percent as of 2015 (Statistics Korea, 2015). The country's suicide rate has been the highest among OECD members in the last ten years, especially among elderly people in rural areas and youths. These figures are presented as a sign of the regression of Korean society; thus, netizens refer to Korea as "hell Chosŏn": the backward-looking society that lacks positive visions. The "well-being" fever has waned because of the costs of gym memberships, therapy, and organic food: young people's primary concern now is to get jobs to stay afloat. Many young people have given up hope for marriage, having children, and even dating due to their lack of economic resources, thus they despairingly call themselves "*samp'o sedae*" (a generation that has given up the aforementioned three social activities). In short, the *mŏkppang* phenomenon reveals the breakdown of the over-performance of status. *Mŏkppang*, contrary to its presentation of fullness and enjoyment, rather demonstrates the mental exhaustion felt by audiences who do not have to be concerned about their performance in front of TV sets and computer screens. The emergence of TV cooking shows can be contextualized in this rather depressing social context in which men play a role in comforting the audience through their performance of culinary masculinity.

Unlike the often exotic-looking dishes created by celebrity professional chefs in Western TV cooking shows, most dishes presented in Korean shows are home-cooked meals created by nonprofessional chefs whose image is marked by familiarity, comfort, and care. It is through the image of care and comfort attached to these home-cooked meals, called *chippap*, that masculinity is negotiated in Korean media. The term *chippap* in fact pops up frequently beyond cooking shows. It also appears in TV dramas when all-too-busy urban dwellers desire a proper meal over the ready-made lunch boxes or rice balls they pick up at a convenience store. It was once entirely natural that people would eat their meals at home, where certain members of the family, most likely women, would prepare them. In other words, these meals have only become known as *chippap* since people's desire for home-cooked meals has grown because of their reduced opportunity to have them.

There has been a tendency in TV cooking shows in the West—North America and Western Europe in particular—to present domestic cooking as a higher form of art and design (Ray 2007, 57). The kinds of food prepared in these shows are a cultural capital of the middle or upper classes who have better purchasing power over their food choices. The target audience of cooking shows in Korea, however, is ordinary citizens whose eating patterns as represented in the shows do not necessarily distinguish their social status, as Bourdieu once observed. The representation of domestic cooking in Korea is not viewed as an aestheticization either; rather, it is the practicality and nostalgia that appeals to the audiences for its association with the ordinariness of food and domesticity. The ordinariness of food in these shows is an important factor to produce the image of belonging among audiences, creating proximity among them. Proximity, as Emmanuel Levinas (1998) once contemplated, helps us to understand the ontology of food because it is connected to the most essential desire: the sense of belonging (74). Even extreme forms of resistance to food, such as nausea and hunger strikes, point to the desire of belonging as well: these forms of rejection rather affirm one's desire to be connected with others. The desire for food can be "a good will," according to Levinas (2001, 28), only if we acknowledge the pleasure and pain of others that may become or have been our own experiences.

Intimacy is stressed with male participation in cooking meals. It visualizes the invisible labor women usually engage in, and promotes care for family and individuals that can be initiated in the most basic thing that concerns all—eating. These shows are a social site that points to some of the pressing social issues that concern the audiences: a hunger for companionship and comfort they seek in real life. It is not the eating that matters; it is the circumstances in which people desire to eat. *Chippap* is not just home-cooked meals; it is meals that are shared among family members at home. These shows, in a way, produce a fantasy of companionship, feeding the eyes of the people who can temporarily escape from their stressful lives and seek alternative ways to feed their hunger for belonging and comfort. However, the seemingly all-inclusive and encompassing notion attached to "togetherness" is not gender neutral. Rather, it points to the serious gender discrimination and hierarchy so pervasive in Korea that cannot be digested easily. Conventional perceptions about food, cooking, and eating are being reproduced in these shows while coating the problem of patriarchy through the performance of culinary masculinity.

FOOD ESCAPE AND FETISHIZING *AJUMMA*

As Krishnendu Ray (2007) points out, some American TV cooking shows produce "syrupy sentimentalism about domestic bliss" (59) through the aestheticization of cooking. And a similar sentimentalism is seen in *Korean Cuisine* (*Han'gugin ŭi papsang*) and *Three Meals a Day* (*Samsi sekki*), in which food and cooking are embellished with nostalgia for the traditional kitchen and motherly love. *Korean Cuisine* is such a show that glamorizes regional cooking traditions passed down from generation to generation by women. It is led by a nationally acclaimed actor, Ch'oe Purham, whose image of a kind, faithful, and responsible father/grandfather fits well with the agenda of the show—that is, searching for the remnants of tradition in women's kitchens. In the show, Ch'oe visits small villages across the peninsula and introduces regional foods. The show usually picks one specific family in a rural village and focuses on the family's culinary specialty. An elderly female member of the family then converses with Ch'oe, explaining her family's and the region's traditions along with a demonstration of cooking processes. In these shows, male members of the family do not usually appear in the kitchen; rather, it is Ch'oe who steps into the woman's kitchen as an observer and a tester (figure 7.1).

The appreciation of women's domestic labor is emphasized in Ch'oe's narration, starting from commenting on the cooking process to the "taste of mothers' love" embodied in the cooked dishes. The male tester rediscovers women's invisible labor, stressing their emotional investment in food and cooking, which is an expression of love and care for their families. The intimacy between the male tester and women in the show plays an important role for the audiences' experience of comfort and belonging that they lack in their everyday lives.

However, the image of these elderly women reproduces the gender stereotype about domestic cooking in the name of nostalgia and tradition. The kind of labor invested in these dishes is appreciated by the narrator but the camera hardly depicts women's enjoyment of food; rather, the camera shows how hard these women try to please their family.

In *Korean Cuisine*, the recognition for women's culinary expertise comes from men and women who remain in their kitchen perpetually through the visual construction of them as *ajumma*—a middle-aged woman with children—whose femininity is solely defined by her domestic role. An *ajumma* is devoid of personality or individuality in the Korean context, a category of women who usually have no professions but put the family first in their lives. The camera aestheticizes women's motherly love, mingling the rural landscape with women's makeup-free, deeply wrinkled faces and simple dresses, as if they are a part of nature. The literal meaning of the title of the

Figure 7.1 Actor Ch'oe Purham in a Traditional Kitchen. *Korean Cuisine*, January 21, 2016. *Source*: Photo courtesy of KBS 1.

show is "Koreans' dinner table," homogenizing the ethnic identity of Koreans through food. In this context, *ajumma* is fetishized with a national rhetoric that ironically does not recognize them as equal at the dinner table: they are the self-sacrificing mothers and the servers whose female subjectivity is veiled behind the nostalgic flavor of food. When food comes to the dining table, it loses its universality and it becomes a symbol of inequality. Food thus represents both possibilities and constraints about our everyday lives because of its social, economic, political, and cultural systems and practices that produce such inequality.

The sense of comfort and belonging forms in rural settings away from urban environments, and this distancing strategy is a success factor for the show. Another popular show, *Three Meals a Day*, is a good example that emphasizes the fantasy of "returning to nature." All participants in *Three Meals* are males, mostly well-known entertainers, and they are dispatched to remote areas away from cities and given limited ingredients and cooking tools. They all live in the same house for one season and have to make three meals a day for themselves. Due to their limited supplies, they go fishing and pick herbs and vegetables from fields and mountains. Most participants have poor cooking skills and knowledge about food, but they make sincere efforts to prepare proper meals. If some members demonstrate good cooking skills, they will be praised by other members in the group. Men praising men for cooking skills is indeed a trend on TV cooking shows, but in *Three Meals*, men's skills are directly related to the survival of all the members because of their isolated location and limited resources.

Like *Korean Cuisine*, it is through men's engagement with domestic work that women's invisible labor is visualized in *Three Meals*. The visualization of this invisibility was largely absent in TV cooking shows in the past when female cooks, with modern kitchen resources, aimed to educate fellow women audiences to become "scientific" toward domestic affairs. Shiny and stylistic cooking tools, the careful measurement of ingredients, and the introduction of Western ingredients were represented as a sign of the advancement of Korean society. Being set up in the wilderness, however, male participants in *Three Meals* are removed from the modern kitchen or supermarket chains; instead they are given the tasks of operating an old furnace, doing dishes in an outdoor water fountain, tending to pets, and even working for farmers in their neighborhood to purchase necessary ingredients. All these tasks mirror what women in rural areas do in *Korean Cuisine*, and yet these men's maneuvering of all their assignments is projected as an entertaining process.

These entertainers' efforts to "feminize" themselves in a remote area gain much attention from audiences. One particular participant, an actor named Ch'a Sŭngwŏn, is hugely popular for his unexpectedly skilled culinary techniques and familiarity with cooking tools, unlike the macho-looking alpha male roles he plays in TV dramas. With a fashion model career in his past, his image as a "mother-like father" for his alternative family became a selling point of the show. Ch'a's willingness to engage in domestic work was received well by audiences, who find his effeminate masculinity refreshing and charming. He is probably the first male entertainer who possesses the ability to oversee housework and provide emotional support for other male members in the show—he is even called "*ajumma* Ch'a [*ch'ajumma*]." Unlike women in real life, though, he acts like a commander, supervising others and correcting others' mistakes. This partially has to do with his age, being the oldest member in the show, but it also mirrors the military style of the professional restaurant business where the cooking team operates like a brigade (Druckman 2010, 30). This male *ajumma* thus assumes the kind of authority a female *ajumma* lacks in real life, being empowered by the kind of femininity that disempowers women in everyday life.

Besides the effeminacy performed by male participants, the friendship among them is another factor for the audiences' positive reception of the show. The rural setting definitely reflects the urban populations' desire to escape cities, and participants "do nothing" but think about what they will cook and eat next. Their devotion of time to food aims to bring awareness of the importance of proper meals that not only nourish their bodies but also enrich their emotional lives. Thus, the development of intimacy among participants creates a fantasy of an ideal relationship that is devoid of the cutthroat competition they are surrounded by "out there." It is through friendly conversations and collaborative preparation of food and cooking for themselves that the male bond develops, and their vitality for life is evidenced through their laughter and expressions of contentment before the camera.

BROMANCE IN THE KITCHEN

While *Korean Cuisine* and *Three Meals* are site-specific cooking shows that stress tradition, self-care, and feminine labor, most shows are set in studios. One of the most popular cooking shows in a studio setting is *Teacher Paek and Home-Cooked Meals* (*Chippap Paek sŏnsaeng*). As its title indicates, *Teacher Paek* presents homey dishes that are cooked by male participants (figure 7.2). The lead of the show, Paek Chongwŏn, is not a professional chef; rather, he is a successful businessman who owns restaurant franchises. The "chef-as-businessman" trend is commonly seen in TV cooking shows in the West (Druckman 2010, 26), but Paek does not have certified credentials as most famous chefs do. He rather projects himself as a foodie who also has a passion for cooking. Led by the success of *Teacher Paek*, he has been running other shows in which he provides knowledge and criticism of various dishes

Figure 7.2 Promotion Poster of *Teacher Paek and Home-Cooked Meals,* March 2016.
Source: Photo courtesy of tvN.

prepared by others, demonstrating his connoisseurship and management ability rather than culinary skills. Nonetheless, Paek's recipes in *Teacher Paek* are known for their simplicity and people-friendly cooking techniques, and his dishes, if one follows his techniques properly, can be made easily and in a relatively short time.

Besides Paek's simple ingredients and cooking techniques, Paek's ability to form a homey atmosphere with other male participants is an attribute in the success of the show. Paek's kitchen is equipped with tools, cupboards, refrigerators, and gas burners, all of which are designed for use at home. Other male participants, though most of them are high-earning entertainers, are presented as average Korean men in terms of their unfamiliarity with the structure of the kitchen, tools, cooking processes, and even ingredients: most of them cannot hold kitchen knives properly and have difficulty identifying ingredients that they commonly consume. Paek appears down-to-earth, non-intimidating, easygoing, and supportive, and he acts like a housewife, sharing practical cooking tips he has accumulated for many years. His techniques are more like skills gained from experience as many housewives might have, and he focuses more on simple processes of cooking for individuals and families who would appreciate simplicity and shortened cooking times. In other words, Paek reverses gender roles by positioning himself as a mother or a housewife. His nickname, *Paekchubu* (housewife Paek), reveals that he is accepted as a role model for men as far as home cooking is concerned.

He assures that "everyone can cook well if taught properly" and shows how pleasant and fulfilling cooking can be. Male participants' reaction to Paek's instruction in turn enhances the image of the pleasure of cooking, transforming them from being the served to the server. The question is why these men have a male teacher rather than a female teacher in the domestic kitchen. Learning from a fellow man can mean a few things for the audiences. On the one hand, it gives male audiences confidence about cooking without being conscious of the social convention of rigid gender boundaries in the kitchen. On the other hand, Paek's family-friendly comments and gestures induce the male participants to admit their negligence of their own families and reliance on their mothers and wives. They might exclaim with joy before the dishes they have created: "I can now cook for my elderly mother!" or "I can feed my kids!" These men's expressions of filial piety and fatherly love through cooking are unusual in the Korean context, in which their duty is mostly related to their work outside the domestic sphere. Domestic bliss is emphasized with men's participation in kitchen work, and their willingness to feed themselves and their families may be seen as a sign of men taking gender equality in the kitchen more seriously than before.

The highlight of the show is the eating time, which was usually omitted in cooking shows in the past. *Teacher Paek* is not the only show that allocates time for eating but it is noteworthy that sharing food among the participants adds a final touch to the construction of companionship among men. Eating becomes a communal enjoyment in this highlight rather than a personal one, indicating how food is such an integral part of social life.

People may eat alone at home but they do not usually eat out alone in Korea; there is a widespread notion that eating out is a social thing. However, the affordability of meals and availability of company has become an issue for many, especially for elderly and young people who face their dinner tables alone. In an attempt to stay in a social circle, some single elderly people in rural areas gather in a community center and share food with fellow elderly villagers, for example. In addition, single-person households are increasing these days: about 9 percent of the population lived alone in 1990 but the number jumped to 27 percent in 2015, and 39 percent of the adult population remains single in 2014, the highest percentage among the OECD countries (Hyŏngu Kim 2015, 155–156). It is said that economic conditions are the major factor behind many people remaining single (H. K. Kim 2016), and the resultant feeling of loneliness affects their social lives significantly.

The flood of TV cooking shows, as some have observed, may have to do with this demographic change: the family-like relationship among participants in these shows gives viewers the chance to experience domestic comfort, albeit temporarily (Hyŏngu Kim 2015, 152). The issue here is the construction of domestic comfort by fetishizing *ajumma* and bromance in the alternative family where women are generally absent. The increase of one-person households does not explain the male dominance of these cooking shows—after all, there is no epistemological or ontological ground to gender the feeling of loneliness and deprivation. The absence of women in these shows derives from the hegemonic notion of cooking as gendered labor that still pervades in the social fabric of Korea. It is true that these male chefs and foodies express their willingness to share domestic labor or look after their individual wellness through cooking. However, their attitude toward cooking shows is shown differently from how women's attitude is generally perceived in public and private spheres, considering cooking as a leisurely thing rather than a daily chore. *Teacher Paek*, like *Three Meals*, is a site where men enjoy the luxury of getting away from suppressing reality by choice and build male bonds that are devoid of the competition they often face at work.

Contrary to the media representation of men as the main players in economic activities, the number of women in the labor market is too significant to ignore: around 53 percent of the female population is employed, whereas 75 percent of the male population is employed as of August 2016, though women earn only 63 percent of the average wage men take as of 2014 (Statistics Korea, 2014). Despite that an increasing number of women with higher education are put into the job market every year, they take up the bottom rung of the economic structure in Korea, being employed as irregular and part-time workers. The marginalization of women in the workforce is nothing new in Korea. Having been treated like temporary workers, they were laid off first by many companies that aimed to reduce wage costs during the IMF crisis (Kim and Finch 2002, 44) and are frequently discouraged from going back to work or barred from promotion after coming back from maternity leave. Regardless of staying single or getting married, it is extremely challenging for women to remain competitive in the neoliberal and patriarchal economic structure; not to mention that they also spend much longer time in the kitchen than men do. Male foodies are given the opportunity to express vitality for life in the culinary escape while women are eliminated from the fantasy. The foodie culture represented in TV cooking shows is highly gendered by reproducing gender stereotypes about food and eating.

FOOD AND MISOGYNY

Although women do not play their role as chefs or cooks in cooking shows, they occasionally appear to "taste" the dishes male participants have created. In *Teacher Paek*, for example, a female actress joined the program recently, and she is the first female "student" of Paek since the opening of the show back in May 2015. The show seems to emphasize her act of eating rather than cooking. Although the camera does not sensualize her act of eating, probably because of the family-like atmosphere the show tries to create, female participants' role to "taste" food, whether it is prepared or delivered by men, is disturbingly sexualized on TV shows at times. One show on a public station, *Food Princess* (*Chal mŏngnŭn sonyŏdŭl*), received vehement criticism for showing various girl group members consuming large amounts of high-calorie dishes. Girl groups in Korea are notoriously underweight, and with their full makeup and tight clothes, their performance of eating heavy dishes creates a sensual spectacle. This kind of spectacle of eating can be described as food porn, which originally referred to "prose and recipes so removed from real life that they cannot be used except as vicarious experience" (O'Neill 2003, 39), but can also be applied to this show for its presentation of the fantasy of young, beautiful, and slim women consuming large amounts of food.

Previous food studies show that women express great concern over weight when they associate themselves with food (Guptill, Copleton, and Lucal 2013, 31) but the female participants in this show demonstrate their passion for food without showing fear of gaining weight. There is a double abuse of the female body in this grotesque culinary stunt: they are pressured to be on a strict diet to stay slim, and at the same time, they are forced to eat to create a spectacle. In both ways, their bodies are sensualized, and the "eating job" enhances their sexual appeal. Male foodies, on the other hand, present their love for food and eating as if it is inherently pleasant and, in many cases, they are either on the plump side or overweight.

This kind of food porn associated with women's eating practice is in fact popular in AfreecaTV (Any Free Casting TV), a video streaming service that broadcasts Broadcasting Jockeys (BJs) consuming excessive amount of food. The conventional notion of gendered ways of eating is evident in AfreecaTV: male BJs make loud noises while chewing their food while most female BJs eat daintily. Male BJs' slim looks are also praised by the audiences, since these BJs reveal that they are not just eating machines but also exercise hard to maintain their fitness. In contrast to the presentation of male BJs' disciplined lifestyles in order to perform well at their "work," female BJs rarely mention their efforts to maintain their slenderness. The looks of female BJs are described as glamorous, skinny, cute, and grotesque, enhancing the existing discrimination against overweight women. The pleasure of eating rather reflects the constraint of freedom that many women feel. Their fearless act of eating excessive amounts of food may give vicarious satisfaction to women, and its grotesque twist of excessiveness and slimness presents a pornographic fantasy to male viewers.

It is not a coincidence that the kinds of food at these BJs' tables have strong tastes with high calories: spicy, salty, and sweet foods that are made of rice cakes, meat, sugar, cheese, noodles, and so forth. BJs' dinner tables or computer desks are full of rawness. They rarely display mild foods but mostly foods that are known for their strong flavors, stimulating the appetite through the spiciness and sweetness of these foods. The rawness and the fullness represented by the BJs perhaps signify the feeling of deprivation or lack the audiences feel in their everyday lives, but this culinary stunt projects a gendered perception on the relationship between body and food. It is especially discomforting to see how female BJs try to overperform their ability to eat when many eating disorders, such as bingeing and bulimia, often stem from social pressure to stay thin. It is not uncommon to see sexist assaults against overweight women in public and domestic spaces in Korea and at times men's attacks on female body shapes through social media are brutally misogynistic. The rawness of female BJs' performances of eating thus cannot be viewed away from this gender politics in Korea, where popular media capitalizes on women's bodies through food.

As Roland Barthes (1957/1972) once stated:

> To eat is a behavior that develops beyond its own ends, replacing, summing up, and signalizing other behaviors. . . . What are these other behaviors? Today we might say all of them: activity, works, sports, effort, leisure, celebration—every one of these situations is expressed through food. (51)

In the case of *mŏkppang*, we see people's behavior of watching food being prepared and eaten, which reveals a breakdown of something that has driven people to this behavior. BJs' demonstration of consuming gigantic amounts of food, for example, signifies a breakdown of social relations, social stability, and mobility in people's desire to watch others eat. The desire is not for the food on the TV or computer screens, but rises from the feeling of social deprivation that manifests in an excessive form. The more hungry people's minds become, the more food they want to watch being eaten, compensating for their mental hunger by the pure materiality of food. This deviancy points to the ways in which people's desire leads them to the core of social life at the time of crisis. However, more often than not, the deviancy associated with food becomes an indicator that directs us to see how social and cultural behaviors are heavily affected by existing gender hierarchies and relations: it seems that abuse of and insults toward women's bodies go in tandem with the crisis of masculinity in South Korea that manifests in violence.

In the past two decades, the number of female victims in Korea has increased dramatically, from 72.2 percent of all the victims of violent crimes in 1995 to 90.2 percent in 2013, and many of them are victims of "crimes with no reason" (*mutchima pŏmjoe*) committed by men who turn their anger and hatred toward women randomly (Yi 2015). At the root of the misogyny is a sense of men's fear of losing social stability in their competitive living conditions, in which not just men but both men and women find it extremely difficult to compete for jobs. As Hyaeweol Choi observes, as women's participation in the labor sector increases, men become antagonistic toward women, viewing women as the cause for their reduced job opportunities despite the fact that women take up the bottom level of the economic hierarchy in contemporary Korea. Violent expressions of misogyny are spreading widely at a startling rate: not only do they manifest in crimes but they also manifest in behavior on social media, where the clash between misogynist groups and feminists happens daily (Choi 2016). Even in the midst of the fast-growing "#MeToo" movement in Korea at this moment, it is not rare to encounter the bashing of women, criticizing them for their consumption-oriented lifestyles while being financially dependent on men. This kind of gender bashing rises prominently when society goes through immense economic crises, and women become an easy target for men whose feelings of fear manifest in their misogynistic expressions, blaming women for their reduced opportunities for social mobility.

CONCLUSION

The "softened" Korean masculinity performed by male chefs and foodies can be aligned with the popularization of the effeminate image of male celebrities culminated in the term *kkotminam* since the early 2000s. *Kkotminam* broadly refers to the hybrid masculinity that combines soft personality and hard bodily images of men—warmhearted, attentive, pretty-looking men with muscular bodies—in Korean popular culture. Its image has been widely consumed beyond Korea as well. Korean *kkotminam* celebrities who possess these traits are very popular in East and Southeast Asia, where they are viewed as an alternative to the overtly controlling patriarchal masculinity (Hirata 2008, 143–156; Jung 2011, 102–116). And yet, it must be noted that Confucian traits underpin this hybrid masculinity, as Sun Jung points out: patriarchal authoritarianism that is deeply embedded in Confucian *yangban* ideology still persists on the matter of female chastity and filial piety (Jung 2011, 103–104). In other words, *kkotminam* is a media-constructed image that may respond to women's expectations of men but seriously lacks a grounding in social reality, whereas hegemonic masculinity continues to mediate men's dominant position over women's daily lives and pressure men to conform to it.

Food is a gateway to seeing the sources and practices of gender inequality that we face in everyday life. As demonstrated in this chapter, the popularity of TV cooking shows in Korea reveals that the existing gender hierarchy and relations persist. The representation of culinary masculinity in these shows indeed challenges the existing gender and class hierarchy associated with cooking. And male participants' investment of emotion, energy, and time into the domestic activity reflects the current social demands to rearrange the controlling, work-driven, and strict Korean masculinity to be increasingly caring and family oriented. However, this chapter attempted to show that these shows disregard women's labor in domestic and professional kitchens by overemphasizing men's willingness to pay attention to family lives and their own wellness. In addition, the close relationships among studios represent male bonding through food, making this site of cooking an escape from their competition-driven workplaces.

While being eliminated from the kitchen where men build intimacy among themselves, women have remained outside the culinary fantasy and food escape. Women's intimacy among themselves is seen elsewhere in these cooking shows, where cooking is not a leisurely activity but an unpaid daily job. Women's domestic labor is indeed visualized in the depiction of traditional food but their labor is coated with nostalgia that is invoked by women's motherly love as expressed in their food preparation for their families. They remain as eternal *ajumma* whose identity is solely determined by their dedication to their families, in contrast to the sexualization of young female bodies in TV cooking and eating shows, indicating that age is another important factor in interrogating the media representation of the relationship between food and women. The representation of domestic comfort associated with male *ajumma* and bromance in TV cooking shows is also problematic, since the fantasy of domestic men seems to belong to a single category of men while failing to address the class differences among them.

NOTES

1. Foodies are "people with a long-standing passion for eating and learning about food but who are not food professionals" (Cairns, Johnston, and Baumann 2010, 592).

2. By hegemonic masculinity, I rely on R. W. Connell's (2005) definition of it "as the configuration of gender practice which embodies the currently accepted answer to the problem of the legitimacy of patriarchy, which guarantees (or is taken to guarantee) the dominant position of men and the subordination of women" (77).

REFERENCES

Ashley, Bob, Joanne Hollows, Steve Jones, and Ben Taylor. 2004. *Food and Cultural Studies*. New York: Routledge.

Barthes, Roland. 1957/1972. *Mythologies*. Translated by Annette Lavers. London: Paladin.

Bourdieu, Pierre. 1984. *Distinction: A Social Critique on the Judgment of Tastes*. Cambridge, MA: Harvard University Press.

Cairns, Kate, Josée Johnston, and Shyon Baumann. 2010. "Caring About Food: Doing Gender in the Foodie Kitchen." *Gender and Society* 24 (5): 591–615.

Choi, Hyaeweol. 2016. "Tragedy in Seoul Brings Misogyny to Light." *East Asia Forum* 3 (August). www.eastasiaforum. org/2016/08/03/tragedy-in-seoul-brings-misogyny-to-light/.

Chung, Hae-Kyung, Hye Jeong Yang, Dayeon Shin, and Kyung Rhan Chung. 2016. "Aesthetics of Korean Foods: The Symbol of Korean Culture." *Journal of Ethnic Food* 3: 178–188.

Connell, R. W. 2005. *Masculinities*, 2nd ed. Berkeley, CA: University of California Press.

DeVault, Marjorie. 1991. *Feeding the Family: The Social Organization of Caring as Gendered Work*. Illinois: University of Chicago Press.

Druckman, Charlotte. 2010. "Why Are There No Great Women Chefs?" *Gastronomica* 10 (1): 24–31.

Elfving-Hwang, Joanna. 2013. "Cosmetic Surgery and Embodying the Moral Self in South Korean Popular Makeover Culture." *The Asia-Pacific Journal* 11 (24): 2. www.japanfocus.org/-Joanna-Elfving_Hwang/3956/article.html.

Gillis, Stacy, and Joanne Hollows, eds. 2009. *Feminism, Domesticity and Popular Culture*. New York: Routledge.

Guptill, Amy E., Denise A. Copleton, and Betsy Lucal. 2013. *Food and Society: Principles and Paradoxes*. Malden, MA: Polity.

Hirata, Yukie. 2008. "Touring 'Dramatic Korea': Japanese Women as Viewers of Hanryu Dramas and Tourists on Hanryu Tours." In *East Asian Pop Culture*, edited by Chua Beng Huat and Koichi Iwabuchi, 143–156. Hong Kong: Hong Kong University Press.

Hyman, Gwen. 2008. "The Taste of Fame: Chefs, Diners, Celebrity, Class." *Gastronomica* 8 (3): 43–52.

Jung, Sun. 2011. *Korean Masculinities and Trans-cultural Consumption: Yonsama, Rain, Oldboy, KPop Idols*. Hong Kong: Hong Kong University Press.

Kim, Hye-Kyung. 2016. "Familist Individualization of Ever-Single Korean Youths in Their Late 30s: Individualization and Transformed Familism in the Neoliberal Era." *Korea Journal* 56 (1): 33–60.

Kim, Hyŏngu. 2015. "1 in kagu wa pangsong t'ŭrend pyŏnhwa: mŏkppang, k'ukppang ŭl chungsim ŭro [Single-person households and the trend in broadcasting: focusing on cooking/eating shows]." *Midŏo wa kyoyuk* 5 (1): 152–171.

Kim, Allen, and Karen Pyke. 2015. "Taming Tiger Dads: Hegemonic American Masculinity and South Korea's Father School." *Gender & Society* 29 (4): 509–533.

Kim, Seung-kyung, and John Finch. 2002. "Confucian Patriarchy Reexamined: Korean Families and the IMF Economic Crisis." *The Good Society* 11 (3): 43–49.

Kwak, Sanga. 2015. "Han'guk i OECE kkolchi ch'ajihan punya 9 kae [The nine categories Korea ranked the lowest in the OECD countries]." Huffpost, Feb. 6. www.huffingtonpost.kr/2015/02/06/ story_n_6628076.html.

Lee, June J. H. 1996. "Health Food as Gendered Commodity: Body, Health, and Sexuality among Middle-Class Korean Men." *International Journal of Politics, Culture, and Society* 10 (1): 73–94.

Levinas, Immanuel. 2001. *Existence and Existents*, 2nd printing. Translated by Alphonso Lingis. Pittsburgh, PA: Duquesne University Press.

———. 1998. *Otherwise than Being or Beyond Essence*. Translated by Alphoso Lingis. Pittsburgh, PA: Duquesne University Press.

Lim, Hyun-Chin, and Jin-Ho Jang. 2006. "Neo-Liberalism in Post-Crisis South Korea: Social Conditions and Outcomes." *Journal of Contemporary Asia* 36 (4): 442–463.

O'Neill, Molly. 2003. "Food Porn." *Columbia Journalism Review* 42 (3): 38–45.

Osetrova, Maria. 2016. "National Food and Gastronationalism in Contemporary Korea." PhD diss., Yonsei University, Seoul, Korea.

Park, Sang Chul. 2016. "Ethnic Food for Longevity Pursuit: Assessment of Korean Ethnic Food." *Journal of Ethnic Food* 3: 167–170.

Ray, Krishnendu. 2007. "Domesticating Cuisine: Food and Aesthetics on American Television." *Gastronomica* 7 (1): 50–63.

Statistics Korea. 2015. *Economically Active Population Survey*. http://kostat.go.kr/portal/eng/surveyOutline/4/1/index.static.

Yi Junu. 2015. "Sarin, kangdo dŭng kangnyŏk pŏmjoe p'ihaeja 90% ga yŏsŏng [90% of victims of violent crimes are women]. Online *Chosun Daily*, Sept. 24, 2015. news.chosun.com/site/data/html_ dir/2015/09/24/2015092400375.html.

Chapter 8

Neoliberal Women's Agency and Time-Space Management in the Cook-and-Save Method, *Tsukurioki*

Chikako Nagayama

INTRODUCTION

> Our modern life gets busier by any means, without allowing [us] to turn back the clock. The time imagined from the word "*ji-tan*" (time reduction) is becoming shorter and shorter, and I receive requests for dishes and recipes to be quickly prepared at any rate. . . .
>
> Anyhow, [we] want to prepare meals quickly!
>
> Even more, [we] want delicious and homemade dishes, as much as [we] can! . . . Your effort to prepare dishes in advance will turn into a precious gift for yourself, the "time to spare" (*yutori*) tomorrow. (Tauchi 2014, 4. Translated by author.)

> Even when I end up not having the [sufficient] time for it, I want to cook meals that I eat by myself [rather than buying prepared dishes or eating at restaurants], and I want to eat several balanced dishes, if I can. Then I came across the *tsukurioki* method (to cook and save) and I started to prepare one or two dishes [to save]. (nozomi 2015, 2. Translated by author.)

Two recent Japanese cookbook titles—*The Basics of Time-Reduction Cooking* (Tauchi 2014) and *Cook and Save All at Once during Weekends* (nozomi, 2015)—exemplify the domination of "time anxiety" (Sennet 2006, 49) in everyday life. The "temporal rhythms of corporate efficiency" are increasingly applied to human activities in noncorporate settings with more emphasis on productivity and management under the expansion of the global economy (Negra 2009, 47). As neoliberalism highlights individual autonomy and choices and "proposes that human well-being can best be advanced by liberating individual entrepreneurial freedoms and skills within an institutional framework" (Harvey 2005, 2), time scarcity emerges as a central concern to solve the problems of the "juggling act" in the domestic sphere (Nathanson 2013, 5). Meanwhile, the domestic sphere and feminized homemaking skills have become a site that women capitalize upon to create their own business enterprises. Through analyzing recipe books featuring in-advance food preparation called *tsukurioki* (or the cook-and-save method), this chapter will critically explore how the intensified pressure for time-space management in the neoliberal age manifests in the discourse of in-advance food preparation.

Tsukurioki has quickly become a cultural phenomenon since the mid-2010s. According to Tōhan,[1] two *tsukurioki* books entered their 2014 top ten best seller list in the practical book category, and another *tsukurioki* book appeared among the top ten of the same category in 2015. The 2016 best seller list included two of nozomi's *tsukurioki* books, including the long seller *Cook and Save All at Once during Weekends* in eleventh place for the general category.[2] What follows presents my analysis of thirteen selected *tsukurioki* cookbooks[3] published between 2015 and 2021 (see table 8.1). In my research, the *tsukurioki* cookbooks are examined both as a commodity and a site of discourse. As a commodity, a cookbook has an economic value, but it also bears cultural values beyond its exchange value and use value (i.e., commodity fetishism; see Appadurai 1988; Sturken and Cartwright 2009). In a visually intensified contemporary culture, a cookbook's appeal tends to be magnified with abundant images that accompany the descriptions of cooking procedures. As the term "food porn" indicates, diverse professionals, such as food stylists and videographers among others, are involved to boost the visual attraction of food (McBride 2010). Moreover, commodities are presented as means for self-fulfillment and problem-solving, and this "therapeutic discourse" is a foundational part of consumer society (Sturken and Cartwright 2009, 269). As a version of the discourse, *tsukurioki* offers a prescription for a perceived crisis in the domestic space—in particular, specific instructions for time and space management.

To paraphrase, the cook-and-save method presents itself as a solution for time scarcity and overwhelming stress for women who handle multiple tasks around pregnancy, child-rearing, and assisting spouses, parents, and in-laws at times, besides their own paid work (see Lee 2010). The cookbook authors argue *tsukurioki*'s smart techniques and in-advance planning create extra time and psychological ease for women troubled by these excessive burdens, while maintaining the high nutrition and heartwarming impact of home-cooked meals. However, their way of addressing the issues of domestic time saving simultaneously forecloses more fundamental questions about women's assumed domestic responsibility. Why does having less time for cooking at home become an issue that women must take charge to solve? *Tsukurioki* must be considered as a discourse that connects the ideological elements of time, space, and gendered agency, constituting an "ideology that discovers its subjects," rather than imagining self-disciplined and time-efficient multitasking female authors simply mirrored on these texts (Grossberg 1986, 53). The rise of time anxiety in a cookbook genre such as *tsukurioki* seems to coincide with a larger sociocultural trend, the "feminization of time crisis," in which women are constructed as "beset by temporal problems that may frequently be resolved through minimization of their ambition and reversion to a more essential femininity" (Negra 2009, 48). Women's labor force participation has steadily increased if full-time and part-time employment are combined,[4] but the gendered division of work has not been fundamentally changed. Instead, the gendered discourse of the "separate spheres" is maintained in society to further intensify women's double shift, resulting in their experience of "time crunch" (Nathanson 2013, 5–6; see also Ito and Muta 2015). As further explored later, the linkage between domestic time scarcity and women's active role therein is not inevitable but forged vis-à-vis the socioeconomic conditions of our time.

Neoliberalism, the Female Power, and Housework

In Japan, the stay-at-home housewife has become a symbol of the modern middle-class family. Until the late nineteenth century, upper-class women did not cook by themselves because their servants prepared their daily meals for them. As the new middle class emerged due to the Industrial Revolution, Western middle-class ideals about home and the family were introduced through intellectual discourse, public education, and popular culture from the late nineteenth century to the beginning of the twentieth century (Inoue 2003; Muta 1994, 1996). While both men and women were—and still are—involved in food processing and cooking on various occasions (Takeuchi 2009), the new norms about family unity and women's central role in it became gradually instilled in society. Cookbooks in the previous Edo era largely featured luxurious, and sometimes playful, food preparation techniques to entertain guests, which were not applicable for daily meals (Ehara 2012, 4). Cookbooks began to address the homemakers of the newly formed middle class in the 1900s (Ishikawa and Ehara 2002, 86–87). The concept of three square meals a day was newly introduced from the West, where industrialization normalized regular work hours (Winterman 2012).

Along with school education and magazines, cookbooks have mediated the dissemination of modern home cooking: the idea of nutritional balance, new food items such as beef and milk, and Western, Chinese, and Japanese culinary skills. Gradually, various forms of Japanese-Western mixed (*wayō*

Table 8.1 Summary of *Tsukurioki* Authors' Background Based on Their Bios and Descriptions

	Author Name	*Sex*	*Publication Year*	*Marital Status*	*Children*	*Current Occupation*	*Previous Occupations*	*Food-Related Qualification*	*Media*
1	Hida, Kazuwo	F	2011	Married	Elementary school student daughter	N/A	Housewife	N/A	N/A
2	Multiple recipe contributors; Edited by Shufuno tomo sha	N/A	2015	N/A	N/A	N/A	N/A	N/A	N/A
3	Mori, Nozomi (aka nozomi)	F	2015	Married	Child(ren)	System engineer, food blogger, and author	System engineer	System engineer	Blog
4	Ito, Akane (aka Ātan mom)	F	2016	Married	3-year-old son	N/A	Worked at patisserie shop	Qualified chef	Blog
5	Ichise, Etsuko	F	2017	Vaguely implied by the word "wagaya" (my home)	N/A	Food researcher, food coordinator	Worked at a food company; assisted various food researchers	N/A	TV, magazines, books
6	Tassen, Sima (aka Shima)	F	2017	Married	Newly born child	Freelance housekeeper; seminars and events	Worked at restaurants in France and Japan	Cooking school graduate (in Japan and France)	Website, TV
7	Wakana, Marie	F	2018	Married	3-year-old son, 1-year-old daughter	Working mother, food blogger	Worked at food-related jobs	BA in food chemical biology	Blog

8	Makita, Zenji (Author)/ Sakashita, Chie (Recipe contributor)	M/F		Married	2 daughters (*b.* 2004 and 2009)	MD (Makita) /Food researcher and dietitian (Sakashita)	A U.S. medical institution researcher; Professor at medical schools (Makita)	MD (Makita)/ Food nutrition major at a woman's 2-year college (Sakashita)	Books (Makita)/ Blog, books (Sakashita)
9	Nakai, Erica	F	2019	Married	Young child	Raising a child; freelance dietitian	Worked at an employee cafeteria	Registered dietitian	Instagram
10	Matsumoto, Yumi (aka Yū-mama)	F	2019	Married	Three sons (16, 12, and 6); also living with parents	Recipe book author, café owner	N/A	N/A	Blog, Instagram, magazines, ads
11	macaroni (Writer's collective)	N/A	2020	N/A	N/A	N/A	N/A	N/A	Website
12	Shoku no sutajio (Editor)/Fujita, Satoshi (Supervisor)	M/F	2020	N/A	N/A	University professor (Fujita)	University positions (Fujita)	U.S. degrees (Fujita)	Books (Fujita)
13	Suga	F	2020	Married	Child(ren)	Company worker, recipe book author	N/A	N/A	Blog, Instagram

secchū) recipes were also created. The first Japanese home-cooking magazine for women readers, *Ryōri no tomo* (Cooking companion), was launched in 1913. As early as the 1930s, magazine articles encouraged homemakers to gain skills to economically cook popular restaurant dishes at home (Ehara 2012, 165–167). Although this trend started from the urban middle class, the 1950s marked a significant turning point for rural households: whereas the nutritional limitations of a traditional diet were addressed and alternative preparation methods and food items were promoted through the New Life Movement (*shin seikatsu undō*),[5] television cooking programs and magazine articles made new recipes accessible to remote areas (Yano 2009, 207–211). Conventionally, food techniques were passed down person-to-person within a family or community. Even though the cookbooks do not fully replace this traditional form of knowledge sharing—for instance, cookbooks assume a basic skill set that the reader has acquired somewhere else—they have become indispensable, and even normalized, in places where a nontraditional diet is seen as healthier and more appealing, like in contemporary Japan.

Faced by domestic and international pressures for gender equality, the Equal Employment Opportunity Law was enacted in Japan in 1986, followed by two major revisions in 1997 and 2006/2007 (Assman 2014). The number of married women with paid jobs has been increasing since the 1980s, and there have been fewer households with a so-called stay-at-home housewife than households with a wife holding a paid job since 1997 (Murata and Masaki 2016, 9). A public opinion survey conducted by *Nihon Hoso Kyokai* (NHK, Japan broadcasting association) shows that the amount of time women spend on home cooking has been declining, which is in parallel with the increased women's employment rate. They have especially spent less time on dinner preparation. At the same time, women have become less frequently involved in cooking at home (Murata and Masaki 2016, 9). Instead of eating at home, options of dining out or buying preprepared dishes have become increasingly accessible (see Yoshizumi 2002).[6] The use of frozen food has increased and it has improved in quality. However, within couples, the majority of food preparation is still done by female partners (Murata and Masaki 2016, 10–11). As Hochschild asserts, housework is women's "second shift" beside their paid jobs (Hochschild and Machung 1989/2012), and food purchasing and preparation constitute a large part of their domestic responsibility. According to the NHK survey cited above, 83 percent of unmarried women regularly cook at home, while 63 percent of unmarried men eat food prepared by their partners and only 29 percent regularly cook for themselves. Although situations vary according to their actual available time, daily cooking falls largely onto the female spouse's shoulders in a heterosexual couple, even though their male partner might offer help (see Dixey 1996).

Kimura (2011) has revealed that participants in a food certificate program called Food Education Leader, who are largely women, share the "naturalized discourse" of the division of labor which designates women as the "primary homemaker, nurturer and caretaker of their families" (477) and food as "women's responsibility" (478), and many enter food education programs because of their interests in health, child-rearing, and/or food safety. While concerns over radiation risks have risen since the meltdown of the Fukushima Daiichi Nuclear Power Plant after a 9.0 magnitude earthquake on March 11, 2011, men's relatively low interest in food safety has been maintained, but they tend to consider radiation as "a threat to financial stability rather than to physical well-being," according to Morioka (2014). Although it is problematic to generalize this dualistic gendered tendency in selected research demographics to the more diverse population of Japan regarding age, socioeconomic class, employment status, race/ethnicity, and (dis)ability, the *tsukurioki* book authors clearly demonstrate the naturalization of women's responsibility for home cooking: most of them are cisgender women, some of whom have food-related qualifications, whereas a small number of publications with an emphasis on specific diet techniques or medical concerns are written by male doctors and scientists (see table 8.1).

In the nuclear family model, the concept of biological difference between the sexes underpins the gendered division of work. However, sexual difference itself is a shifting construct and some conceptual developments can be observed from the period of modern nation-state building (1868–) to the contemporary *tsukurioki* discourse. As a crucial foundation of the nation-state, the "good wife and wise mother" ideology in the Meiji period (1868–1912) was employed to implement girls' school education; under this ideology, women's dedication to child-rearing and support for their husband was a way for them to carry out their gendered citizenship and make contributions to the state and society while being categorically excluded from the public sphere (Uno 2005; Kietlinski 2013). As national leaders strived to consolidate the nation's resources and mobilized the population for wars, national progress and military strength were inseparable from the goal of women's education, and Japan's state of domestic affairs was often compared with, and claimed to be superior to, that of neighboring nations, to justify its dominance in Asia (Uno 2005).

A neoliberal notion of the female power, *joshiryoku* (女子力) is today's reincarnation of the good wife and wise mother ideology, in the sense that it presupposes girls and women to "voluntarily follow the traditional gender norm" and achieve excellence in domestic skills, clean and pretty looks, and careful attention to men's needs and moods (Kikuchi 2019, 87). But *joshiryoku* is not considered to naturally emerge from women's biological difference from men. It is presupposed that women's own efforts are needed to acquire and perform these skills in an excellent manner. Furthermore, acquiring *joshiryoku* is considered equally important for women regardless of their varying socioeconomic status: her domestic skills would not compensate for her lack of social stability or achievements, and vice versa. I consider *tsukurioki* as a variation of this neoliberal notion of female power. It renews the preceding concept of *haha no aji*. Symbolically and materially, mothers have been central to family unity. *Haha no aji* is literally translated as "mother's flavor," but it connotes a mother's heartwarming meal that cannot be monetized but appeals to subjective values associated with family bonds. Today's *tsukurioki* boom rather embraces the economy of time and space and the self-discipline of women, which are objectively valued and calculated. It provides a revised model of femininity in which the significance of women's cooking hinges upon their management skills and continuing efforts, while the gendered division of work is not fundamentally challenged in ideology or practice.

As discussed earlier, *tsukurioki* constitutes a part of "discursive formation" involving food and cooking, in accordance with food education and economy, that maintains the construction of the domestic sphere as feminine (Grossberg 1986, 53). What follows demonstrates how woman's agency is constructed through this discourse in my selected sample of cook-and-save books.

Tsukurioki Authors as Female Entrepreneurs

The *tsukurioki* discourse might hardly appear to be a social norm linked with the good wife and wise mother ideology. It might rather look like a form of resistance against the status quo; it spotlights the voices of female food entrepreneurs who earn their own income, and speaks to busy women with paid jobs as its intended audience. Whether or not they were employed at one point, the authors' biographies indicate that they had established their entrepreneurship as food-related professionals prior to publishing their cook-and-save books. In a way, these figures—from a famous recipe blogger to a food storeowner—reflect the spread of entrepreneurs in the neoliberal economy (Scharff 2015). Many authors share their recipes, food photos, and cook-and-save methods through their blogs and Instagram as well as their books (table 8.1). They are commodifying their domestic skills and knowledge, investing their activities in the private sphere as a human capital (Kikuchi 2019, 60–61), while new technologies blur the boundary between the private and the public, hobbies and work, and allow the creation of workspaces at home (Kaufman-Scarborough 2006). When women's access to the public domain is still limited and the burden of care work has not been lifted from their shoulders (Assman 2014), the dissolution of the public and private spheres might result in increasing tasks for them to simultaneously handle.

"If I have got *tsukurioki* [saved dishes], I don't have to mind dinner [preparation] when I come home late from work. I don't have to think about what to cook every day, which is also a relief" (nozomi 2015, 2). Time saving is the central concern that the cook-and-save method focuses upon. The concept of time saving presumes it as a resource: in a capitalist society, time has become commodified, and "like money, we can say that time can be wasted, saved or spent" (Walker 2009, 486). Some authors use a day during the week or on the weekend for food preparation and consume the cooked food during the rest of the week (see table 8.1). For ultimate time saving, Mori Nozomi (aka nozomi) encourages her readers to cook ten dishes within two hours, each of which will be put in a container and preserved in a refrigerator for a week. A *tsukurioki* vlogger Aonīna states that she can cook seventeen dishes within three-and-a-half hours, and her edited videos with voice-overs show her preparation of twelve to seventeen dishes to eat throughout a week. Some other authors recommend finding and maximizing the "time in between" (*sukima jikan*) various tasks to cook and save one or two dishes at a time (Wakana 2018).

To simultaneously and speedily handle multiple cooking processes in a limited time, time-efficient cooking methods are heavily utilized in *tsukurioki* recipes. To name just a few:

(1) *Renchin*: Heating up food items with the microwave. You do not have to closely attend them but can do other things—perhaps cutting, stir-frying, boiling, washing, and so on—while they cook. The cook can rely on the machine to take care of the most important aspects of cooking, such as timing, which actually changes the notion of cooking skill in a fundamental way. Moreover, this can reduce the amount of dirty pots and pans to be washed after meals are prepared.

(2) Mixing: Instead of vegetable stews, which may take over an hour to prepare, marinated vegetables and salads are preferred because this radically reduces preparation time per food item. Perhaps the modern notion of "the fresher, the better" accelerates reliance on this method rather than slow cooking.

(3) Careful planning and ordering of procedures: When you start cooking, you should have a clear idea of what dishes you are cooking today. Ideally, you do not have to consult a recipe while cooking, because you are already familiar with them. Meat, poultry, and fish are seasoned or marinated a night before or earlier. Boiling vegetables for different dishes can be done in a sequence in the same pot, during which the pot does not have to be thoroughly cleaned with soap but just quickly rinsed with water

(nozomi 2015, 77). Vegetables, fish, and meat can be cut into pieces while boiling or in-between cooking procedures (nozomi 2015, 77).

(4) Prep and save: Even better, a large quantity of a frequently used food items (i.e., onion, green onion, ginger, meat, etc.) can be sliced, divided into small portions, and preserved in the freezer. When you enter the kitchen, you can then skip washing and cutting/slicing ingredients to immediately warm up a pan and start stir-frying or boiling selected items from the freezer. Along the same line, ground and seasoned meat in large quantities can be cooked and saved for one to three days in the fridge or longer in the freezer, and you can take out and cook a necessary portion again with vegetables. This ingredient can be used in fried noodles, pasta sauce, fried rice, and so on, leaving some recipe options to explore.

(5) Marinating: This technique reflects the ideas of (3) and (4) above, but the time you spend in the kitchen can be reduced through marinating. This is a technique that lets food take care of itself on its own, so to speak, for hours while the cook is handling other tasks. A variety of seasonings and marinating sauces—for example, *miso* (fermented soybeans); *koji* (rice malt); curry powder and yogurt; mixed soy sauce, grated garlic, and ginger—can turn poultry, pork, or fish into totally different dishes with rich flavors, although the last step of the cooking process can still be quite basic, such as grilling. Pre-seasoning also helps to extend the life of meat, fish, and poultry in the refrigerator.

In addition to saving time in the kitchen, what is encouraged is the improvement of space management in the fridge. Besides the refrigerator, the freezer is constantly used for the preservation of cooked and uncooked items. When you pick up a cook-and-save recipe book from a bookstore shelf, the first thing you will notice is its cover design. It typically shows a cooked dish in a glass or enamel container, or multiple dishes in multiple containers. This image quickly delivers what *tsukurioki* is all about: it is a method of compartmentalization. It compartmentalizes cooked dishes—and simultaneously time, space, and money—so that home cooks can most effectively manage them while busily juggling other tasks of domestic work and paid jobs.

A clean container with a transparent or semitransparent lid is key for both lasting preservation and making the most of the limited space in the refrigerator and freezer. For keeping cooked dishes in the freezer, plastic bags become handy, too. Their transparency and flexibility, and their capacity to turn into a slim container once the contents are frozen, make them superior to glass, plastic, and enamel containers whose sizes are fixed. Transparent materials—mostly glass or plastic—for containers, their lids, or bags are crucial for saving time, too. When a home cook has limited time, the ability to instantly grasp what is in an individual container is vital. The visual clues also offer great help for the cook to figure out possible combinations of food items that can be served at a time. Prepared *tsukurioki* dishes are served for breakfast and dinner, or put in a lunch box. The same dish can be divided into different portions, part of which can be used as is and another part of which can be cooked again with new seasonings into a different dish.

By maximizing the refrigerator's capacity for food preservation, the cook-and-save method projects the idea that the progression of time has only a negative impact on food items. If food is left alone without being cooked, it "goes bad." However, in traditional food-processing methods, such as drying, pickling, and fermentation, taking a certain amount of time is an essential part of processing: it increases nutrients and adds unique flavor to vegetables, beans, meat, poultry, and fish. On the contrary, the cook-and-save method seeks to minimize the time for food processing so that time can be "saved" for other activities.

Besides the time and space management, the concept of wise distribution of one's energy frequently appears in *tsukurioki* books:

> I often hear [from my readers and television audience] that "I have no time to make *tsukurioki* dishes," or "I can't push myself so hard," not only during weekdays, but also on weekends. So I have developed simple recipes for you to quickly and effortlessly prepare dishes with. . . .
>
> In my household, I make it a habit to swiftly prepare one dish with vegetables that I purchase in a large quantity, in addition to a kind of pickles and two or three kinds of all-purpose sauce saved in jars. Although they are small in number, it really helps [to always have them in the fridge]. . . .
>
> The goal [that this cookbook provides for you] is to feel grateful that you have cooked in advance while you didn't push yourself too hard. (Ichise 2017, 3, my translation)

> It is not about making many dishes, but about continuing what you can do every week without pushing yourself too hard. (nozomi 2015, 3, my translation)

Authors encourage their readers not to "push yourself too hard" (*muri wo shinai*) and recommend recipes that "reduce your burdens" (*futan ga karuku naru*) (Ito 2016, 2). As the authors emphasize, the main purpose of *tsukurioki* is not to increase the quantity of total dishes to be made at once, but smart management of one's time and energy. Aligned with the neoliberal discourse of entrepreneurship, the authors remind the readers to view themselves as a business: they need to monitor themselves physically and mentally so that they can wisely use their resources. When people are seen as a business, they are "a collection of assets that must be continually invested in, nurtured, managed, and developed" (Martin 2000, 582, cited in Garshon 2011). This is a characteristic of a neoliberal agency that takes a reflexive position toward itself:

> People are subjects for themselves—a collection of processes to be managed. There is always already a presumed distance to oneself as an actor. One is never "in the moment"; rather, one is always faced with one's self as a project that must be consciously steered through various possible alliances and obstacles. This is a self that is produced through an engagement with a market, that is, neoliberal markets require participants to be reflexive managers of their abilities and alliances. (Garshon 2011, 539)

Tsukurioki's time and space management technique projects this agency that keeps adequate objectivity toward one's actions, regularly assesses their performance and whether or not it meets their expectations, constantly acquires new skills for improvement, and takes a rest for better productivity. Even book titles and other texts on their covers highlight that purchasing them is a smart investment: "[You would] want to try every recipe [in the book]; [and you would] want to eat it again and again!" (Ito 2016, cover band); "Best *tsukurioki* [recipes] you can use for a lifetime" (Suga 2020, title).

The "Intimate Public Sphere" of Cookbooks

While a *tsukurioki* book normally has the practical appearance of a food recipe collection, its author's short descriptions are also included in the introduction, at the beginnings of chapters, or in the author biography, allowing an intimate look into her family life. All female authors in my sample are married cisgender women, with or without children, as specified or indicated by their descriptions. In addition to their marital status, their bios often specify the number of children they have and the gender and age of each child, mimicking the way they would introduce themselves to other mothers of young children when they meet in school or at a neighborhood playground while accompanying their child(ren). Occasionally the author's mother, mother-in-law, and remote hometown are mentioned in relation to a particular recipe, indicating that it has been inherited through an author's maternal lineage.

This personal touch not only adds a distinctive character to each volume but also offers a sense of peer-to-peer sharing, in which the female authors deliver cooking tips and food-related memories to the assumed reader through their subjective voices:[7] "Because you have taken this [book] in your hand . . . I think you are worried about [how to prepare] lunch boxes [for your family] every day. . . . By dividing each dish into small portions and keeping them in the freezer, your lunch box preparation will be surprisingly easier" (Matsumoto 2019, 8).

Their personal descriptions illuminate how food is crucial in their relationship with their husband and/or children, while revealing not only heartwarming moments in ordinary interactions but also their struggles and pains in not having enough time for every role that they are desired to fulfill as a mother and wife:

> I introduced *tsukurioki* into my daily routine when I couldn't even take a breath while juggling my job and childrearing. It offered a strong support for my family's health and allowed me to have a relaxing moment. Now, my childrearing is over and my work conditions have been improved, but I continue my cook-and-save routine. (Suga 2020, my translation)

> Originally I liked cooking and enjoyed making well-planned, nutritious meals at home. But after I got married and had children, I could not take as much time for cooking as I wished. Therefore I started to cook and save. (Nakai 2019, my translation)

> Since childhood, I was interested in food and cooking; and I studied food biochemistry at university and worked in food-related jobs. I began to cook and save four years ago, when I first got pregnant with my first child. I was [normally] too tired to support my body by myself in the kitchen, so I began *tsukurioki* when I felt better. (Wakaba 2018, my translation)

In their intimate narratives, what has caught my attention is the authors' revelation of challenges in their housework, described alongside their persistent hope to somehow resolve it. In a short essay, Kazuwo Hida reveals her husband's insatiable craving for macaroni salad and her mindful efforts to cook a limited amount of it at once—because he eats it all. When an editorial team came for a photo shoot of her *tsukurioki* dishes, the staff "took care to leave behind" a portion of macaroni salad, which she was "looking forward to having" after they were gone. But when she was "taking a bath, my husband [came to the kitchen and] just finished it all in a second. There was plenty of it, though. . . . According to him, it was so delicious that he could not spare it for his daughter or wife." So the author firmly decided to "divide it into portions and save them in separate containers from the next time" (Hida 2011, back of the front cover). This story's multiple implications intrigue me—she talks lovingly about her husband, boasts about her perfect knowledge of his soft spot, and educates the reader about what a home-cooked meal can do to maintain the family bond—but am I reading too much into it if I hear a sigh and indirect complaint in this? "After all," I hear, "what could I do now to change my longtime husband's self-centeredness?"

As the book title *The Female Complaint* indicates, Lauren Berlant's emphasis in her interrogation of so-called women's culture is its complex relationships with, and sustained attachment to, the status quo in spite of women's expressed sufferings and disappointments:

> What makes a public sphere intimate is an expectation that the consumers of its particular stuff already share a worldview and emotional knowledge that they have derived from a broadly common historical experience. . . . Its consumer participants are perceived to be marked by a commonly lived history; its narratives and things are deemed expressive of that history while also shaping its conventions of belonging; and expressing the sensational, embodied experience of living as a certain kind of being in the world, it promises also to provide a better experience of social belonging—partly through participation in the relevant commodity culture, and partly because of its revelations about how people can live. (Berlant 2008, viii)

Similar to this "intimate public" that Berlant describes, the *tsukurioki* narratives postulate an existing community of women who share a common joy and sorrow and circulate a collective category of women that a reader can identify with. The personal stories assure the readers that "you are not alone (in your struggles, desires, pleasures)" (Berlant 2008, ix), and yet, the status of the narratives remain personal. Moreover, this sense of belonging is a kind of "fantasy" enabled through commodity culture (Berlant 2008, ix).

Because of this intimate setting, the *tsukurioki* discourse does not present itself as a social norm imposed upon women but merely a matter of technique. Apparently, it is an individual, voluntary choice by home cooks; they can do it if they are just willing. But the significance of eating at home is determined by the perceived superior status and cultural values associated with it. Contemporary cookbooks reproduce the idea that the best meal must be speedy, healthy, economical, tasty, and visually appealing. The status quo is that homemade food is far superior to ready-made dishes purchased at stores and meals served at restaurants, because it fulfills all the criteria above. Home-cooked meals, it is widely assumed, can save money and are healthier, with less sodium and oil consumption and more vegetables. This idea of home food superiority does not always reflect the actual ability of those in charge of cooking at home.

As discussed earlier, alternative eating options other than home-cooked meals have increasingly been acknowledged in Japanese society, but the cookbook discourse and the food industry tend to put home cooking in competition with external eating options, such as eating out and purchasing precooked dishes, and eating at home is compared with the other options' costs and effects—price, time, nutrition values, and psychological benefits. In order to win this competition, home cooks need to make food cheaper, faster, and healthier, and the cookbooks contend that they can.

But in order for a home cook to keep serving economical and delicious meals regularly on their table, their developed skills, efforts, and the systemic organization of time and space in their daily routine is a must. This distinctive status of homemade meals can be seen as a social norm that "operates within social practices as the implicit standard of *normalization*. . . . Norms may or may not be explicit, and when they operate as the normalizing principle in social practice, they usually remain implicit, difficult to read, discernible most clearly and dramatically in the effects that they produce" (Butler 2004, 41, emphasis in original). Although minor in number compared to *tsukurioki*, other recently published cookbooks highlight fuss-free, easy procedures and call this type of cooking *zubora meshi* or lazy meal (see, for example, *"Hitori gurashi wo tokoton tanosimu" henshū bu* 2014). This buzzword indicates that putting a degree of effort into home cooking is still the norm, and cutting corners in food preparation is not ideal and implies a moral deficiency, such as laziness. Through female authors' voices and by projecting an intimate reader community, the *tsukurioki* books normalize women's domestic responsibilities and their commitment to time-saving efforts, while providing women a temporal, imaginative space where they can share their hopes and struggles to cultivate a sense of belonging.

CONCLUSION

The *tsukurioki* discourse typically assumes contemporary Japanese women's need to multitask, whereas it does not essentially challenge the unpaid and feminized status of domestic work. *Tsukurioki* is a therapeutic discourse of consumer culture that provides practical tools for home cooks to acquire and develop their time- and space-managing skills. In combining business and cooking, the *tsukurioki* authors exemplify the entrepreneurs of the neoliberal era, turning their personal affairs into monetizable resources for economic achievements, and in their writings, time is also a scarce resource that should not be wasted in the kitchen but saved for other productive activities. The authors' publicly active profiles disrupt the established perception of the gender binary associated with home cooking, but do not destabilize it. Furthermore, *tsukurioki*'s particular notion of time-space management masks the limited power a consumer has toward the intensifying conditions of a globalized neoliberal economy.

To further contextualize the anxiety expressed through the cook-and-save books, it would be beneficial to consider wider socioeconomic conditions surrounding this mentality. Under post-industrialized global capitalism, the systems of production and economic transactions heavily rely on Information and Communication Technologies (ICTs), and large- and small-scale mergers and acquisitions can occur at any moment, which demands workers' flexibility to acquire new skills and adapt to unfamiliar environments (Sassen 2005; Kunda, Barley, and Evans 2002). In short, workers are constantly pressured to not only save time but also catch up with time. As "space becomes virtual and global transactions occur in 'real time'" (Walker 2009, 487), ongoing wide-scale crises such as global warming, wars, and pandemics also add a common sense of urgency. "This sense of being unable to control time coupled with the normative assumption that we should control, and in fact master it, creates a paradox which manifests itself in heightened feelings of anxiety and powerlessness" (Walker 2009, 488). In agreement with current neoliberal tendencies elsewhere, the *tsukurioki* discourse does not offer "political perspectives that highlight the need for social change. Instead, desires for change are directed away from the sociopolitical sphere and turned inward. Social critique is transformed into self-critique, resulting in a prevalence of self-doubt and anxiety" (Scharff 2015, 108). Words such as *anshin* (relief) and *raku* (relax, or saving one's energy) repeatedly appear throughout the cook-and-save discourse, drawing the reader's attention to the domestic cook's skills to overcome their anxiety on their own by improving their home management ability.

The dilemma between women's agency and the pressure upon them to "achieve the perfect" (McRobbie 2015, 3) through the cook-and-save method illustrates a Japanese variation of "postfeminist femininity" (Nathanson 2013, 7) that replaces the conventional idea of mother's homemade food (*haha no aji*) based upon the biologically inherited capacity of the female body and emotions. Women are not naturally entitled to belong to the domestic sphere; but they are expected to return there and secure their place through constantly working to maximize their capacity of home management. Inadvertently, *tsukurioki* books reveal the peculiar ambivalence in which middle-class women are situated in relationship with their homes.

NOTES

1. Tōhan is a top trading company based in Tokyo that handles books and other publications.

2. A total of 537 cookbooks published from 1984 until 2020 had the word *tsukurioki* in their titles, among which 511 were published after 2010, according to the National Diet Library catalogue.

3. I selected the books for this study based on their accessibility, popularity, and variety, while avoiding the duplication of authors. Besides two *tsukurioki* books by well-known authors that I already owned (nozomi 2015 and Hida 2016), I randomly picked three books (Ito 2016, Matsumoto 2019, Suga 2020) at a Junkudō bookstore in Nagoya, Japan, in March 2020. In addition, I obtained a book developed from a 2014 best-selling book which spearheaded the *tsukurioki* recipe boom (Shufu no tomo sha 2015); seven others were chosen based on lifestyle blogs' recommendations and Amazon.co.jp's best seller list in December 2020. Among these seven books, six

authors such as Shima (2017), Ichise (2017), Wakana (2018), Makita (2019), and Shoku no sutajio (2020) have published multiple *tsukurioki* books, and so did the other five authors for the books that I initially obtained. The editorial team at Shufuno tomo sha has also published several cook-and-save books.

4. This generic explanation does not reflect women's massive job loss due to government interventions and other public responses triggered by the Covid-19 pandemic since the spring of 2020. A further investigation would be needed to grasp the impact of changing social and economic conditions for the gendered division of work after the outbreak of the virus.

5. New food items such as butter, salad oil, and black pepper were introduced in recipes such as salad, fish fillet sautéed with butter, pumpkin croquette, and so on. When the new cooking methods were first demonstrated, many ingredients were not accessible in remote communities. But "the cooking lessons [offered by the New Life Movement] allowed rural women to have a glimpse of a new diet as their possibility" and "made them feel closer to it" (Yano 2009, 209).

6. Eating preprepared, purchased meals at home is sometimes called *chushoku*, or eating in the middle. According to a Management and Coordination Agency survey, eating out constituted 7.2 percent, and "eating in the middle" made up 3 percent of Japanese households' average dietary expenses in 1965. Meanwhile, these ratios doubled in 1985 with eating out constituting 6.3 percent, and "eating in the middle" making up 15.1 percent (Ishikawa and Ehara 2002) of the households' dietary expenses.

7. Among the thirteen selected *tsukurioki* books for my sample, eleven identify their authors with a short biography while two others had a collective of recipe contributors without individual descriptions of them. Nine were written by female authors, all of whom included detailed descriptions about their lives and families. Meanwhile, the male doctor and the male scientist, who were in charge of the other two *tsukurioki* books, did not reveal their own family structure or engagement with domestic work, but their biographies present their career trajectory through highlighting their past and present institutional affiliations (see table 8.1).

REFERENCES

Appadurai, Arjun. 1988. "Introduction: Commodities and the Politics of Value." In *The Social Life of Things: Commodities in Cultural Perspective*, edited by A. Appadurai, 3–63. Cambridge: Cambridge University Press.

Assman, Stephanie. 2014. "Gender Inequality in Japan: The Equal Employment Opportunity Law Revisited." *The Asia Pacific Journal* 12 (45, no. 2).

Berlant, Lauren. 2008. *The Female Complaint: The Unfinished Business of Sentimentality in American Culture*. Durham: Duke University Press.

Butler, Judith. 2004. *Undoing Gender*. New York: Routledge.

Dixey, Rachael. 1996. "Gender Perspectives on Food and Cooking Skills." *British Food Journal* 98 (10): 35–41.

Ehara, Ayako. 2012. *Katei ryōri no kindai* (The modernity of home cooking). Tokyo: Yoshikawa kōbunkan.

Garson, Ilana. 2011. "Neoliberal Agency." *Current Anthropology* 52 (4): 537–555.

Grossberg, Lawrence. 1986. "On Postmodernism and Articulation: An Interview with Stuart Hall." *Journal of Communication Inquiry* 10: 45–60.

Harvey, David. 2005. *Brief History of Neoliberalism*. Oxford: Oxford University Press.

Hida, Kazuwo. 2011. *Jōbisai* (Regularly saved dishes). Tokyo: Shufu to seikatsu sha.

———. 2016. *Jōbisai* (Regularly saved dishes), vol. 2. Tokyo: Shufu to seikatsu sha.

"*Hitori gurashi wo tokoton tanosimu*" *henshu bu* 2014. *Hitori gurashi no zubora meshi* (Lazy meal recipes for living alone). Tokyo: Shufu no tomo sha.

Hochschild, Arlie, and Anne Machung. 1989/2012. *The Second Shift*. New York: Penguin Group.

Ichise, Etsuko. 2017. *Rakuchin okazu tsukurioki 200* (Easy dishes to cook and save 200). Tokyo: Shufu to seikatsu sha.

Inoue, Mariko. 2003. "Regendering Domestic Space: Modern Housing in Prewar Tokyo." *Monumenta Nipponica* 58 (1): 79–102.

Ishikawa, Hiroko, and Ehara Ayako. 2002. *Kingendai no shoku bunka* (Modern and contemporary food culture). Kawasaki: I & K Corporation.

Ito, Akane. 2016. *Kantan nanoni honkaku!: Zeppin tsukurioki* (Easy but authentic!: Excellent cook-and-save dishes). Tokyo: Subarusha.

Ito, Kimio, and Kazue Muta. 2015. *Jendā de manabu shakaigaku* (Sociology learned through gender). Kyoto: Sekai shisosha.

Kaufmann-Scarborough, Carol. 2006. "Time Use and the Impact of Technology." *Time & Society* 15 (1): 57–70.

Kietlinski, Robin. 2013. "Sports, Motherhood, and the Female Body in Contemporary Japan." *The Asia-Pacific Journal* 11 (27, no. 3).

Kikuchi, Natsuno. 2019. *Nihon no posuto feminizumu: Joshiryoku to neoriberarizumu* (Japan's Postfeminism: The female power and neoliberalism). Tokyo: Ōtsuki shoten.

Kimura, Aya H. 2011. "Food Education as Food Literacy: Privatized and Gendered Food Knowledge in Contemporary Japan." *Agriculture and Human Values* 28 (4): 465–482.

Kunda, G., S. R. Barley, and J. Evans. 2002. "Why Do Contractors Contract?: The Experience of Highly Skilled Technical Professionals in a Contingent Labor Market." *Industrial and Labor Relations Review* 55 (2): 234–261.

Lee, Kristen Schultz. 2010. "Gender, Care Work, and the Complexity of Family Membership in Japan." *Gender and Society* 24 (5): 647–671.

macaroni. 2020. *365 nichi no tsukurioki: mainichi kantan, mainichi oishii* (Tsukurioki for 365 days: easy every day, tasty every day). Tokyo: KADOKAWA.

Makita, Zenji. 2018. *Tōshitsu ofu no yaseru tsukurioki* (Cook-and-save method to cut off sugar and lose weight), with recipes by Chie Sakashita. Tokyo: Shinsei shuppansha.

Matsumoto, Yūmi. 2019. *Maiasa rakusuru tsukurioki no bentō* (Cook-and-save bento box that allows you to save your energy every morning). Tokyo: Fusōsha.

McBride, Anne E. 2010. "Food Porn." *Gastronomica* 10: 38–46.

McRobbie, Angela. 2015. "Notes on the Perfect: Competitive Femininity in Neoliberal Times." *Australian Feminist Studies* 30 (83): 3–20.
Morioka, Rika. 2014. "Gender Difference in the Health Risk Perception of Radiation from Fukushima in Japan: The Role of Hegemonic Masculinity." *Social Science and Medicine* 107: 105–112.
Murata, Hiroko, and Masaki Miki. 2016. "*Kazoku to shoku no kankei wa kawaru noka: Shokuseikatsu ni kansuru seron chōsa kara* 2" (Will the relations between the family and food change?: From a public opinion survey on dietary habits, continued). *Hōsōkenkyū to chōsa* (Broadcasting Research and Survey) 66 (11): 2–20.
Muta Kazue. 1994. "Images of the Family in Meiji Periodicals: The Paradox Underlying the Emergence of the 'Home.'" Translated by Marchella S. Gregory. *U.S.-Japan Women's Journal: English Supplement* 7: 53–71.
———. 1996. *Senryaku to shite no kazoku* (The family as strategy). Tokyo: Shinyōsha.
Nakai, Erika. 2019. *Yasai ga oishi sugiru tsukurioki* (Cook-and-save dishes with super yummy vegetables). Tokyo: MdN Corporation.
Nathanson, Elizabeth. 2013. *Television and Postfeminist Housekeeping: No Time for Mother*. New York: Routledge.
Negra, Diana. 2009. *What a Girl Wants?: Fantasizing the Reclamation of Self in Postfeminism*. Milton Park, Abingdon, Oxon: Routledge.
nozomi (a.k.a. Mori, Nozomi). 2015. *Tsukuoki: Shūmatsu matomete tsukurioki reshipi* (Tsukuoki: Recipes to cook and save during weekends). Tokyo: Kobunsha.
Sassen, Saskia. 2005. "The Global City: Introducing a Concept." *The Brown Journal of Global Affairs* 11 (2): 27–43.
Scharff, Cristina. 2015. "The Psychic Life of Neoliberalism: Mapping the Contours of Entrepreneurial Subjectivity." *Theory, Culture and Society* 33 (6): 107–122.
Sennett, Richard. 2006. *The Culture of the New Capitalism*. New Haven: Yale University Press.
Shima. 2017. *Shima-san no puremiamu na tsukurioki* (Shima's premium cook-and-save method). Tokyo: Daiamondo sha.
Shoku no sutajio. 2020. *Shikkari tabete kirei ni naru: Tanpakushitsu no tsukurioki & rakuhaya okazu* (To sufficiently eat and become pretty: *Tsukurioki* and easy quick dishes with protein). Supervised by Satoshi Fujita. Tokyo: Shinsei shuppansha.
Shufu no tomo sha, ed. 2020. *Tsukurioki sōzai* (Cook-and-save dishes). Tokyo: Shufuno tomo sha.
Sturken, Marita, and Lisa Cartwright. 2009. *Practices of Looking: An Introduction to Visual Culture*, 2nd ed. Oxford: Oxford University Press.
Suga. 2020. *Motto rakusuru: Isshō tsukaeru tsuskurioki besuto* (Save your energy more: the best *tsukurioki* recipes that you can use for the rest of your life). Tokyo: Fusōsha.
Takeuchi, Yukiko. 2009. "*Chōri to gendā*" (Cooking and gender). In *Shokubunka kara shakaiga wakaru! (You can understand a society from its food culture!)* by Nobuo Hara, Ayako Ehara, Yukiko Takeuchi and Keiichi Yano, 101–146. Tokyo: Seikyūsha.

Tauchi, Shoko. 2014. *Jitan ryori no kihon* (The basics of time-reduction cooking). Tokyo: Soshisha.

Uno, Kathleen S. 2005. "Womanhood, War and Empire." In *Gendering Modern Japanese History*, edited by B. Molony and K. Uno, 493–519. Cambridge, MA: Harvard University Press.

Wakana, Marie. 2018. *Isogashī hito sen'yō: Tskurioki shokudō no chōkantan reshipi* (Especially for busy persons: *Tsukurioki* Diner's extremely easy recipes). Tokyo: Fusōsha.

Walker, Judith. 2009. "Time as the Fourth Dimension in the Globalization of Higher Education." *The Journal of Higher Education* 80 (5): 483–509.

Winterman, Denise. 2012. "Breakfast, Lunch and Dinner: Have We Always Eaten Them?" *BBC News Magazine*, November 15. https://www.bbc.com/news/magazine-20243692.

Yano, Keiichi. 2009. "*Ikka danran no aji to kōdo seichōki*" (The taste of family unity and the high growth period). In *Shokubunka kara shakaiga wakaru! (You can understand a society from its food culture!)* by Nobuo Hara, Ayako Ehara, Yukiko Takeuchi and Keiichi Yano, 183–217. Tokyo: Seikyūsha.

Yoshizumi, Kyoko. 2002. "*Shoku to Kazoku*" (Food and the family). In *'Shoku' no ningen gaku* (The study of humanity regarding 'diet'), edited by Yoshikuni Yatani and Hiroshi Yamamoto, 188–191. Kyoto: Nakanishiya shuppan.

Chapter 9

Eating as a Way of Performing Gender

The Intersection of Food, Gender, and Human Capital in Taiwan

Amélie Keyser-Verreault

ABSTRACT

This chapter seeks to inaugurate a discussion on the relationship between food and the quest for beauty in Taiwan's neoliberal context. Focusing on analyzing how women use specific ways of eating in performing gender, I draw on seventy in-depth interviews with highly educated, urban Taiwanese women and ethnographic work in Taiwan conducted between 2010 and 2017. My insights are drawn from Foucault's critique of the theory of human capital and his emphasis on how neoliberalism redefined individuals as "entrepreneurs" who attentively and constantly invest, manage, and improve their "human capital." I argue that beauty is a determinant part of women's human capital and therefore neoliberal subjects must continually carry out important aesthetic labor, including food-related practices, to keep their capital attractive. Consequently, it is important that women struggle to balance their eating habits and regulate their body weight. I also emphasized that the link between eating, womanhood, and managing one's embodied human capital is a continuous process of entrepreneurial tasks spanning adulthood, pregnancy, and motherhood.

INTRODUCTION

This chapter explores gendered food selection and intake in contemporary Taiwan. It attempts to explain the sociocultural pressure for women to stay thin and the individual's desire for and pursuit of a slim figure, both of which are present in and determinants of women's eating behavior. In other words, not only are women socialized to eat in a feminine manner—given the significant amount of appearance-related pressure—but many of them choose their food actively and consciously to keep, maximize, or, at least, fight the depreciation of their figure. In Taiwan, as I will show, beauty is seen as a crucial component of women's embodied human capital that can be converted into many material and immaterial benefits, and thinness is the most important part of the Taiwanese ideal of beauty. Consequently, it is essential and important that women struggle to balance their eating habits and regulate their body weight. I will argue that not only gender difference plays a key role in food-choice motives and attitudes toward food, but also eating behaviors are highly linked to unrealistic body-weight goals, dissatisfaction with body weight, and weight-loss experiences. Therefore, it is crucial to examine the relationships between food, gender, and women's desire to keep their beauty capital attractive.

Some scholars have already stressed the strong and enduring association between femininity and body work implied by the ideal of beauty in other countries. For example, Lazar (2011, 37) cogently points out that "in many societies, 'doing' beauty is a vital component of 'doing' femininity: being beautiful, as defined by the norms of a society [. . .] and working towards achieving those conventional standards are an accepted (and expected) part of what women do by virtue of being 'women.'" Wen (2013, 93) stressed that, in Chinese culture, as well as in Taiwan, appearance is a gendered expectation and a long-standing cultural value: "The obsession with female beauty is rooted in stereotypical gender roles for women." Yet, while the sociocultural factors of beauty norms are indispensable in explaining women's bodily beautification and eating-related attitudes, I highlight women's agency and their aspirations for empowerment that underlie aesthetic labor including diet, food selection, and so on. As Oksala (2013, 39) argues:

> The spread and intensification of neoliberal governmentality have meant that women have also come to be seen, and to see themselves, increasingly as neoliberal subjects—egoistical subjects of interest making free choices based on rational economic calculations. No more do women only want a happy home; they too want money, power and success.

In Taiwan's neoliberal context, where appearance is considered one of the most important personal assets for women, beauty is a monopolistic capital that could be converted into many advantages (e.g., marrying a wealthy man, a good job). Therefore, bodily beautification is largely considered a form of capital in which one can invest, and physical attractiveness can be used as a practical strategy to reshape the various fields (e.g., marriage, workplace, etc.) surrounding them. In this sense, influenced by local feminist movements and Western individualism, Taiwanese women have become increasingly emancipated from traditional gendered roles and expectations. Therefore, women are not totally victims of the beauty myth or merely cultural dupes; rather, they try to reappropriate gendered norms to empower themselves and to gain many forms of personal advantages. In Chen's (2013) words, neoliberal individualism often "equates the patriarchal norm with rationality" (446). Moreover, I highlight that women's active control of their bodies comes not only from the societal expectations imposed on them, but also from a desire to realize their own ideal. In other words, rather than a reduced explanation that describes body work and eating behaviors simply as patriarchal coercion, I emphasize the role of pleasure in this bodily beautification and that it may be more helpful to see such intensified aesthetic labor as an agentic process for producing individual enjoyment. This analysis is akin to what Elias and Gill (2018) argue, that bodily discipline is often "wrapped in discourses that highlight pleasure, choice, agency, confidence and pleasing oneself" (64).

Thus, this point—that women's attitudes and behaviors regarding eating are highly influenced and determined by body-shape concerns—is a central concern of this chapter. In the following sections, I will analyze how, for the women in our study, body-shape concerns, eating motives, eating styles, and quantity of food are highly interrelated. While pleasure is at stake in women's choices concerning food, through eating, women also want to become slimmer to avoid depreciating their beauty capital. Accordingly, *eating* is more than feeding oneself and enjoying the pleasure of being a gourmet; it is also an entrepreneurial activity by which women seek to maintain their figure, which is seen as a crucial asset of their human capital.

This article is divided into three sections. After presenting the theoretical framework and methodological considerations, I will then show how eating and doing gender are highly linked. Although there are many eating styles among participants, they have a common goal—that is, taking pleasure in eating but trying to stay as slender as possible. Next, I will present particular social norms and personal practices concerning food and eating behaviors during and after pregnancy. Finally, I will discuss how participants, who are mothers, transmit certain values and eating habits to their daughters. In fact, emphasis on different periods in a lifetime results from the interaction between social norms and some of the key moments in a woman's life. In Taiwan, marriage, childbirth, and motherhood are crucial events that influence women's aesthetic labor and self-perception. Therefore, this analysis/chapter provides a holistic view of the linkage between gender and food-related norms in modern Taiwan.

Beauty, Human Capital, and Neoliberalism

The analysis presented here is inspired by the work of Foucault (2004) on neoliberalism. Though it is centered on what is generally referred to as the Western world, here we adopt his emphasis that the ideology behind neoliberalism disseminates the *model of the market* to all domains and activities, even domains that have nothing to do with money or even materiality, including social phenomena and private life (Foucault 2004, 245–246). Thus, the ideology of neoliberalism is slowly colonizing every aspect of our world (Harvey 2005) and, according to this logic, human subjects are being reformatted as "human capital." This means that "the rise of human capital as a dominant subjectivity form is a defining feature of neoliberalism" (Feher 2009, 24). Hereafter, every aspect of life can be expressed as an investment in one's human capital (Foucault 2004, 249).

From these sources one can conclude that human capital includes all that is inherited or acquired and that can be appreciated in the form of revenue in a specific context (Foucault 2004, 230). Capital could be any skills or abilities that could produce some kind of income, which then includes all physical and psychological factors used to acquire benefits. In this analytical approach, the individual is redefined as a stock of capacities and "my human capital is me, as a set of skills and capacities that is modified by all that affects me and all that I effect" (Feher 2009, 26). In addition, I would like to emphasize the importance of the body and body control in women's management of their human capital, as Winch (2015) stressed: "The body is recognised as the object of women's labour: it is her asset, her product, her brand and her gateway to freedom and empowerment in a neoliberal market economy" (21). Self-improvement in neoliberal rationality is therefore an *embodied* directive where, under the influence of the quest for beauty and for thinness, body-shape concerns and body-weight regulation are determinant factors for women.

In short, the rapid spread of neoliberal ideology can favor the inclusion of beauty as part of human capital and non-Western societies can be thought of as directly affected by this global beauty culture (regarding the penetration of neoliberalism in Taiwan and its influence on women's bodily regulation, see my previous work: Keyser-Verreault 2018a, 2018b, 2020). If beauty and its vital component, thinness, are determinant parts of women's human capital, as I shall explore later, then neoliberal subjects must continually carry out important aesthetic labor to keep their capital attractive, which includes food-related practices and behaviors. Thus, I consider women's regulation of their eating behaviors an indispensable part of their entrepreneurial activities.

Methodology

This study is based on thirty-three months of ethnographic fieldwork, between 2014 and 2017, during which I conducted a large research project involving highly educated, urban Taiwanese women's beauty practices. For the purpose of this chapter, I selected sixty in-depth, open-ended interviews I conducted with women who were pregnant or who already have children. These women all hold master's or PhD degrees from top-ranking Taiwanese universities or from foreign universities. They are all heterosexual and identify themselves as middle class. The women in the study ranged in age from twenty-nine to thirty-nine and they were employed in a wide range of positions. They were all living in the capital, Taipei, and are part of the main ethnic group, Han.

I recruited women through personal networks and snowball sampling, and this ethnographic work was all conducted through in-person interviews and in Mandarin Chinese, a language in which I am fluent. In-depth interviews allow participants to talk about their perceptions and feelings and allow me to observe diverse sources of information such as body language, clothing style, facial cues, or tone of voice. Respondents were asked to talk about women's beauty in Taiwan and my questions covered the definition of beauty, the role of appearance in society and in their lives, and their concrete beauty practices—including their eating habits and food-selection behaviors. Participants who have children were asked about their feelings regarding their pregnancy and postpartum body as well as about a significant other's feelings about them, and about the feelings of others; I also asked about their special beauty practices during and after pregnancy. In addition to interviews, data was also gathered through close ethnographic participation. Taiwan is known for its rich food culture; food is available ranging from gourmet to light refreshments, local snack bars, and every kind of eating establishment. Many restaurants and night markets stay open until midnight, or even later. It is easy to see that, in Taiwan, lunch with colleagues, afternoon tea at a café with friends, or dining at a restaurant with the family are important parts of everyday social life. As a mother of three, I took part in many gatherings at many child-friendly restaurants (*qinzicanting* 親子餐廳) with friends and study participants who are mothers. Living in Taiwan more than three years and having many friends and in-laws there, I took part in food-related social events; these experiences as well constitute part of the data of this study.

In the process of moving between data and analysis, I first combined the interview transcripts with my field notes to form one large data set. I did line-by-line coding for core themes and subthemes or patterns inviting further explanation. I also employed the method of constant comparative analysis, moving back and forth between data collection and analysis and focusing on coding for examples and counterexamples.

Ethics approval was granted by my university and all names used in this article are pseudonyms.

"I Am a Gourmet Eater, but I Should Stay Thin"

Beauty as a Dominant Human Capital for Women

Before continuing, it may be helpful to portray the social context that frames the interaction between gender, food, and body-shape concerns. In fact, although the idea of a close linkage between beauty and womanhood certainly is not new, recent feminist research on women's experience of body transformation underscores that beauty pressure is at an unprecedented level in contemporary societies. For instance, Elias, Gill, and Scharff (2017) note that "beauty pressure is not just intensifying, but also extensifying" (28). The unprecedented degree of scrutiny of women's bodies is what McRobbie (2015) calls "the tyranny of perfect." Widdows (2018) not only argues that "the gradual increase in minimum standards in the context of a dominant and ethical beauty ideal is significant in that what is required to be normal is increasingly demanding," but also points out that "the primary feature of the dominant beauty ideal is that of thinness" (21).

In Taiwan, I observed as well close links within the trinity of beauty, slenderness, and womanhood. For many Taiwanese women, beauty significantly contributes to a successful life and there is still strong social pressure for women to get married and have children to continue the paternal lineage. To compete with other women and solicit male candidates with good social standing, the participants interviewed in this study overwhelmingly regard beauty as women's greatest capital. I was repeatedly told of the paramount importance of appearance. Sara noted that, for men, women's appearance is paramount. Echoing her, Re-Lin said, "For most Taiwanese men, the personal quality of a woman is much less important than her appearance." Qing emphasized that her spouse's opinion is very representative of men's way of thinking in Taiwan: "For him, the most important thing for a girl is whether she is beautiful or not; other things, like personality, are merely a secondary advantage."

Moreover, observations during fieldwork and interviews enabled me to identify elements that form the predominant canon of beauty and that are essential for a woman to be judged beautiful and also make her feel beautiful. In Chinese, a great compliment for a woman is to be called *zhenmei* (正妹), which means that she is pretty. A beautiful girl, someone who is *zhenmei*, is very thin, has white skin, big eyes, long silky hair, and is a cute woman. It is the dominant ideal of beauty and study participants clearly indicated that any other kind of beauty would be marginally acceptable.

It should also be noted that the most important criteria on which beauty is judged are thinness first and then white skin. Qian Xiao San's remark is typical in this regard: "It matters very much if someone tells me that I gained weight or my skin is darker than it was. We equate beauty with slenderness and having white skin." In other words, for this study's participants, being beautiful mainly means staying thin and most of them confirm that if a woman is not very thin, she will not be considered a pretty girl. Momo told me, "In Taiwan women pursue extreme slenderness. There is a popular expression: An attractive girl is one who is as thin as paper (*zhi pian ren* 紙片人)." As a result, "in Taiwan, every woman wants and needs to undertake a regimen—even a girl who is already very slim thinks about going on a diet to lose weight," said Lu-Lin. Therefore, we can conclude that staying fit and looking good continually play key roles in the contemporary production of the gendered body in Taiwan.

Finally, we can illustrate the link between womanhood and the Taiwanese ideal of beauty by examining the now-famous 2021 *food calendar* (*shiling rili* 食令日曆). This calendar, which highlights and describes local Taiwanese food specialties, has caused a scandal because the text is imbedded with sexism and popular misconceptions. For example, from the July 7, 2021, page: "Attracting a lot of flies? Maybe because you are delicious like a dried scallop!" In this statement, not only are women equated with food, but also implicit is that a beautiful woman is like *delicious food* that attracts many flies (hinting at suitors, or any kind of sexual harassment). A few of the participants told me that many Taiwanese men like cute, docile, and weak women and, if they find them attractive—especially sexually—they often say that she looks "delicious" (*kekou* 可口).

Another interesting example is the December 1, 2021, page: "Even if you became a wife, you should stay 'juicy' as a clementine." Here, the word "juicy" (from Taiwanese Hokkien) can be translated literally as "water, water" (*shui shui* 水水) and it means "beautiful." Since Taiwanese is a very commonly spoken language in Taiwan, this expression (*shui shui* 水水) has become a synonym for *being pretty* in the (popular) vernacular. Moreover, in the subtext, there is advice on how to choose a juicy clementine that "tastes as juicy (*shui shui* 水水) as you"; again, this is a direct reference to women, beauty, and food.

On the February 15 page, we read that "Both monkey head mushrooms [*Hericium erinaceus*] and women seek pure whiteness." The subtext states, "Choose white monkey head mushrooms, which look like you who are always white and beautiful even on holiday."

In this section, I have explained the close association between food, beauty, and womanhood in Taiwan's context; this linkage is often maintained and strengthened through various social pressures.

Women's Bodies under Surveillance

It must be pointed out that because of the climate of open critique of women's bodies, eating behaviors have often become the object of observers' comments. For example, Chun-Fang told me: "Since beauty is so linked to womanhood, if I don't keep myself beautiful, everybody—even an unknown taxi driver—will advise or criticize you, saying that you should undertake a regimen!" Moreover, compared to men, women received many more comments from their mothers regarding weight and shape, and about the importance of physical appearance. Many participants told me that their mothers (or sometimes an older female family member) closely control what they eat. Some mothers—judging their daughters already overweight—regularly say to them, "Eat less!" or "Stop, that's enough!" Family dinners, especially during the Chinese New Year, are a huge source of stress because "we are always compared with other female relatives according to who is thinner and if we have lost or gained weight," stated one participant. Meili's experience is quite common, based on this study:

> At a family dinner, one of our aunts said to my cousin, "Wow! You must have lost a lot of weight! You look great! You've become so pretty!" Then she turned to me and said, "Oh! My god! Why did you become such a fatty?"

In fact, the pressure demanding that women stay slim comes not only from family but also from friends and colleagues or anyone. Xiao Ye's experience was typical in this regard: "Once, I had lunch with many colleagues in a restaurant near our office. One female colleague told me, in a contemptuous tone, 'Did you notice that you are the only one who has eaten all the food on your plate?' But I was so hungry!"

Finally, I would like to underline two important points. First, in Taiwan, women's bodies often become the object of remarks, jokes, and critiques in public spaces, and this phenomenon is highly tolerated. In other words, the boundary between the private and the public is ambiguous, especially regarding women's bodies. Second, social pressure about eating, endured by many more women than men in the Taiwanese context, is due to the fact that the regulation of food is often the only way of controlling one's body weight. Although doing sports to maintain a healthy body is commonly advised in Taiwan, many participants emphasized that women don't do this much, partly because men prefer weak women and also because women with muscles and who sweat are seen negatively by men. In fact, many participants explained that, if they go to the gym, there are always some men who stare rudely at them and especially at their moving breasts. A few participants mentioned that they sometimes go to a women-only gym or choose night jogging to avoid strange looks or glances with a sexual connotation, and also to avoid darkening their white skin when jogging on a sunny day. Under these circumstances, for women, maintaining a slim figure mainly means controlling one's quantity of food. Thus, eating behaviors are not only affected by unique social pressures, but are the main object of women's self-surveillance.

A Thousand Ways of Eating with One Goal: Staying Slender

In this study, I found that, on the most obvious level, there are many different eating styles and every participant has her own way of eating. Yet, on closer inspection, participants' food selections are significantly influenced and determined by concern about socially prescribed body shapes and a desire to be as thin as possible. Food represents a mixture of the pleasure of eating and the pressure and anxiety that come from appearance-related concerns. What women actually eat often results from a combination of several factors including personal physique, personal taste, and the effects of weight gain. In other words, women will choose food based on their physical build and preferences but also, most importantly, foods that "do not fatten me up (*bu hui rang wo bian peng* 不會讓我變胖)," which is what many participants reported. For instance, Chen-Chi said:

> I like food and refreshments and I am a picky eater; there are a lot of things that I never touch. For some, I do not like the taste, but most are foods that make me gain weight easily. Women cannot eat too much, because being plump is a very negative thing for us. So there is a limit to how much I can eat—I doubtlessly choose the dish that will not make me chubby.

Another example is from Chun-Fang, who explained how staying slender is always associated with food intake:

> I eat mainly vegetables and fruit, sometimes a little meat. When I cook, I often prepare congee instead of a bowl of rice, because I will eat less rice and I'll feel full more quickly. As a rule, staying thin and beautiful requires a lot of self-discipline so I don't eat any sweets or fruit after noontime because there's a lot of sugar in them. Also, I don't eat anything three or four hours before going to bed but if I'm really hungry, I will eat some unsweetened yogurt to stop the hunger.

In the following description from Qing, it is clear that every detail of food intake is calculated to balance the pleasure of eating and the desire to maintain a slender figure:

> In order to keep a thin figure, it is most important to choose the right kind of food on the one hand, as well as the quantity of food and the time to eat on the other. Everyone's body is different, and you have to find the food that doesn't make you fat. Of course, we can't eat too much and, over a span of twenty-four hours, there are times that food will more easily become fat. So, for example, I don't eat after dinner because it will make me gain weight quickly. [. . .] According to my observations, in regard to keeping a slender figure, every woman has her own ideal menu. I prefer quinoa, which is now very popular in Taiwan because, compared to rice or noodles, there are fewer calories and more fiber, protein, and other nutrients. So, when I undertake a diet, I'll eat only quinoa salad and vegetable broth.

Echoing Qing, On-Ru shared her "rules of the game" regarding a way of eating to keep one's figure:

> I eat a lot of fruit because fruit is indispensable for women's beauty. Yet, in some fruit there are a lot of sugar and calories, so I eat them only in the morning. If you don't want to become heavy, you should have very strict self-control and self-restraint. For example, I have many rules for myself: when I finish a meal, I don't sit down and I try to stand as long as possible so that I burn calories; I never have late-night snacks; every morning, the first thing I do is drink a mug of lemon water so that I have a radiant glow; for dinner, I eat very little starch; if I eat out, I generally order salad; if there is a chicken thigh, I will avoid the skin; if there is oil on my food, for example vegetables, I will rinse it in a glass of water (*xiyou* 吸油), and so on.

On-Ru's food-related notes are very typical, and I met many participants who have their own "must eat" and "prohibited food" lists for losing weight. I gathered various types of food-related lists from many other women during this fieldwork. I contend that women's ways of eating are often the result of interactions between personal taste, an individual's physical build, and a common desire to stay slim.

Furthermore, in the interview excerpts above, it is noteworthy that participants underlined the importance of discipline and self-control. Doing gender and eating are held on a continuum that ties two contradictory aspirations: a ceaseless fight between gluttony and the pleasure of eating on the one hand, and control, constraint, or hindrance on the other. Eating always represents uncertain combat between *laisser-aller* (letting go) and sobriety, or moderation. Yet, I emphasize that self-commands regarding the kind or quantity of food and timing of eating are not merely drawbacks or deterrents controlling unchecked longings to eat more or eat what one wants; they are also a source of pleasure or self-satisfaction. At the expense of the enjoyment in being a gourmet, women gain the recompense of staying slender and maintaining their attractiveness, their embodied human capital. Winch (2016) cogently points out not only that to "be in the process of erasing, fighting, controlling fat is privileged as an essential element of women's labor," but that "control is erotic" (905) since "pleasure is accumulated through the body's control and surveillance of fat" (909).

In the following section, I show how the regulation of food and quest for slenderness continue and metamorphose during maternity.

"I Am Pregnant and I Am Often Hungry, but I Should Think about Getting My Body Back"

The existing works on pregnancy and beauty, which focus on a Western context, are contradictory (Nash 2014, 242), particularly in regard to how expectant mothers cope with weight gain and how women feel about their pregnant bodies. There are two major interpretive directions. Some scholars (Bailey 2001; Fox and Neiterman 2015; Huntley 2000; Upton and Han 2003; Young 2005) frame pregnancy as a release from beauty pressure and contend that pregnant women and motherhood are associated with asexuality and the functional conception of women's bodies. For instance, Bailey (2001) notes that "for some of the women, the norms of slender body management that are part of the dominant representation of femininity were felt no longer to apply" (121). Part of this is due to "the desexualization of their bodies in discourses around pregnancy and motherhood [that] led to a redefining of their bodies as existing for another" (124). Young (2005) holds that this asexualizing discourse releases women "from the sexually objectifying gaze that alienates and instrumentalizes [a pregnant woman] when in her nonpregnant state" (54).

In contrast, contemporary writing emphasizes the colonization of pregnancy and motherhood by beauty culture. Tyler (2011) contends that "pregnant women are no longer released, however briefly, from either the relentless pursuit of beauty or the pressure to perform sexual availability" (27). Echoing this, important and increasing scholarship stresses the redefinition of the pregnant body and motherhood due to recently intensified beauty pressure: from the "yummy mummy" (Littler 2013), "pregnant beauty" (Tyler 2011), and "pregnancy chic" (Musial 2014) to some more sophisticated descriptions such as "getting your body back" as "the third shift of bodywork" (Dworkin and Wachs 2004), or the task of performing "aesthetic/maternal labour" (De

Benedictis and Orgad 2017, 105). Littler (2013) concludes that "it involves the extension of a fashion and beauty complex to the pregnant and post-pregnant body" (230).

Accordingly, in Taiwan, the necessity of keeping an attractive appearance and desirable body has shifted more deeply into pregnancy and motherhood. Becoming a pregnant beauty (Tyler 2011) and a yummy mummy (Litter 2013; Keyser-Verreault 2020) after childbirth and always looking good have become a normative choice and an ongoing project of self-governance. Taiwanese mothers want to measure up to the ideal body of models and celebrities presented in mass media and popular culture. In my own research, almost all the women interviewed stressed the importance of body beautification during pregnancy and the imperative of getting back into shape as quickly as possible after childbirth.

Furthermore, pregnancy and childbirth are seen by many participants as a depreciation of women's beauty capital. Even many women who had not yet had a child had strongly prejudged the impact of maternity on women's appearance. For instance, Wen Pei confessed that, "for me, a woman who becomes a mother is really ugly. Her belly looks like a watermelon and it never regains its former shape, her breasts sag, nipples become bigger and darker, and her skin becomes something like orange bark." For many participants, becoming a mother means, among other disadvantages, suffering from the loss of one's physical attractiveness and many gendered advantages relating to women's beauty. Re-Lin concluded that "the body of a woman who did not have kids is better and everybody agrees with that." Some of my informants literally said that pregnancy "breaks" (*pohui* 破壞) women's bodies—their beauty. As a result, many expectant mothers feel obliged to do important—even very intense—aesthetic labor to counter the depreciation of their beauty asset and the inevitable weight gain due to pregnancy. Many participants reported significant food-related practices during and after pregnancy and, among them, the goal of "nurturing the fetus, not the fat" was seen as crucial. This is an expression I frequently heard during my conversations with participants, which was sometimes expressed as "nursing the baby, not the unnecessary flesh." Regarding this, Lisa's comment is representative:

> We Taiwanese mothers want to stay slim even if we are supposed to put on weight during pregnancy. The trend during pregnancy is that "you nurture the baby, not yourself." If your baby has enough and is a normal weight but you gain weight as well, it is not the greatest situation. The best-case scenario is a chubby baby with a slender mum and it's the dream all expectant mothers want to realize.

To accomplish this goal, it is crucial—from the beginning of the pregnancy—for women to closely monitor what they eat and to gain as little weight as possible; women in the study frequently reported that this is a very common practice. Lara's case is typical in this regard and her comment is representative of what many women experience, the dilemma of gluttony versus the desire to keep their figures:

> When I was pregnant, I could not eat sweets or have fast food and I had to weigh myself every day. For Taiwanese women it is very important to look as slim and young after pregnancy as before. I am so scared of not getting into shape. [. . .] There is a book, *Pregnant and Skinny* (*Shou Yun* 瘦孕), which is very influential. Now there is kind of a concept to be pregnant and skinny. We should not gain more than 8 kg during pregnancy!! [. . .] Sometimes I'm getting sick of that. I have mood swings—there are the hormones. Why do I have to be skinny! I want to eat! [. . .] But for us it is very important to get into shape very quickly after the pregnancy.

Lara felt angry about those unfair demands on her own body and, as do many pregnant women, she had distinctive cravings during pregnancy—but she didn't challenge the skinny pregnancy norm and continued to avoid gaining weight.

After delivery, the project of regaining one's body begins. The majority of my informants reported that, as is widely said, the first six months after childbirth is the "best period for regaining one's pre-pregnancy figure." Yet, one of the strong themes that emerged from interviews was that, in this competition to get back into shape, the real difficulty of bouncing back often comes less from personal determination than from dealing with delicate social relationships. Because of complicated kinship and social relationships, women could not freely do their bodily beautification, choosing what and how much they eat. For instance, Qin-Qin also remarked about the dramatic experience of her after-childbirth diet during the postpartum month (*yuezi* 月子):

> I want to lose weight quickly after childbirth so I diet, but it is really tough because there is someone always talking to me about what to eat and pressing me to eat more. Even worse, many people—relatives or friends—prepare meals for me and bring me a lot of food. [. . .] But it is clear that I can't eat a whole chicken every day—I'd rapidly become chubby!! I soon decided to order prepared *yuezi* meals because these meal companies know that we mothers want to lose weight quickly, so their meals are nutritious without many calories. I said to this elder that I got free meals as a gift from one of my close friends and I had no right to refuse!

Indeed, in my analysis (Keyser-Verreault 2018b, 54–55) of advertisements from the postpartum meal industry, a popular service in Taiwan, I point out that the main focus of these ads is regaining one's body/figure, which almost replaces the importance of health: These advertisements use the theme/motif of personal sharing between women who are mothers. What is emphasized is not the health of mothers but regaining their figure after delivery. For example, one ad states:

> Many mothers worry a lot about gaining weight due to traditional high-calorie postpartum meals. In fact, I have gained 27 kg during pregnancy but, due to these specialized meals, in less than five months I still have only 4 kg to lose.

Another issue regarding gender and food is the fear of one's skin becoming darker during pregnancy. Thus, after thinness, white skin is an important component in the Taiwanese ideal of beauty. There is a relevant Chinese saying: "A white complexion hides three flaws." White skin is also a sign of social class, because people in Taiwan associate dark skin with the working class or migrant workers (mainly from Southeast Asia). At a dinner party in a restaurant, I once heard a father—a rich businessman and a close friend of my husband's family—introduce his nine-year-old daughter in an embarrassed manner: "She has a defective appearance. I often joke that she looks like a migrant worker!"[1] A few of the study participants told me that, during pregnancy, to keep their skin white they avoid eating dark-colored food like chocolate, soy sauce, or black tea. They said that consuming these foods may darken their skin and that of their unborn child, and they didn't want to risk having a dark-skinned baby girl. At a teahouse in the Tianmü District (天母) of Taipei, I met an elegant woman who told me about the influence of food on the skin color of the baby:

> I like tea so much, so I couldn't stop drinking it during my pregnancy. It is often said that if we have dark-colored foods like tea or coffee during pregnancy, not only will the expectant mother end up with a dark complexion, but it is highly possible that our babies will have a darker skin tone. Despite my worries, I continued having a cup of oolong every morning. In the end, I had a dark-skinned child! Many people blamed me for drinking too much tea!

Conversely, a few participants chose to consume certain foods to whiten their skin and the most popular product is pearl powder. Many participants informed me that pearl powder is widely believed to not only remedy the problem of low skin sheen, but also help whiten the skin of the unborn child. In addition, collagen and edible bird's nest (*yanwo* 燕窩) are two other products that are believed to have great effect on pregnant women's skin; I saw many advertisements for these three products in the country's major maternity magazines, which presented them as "the best and indispensable nourishment for the beauty of pregnant women" (Keyser-Verreault 2018b, 66–67).

In summary, in this section I have shown that women undertake extensive eating-related aesthetic labor during and after pregnancy. This Taiwan study confirmed that pregnancy is no longer a release from beauty pressure and the pursuit of slenderness. Food-related practices such as undertaking severe diets and the quest for white skin—during and after pregnancy—bear witness to the penetration into motherhood of the cult of beauty. Consistent with previous findings, mine support De Benedictis and Orgad's (2017, 103–104) argument:

> A growing body of scholarship on maternity under neoliberalism interrogates the incorporation, intensification and legitimation of aesthetic labour into maternal subjectivities. Mediated figures such as "yummy mummy" or "pregnant beauty" have emerged recently, emphasising how maternal identities are increasingly reliant upon and articulated through beauty practice and body projects such as dieting, exercise and cosmetic surgery.

In the following section, I explain that the pursuit of thinness and management of women's embodied human capital are also familial and intergenerational phenomena.

"Mothers Should Encourage Their Daughters to Eat Small Portions"

"I would like to have a daughter because I want to dress her like a princess!" I heard this so many times from expectant women or mothers who only have sons. But a princess, like a woman, should be beautiful and, consequently, thin.

In a park, there were two little girls playing near their mothers. One of these mothers called to her daughter, saying, "Come and have some snacks! You should eat in order to be pretty!" She turned to her friend and continued in a proud tone: "She eats very little meat, but a lot of vegetables and she often leaves her rice bowl unfinished!" Another mother responded: "Wow! It's wonderful! She is naturally on a diet! You do not need to worry about her future!"

This anecdote is representative of the food-related relationship between mothers and daughters, in two ways. First, girls like the one in this anecdote are socialized to eat in a feminine manner (eat little; eat as little starch as possible; prefer vegetables over meat, and so on). Children certainly understand the connection between eating and body weight, and girls are most likely to experience such concerns. Second, like many study participants who are mothers, these mothers in the park are convinced that a slender body, resulting from one's eating habits, is important and advantageous for women.

Another anecdote illustrates the gendered difference in the food-related education parents provide. I was invited by two study participants—Sylvia, a university professor, and Bai-Xue, a high schoolteacher—to an afternoon family gathering in Guanmiao (關廟), a little city near Tainan, the capital of Southern Taiwan. Every family member brought some prepared dish and all kinds of fruit and snacks, and the eldest male family member prepared oolong tea for everyone. There was plenty of delicious food on the long table in the garden and, while the adults were chatting, children played and grabbed snacks and refreshments from time to time. Suddenly, I heard someone yelling, "Little sister, stop eating! Your belly is big enough!" It was Sylvia talking to her daughter. However, this little girl tried to take a last piece of cake. I heard a "clap" sound—Sylvia had just given her daughter a slap for behaving "badly." Yet her son, only sixteen months older, continued eating and no one made any comments. Afterward, Sylvia explained to me that to keep her daughter from becoming fat, she must control the quantity of her snacks and meals; then she continued:

> My niece, Bai-Xue's daughter, is already too big and my older sister doesn't do anything to improve this situation! Sometimes when I'm at her home, my niece eats a big piece of chocolate cake while watching TV at three o'clock in the afternoon! This girl is chubby, and everyone worries about her. A heavy woman can't find a boyfriend or a good job easily—everyone in Taiwan knows that.

In fact, many participants confirmed that, from childhood, they are taught and encouraged to eat in small bites, which is seen as a *girl's* way of eating or a feminine manner. Some women in this study reported that, even as adults, their mothers control and oversee their figure and what they eat. Lara shared her experience:

> For my mother, a woman's figure is very important, and she oversees what I eat and how much I weigh. Even when I was a university student, during our telephone calls she always asked me what I ate or if I had gained weight. She even invented a funny game—every time I returned to my parents' home, she would weigh me and, if I had succeeded in losing 1 kg, she would give me NT$1000 [approx. US$33]!

The way these Taiwanese mothers manage their daughters conflicts with the findings from related studies of Western mothers. For example, Maor and Cwikel (2016) report mothers' strategies that promote a healthy body image for their daughters. In fact, according to my field observations and in many competitive societies in East Asia, concerning personal and professional success, only a minority of parents are conscious of the difference between perceiving children as human capital and pursuing a child's well-being (a Western concept). A few parents, especially mothers, tried hard to balance the well-being of their children with the pragmatic considerations of preparing them to be what we analyze as future entrepreneurs of the self. To ensure that their children stand out from others they will contend with in their future lives, parents in Taiwan tend to take a realistic, businesslike, and down-to-earth approach to children. I contend that, given this logic, many study participants adapt an entrepreneurial perspective of their daughters' eating behaviors.

In summary, the link between food, gender, and beauty—women's most important human capital asset (especially thinness)—is also a transgenerational relationship; appearance-related pressure within the family exists and was often mentioned by the participants of this study, especially in the mother-daughter relationship.

CONCLUSION

In this chapter, I regard women's control and regulation of eating behaviors as indispensable parts of their entrepreneurial activities and food intake to be an integral part of women's embodied human capital investment and management. Stated differently, while there are many kinds of eating behaviors, selecting certain foods is interwoven with body-weight concern and weight control in maintaining a slender figure. I also emphasized that the link between eating, womanhood, and managing one's embodied human capital is a continuous process of entrepreneurial tasks spanning adulthood, pregnancy, and motherhood. Thus, the "nurture only the unborn child and stay slim" imperative during pregnancy and trying to snap back into shape after childbirth are considered the main ways to avoid depreciating women's physical attractiveness after maternity. The quest for slenderness through the regulation of eating behaviors is also an intergenerational phenomenon, since many mothers in this study encourage their daughters to eat in a "feminine way." For many mothers, little girls are seen as and socialized to be future beauty capital entrepreneurs; thus, they are encouraged to undertake a gendered way of eating.

Finally, in Taiwan, the quest to be pretty seems to be an open-ended imperative; many study participants talk about the ideal of the "beautiful witch" (*meimonü* 美魔女) for mothers whose children are already teenagers or adults. A *beautiful witch* is praised for her magic powers to resist the natural aging process. Consequently, it would be interesting to observe anxiety about aging based on particular ways of eating. Since youth is a crucial component of the Taiwanese ideal of beauty and there is a strong culture of "wellness" or "preserving one's health" (*yangshen* 養生) due to the influence of Chinese medicine, it would be relevant to explore—considering the cult of thinness and youth—the intersection between food, gender, and aging in contemporary Taiwan.

NOTE

1. It is important to underline that there is a lot of discrimination against migrant workers in Taiwan. Therefore, the comment of that father regarding his daughter was not a compliment. I underline that, as this example has shown, social norms regarding beauty and light skin are closely linked with the discourse on social class and race in addition to gender (e.g., Glenn 2008).

REFERENCES

Bailey, Lucy. 2001. "Gender Show: First-Time Mothers and Embodied Selves." *Gender & Society* 15 (1): 110–129.

Chen, Eva. 2013. "Neoliberalism and Popular Women's Culture: Rethinking Choice, Freedom and Agency." *European Journal of Cultural Studies* 16 (4): 440–452.

De Benedictis, Sara, and Shani Orgad. 2017. "The Escalating Price of Motherhood: Aesthetic Labour in Popular Representation of 'Stay-at-Home' Mother." In *Aesthetic Labour: Rethinking Beauty Politics in Neoliberalism*, edited by Ana Sofia Elias, Rosalind Gill, and Christina Scharff, 101–116. London: Palgrave.

Dworkin, Shari, and Faye Linda Wachs. 2004. "Getting Your Body Back: Postindustrial Fit Motherhood in Shape Fit Pregnancy Magazine." *Gender & Society* 18 (5): 610–624.

Elias, Ana Sofia, and Rosalind Gill. 2018. "Beauty Surveillance: The Digital Self-monitoring Cultures of Neoliberalism." *European Journal of Cultural Studies* 21 (1): 59–77.

Elias, Ana Sofia, Rosalind Gill, and Christina Scharff. 2017. "Aesthetic Labour: Beauty Politics in Neoliberalism." In *Aesthetic Labour: Rethinking Beauty Politics in Neoliberalism*, edited by Ana Sofia Elias, Rosalind Gill, and Christina Scharff, 3–49. London: Palgrave.

Feher, Michel. 2009. "Self-appreciation or the Aspiration of Human Capital." *Public Culture* 21 (1): 21–41.
Foucault, Michel. 2004. *Naissance de biopolitique*. Paris: Gallimard/Seuil.
Fox, Bonnie, and Elena Neiterman. 2015. "Embodied Motherhood: Women's Feeling about their Postpartum Bodies." *Gender & Society* 29 (5): 670–693.
Glenn, Evelyn Nakano. 2008. "Yearning for Lightness: Transnational Circuits in the Marketing and Consumption of Skin Lighteners." *Gender & Society* 22 (3): 281–302.
Harvey, David. 2005. *A Brief History of Neoliberalism*. Oxford: Oxford University Press.
Huntley, Rebecca. 2000. "Sexing the Belly: An Exploration of Sex and the Pregnant Body." *Sexualities* 3 (3): 347–362.
Keyser-Verreault, Amélie. 2018a. "Zuiqiu meimao yu biancheng müqing de liang nan: yi gao wenping de duhui nüxing weili" [Quest for beauty and becoming a mother: a painful paradox for highly educated, urban Taiwanese women]. *Taiwan Journal of Anthropology* 16 (1): 97–158.
———. 2018b. "Huifu zixin meiti: meixue jinying zhuyi xia de müxing zhuti yu huaiyun shenchan" [Recover a self-confident body: pregnancy and childbirth under aesthetic entrepreneurship]. *Journal of Women's and Gender Studies* 43 (2): 1–28.
———. 2020. "I Want to Look as if I am My Child's Big Sister": Self-satisfaction and the Yummy Mummy in Taiwan." *Feminism and Psychology*. https://doi.org/10.1177%2F0959353520973572.
Lazar, Michelle. 2011. "The Right to Be Beautiful: Postfeminist Identity and Consumer Beauty Advertising." In *New Femininities: Postfeminism, Neoliberalism and Subjectivity*, edited by Rosalind Gill and Christina Scharff, 37–51. New York: Palgrave Macmillan.
Littler, Jo. 2013. "The Rise of the 'Yummy Mummy': Popular Conservatism and the Neoliberal Maternal in Contemporary British Culture." *Communication, Culture & Critique* 6: 227–243.
Maor, Maya, and Julie Cwikel. 2016. "Mothers' Strategies to Strengthen Their Daughters' body image." *Feminism & Psychology* 26 (1): 11–29.
McRobbie, A. (2015). "Notes on the Perfect." *Australian Feminist Studies* 30 (83): 3–20. https://doi.org/10.1080/08164649.2015.1011485.
Musial, Jennifer. 2014. "From Madonna to Whore: Sexuality, Pregnancy, and Popular Culture." *Sexualities* 17 (4): 394–411.
Nash, Meredith. 2014. "Picturing Mothers: A Photovoice Study of Body Image in Pregnancy." *Health Sociology Review* 23 (3): 242–253.
Oksala, Johanna. 2013. "Feminism and Neoliberal Governmentality." *Foucault Studies* 16: 32–53.
Tyler, Imogen. 2011. "Pregnant Beauty: Maternal Femininities under Neoliberalism." In *New Femininities: Postfeminism, Neoliberalism and Subjectivity*, edited by Rosalind Gill and Christina Scharff, 21–36. New York: Palgrave Macmillan.
Upton, Rebecca, and Sallie Han. 2003. "Maternity and its Discontents." *Journal of Contemporary Ethnography* 32 (6): 670–692.
Wen, Hua. 2013. *Buying Beauty: Cosmetic Surgery in China*. Hong Kong: Hong Kong University Press.

Widdows, Heather. 2018. *Perfect Me: Beauty as an Ethical Ideal*. Princeton and Oxford: Princeton University Press.
Winch, Alison. 2015. "Brand Intimacy, Female Friendship and Digital Surveillance Networks." *New Formations* 84: 228–245.
———. 2016. "I Just Think it's Dirty and Lazy: Fat Surveillance and Erotic Capital." *Sexualities* 19 (8): 898–913.
Young, Iris Marion. 2005. *On Female Body Experience: Throwing Like a Girl and Other Essays*. Oxford: Oxford University Press.

Chapter 10

(Post-)traumatic Logic of Socialism, Hunger, and Masculinity in Zhang Xianliang's *Mimosa* (1984)

Gabriel F. Y. Tsang

ABSTRACT

Zhang Xianliang was officially stigmatized as a rightist in the Anti-Rightist Movement because of his published long poem "The Song of Hurricane" (1957) and then expelled to Xihu Farm in Yinchuan for nineteen years. After Mao Zedong died in 1976 and Deng Xiaoping relaxed the freedom of artistic creation in the Fourth Congress of Chinese Art Workers on October 30, 1979, many older-generation Chinese intellectuals, including Zhang, were rehabilitated and then resumed writing, collectively reiterating their shared experiences of political mistreatment, hunger, boredom, insufferable labor, family separation, repressed romantic desires, and so on through fictional creation. Their reiteration encodes a powerful reevaluation of Mao's history in an era of ideological transition.

This chapter focuses on Zhang Xianliang's reflective novella *Mimosa* (1984), which epitomizes the anti-intellectual history of Mao's China with its fictional record of personal experiences in early Deng's era. Food is a key to accessing the intersection of post-traumatic memories and reimagined gender politics that marked the specific ambivalence of Zhang. An illustration of the representation of food, as a pivotal signifier to determine the power relation between two protagonists during a famine, supports my argument that the narrative responses to hunger could modify masculinity and empower women beyond socialist regulations and patriarchal conventions.

INTRODUCTION

There have been in-depth discussions concerning how capitalism generally reforms contemporary cultural logics, such as those initiated by Fredric Jameson and cultural Marxists. Socialism, as the stage between capitalist exploitation and Communist ideal according to Karl Marx's ideological evolutionism, is commonly a contextualized topic to help evaluate the phenomenal consequence of planned economy, propaganda politics, and official manipulation of state apparatuses. As a nation that had experienced aggressive communism after the charismatic and idealistic leader Mao Zedong's initiation of the "Three Red Banners Movement" in the late 1950s (which consisted of the General Line for Socialist Construction, the Great Leap Forward, and the People's Communes) and then nominally retreated to socialism after Deng Xiaoping launched capitalization and modernization in the late 1970s, the People's Republic of China (PRC) encountered a critical period of ideological transition during the 1980s. Beyond the official theoretical systemization of "socialism with Chinese characteristics" to mediate between the developmental needs of connecting to the global market and maintaining the Chinese Communist Party's (CCP) authority, Deng Xiaoping enabled Chinese intellectuals, as the representatives of the public that survived the Cultural Revolution (from 1966 to 1976), to incrementally recover from the catastrophe of both economy and humanity through literary representation of the memory of trauma until the June Fourth Incident,[1] after which severe censorship filtered retrospective writing and hindered public understanding of the past.

On October 30, 1979, Deng Xiaoping delivered a speech in the Fourth Congress of Chinese Art Workers to relax the freedom of artistic creation. Previously besieged by "high-level assemblies, political reeducation classes, land reform activities, registration drives" and "bodily, literary, aural, artistic, and other forms [of] meanings and symbolisms inscribed upon the subject" (U 2019, xiv), Chinese intellectuals then collectively reiterated their shared experiences of political mistreatment, hunger, boredom, insufferable labor, family separation, repressed romantic desires, and so on, leading to a literary fashion called "scar literature,"[2] which mainly took the form of fiction.[3] This fashion lasted from the late 1970s to the early 1980s, and was soon transformed into a powerful but short-lasting reevaluation of Mao's history.

The older-generation writer Zhang Xianliang's reflective novella *Mimosa* (1984)[4] is a representative piece during the emancipated 1980s with an interplay of enduring starvation and subordinated masculinity. It deserves attention, as, according to David Wang's summary, it (together with Wang Ruowang's *Hunger Trilogy* [1980]) "use[s] hunger as a point of reference for chronicling the Maoist coercion of intellectuals" (Wang 2004, 145). This does not "eschew class politics," as Judith Farquhar (2002, 30) summarizes the post-Mao reform novel, and offers a lens to view how physical perception of shortage and tolerance intertwines with autobiographical reflection on traumatic dailiness. Moreover, *Mimosa* records the continuity and disruption of socialism from Mao's era that Zhang experienced through to Deng's era in which Zhang wrote his story about Mao's past. This sort of writing across the contexts of Mao and Deng is what I would like to term "[post-]traumatic" or "[post-]socialist."

Zhang's description of food in *Mimosa* bears importance, relevant to the grand history of intellectuals' suffering and also the interpersonal dynamics between men and women that correspond to the author's memory and reveal a mix of gender conception in the past and the present. This chapter will focus on the post-traumatic representation of food, a pivotal signifier of *Mimosa* that determines the power relation between two protagonists by placing the female as a dominant supplier during the male's starvation. It connects the traumatic imagination of the story to the author's exile to Southwest China, and delineates the operation and malfunction of a socialist control over individuals' material possessions, love, personal identification, and power related to gender. An interpretation of *Mimosa* will further an understanding of the intersectional transcendence of food over socialist regulations and patriarchal conventions.

Interpretation of Hunger, Labor, and Intellectuals in the (Post-)socialist Context

In the introduction of her translation of Wang Ruowang's *Hunger Trilogy*, Kyna Rubin expounds on the anthropological significance of food and its relation to literary representation in the Chinese context. With a focus on the absence of food, namely hunger, she states that "one cannot fully appreciate the special implications of hunger in China without an awareness of the overriding importance of food in Chinese culture" (Rubin 1992, xvii). Agreeing with K. C. Chang's claim that "food and eating are among things central to the Chinese way of life and part of the Chinese ethos" (Chang 1977, 13–14, cited in Rubin 1992, xvii), she illustrates the transfigurative influence of eating on politics, religions, linguistics, and everyday life of Chinese people. Although the notion of food as central to quotidian practices is common in East Asian cultures, and perhaps also many parts of the world, the desire for satiation and taste is specifically significant to modern China, which had profound shared experiences of famine intersected with traumatic historicity. In *Hunger Trilogy*, the narrator's failure to negotiate for more food through a hunger strike in the CCP's prison in 1966, hence starving enough to eat toothpaste (Wang 1992, 93), marks the extreme of his passivity in food politics, reflecting also a disconnection from the diverse Chinese tradition sustained by localized dietetic habits. This could be attributed to the loss of democratic efficiency, economic mismanagement, arbitrary subordination of intellectuals, and so on.

From a contextual perspective, the hungriest moment of Wang Ruowang's narrator is close to that of Zhang Xianliang's narrator. It is drawn from a time period that prepared hunger narratives to be represented in a more affluent period. The story of *Mimosa* is set from a time before 1959 up to 1983 (the year of completion). In 1958, Mao launched the Great Leap Forward in order to rapidly industrialize rural areas and collectivize the production system. Its aggressive plan to "surpass Great Britain and then catch up with the United States" with an upsurge of steel output at all costs soon resulted in the great famine that lasted from 1958 to 1961. Oliver Rubin estimated that thirty million people in mainland China died in the great famine and hence regarded it as "result[ing] in the highest famine-related death toll ever recorded in the world" (Rubin 2012, 9). Redefining the period of the great famine as from 1958 to 1962, Frank Dikötter (2011, 333) made calculations with the data collected from local governments in China, and concluded that the number of deaths in this catastrophe reached a minimum of forty-five million.

After the great famine, Liu Shaoqi, the then chairman of China, conclusively attributed this catastrophe 30 percent to natural disasters and 70 percent to man-made errors in early 1962, with a wish to resolve the food issue through capitalist reform. However, Liu's practical review of official mistakes could not help improve agricultural productivity and bureaucratic management of the economy (such as local cadres' common exaggeration of local productivity instead of offering real statistics to the central government for better planning) and even rationalized Mao Zedong's criticism against his political rivals, including Liu himself, a targeted "capitalist roader" who was eventually persecuted to death in 1969. Jasper Becker summarized the situation of food production in China in the two decades before the end of the Cultural Revolution, stating, "Not until after Mao's death in 1976 did per capita grain production reach the level of 1957, and in the early 1970s food production actually fell once more to levels seen during the famine" (Becker 1998, 255). He reveals that food shortage in Mao's China remained unsolved after the failure of the Great Leap Forward and became a severe problem again after the outbreak of the Cultural Revolution. In the analysis of Zhang Qihua et al., even two years after the end of the Cultural Revolution, "there were still 250 million people unable to solve their own food problems" (Zhang et al. 1997, 225). This means that around a quarter of Chinese people were still under the risk of death due to socialist and collectivist production management at the very beginning of Deng's era.

Besides the bureaucratic reason, the economic mismanagement that caused the shared trauma is also a result of the ideological overemphasis on the peasant class, to which Mao Zedong subordinated the intellectuals with professional knowledge. Since the establishment of the PRC in 1949, Mao utilized a labor ethic in place of democracy to pursue egalitarian betterment and social stability. However, this ethic not only disrupted national developments, but also traumatized the educated ones who were under Mao's rural pedagogy composed of guidance from the illiterate, political stigmatization, physical hardship, poverty, repressed wants, hunger, and inescapable countryside.

In *Capital*, Karl Marx discusses labor in terms of its materialistic value. He analyzes the economic and instrumental value of labor, the limitations of exploited laborers, and the objectification of subjects during productive activities in nature. Regarding himself as an orthodox Marxist,[5] Mao Zedong subjected nature to "transformation and reconstitution as part of the process of creating new revolutionary subjects" (Chen 2012, 161). He interpreted labor as moral, instead of capitalistic and contractual, and granted positive value to heavy workloads, which were originally recognized as a result of the employers' exploitation. In many public speeches, Mao characterized the hardship of labor as contributing directly to the national good, and as a form of personal training for revolution. As he stated: "The establishment of socialism opened a road for us to reach the ideal; however, the actualisation of the ideal requires our diligent labour" (Mao 1957, 386). This kind of positivist labor discourse, with claims such as "the countryside is a vast expanse of heaven and earth where we can flourish," had effectively motivated young urban intellectuals to be rusticated during the Down to the Countryside Movement from the late 1960s to the late 1970s, as Mao's solution to the Red Guard riots during the early stage of the Cultural Revolution.[6]

Parallel to his optimistic promotion of labor, Mao Zedong utilized labor as a punishment (presented as a "reform through labor") for political dissidence, to standardize the minds of the older-generation intellectuals (the ones older than the abovementioned voluntarily rusticated educated youth) up to his Communist ideal. Since the 1950s, the central government had been sending intellectuals to the countryside and the national border, compelling them to labor with high intensity. Zhang Xianliang, who was officially criticized in the Anti-Rightist Movement (from 1957 to 1959) because of his published long poem "The Song of Hurricane" (1957) and then expelled to Xihu Farm in Yinchuan for nineteen years,[7] is one of the uncountable examples. After his personalized hurricane's lyrical declaration that "a new era had come"[8] (reminiscent of Percy Bysshe Shelly's "Ode to West Wind" [1819], laden with revolutionary enthusiasm) received criticisms, such as Gong Liu's summarization of "The Song of Hurricane" as "an antagonistic work that doubts about and curses the socialist society" (Gong 1957), Zhang Xianliang ceased to write until the end of labor education.

Embodied hunger and repressed creativity are key features of Mao's intellectuals, and also the drive to diversify expression in Deng Xiaoping's era. The year 1979 was the year of Deng Xiaoping's provisional relaxation of speech control and also of Zhang Xianliang's rehabilitation. Zhang soon resumed writing and published a short story called "Spirit and Flesh" in 1980, in which the male protagonist, like Zhang, is labeled as a rightist and labors on a farm, losing career opportunities and family bonding due to unpredictable political changes. When he did not encounter criticism and censorship as before,[9] Zhang Xianliang cautiously continued his fictional recording of personal traumas, moving on from his general reflection on historical passivity of intellectual individuals to focuses on politics of food and sexuality in *Mimosa* (1984) and *Half of Man Is Woman* (1985) respectively. Material shortage and sexual repression, as heuristic components of labor education, engraved specific experiences on Zhang's body in the past and became concrete when his embodied experiences were increasingly permitted to disseminate through fiction in Deng Xiaoping's era.[10]

Corresponding to the collective starvation in the past, David Der-wei Wang (2004, 145) observed that hunger became a "popular subject" in Chinese literature from the 1980s[11] and Howard Y. F. Choy discovered that many noticeable contemporary fictional characters were named for food, such as "Sima Grain in Mo Yan's *Big Breasts and Wide Hips*, Rice Boy in Su Tong's *Rice*, as well as the five children—Buckwheat, Soybean, Little Pea, Red Bean, and Millet—in Liu Heng's 'Dogshit Food'" (Choy 2008, 188–189). The narration of hunger and food delivers a folk record of the near past, a satire of politics, an urge of reconstructing Chinese traditional culture, and so on. It reflects not simply personal or public desires for satiation and taste enjoyment. The sophisticated metaphorical and metonymical significance of hungry bodies in fiction offers diverse ways of interpretation that enable a connection between fiction and reality. Concerning *Mimosa*, David Wang regards the dietetic cycle of characters as a vehicle that the older-generation author used for compiling his own intellectual history. Similar to *Hunger Trilogy*, *Mimosa* is personal and ironic, autobiographically telling a story related to hunger in chronological order. In both fictional stories, personal hunger can signify national inferiority and poverty; food shortage that first-person narrators encounter could imply the failure of socialism or the CCP in bringing satisfactory everyday life to the public.

While *Hunger Trilogy* was banned in mainland China due to its comparison of food supplies between the prisons of Kuomintang and the CCP, *Mimosa* was still permitted to circulate with its exposure of a traumatic history that the Party was dedicated to erasing. The trick, reminiscent of the male protagonist Zhang Yonglin's wise use of an American milk powder can to obtain a bit more congee from the cook in *Mimosa* (Zhang 2013, 9–10),[12] laid on his cautious understanding of institutional rules. Zhang Xianliang was sensitive to ideological dynamics and hence wrote in the "Author's Preface" of *Mimosa* that Deng Xiaoping's economic reform would resolve food problems with modified socialism (Zhang 1985, 7–8).[13] He made a historical distinction between Mao's regime and Deng's regime, implicitly safeguarding the authority of the CCP headed by Deng with his authorial interpretation of hunger as an already ended tragic experience.[14] Likewise, at the end of the story, the narrator comments that "[in 1983,] our nation and I had got rid of misfortune, paying off the bill that history requires us to pay" and praises the national anthem that connotes the spirit of struggling (135–136). He necessitates the value of sacrifice for validating his fiction under the risk of still-existing censorship (in spite of Deng's declaration of creative freedom). As *Mimosa* is still openly circulated and even canonized in mainland China, this kind of summarization of hunger narration before and at the end of his story has finally proved successful, regardless of whether Zhang Xianliang sincerely held a pro-government and pro-Party stance at the time of his writing.

In *Mimosa*, Zhang Xianliang largely highlights traumatic hunger during the intellectual protagonist Zhang Yonglin's reflective labor. At the beginning of the story, the narrator enters the farm where he has been assigned. It is a space with backward facilities (such as a simple and broken wooden bridge), unfavorable geographical conditions (dry, icy, infertile), and severely unhealthy livestock (3). Zhang meticulously depicts the physical features of three piteous horses: "breathing with *fuha-fuha* noise and leaning towards east and west"; "folding up their begging eyes to appear white"; "while using their strength, exposing worn-down and yellow teeth from a little gap of their mouths"; "nervously shaking their ears again and again"; and so on (3). The narrator regards them as even weaker than himself, who is "1.78 m tall with weight only 44 kg" and "has only skin to cover bones"—the doctor of his labor-reform team even regards his survival as a miracle (3). The gaze of the narrator presumes the upcoming deterioration of his body after compulsory labor that has tortured the imprisoned horses. Through the omniscient narrator's sympathy for the horses, which is also sympathy for himself who knows what is happening next, the story foregrounds the punitive nature of labor in Mao's era, which is in a non-rewarding form more exploitative than capitalistic labor.

The superficial utilization of suffering and hunger for an educational purpose serves political leaders' manipulation over political dissent and failed economy. It binds the narrator, who is supposed to labor like the horses, with the sublime ethic of labor under the CCP's surveillance that does not guarantee individual autonomy, flexibility, and mobility, and even discursively validates the negligence of basic needs. In the following plot, the narrator compares himself with the "Manager of Sales Department," a stigmatized rightist. Both of them recognize their acquisition of more food than is generally allotted as a matter of luck and trickery, instead of effort. The punitive labor system with its socialist aura of altruism has restricted them, as capitalist prisoners, from the "more pain, more gain" capitalist logic. They are expected to repress their desire of satiation and reflect on their hunger in order to be socialistically qualified. Their eagerness for food is hence private and only made public after rehabilitation. This matches Zhang Xianliang's semi-autobiographical retrospection of his imprisonment through a series of fictional writing.

A Portrayal of an Emasculated, Hungry Male Intellectual

A year before the release of Wang Anyi's *Love in a Small Town*, a Chinese feminist erotic classic, Zhang Xianliang published *Half of Man Is Woman* (1985), which, in Zhong Xueping's view, combined "eroticism and political implications" and hence "attracted much critical attention" (Zhong 1994, 175).[15] Those implications, grounded on a political penalty of endless food production, could connect land productivity to willing loyalty to the nation, which produces laborers through personal love and sex. This novel innovatively politicizes the male body of Zhang Yonglin (the same name as *Mimosa*'s protagonist), whose bourgeois background leads to compulsory labor on a national farm and subsequently long sexual repression. He finds himself impotent on the night he marries his dream woman whose nude body haunted him eight years ago. The representation of this haunting is brief, as the narrative minimizes the personal stream of consciousness and skips the duration of missing her. Due to the extramarital affairs of his wife, he is finally fertile again but decides to divorce her.

Half of Man Is Woman reveals Zhang Xianliang's implicit search for creatively symbolizing sex. After *Mimosa* completed an introspective integration of the significance of Marxism, hunger, and sense of belonging, *Half of Man Is Woman* extended an enquiry into unromantic love and libidinal sex on the same memorized land of unrewarding production. On the one hand, Zhang cautiously expanded the borders of signifying forbidden terms and themes, bargaining for a wider scope of free expression. For instance, his sentence-by-sentence use of "boiling swamp," "volcano with splashing magma," "a beautiful nautilus," "a colorful sponge on white coral," "a mirage in the desert," "an oasis in a mirage," "the garden of the fairy-tale giant," and "the most ancient fairy tale" (Zhang 2006, 173) diversely portrays the tabooed vagina that the male protagonist explores for the first time in his life; besides, his vivid metaphor for the female protagonist's breasts as "two giant snowy-white lotuses" with "ruby-red stamen in the middle" (Zhang 2006, 204) further visualizes the erotic figures that were severely forbidden in Mao's discourse. On the other hand, these few but enticing symbols contrast the male protagonist's malfunctioned desire in the era of political impotence, and are hence satirical. Such a cautious design of symbolism corresponds to the narrative binding of sex and politics. At the end of the story, despite his final rehabilitation from being a "disabled" and "half" man (Zhang 2006, 176), Zhang Yonglin has been unable to "appropriately grasp the sentiment" (Zhang 2006, 236). This kind of plot arrangement both politicizes sex and sexualizes politics beyond the most basic dietetic needs, creating conceptual ambiguity related to the penetration of politics into intellectuals' private affection and the empowerment of the self through explicit sex that might threaten collectivist ideology.

As preparation for pioneering erotic narration, *Mimosa* had explored the subtle power relations between men and women, challenging the unspeakable but publicly known regulation of gender roles. Without erotic plots but with abundant narratives related to hunger and food, Zhang Yonglin in *Mimosa* similarly fails to perform the conventionally regulated and culturally inscribed manhood retained from the past, arousing reflection on engendered division of labor. To further elaborate, it is crucial to first contextualize Chinese masculinity. Kam Louie has applied the endless, dynamic interaction between yin and yang to dissolve absolute characterization of Chinese masculinity, but identifies a twofold representation of Chinese masculinity from his interrogation of the elements of *wen* (cultural attainment) and *wu* (martial valor) rendered in historical and artistic male images. In his view, masculinity not only refers to "physical strength and military prowess," but also, especially in the context of traditional China before the Cultural Revolution, includes "refined qualities that were associated with literary and artistic pursuits of the classical scholars" (Kam 2002, 14). This dichotomy of *wen* and *wu* somehow continued in Mao's era that appreciated muscular devotion to national construction, as presented in numerous propaganda posters, and intelligent contemplation of Marxist and Maoist thoughts.

However, one should note that, up until the decade-long Cultural Revolution, Mao Zedong had utilized a series of mass movements, such as the Yan'an Rectification Campaign (1942–1944), the Anti-Hu Feng Campaign (1955), and the Anti-Rightist Movement, to criticize and then persecute intellectuals who were dominantly male. He placed peasants at the highest position of political hierarchy, regarding them as the ones who knew revolution the most and could effectively demonstrate their historical value through diligent labor. This aided his anti-capitalist labor ethics and obscurantism against intellectuals for stability. In such a context, the knowledge and wisdom of male intellectuals were a hindrance to their self-actualization, and the male intellectuals were pushed to comply with the peasants' reeducation in the countryside and rigorously engage in productive activities in order to perform masculinity according to their social identity and biological sex.

Corresponding to the Zhang Yonglin in *Half of Man Is Woman*, whose impotence furthers his physical incapability to contribute to collective productivity with his offspring, the Zhang Yonglin in *Mimosa* is also not socialistically masculine enough. Having been stereotyped as politically unfaithful, he appears feeble and prioritizes personal satiation, instead of any sublime ideals. Despite not being sensitive to his biological sex, he is conscious of his failed fulfillment of the duties traditionally imposed on male intellectuals. When he successfully utilizes his understanding of collimation error to obtain 100 milliliters more congee than "Manager of Sales Department," he exclaims, "My cultural knowledge is used on this!" (10). His contempt for gluttonous desires, especially due to seeing "congee" as cheap, water-like, and unsatiating food that seems to harm the baseline of his dignity for the sake of survival, implies an unwanted violation of pre-Maoist/intellectualist expectations on men to acquire career success and spiritual self-actualization through intelligence. In another scene, Zhang Yonglin "frequently glimpses the window" of food allocation while talking about Hegel and Marx with a philosophy lecturer who has already taken a bowl of thin soup (7). His attention to the closing of the window and later pleasure over obtaining one-and-a-half ladles of sticky rice with vegetable leaves reveal his focuses on materiality that could give him instant and chiefly basic satisfaction, instead of potential contribution to his nation through reasoning. When either *wenwu* or Mao's desired manhood needs to be qualified by political evaluation, and when food is insufficiently rationed to imprisoned intellectuals, this male rightist, perhaps epitomizing many others in Mao's reality, is opposed to the formulated ideal. He represents a new type of masculinity (or counter-masculinity) that fictionally emerged in early Deng Xiaoping's era as a result of the author's cautious avoidance of censorship and close attention to trauma. Beyond masculinity, Zhang Xianliang's composition of the male's innate romantic desire for women follows the Chinese literary trajectory of romanticism but also contravenes it with anti-capitalist revolutionism that deserves further attention. It encodes a powerless intellectual's conflicts between his social and biological sexes.

Capitalist Gender Politics in Socialist Space

While Deng Xiaoping's Open Door Policy was dismantling Mao Zedong's Communist wish, Zhang Xianliang autobiographically configured fictional characters to contain the imagination of men previously forbidden or hidden by Mao's ideology. He, as a reflective revenant—a term Chen Sihe (2006,

204) coined to refer to the writers who entered the Chinese literary arena in the 1950s and then returned from the late 1970s—was recalling rather socialist memories in a rather capitalist context. Trickily corresponding in *Mimosa* is that there is a materialistic exchange of gender power, which could evoke the readers' doubt about the authority and purity of older political orders in the course of Deng's modernization.

In the story, Zhang Xianliang frequently highlights Zhang Yonglin's hunger, despite his final defense for the Party's authority with his enlightenment from trauma. "Manager of Sales Department" is jealous about his purely bourgeois identity and regards the narrator's imprisonment with hardship and starvation as deserved (5). He imaginatively considers capitalist life equivalent to enjoyment, and hence superior to socialist life. Although the narrator does not explicitly complain about his socialist life, food becomes a materialistic core to confirm his preference for capitalism. For instance, after he finds his two tare buns eaten by mice, he nearly faints and comments:

> If these two tare buns were not lost, I would not have any feeling even though I do not eat them. This huge loss deepens my anxiety, letting me feel extremely hungry. Hunger becomes an object with weight and size, dashing in my stomach; and it voices out, shouting at every nerve of my body: To eat! To eat! To eat! . . . I have no strength to move and no mind to think, but only a sudden thought: Must salvage back a double of what has been lost. (24)

The narrator cherishes his buns and only feels safe with them, corresponding to the capitalist emphasis on personal property. He hopes to accumulate food, creating surplus value for himself, and is dedicated to maximizing the quantity of his food especially when socialist welfare cannot guarantee satiation. This emphasis is congruent with his attachment to the female power of Mimosa, the female protagonist with a vivid name identical to the novella title in English but different in Chinese (*Ma Yinghua* 馬纓花 versus the Chinese title *Luhua shu* 綠化樹),[16] whose possession of food directs their romantic relationship.

Configured in a transitional era, Mimosa is an engendered hybrid of socialism and capitalism. In terms of socialist norms, women were seen as a female collective rather than female individuals. Idolized as "iron ladies" as Mao Zedong had promoted since the late 1950s, they had to work and comply with the Party's command as men, in exchange for limited equality. Under the ideological influence of the Party-state, which "redefined proper women as those who worked" (Rofel 1994, 237), they were subject to institutional patriarchy that expected them to be tough in the public space and mindful of their family responsibilities. To a certain extent, this resembles the condition of working women in modern bourgeois society. Lisa Rofel has criticized that this kind of "women's liberation rhetoric" burdened the iron ladies with duties both inside and outside their own family (Rofel 1994, 231). However, without any complaint, the character Mimosa appears positive about this rhetoric. She enters the story while harmoniously breaking feces as fertilizer on farmland with other women. Despite being sufficiently provided for by men who fancy her (though this potentially violates the self-sufficient image of iron ladies), she is willing to labor with others in public. Besides, she independently plays a qualified family role, optimistically raising her daughter and managing the interior space of her home without a husband, who is absent in Mao's iron-lady discourse. Nevertheless, the corporeality of Mimosa is rather capitalist. An iron lady is supposed to be either asexual or masculine, dressing like a soldier rather than a Western bourgeois woman, and should hide or remove her gender characteristics, such as breasts, soft skin, long hair, and pretty appearance. Although Mimosa does not dress in a feminine style, her voice is soft and her feminine appearance surprises the narrator (28, 53). She partially violates the ideal socialist image in exchange for food that she can utilize to bargain for love. In the context that cash is not a common currency in the planned economy dominated by rations, female charisma becomes a more solid capital to earn materials and connection to men.

The most significant plots of the story surround the private space of "American Restaurant," the home of Mimosa that is reminiscent of anti-socialist logics, satisfaction, and moral corruption.[17] Gang Yue's monograph on modern Chinese food narrative regards this as "transgress[ing] the ideological and political mapping of the world" (Yue 1999, 199). He argues that Chinese peasants in the story are remapping space according to international politics, in contrast to their exterior Chinese, impoverished, rural space. American Restaurant appears as a capitalist space with abundant food inside the socialist farms, in which intellectuals cannot exchange tedious labor for food.

As a bachelor who had not seen women during his four years of labor-reform (27), the narrator gets Mimosa's permission to enter American Restaurant to take a stove during their first meeting (28). He is then attracted by the potential intimacy and satiation that this exotically named house with its normal Chinese settings can grant. As the host of the restaurant, Mimosa lets the narrator feel at home, and her hospitality triggers his ambivalence about staying in it. He reflects, "I really feel sorry for her and also shameful for myself about eating and drinking without pay. However, I deeply want to go there. In her home, there is a kind of obscure bliss, happiness, comfort and freedom attracting me" (65). While habitually rejecting her food offers and eating to be full every day, the narrator appreciates the stock of Mimosa's grains (flour, rice, yellow rice, corn, sorghum, soybeans, peas, and so on) and her cooking, feels self-abased because of her generosity, and worries about their exchange of food and love to be suspected as adultery between a male political exile and a local single mother. There is a slight switch in traditional gender roles: the narrator could be perceived from his status to be a cautious recipient, not a proactive provider, whereas Mimosa is a resources controller despite also being an indoor caretaker. This switch challenges the inert power structure that had long empowered the biological men who acquired and manipulated materials for the female leader of a family to distribute at home.

As Mao's authorization of women to share male power does not specify the domestic realm, the author's prominent emphasis on the asymmetric relationship between two characters in American Restaurant seems to suggest that only a capitalist private space could offer a practical ground for eliminating gender bias. As the female protagonist can flexibly control resources and intimacy in a site outside of socialist surveillance, this allows food in a famine to supersede engendered norms that conventionally privilege men in a romantic relationship.

According to Gillian Rose, "Examining the lives of women requires attention to the ordinary, to the unexceptional, because women are excluded from arenas of power and prestige" (Rose 1993, 22). Her argument against a universal and masculinist perspective of time geography (the discipline that includes temporal dimension and daily routines in conception of space) problematizes the male spatial construction of domestic regulation over women. In this regard, Zhang Xianliang, as a literary architect of American Restaurant, sets up the private normalcy of an empowered woman through his male gaze. Within the frame of telling a story about a weak man and a strong woman, Mimosa's domestic activities follow the male author's "ordinary" and "unexceptional" reversal of certain gender roles that may simplify the affectation and desire of women.

Moreover, although Mimosa is suspected to have complicated relationships with many men and has a fatherless daughter, she is configured as being bold before the narrator, not ashamed of her scandals. In her communication with the narrator, the potatoes and fine buns that the narrator lacks and longs for authorize her to speak rudely and direct his career path toward practices of knowledge from books. Such a reversal of androcentric gender politics by food is chiefly founded on the innate attractiveness of femininity, which somehow consolidates her gender identity and performance to serve the core theme surrounding a male intellectual's enlightenment. In a latter part of the story, the narrator's competitor for Mimosa's love reveals, "The so-called 'American Restaurant' is just what the people fabricate. I know that she-devil is very clever. One can give her something but can't touch her body" (119). This plot discloses not only the innocence of Mimosa and her faithful love to the narrator, but also the financial source of American Restaurant. It is Mimosa's tactical use of intimacy and estrangement, instead of erotic sex, to maintain the food flow of her home. The core capital is her feminine charm that breaks the rules of material exchange and voluntary devotion, enabling her to collect food offerings from men and then use them, mixed with her attraction, as the incentive to guide the narrator according to her will. Under Zhang's narration, her personal strategy thoroughly follows her biological advantages, rather than asexual formulation according to Mao's discourse.

Toward the end of the story, the narrator reads Marx's *Capital* and is deeply enlightened by it, beginning to appreciate the simplicity and selflessness of Chinese laborers. His interest in Karl Marx's theory, which shades a socialist aura on this fictional work, does not exist at the beginning of the story; it originates from the satiation and encouragement from Mimosa, who despises men without knowledge. The ending of this heuristic bildungsroman is paradoxical in the sense that Mimosa loves and feeds the narrator merely because of his identity as an intellectual, not his status as a worker or a peasant that used to be adored in the revolutionary discourse since the establishment of the CCP in 1921. The narrator's victory from his competition with male food suppliers for the love of Mimosa reveals an intellectual complex that drove the author to recognize the reflective achievement of the narrator while confirming "food determinism." This does not deter our understanding of Mao's political hierarchization as disadvantaging male intellectuals and empowering women through their potential reliance, because food is thoroughly the base structure in the story to determine gender balance and self-recognition.

To briefly conclude, food connects the intellectual identity and rusticated experiences of Zhang Xianliang as he was a starving and reflective laborer deprived of political rights and material satisfaction during Mao Zedong's era. When Deng Xiaoping reigned, alleviated censorship allowed Zhang Xianliang to semi-autobiographically reiterate traumatic hunger with imaginative enquiries into gender, love, and sex. *Mimosa* represents his configuration of a woman partially corresponding to the socialist iron lady and keeping her feminine features to serve his masculinist plot arrangement. As the space that centralizes the main characters' interaction, American Restaurant regulates the daily life of the female protagonist, where food is not simply for satiation, but also for reversal of gender roles, domination in a relationship, affective transaction/exchange, and heuristic interpretation. In the narrative, famine reinforces the biological power of engendered charm beyond intellectual dignity and socialist ideology. All these perspectives delivered in a fictional form deserve historical or sociological research to further explore their validity and contextual implications.

NOTES

1. A large group of Beijing university students, growing up after the generation of the educated youth, demonstrated for radical democratization in China. Their protest was suppressed by the People's Liberation Army under Deng Xiaoping's command. According to Richard Baum, the total number of dead was between 600 and 1,200, and the number of injuries was around 6,000 (Baum 2011, 452–453). The death and injury were followed by identifying the student movement as "counterrevolutionary rebellion" (457), launching arrests throughout the big cities (458), controlling the content of news reports which, for example, asserted that "not a single student had been killed by troops during the operation to clear Tiananmen Square" (459), and removing Zhao Ziyang and Hu Qili, who were supporters of the students, "from the Politburo and the Central Secretariat" (460).

2. Scar literature, named after Lu Xinhua's short story "Scar" published in 1978, refers to mainstream writings from the late 1970s to the early 1980s that were concerned with the shared traumatic past of the majority of the Chinese public. Different generations of intellectuals held the same wish to share their memories and experiences in order to resist the unpredictable political power that previously suppressed them.

3. According to Yomi Braester, in the early post-Mao period, while Scar literature prospered, writers had to "check the limits of expression under Deng, explor[e] the potential of public discourses and assess the inner resources needed for speaking up and bearing witnesses." The publication of nonfictional writing about the traumatic past was increasingly allowed in mainland China since the mid-1980s. See Braester (2003, 146).

4. *Mimosa* was written between September and November in 1983, and then published in February in 1984.

5. Mao regarded himself as an orthodox Marxist since Khrushchev replaced Stalin as the leader of the Soviet Union. The deteriorating relationship between China and the Soviet Union urged him to launch a discussion of revisionism and validate his identity as a non-revisionist. See Radchenko (2009, 51–56).

6. Michel Bonnin asserts that Mao Zedong's strategic expulsion of a generation of youngsters was an adaptation of Li Dazhao's perspective of rustication developed from Russian populism. See (Bonnin 2009, 34). Different from populist rustication, which aims to spontaneously evoke the compassion of urban individuals toward rural ones through experiencing their daily lives, Mao's rustication purposefully subordinated the urban young intellectuals into peasants and government officers for maintaining political stability, especially as these idle but aggressive helpers of the Cultural Revolution had become a social and political risk.

7. Zhang Xianliang was first in prison from 1957 to 1960. In 1960, he escaped from there for three years and then returned and stayed imprisoned until 1979.

8. This repeats twice: at the end of the first stanza and the end of the whole poem. See Zhang (1957, 11–16).

9. The censorship in Mao Zedong's era limited fictional writing to representation of rigid political formulas, such as "three emphases," which emphasizes a narrative

hierarchy of positive characters, heroic characters, and a leading heroic character in the service of the personality cult of Mao.

10. One has to note that the oppressive labor system caused multidimensional trauma; its control over even the speech of laborers resulted in postponed and distorted representation of traumatic experiences. In his analysis of Zhang Xianliang's autobiographical novel *My Bodhi Tree* (1994), Yomi Braester regards narrating mental scars as "reactivat[ing] suppressed mnemonic and linguistic skills" and the delayed representation of personal trauma in Zhang's case as a psychological effect (see Braester 2003, 157). Zhang's narration of his personal trauma with twenty-two years of imprisonment, fifteen years after his rehabilitation in 1979, is biographically specific, different from the writing of educated youth writers and also those rightist writers of his generation.

11. Meng Sui, who wrote the only journal paper concerning the hunger-themed literature in the early Reformation period, discussed some earlier literary works related to hunger and food, such as Ru Zhijuan's "The Story with Editing Mistakes" (1979), Gao Xiaosheng's "The Owner of a 'Funnel Unit'" (1979), Liu Zhen's "She Seems to Know a Little Bit More" (1979), Ye Weilin's "On the River without Navigation Marks" (1980), Zhang Yigong's "The Story of Criminal Li Tonzhong" (1980), Niu Zhenhuan's "The Vast Snowy Storm" (1980), Ding Zhegquan's "Tian Sanniang Cooks Liver" (1982), and Zhang Xianliang's "Descendants of the River" (1983). See Sui (2014, 117–122).

12. Since this chapter mainly refers to this book, I will insert page numbers only for all its following quotations.

13. In the "Author's Preface," he attributes the Great Famine to collective aggressive belief in personal power and implies that the economic reform launched by Deng Xiaoping is resolving famine in China. He regards the narrator as a victim of a series of political movements, such as the Great Leap Forward. However, he does not draw readers' attention to the specificity of his personal hunger exhaustively transfigured in the story, but centralizes his claim of trust in Marxism instead.

14. Zhang Xianliang states in the first paragraph of the "Author's Preface," "In 1958, because we placed too much emphasis on the effect of the subjective will, the movement known as the Great Leap Forward was initiated, and we dreamt of reality, we hardly even left the ground, and we paid the penalty exacted by economic laws and ultimately plunged into hell. A dreadful famine spread throughout the country. As *Mimosa* begins, this period of famine is already nearing its end" (Zhang 1985, 7). He deems the Great Famine a result of collective blind participation in the Great Leap Forward, and later shows his optimistic attitude toward Deng's modernization, which is supposed to improve the dietetic conditions of the Chinese public.

15. Liu Jianmei illustrates the controversy of *Half of Man Is Woman*: "The Chinese reader, accustomed to traditional as well as revolutionary morality in judging sex, was stunned by this new literature flooded with men's and women's sexy bodies, primitive sensations, libidinal energy, and erotic desire. This phenomenon provoked great controversy because critics could no longer categorise it with their familiar Marxist approaches" (Liu 2003, 24).

16. The Chinese name of Mimosa and the Chinese title signify "red rhododendron" and "greening tree" respectively, both delivering a sense of vitality and

positivity. The author did not provide an explanation for the naming and, according to my reading, the difference of the two names in Chinese does not serve a particular symbolic function.

17. As Zhang Xianliang narrates, "To the farmhands America was an outlandish, promiscuous, immoral country, but so rich that no one worried about food and clothing." See Zhang (1985, 85–86).

REFERENCES

Baum, Richard. 2011. "The Road to Tiananmen: Chinese Politics in the 1980s." In *The Politics of China: Sixty Years of The People Republic of China (Third Edition)*, edited by Roderick MacFarquhar, 337–467. Cambridge: Cambridge University Press.

Becker, Jasper. 1998. *Hungry Ghosts: Mao's Secret Famine (Reprint edition)*. New York: Holt Paperbacks.

Bonnin, Michel. 2009. *Shiluo de yidai: zhongguo de shangshan xiaxiang yundong · 1968–1980* (The lost generation: China's down to the countryside movement 1968–1980). Beijing: Encyclopedia of China Publishing House.

Braester, Yomi. 1977. *Witness Against History: Literature, Film, and Public Discourse in Twentieth-Century China*. Stanford, CA: Stanford University Press, 2003.

Chang, C. K. *Food in Chinese Culture: Anthropological and Historical Perspectives*. New Haven: Yale University Press.

Chen, Sihe. 2006. *Zhongguo dangdai wenxueshi jiaocheng* (A course of Chinese contemporary literary history). Shanghai: Fudan University Press.

Chen, Tina Mai. 2012. "The Human-Machine Continuum in Maoism: The Intersection of Soviet Socialist Realism, Japanese Theoretical Physics, and Chinese Revolutionary Theory." *Cultural Critique* 80: 151–182.

Choy, Howard Y. F. 2008. *Remapping the Past: Fictions of History in Deng's China, 1979–1997*. Leiden: Brill.

Dikötter, Frank. 2011. *Mao's Great Famine: The History of China's Most Devastating Catastrophe, 1958–62*. London: Bloomsbury.

Farquhar, Judith. 2002. *Appetites: Food and Sex in Post-Socialist China*. Durham: Duke University Press.

Gong Liu. 1957. "Chi 'Dafeng Ge'" (Rebuking "the song of hurricane"). *People's Daily*, Sep. 1.

Kam, Louie. 2002. *Theorising Chinese Masculinity: Society and Gender in China*. Cambridge: Cambridge University Press.

Liu, Jianmei. 2003. *Revolution plus Love: Literary History, Women's Bodies, and Thematic Repetition in Twentieth-century Chinese Fiction*. Honolulu: University of Hawai'i Press.

Mao, Zedong. 1957. *Mao Zedong xuanji—diwujuan* (Selected works of Mao Zedong—volume v). Beijing: People's Publishing House.

Marx, Karl. 2013. *Capital*. London: Wordsworth Editions Limited.

Meng, Sui. 2014. "The Political Logics of the Hunger—Themed Literature in Beginning of the Chinese Reform Times." *Journal of Xiangtan University (Philosophy and Social Sciences)*, no. 4: 117–122.

Radchenko, Sergery. 2009. *Two Suns in the Heavens: The Sino-Soviet Struggle for Supremacy, 1962–1967*. Chicago: Woodrow Wilson Center Press and Stanford University Press.

Rofel, Lisa. 1994. "Liberation Nostalgia and a Yearning for Modernity." In *Engendering China: Women, Culture, and the State*, edited by Christina K. Gilmartin et al., 226–249. Cambridge, MA: Harvard University Press.

Rose, Gillian. 1993. *Feminism and Geography: The Limits of Geographical Knowledge*. Cambridge: Polity Press.

Rubin, Kyna. 1992. "Introduction: The Growth of a Nation and an Intellectual." In Wang Ruowang, *Hunger Trilogy*. Translated by Kyna Rubin and Ira Kasoff, xi–xxxvii. New York: An East Gate Book.

Rubin, Oliver. 2012. *Democracy and Famine*. New York: Routledge.

U, Eddy. 2019. *Creating the Intellectual: Chinese Communism and the Rise of a Classification*. Oakland: University of California Press.

Wang, David Der-wai. 2004. *The Monster that is History: History, Violence, and Fictional Writing in Twentieth-Century China*. Berkeley: University of California Press.

Wang, Ruowang. 1992. *Hunger Trilogy*. Translated by Kyna Rubin and Ira Kasoff. New York: An East Gate Book.

Yue, Gang. 1999. *The Mouth that Begs: Hunger, Cannibalism, and the Politics of Eating in Modern China*. Durham: Duke University Press.

Zhang Qihua et al. 1997. *Zhonghua Renmin Gongheguo shi jianbian* (A brief history of the People's Republic of China). Beijing: Contemporary China Publishing House.

Zhang Xiangliang. 1957. "Dafeng Ge" (The Song of Hurricane). *Yanhe* 7: 11–16.

———. 1985. *Mimosa and Other Stories*. Translated by Hu Zhihui and Wang Mingjie. Beijing: Panda Books.

———. 2006. *Zhang Xianliang Jingxuan Ji* (Collection of Zhang Xiangliang's best works). Beijing: Beijing Yanshan Press.

———. 2013. *Lühua Shu* (Mimosa). Guiyang: Guizhou People's Press.

Zhong Xueping. 1994. "Male Suffering and Male Desire: The Politics of Reading *Half of Man is Woman* by Zhang Xianliang." In *Engendering China: Women, Culture, and the State*, edited by Christina K. Gilmartin et al., 175–191. Cambridge, MA: Harvard University Press.

Part IV

TRANSNATIONAL PRACTICE OF FOOD AND GENDER

Chapter 11

Fashioning K-Food

New Gendered Space and Culture in South Korea

Eric Ping Hung Li, Somin Lee, and Matt M. Husain

ABSTRACT

In this chapter, we employ Lefebvre's (1991) conception of space to illustrate the interrelationship of gender, food, and space in the context of urban Korean popular food (K-Food) culture. We first examine the surge of "K-Food" as a part of the *Hallyu* (or "Korean Wave") culture and as a new trend in the local food culture in urban settings. We then adopt Lefebvre's framework to showcase the market construction of gendered representations in retail food space. Through the qualitative case studies of food retailers in Korea, we unpack the complexity, multiplicity, and dynamicity of market-mediated gendered food consumption. We argue that the spatial setting of K-Food not only renews the definitions and standards of "taste" but also employs gender performativity to reinforce gender representations in contemporary urban Korea.

INTRODUCTION

In the past two decades, Korean popular culture (or K-pop) has illustrated its dominance in East Asian and Southeast Asian societies. Korean drama, pop music, food, and beauty products/services have become new trends for generations of Asian consumers. In 2019, the K-pop industry generated a sales revenue of around 6.1 trillion South Korean won (US$5.6 billion). It is anticipated the K-pop market will experience further growth in the next decade (Waldeck 2020). While Korean popular culture creates tremendous economic benefits for the Korean entertainment and tourism industries, the majority of the studies on K-pop have focused on its external impact (e.g., Messerlin and Shin 2017; Yoon 2019). Few scholarly studies have explored the impact of these new cultural and market trends on the social structures and everyday life practices within Korean society. In this chapter, we focus on exploring how the new food culture in South Korea (or K-Food) influences the country's food consumption and existing gender identities and roles.

In Korea, K-Food has immersed itself into the popular culture as Koreans discuss food, differentiate their social class through the restaurants they visit, watch cooking shows and competitions on television, as well as buy cookbooks or attend culinary schools to learn to be better chefs or consumers (Rhee 2019). K-Food generally refers to the newly emerged, localized versions of imported food items in contemporary Korean culture, such as the Paris Baguette chain of restaurants. K-Food also refers to a global phenomenon because a number of Korean food items, including kimchi and bibimbap, are considered globalized (Rhee and Otmazgin 2016). However, in this chapter, we focus on imported food items in urban Korea that have sustained themselves by employing a localized version. In this context, Paris Baguette is an ideal example. Building on that definition and with an urban focus, we argue that food has become an identity marker in a Korean consumer society as it defines social status, personality, competency, worldview, and relationship as well as "taste" in Bourdieu's (1984) conception.

We also argue that K-Food employs gender performativity to reinforce hegemonic gender identities and roles in Korean society. In traditional Korean culture, preparation of food such as family meals and kimchi falls on female family members' (i.e., wives' or mothers') shoulders. As the preparation of kimchi requires skills, diligence, and work ethic, there is an old saying that "making good kimchi is the way to get a marriage (or a good husband)." Such cultural myths have continuously been influencing the expectations of women in Korean society, in particular, up until contemporary times. Building on that foundation, the examples illustrated in this chapter reaffirm a phenomenon in which traditional gender roles are consolidated.

In her analyses on the assumed ontological status of gender categories, Butler (1990, 2011) problematizes the binary roles of gender and explains that gender is performative, suggesting that gender is a phenomenon that is being produced all the time and reproduced continuously. In a similar vein, Arsel, Eraranta, and Moisander (2015) demystified that gender is rather a cultural category that is underpinned by socially constructed and contested assumptions and norms about identity and sexuality (1553). Drawing insight from these conceptualizations, in this chapter we examine the correlation between food and gender in Korea as well as the instrumental factors that heterosexual men and women consider in choosing a food or a restaurant. Our two interconnected inquiries include (1) how do globalization and habitus reinforce the gendered foodscape in contemporary Korean society? and (2) how do Korean consumers negotiate gender roles and gender identities through food consumption?

We first examine the sociohistorical development of Korean food culture and the surge of "K-Food" as a part of the *Hallyu* culture (or "Korean Wave") as a new cultural trend and a global phenomenon (Rhee and Otmazgin 2016). We draw a theoretical framework employing Lefebvre's (1991) conception of space to illustrate the interrelationship of gender, food, and space in the context of K-Food. By analyzing a variety of scholarly articles and literature on K-Food, Korean women, and men, we identified a relation between food and gender in Korean urban space. K-Food captures the center stage for local popular culture and offers varieties and choices for everyone. We also conducted two case studies on food retailers: (1) Paris Baguette for women and (2) drivers' restaurants for men. Our selection is based on the popularity of these dining outlets in Korea and their connection to urban Koreans' everyday life. Our findings reveal that Korean women tend to prefer eating Westernized food, while Korean men prefer traditional Korean food. The findings further reveal that women and men have preferences toward specific food items, and the space or setting of restaurants plays important consideration for women and men when they are picking a place for consuming food and socializing with peers. We explain this phenomenon by employing Butler's (1990) gender performativity. We argue that gender differences play a crucial role in the spatial setting of K-Food. Gender differences also renew the definitions and standards of "taste" by reinforcing the gender representations in contemporary Korean society.

The Sociohistorical Development of Korean Food Culture

Korean food is historically tied to Northeast Asian culture, which comprises many ethnic groups now referred to as Chinese, Mongolian, Korean, Japanese, and Russian (Siberian). According to previous historical studies (e.g., Kwon and Chung 2018; Lee, Moon, and Kim 2015; Lee and Kwon 2005) on the sociohistorical development of the Korean Peninsula, rice cultivation was a common practice during the Three Kingdoms Period (57 BC to AD 668) of Korea. Other agricultural products, such as soybeans, were introduced to the Korean diet by early settlers to maintain a stable protein source. Besides these farming practices, Korean people have long known about fermentation and preservation technologies (Kwon 2015; M.-O. Lee 2018). Soybean fermentation and rice-wine–making technologies were transferred to Japan during the Koryŏ dynasties (AD 935 to 1392). Iconic Korean food such as kimchi (salted and fermented cabbage and Korean radish) and *kochujang* (Korean red chili paste) are some of the products of Korean's advanced food-processing technologies.

Korean foodways experienced dramatic changes in the past century. After Korea opened its gates to Western countries in the 1870s, European diplomats, Russians, and missionaries from America introduced cakes and coffee to Korean people. However, the Japanese invasion (from 1910 to 1945) and the Korean War (from 1950 to 1953) created a major shortage of food, leading to starvation and forcing Korean people to adapt to milk products, such as milk porridge (Lee 1995). With the emergence of globalization, the rapid development of the food industry in the past four decades in Korea has significantly changed people's dietary practices. As a result, Korean people these days enjoy a variety of foods that are both evolved from their local culture and imported from other Asian and Western societies. At the same time, interestingly, Korean food (or K-Food) has occupied an important place in the global foodscape. For instance, kimchi has very much become the ambassador of Korean food. Bibimbap, a dish made with various vegetables, eggs, rice, and *kochujang*, has become one of the most popular Korean dishes globally (Hwang et al. 2018). Many of these Korean dishes possess symbolic meanings. For example, mixing the chili paste, rice, and vegetables all together while consuming bibimbap is similar to Koreans' emphasis on grouping and mingling with others. Sometimes people refer to Korean culture as a "bundled culture," in which Koreans tend to care about other people both in positive and negative ways. Koreans often use the term *chŏng* to highlight the importance of attaching to others.

In the early 2000s, the Korean Wave began to dominate East Asian media and popular culture. K-Food, in line with other *Hallyu* products, started gaining global consumers' attention. M.-O. Lee (2018) found that consumers' preference for K-drama, K-pop, *Hallyu* (or K-Wave), and K-friends had a positive influence on their choice, satisfaction level, and repurchase intention for Korean food. However, as Korean food becomes more globalized, Korea's younger generation appears to be losing its affinity toward local food. Therefore, the Korean government is raising the profile of traditional Korean food through an incremental media presence (Chung et al. 2016). Media, especially TV shows, introduce Korean food recipes and various traditional Korean food to target not only a national audience but also a global one; due to the popularity of K-pop and K-beauty, more international tourists are visiting Korea and experiencing Korean food while traveling. An interesting part of these Korean cooking shows is the chef. Unlike Korean traditional gender roles (where cooking was a women's job), most chefs on TV shows are men. For instance, according to Rhee (2019), cooking shows such as *Korean Cuisine*, *Three Meals a Day*, *Teacher Paek*, and *Home-Cooked Meals* are composed with male chefs as the main character. She also reports that the surge of male chefs and "foodies" in Korean TV cooking shows is ambivalent in terms of men's attentiveness to domestic affairs as well as the male dominance and gender hierarchy in society.

In Korea, food also reflects gender roles and gender hierarchy in society. In traditional Korean media, women were often portrayed as mothers or wives whose jobs were limited to the household (KOIS 2020). Since women's main role was housework, cooking and providing food were seen exclusively as women's functions. On the other hand, men were portrayed as workers or commanders responsible for taking care of the family. That narrative depicted men as food consumers who did not need to do housework (KOIS 2020). Gender roles began to change and consequentially gained solid momentum vis-à-vis altering gender norms and hierarchy in the late 1980s with the creation of an increasing number of opportunities for women's education (Rose 1993). In contrast to the restrictive roles of the past, today women are engaging in various business activities (KOIS 2020). These changes have led to different gender preferences toward food choices as women are no longer stuck in the "homemakers" role. Female professionals and entrepreneurs have become some of the possible career destinations for young women in Korea. The growing independence of women in Korea also represents emerging market segments in the food industry. In a recent survey of dietary behaviors in Korea, Lee and Lee (2018) found that while women prepared meals more often than men did, women also consumed more instant and frozen food than men. Their survey also found that men often associated eating by themselves with negative emotions such as "lonely" or "boring," while women related more positive emotions such as "free," "joy," and "my own time" in similar circumstances (Lee and Lee 2018, 531). All these observations indicate the differences in food consumption behavior among women and men in Korea.

In the past two decades, scholars have moved beyond the essentialist conceptualizations (i.e., food as a basic human necessity and a fundamental element of human culture), which derived from structuralist normativism, and moved on by adopting alternatives—in particular, a feminist point of view to problematize the market hegemony and male-dominant social hierarchy (Arsel, Eraranta, and Moisander 2015). These scholars undertake Butler's (1990, 2011) work as precursors: "[Gender categories are] the effects of institutions, practices, discourses with multiple and diffuse points of origin" rather than natural givens (179). For instance, several studies critically examine the gendered consumer identity projects, consumer cultural models, and consumption practices. Stalker (2016), for example, found that the increasing numbers of *gurume* manga and TV dramas (e.g., *Gourmet Samurai* and *Solitary Gourmet*) continuously engendered foodways in the past decades. He connected the rising popularity of *B-kyū gurume* (second-class gourmet) cuisine to the emerging "gourmet samurai" and "masculine loners" archetypes in Japan as a reflection of a steep decline in the marriage rate. These emergent archetypes represent new gourmet culture among single adults, particularly single men, in East Asia. In regards to Korea, while K-Food has connected with gender and many popular cultural activities in contemporary Korean society, there are limited studies focused on the interrelationship between food and space. The fast-growing business sector, the increasing variety of food and dining spaces, as well as the changing tastes among Korean women and men offer new opportunities to examine the intersectionality of food, gender, and space. Since behavior and space are mutually dependent, in this chapter, we seek to further explain the relationship of food and gender in a commercialized (i.e., public) space through the spatial theoretical lens.

Theoretical Foundation: Lefebvre's Theory of Space

In Lefebvre's (1991) spatial theory, space is produced by dynamic interrelationships between representations of space (i.e., maps, plans, models, and designs), representational space (i.e., ideas, imagination, theory, and visions), and practice (i.e., daily routine and urban reality) over time (41–52; 116) (figure 11.1). For "representations of space," Lefebvre refers to the infusion of dominant ideological, linguistic, and symbolic conceptions of space into the spatial practices and people's lived experiences. The ability to determine and represent spatial (un)desirability hinges on the symbolic power the dominant group can wield to affect discourses of "proper" space (Loveman 2005) and the resistance dissenters pose to the group's hegemony.

For "representational space," Lefebvre (1991) refers to the directly lived space of everyday life. Soja (1999) interprets such spaces as "spaces in the margins of hegemonic discourses, social spaces carved in the interstices of institutions and the chinks and cracks of the power-knowledge apparatus" (272–273). Duncan (1996) argues that this space allows the best observations of the effects

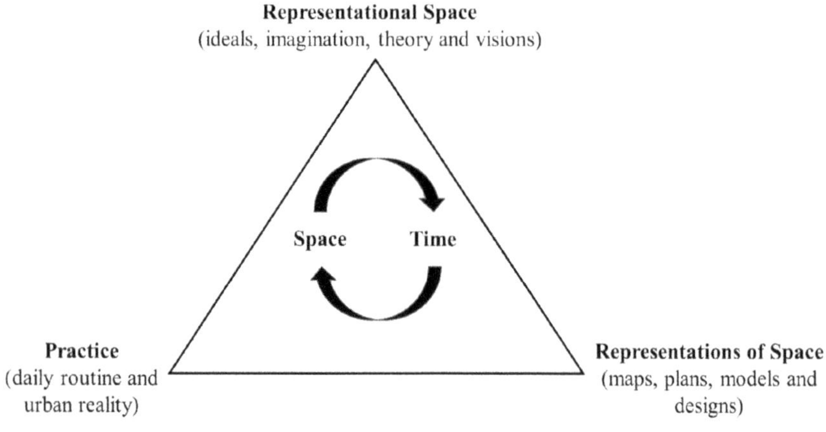

Figure 11.1 Lefebvre's (1991) Spatial Theory. *Source*: Created by Authors.

of power relationships as the banality of everyday life renders representational space taken for granted and invisible.

The last component of Lefebvre's spatial theory, "spatial practices," refers to how people orient themselves geographically through their perceptions of space, such as the ways they move around places and where they want to go or avoid (Lefebvre 1991). Soja (1999) suggests that these spatially observable practices are "the directly experienced world of empirically measurable and mappable phenomena" (265). In other words, individuals' performance and behavior show how dominant discourses influence habitus formation and reflect how individuals perceive and react to the social world around them (see also Bourdieu 1977).

In the past decades, urban studies and consumer researchers have adopted the spatial theory to elaborate new phenomena such as urban regeneration, urban revitalization, experiential consumption, and the development of retailscape (Belk and Costa 1998; Castilhos, Dolbec, and Veresiu 2017; Karababa and Ger 2011; Kozinets 2002; Kozinets et al. 2004; Peñaloza 2000, 2001). Oldenburg (1989, 2001), for instance, uses the term "third places" to describe the role of pubs, cafés, and coffeehouses in shaping citizens' everyday lives and the community's social vitality. For him, third places serve as the transition spaces between the "first place" (home) and the "second place" (workplace) in which citizens can develop new social spheres and enjoy "work-free" (free from "work" and "housework") time and space.

In addition to urban geographers, consumer researchers also explore market dynamics from various dimensions of spatiality. Jessop, Brenner, and Jones (2008) associated the market systems with four dominant dimensions of space (place, territory, scale, and network). These dimensions showcase the variations of the examination of the spatial relationship between consumers and market agents in consumer society. Previous works on consumer culture also addressed such spatial relationships. Belk and Costa's (1998) study on the mountain men myth featuring the Rocky Mountain American West during the fur-trade rendezvous held in the first half of the nineteenth century featured the market-constructed fantasy associated with time and space. Spatial analysis in consumer research also highlights the temporality of space and consumer experience. Peñaloza (2000, 2001), for instance, presents how rodeo shows reinforce the American West culture. Kozinets's (2002) work on the Burning Man Festival also connects the notion of "escape" with the temporal delineation from consumers' everyday lives. Space theory also applies to more permanent and retail settings. In their sociohistorical analysis of early modern Ottoman coffeehouses, Karababa and Ger (2011) found that retail spaces such as coffeehouses and public dining settings have a long history in shaping consumer subjectivity. Kozinets et al.'s (2004) ethnographic engagement with the ESPN Zone in Chicago presents how retail spectacle shapes consumption experience and consumer agency. All these consumption sites featured how market agents constructed site-specific consumer experience.

At the same time, gendered consumption spaces demand empirical exploration (Sredl 2018) as there are limited studies to contextualize the intersectionality of space, food, and gender. Feminist scholars, for example, Ardener (1981), Gregory (1986), and Rose (1993), critique that traditional spatial structures produce and reproduce masculinist societies through which the "social map" of patriarchy has been translated into "ground rules" of spatial behavior. These scholars interpret the division between public space and private space as one of the most oppressive aspects of everyday life. As Gregory puts it, "Spatial structure [was] seen not merely as an arena *in which* social life unfolds but as a medium *through which* social life is produced and reproduced" (Gregory 1986, 451) (Emphasis in original). Butler (1990, 2011) interprets this as a phenomenon that produces a series of effects that consolidate an impression, for example, being a man, being a woman. These critiques provide a powerful tool to contextualize the findings as illustrated through our case studies. Although Gillian Rose mainly paralleled the gender binary with the distinction between the domestic and public spaces, our chapter employs the theory of space to address the interactions of food and gender in commercialized space in contemporary South Korea.

Illustrative Case Analyses

To better understand the construction of a gendered foodscape, we employ the qualitative case study approach (Yin 2003) to understand how food retailers construct a gendered dining experience and foodways as a strategy to develop competitive advantages and unique positions in the K-Food market. We purposely selected Paris Baguette and drivers' restaurants as the core cases for our comparative case analysis (table 11.1).

Our data include materials obtained from food retailers' official websites, online blogs, and news articles associated with the retailers' operations; commentaries and reports from business analysts; and academic literature. To effectively organize the collected data, two authors connect key insights with the spatial theoretical framework (figure 11.1). The authors also compare and contrast their observations and further discuss strategies for interpretation.

Case 1: Paris Baguette

Paris Baguette is a nationwide bakery franchise with more than 3,000 stores in Korea. Since its first store launched in Seoul's Gwanghwamun district in 1988, the franchise has offered freshly baked bread and high-end bakery products to consumers and has become very popular among Koreans. Over the years, Paris

Table 11.1 Summary of the Qualitative Cases: Paris Baguette and Drivers' Restaurants in Korea

	Paris Baguette	*Drivers' Restaurants (*Kisa sikdang*)*
Description	An international bakery specializing in French-inspired goods	Restaurants serving traditional or authentic Korean food (soups, stews, grilled meat)
Food Served	Baked goods (cakes, pastries, sandwiches), salads, coffee/tea, bottled beverages	Traditional Korean rice and soup-based dishes such as *kukbap*, usually served in large portions at affordable/reasonable prices
Spatial Settings	Elegant, Westernized decor, feminine	Simple, convenience-oriented, food-court style
Target Customers	Women, particularly housewives with school-aged children	Men, particularly "drivers" (e.g., taxi drivers, truck drivers) or salesmen who need to constantly travel around the city or regions for business

Baguette has outperformed many globally known franchises and maintained the number one position among bakery franchises in the Korean market since 1997 (Kim 2015). In her new study, H.-W. Kim (2019) shares that among all bakeries and burger brands, Koreans spent the most at Paris Baguette and Paris Croissant, which is the parent organization of Paris Baguette. In the year 2019, Koreans spent approximately 159 billion Korean won (US$134 million) at Paris Baguette and Paris Croissant, and McDonald's ranked second highest with 59.7 billion Korean won (US$50 million).

Paris Baguette emphasizes "quality first," and this core value has been repeatedly highlighted by the founder, Hur Young-in, whose father owned a small bakery in the mid-twentieth century:

> We bake millions of loaves of bread, but a customer may judge us from trying one loaf of our bread. If that one loaf tastes bad, *she* may think the same of all our bread. (Kim 2015, 15, emphasis mine)

Paris Baguette also keeps innovating new bakery items such as toast bread, sandwich bread, Korean wheat bread, and rice bread to satisfy consumers' diversified tastes (Kim 2015). Most of the patrons of this high-end bakery franchise are women: middle-class or middle-upper-class housewives, female professionals, and young women in particular. For middle-class or middle-upper-class housewives, such a space enables them to spend time with other housewives after sending children to day care or school and to share, learn, and exchange information with each other, for example, in regards to children's education. Having said that, the time these housewives spend at Paris Baguette is not entirely considered "leisure time." In fact, their time at Paris Baguette has become an important site for elaborating and performing their domestic labor in a public space. This example illustrates how the space at Paris Baguette conforms to specific gender performativity.

Interestingly, Paris Baguette launched a number of customer engagement programs to better understand its core customers' tastes and desires. Since 2000, the bakery franchise has run the "Séance"[1] and "Séance Jeunesses" customer monitoring programs to engage housewives aged between twenty-five and forty-five, as well as undergraduate and graduate female students aged between nineteen and twenty-eight, to gauge opinions about the quality of their products and services. The same initiative also invited participants to evaluate new products' tastes, designs, and prices (Kim 2015). All these examples exhibit gendering in a commercialized (i.e., public) space through strategic target marketing.

In addition to the new product development and customer monitoring programs, Paris Baguette has been very active in the digital space. On their official website (www.paris.co.kr), the bakery franchise employs mostly female models in their advertising videos for new products (i.e., whipped-cream cakes), festivals, and cooking shows. It is clear that the majority of these videos target homemakers that have school-aged children. The female actors featured in these videos, to some extent, appear as the "ideal housewife" archetype for Korean women, and they represent the central message of Paris Baguette's marketing campaign: Korean moms or housewives should purchase its tasty, healthy, and high-quality baked goods for the family. These examples reinforce gendering in a commercialized (i.e., public) space (figure 11.2).

Paris Baguette's Westernized representations matter for many Korean women as they could also indicate their elevated social status. It is very common to find middle-aged women in Paris Baguette stores enjoying hot beverages and baked goods or desserts. The atmosphere and other related nuances and aesthetics add to the expectations of "women-only" space. Oldenburg (2001) considers Paris Baguette to fit the definition of a "third space" for Korean women after their home and family. In many cases, most Korean women prefer restaurants with comfortable and quiet spaces, and middle-class women—or middle-class Korean moms, in particular—prefer having afternoon tea in elegant, luxurious places where they can stay for a long time. Thus, Paris Baguette has become a great fit for them. According to Lee and Lee (2018), Korean women spend more time on eating when they are with others than men do, which could indicate why women consider not only the taste of the food but also the restaurant space when choosing food. Paris Baguette is one of those places that offers an ambient environment for housewives, female professionals, and young women enjoying a "female-only" (or "female-dominant") time and space in the busy and highly competitive urban Korean society. These

Figure 11.2 Bakery Goods in Paris Baguette. *Source*: Image by Somin Lee.

examples emphasize "women's space" away from domestic space (e.g., home, kitchen) as it materializes in a commercialized (i.e., public) space (figure 11.3).

The majority of Paris Baguette clients are women, and this could create an awkward atmosphere for men who go to these outlets. The brand is also actively generating an image of the shop as a place for mothers and female professionals. Paris Baguette's advertising videos on their website display moms as houseworkers who take care of family meals. One video shows a mom going to Paris Baguette to buy bread for her family; the same production has women as tellers and chefs. Compared to a typical Korean traditional breakfast outlet, which serves rice, soup, and side dishes, the contemporary breakfast style in Korea has changed to be less restricted and with more variety. A mom's traditional roles have changed a lot in the past decades in Korea; however, some elements still remain. Instead of cooking and making traditional food such as kimchi at home, these moms are anticipated to purchase and prepare good-quality food for the family on a daily basis. In other words, homemakers (or

Figure 11.3 Female Patrons Hanging Out at Paris Baguette. *Source*: Image by Somin Lee.

mothers) are the ones taking care of the family's meals and nutrition, which are still tied to traditional expectations of women in Korea.

In addition to the "moms" category, female working professionals and young women are also target customers for Paris Baguette. In recent years, the bakery franchise has engaged various female professions such as skateboarders, DJs, florists, drummers, food stylists, and shoemakers in their ambassador program. These female professionals are mostly considered to be entrepreneurs or members of the trendsetting middle class. As many young Korean women have started joining the workforce, Paris Baguette has moved beyond its "housewives' brand" image and actively draws attention from professional and young women.

To some extent, Paris Baguette shows its intention to empower Korean women to further explore and pursue their careers and dreams. While DJing, skateboarding, and drumming are often known as "male" professions in Korea, the bakery franchise intentionally picks female DJs, skateboarders, and drummers as their promotional ambassadors. For instance, since skateboarding became a popular trend in Korea, Paris Baguette has featured a female skateboarder to show women can also be passionate about their dreams and achieve their desired jobs. This example illustrates how Paris Baguette draws the interest of the younger women market segment by symbolizing overcoming traditional gender norms as well as by emphasizing that the "women's space" away from domestic space marks freedom and new opportunities. These empowering acts, gestures, and interpretations seek to intrigue and inspire independent and professional women to pursue their dreams and act against gender norms.

Figure 11.4 Interior of Paris Baguette. *Source*: Image by Somin Lee.

In summary, Paris Baguette serves as an exemplar of a market-constructed female space. The bakery franchise invests tremendous resources in redefining female identities and roles in South Korea. Not surprisingly, Paris Baguette continues to gain popularity among female customers by paying special attention to its interior design and dining atmosphere. The "Western" (or "French-style") interiors and atmosphere visually differentiate the bakery from traditional Korean bakeries as well as many American fast-food chains. The main interior colors are blue and white, and bread is displayed in the middle of the store (figure 11.4). The display of the bakery items and other products become a representation of Western/European cultures and lifestyle. The emphasis on an elegant lifestyle and Westernized taste echoes new opportunities in the lives of Korean women presented by Western life (figure 11.5).

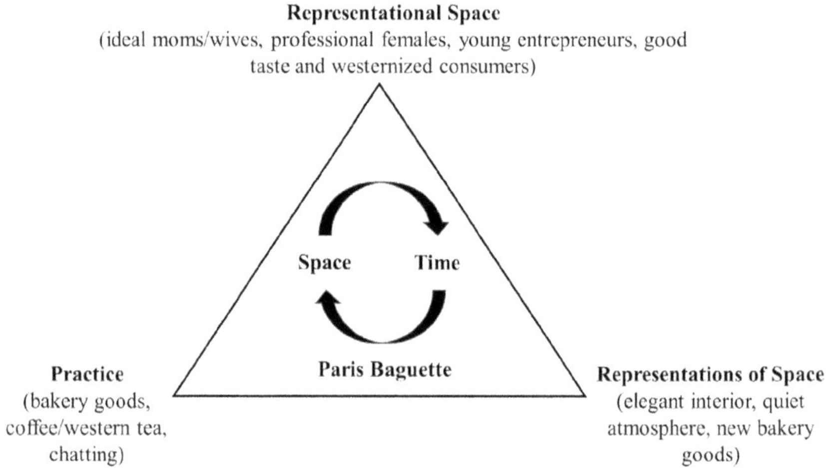

Figure 11.5 Paris Baguette and the Construction of "Female Space." *Source*: Created by Authors.

Case 2: Drivers' Restaurants (*Kisa sikdang*)

Professional drivers, particularly taxi drivers, are one of the media-dominant representations of working-class men in Korea. As one example, a recent Korean film, *A Taxi Driver* (released in 2017), rescreened the historical Gwangju Uprising featuring an ordinary male citizen and showed what a typical taxi driver's life was like in Korea. The Oscar-nominated film *Parasite* (2019) also brought the globe's attention to the grassroots Korean's everyday life. Unlike the hyperreal imageries that *Hallyu* culture often portrays, the increasing public interest in the "ordinary" Korean lifestyle gave opportunities to many grassroots operations.

Taxi drivers in Korea are known to work long hours (up to fourteen to fifteen hours a day) and receive relatively low wages (H. Kim 2019). At the same time, the taxi industry is strong, with over 100,000 drivers in Seoul alone. In our second case, "drivers' restaurants" refers to restaurants drawing in taxi drivers or other commercial drivers and workers (i.e., sales representatives) who travel in and around cities for business. Many of these restaurants serve traditional Korean dishes, like *kukbap* ("kuk" means soup and "bap" refers to rice) or bibimbap, and are usually designed to serve drivers who have limited flexibility and short breaks during the day. The "all-in-one" set meal is, therefore, essential for drivers to refresh themselves with fast and filling foods at an affordable rate. Most of the restaurants offer unlimited refills of rice, banchan, and instant coffee to patrons (Kim 2020). Many of the drivers' restaurants are located next to highway exits or in high-traffic areas. These restaurants often have big parking lots, where drivers have easy access and can dine in within a short period.

Since the majority of taxi and bus drivers in Korea are men, most of the customers in drivers' restaurants are men. The interiors of drivers' restaurants are traditional and simple with limited or no elegant decoration (figure 11.6).

Figure 11.6 Deokpyeong Beef Kukbap: A Well-Known Drivers' Restaurant in Korea. *Source*: Image by Somin Lee.

The food is inexpensive for drivers and mostly costs below 10,000 won (US$7) (figure 11.7). Most of their servings are for one person.

Figure 11.7 Food Items Served at Typical Drivers' Restaurant. *Source*: Image by Somin Lee.

In the past decades, the increasing popularity of K-drama and K-pop made drivers' restaurants a stereotypical "male space" in Korea. The popular Korean reality show *Running Man* (SBS) featured a drivers' restaurant in one episode (Ep.262) in 2016. The episode showcased different traditional dishes and illustrated the everyday lives of drivers and working-class men in Korea. Drivers' restaurants are commonly perceived as spaces for drivers to eat, relax, and gather with other drivers to take a break (figure 11.8). This sociospatial connection echoes a phenomenon that produces and reproduces a consolidated male impression.

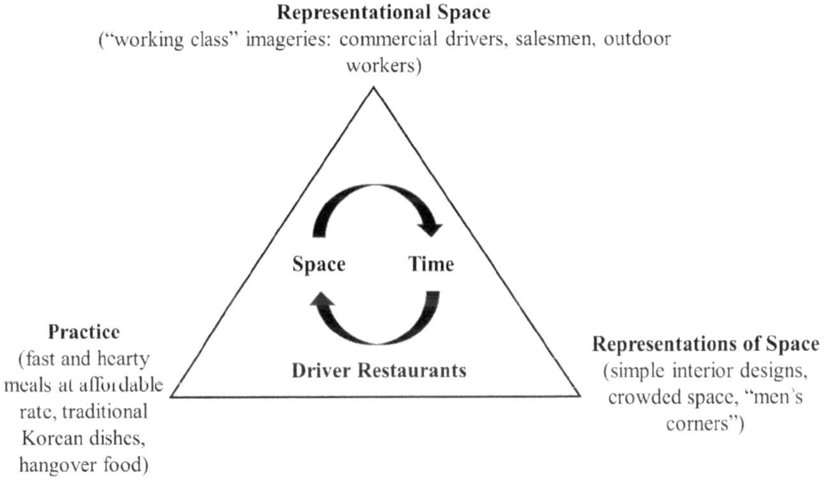

Figure 11.8 Drivers' Restaurants and the Construction of Male-Space. *Source*: Created by Authors.

Food served in drivers' restaurants plays a vital role in defining the working-class male imagery in contemporary Korean society. As mentioned earlier, taxi drivers and other commercial drivers do not receive a high salary even though many work long hours. Drivers' restaurants offer affordable food to support such grassroots communities. Eventually, these dining spaces became "men's corners" as most commercial drivers are men in South Korea.

In this "men-only" space, the drivers' restaurants also offer traditional "comfort foods" such as *kukbap* for their busy customers. *Kukbap* was historically known as peasant laborers' food in premodern Korea and is also considered a men's dish because most peasant laborers were men. Moreover, in the old days, Korean peasant laborers consumed *kukbap* to regain energy so that they could return to work after the meal. Unlike other traditional Korean meals that normally include a number of side dishes, *kukbap* includes both soup and rice in the same pot, which enables diners to consume their meals faster during their breaks.

Kukbap (figure 11.9), however, has changed its meaning dramatically in recent years. The dish is now considered "hangover" food as most Korean men instinctively crave *haejangguk*, a hot pot of soup, in order to overcome their hangovers. Most drivers' restaurants open early in the morning or remain open twenty-four hours a day. Korean men come to eat *kukbap* in the early morning to soothe their stomachs or come at night to have *kukbap* with a drink after work. *Kukbap*, therefore, is a representation of Korean men's practice.

Figure 11.9 ***Kukbap.*** *Source*: Image by Somin Lee.

Compared to women who have afternoon tea in Paris Baguette after sending their children to school, Korean men look for *kukbap* after a late night's work or after consuming alcohol. Since *kukbap* is also one of the traditional Korean foods, Korean men crave it as their comfort food (*Korea Herald* 2016). The division of labor across gender boundaries had been quite rigid in Korea until the late twentieth century: women were not encouraged to work outside the home while men worked outside and took care of their families. That part of the patriarchal mindset still persists in Korean male psyches, as in many cases men have the responsibility to earn enough to keep their families nourished and safe. Due to this mindset, men often worked long hours outside their homes and consumed food based on what is available while working. In many cases, *kukbap* fulfilled their hunger and gave the overworked Korean men a taste of homemade food. *Kukbap*, in this sense, is more than a meal because it symbolizes an embedded cultural feature that confirms men to be masculine and productive.

Today's Korean men like to reproduce that phenomenon to consolidate their masculinity in a commercialized public space.

Discussion: Market Construction of a Gendered Foodscape

For Lefebvre, (social) space is a (social) product (Schmid 2008, 28). The two cases show how the new food options intersect with the traditional foodways in Korea under the K-Food phenomenon. While Korean TV dramas often feature food and restaurants, now food marketers, restaurant brands, and food producers are actively redefining the representations of K-Food. Gender, as shown in our case analyses, intersects with food consumption practices where gendered lifestyles and gendered spaces have developed in this ever-diversifying Korean foodscape. Paris Baguette reconfigures the "female space" in urban Korea. Its Western food culture and European decor not only create a Westernized atmosphere for its patrons but also create a "third space" for women where they can comfortably enjoy time with their female friends over coffee or tea as well as Western-style baked goods. On the contrary, the drivers' restaurants create a "man cave" for Korean working men. The roadside restaurants not only provide quick access to comfort foods like *kukbap* but also create a "time-off" space for busy working professionals. Men's evident preference of spicy and filling food as well as women's preference for creamy food also echoes Bruno's (2017) research findings: "Creamy and greasy food helps women get rid of stress while spicy and cheap food in ample quantities and strong drinks are the best solution for men to enjoy" (116). Bruno's study also highlights that women are more open to experimenting with unknown food and foreign food than men and older people, who prefer traditional food and more nutritious food.

Moreover, Korean women and men differ in regards to how they pick a restaurant. Not only the taste of the food but also the environment, atmosphere, and space matter for women when choosing restaurants. Interiors of Westernized restaurants are mostly sophisticated and refined, and decorated with luxury furniture, while the interiors of drivers' restaurants are very traditional and not close to elegance.

The two cases in this chapter present how food retailers and marketers strategically construct and reinforce gender roles and gender identities through the new foodscape in Korea (figure 11.10). Market segmentation and market targeting are typical marketing strategies that brands employ to define their positions in the mass market. Gender is often used in market segmentation as it is the most visible and easy-to-apply dimension. In Korea, gender is also closely connected to the ever-growing *Hallyu* phenomena such as K-beauty and K-fashion (Li, Min, and Lee 2021). The commodification of K-Food, in this context, also adopts gendered strategies by creating different gendered ideals that tie into particular food preferences and consumption practices. The

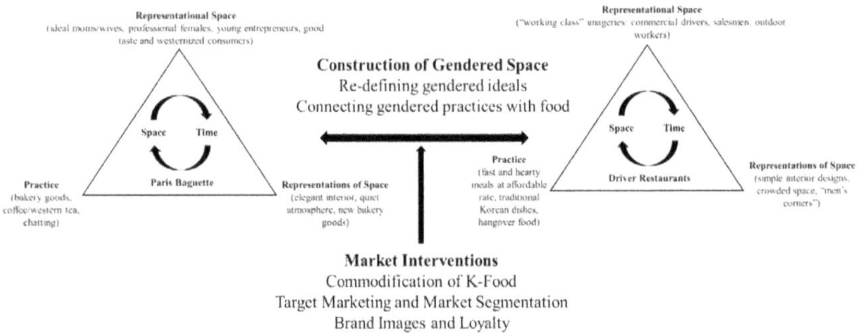

Figure 11.10 Market Construction of a Gendered Foodscape. *Source*: Created by Authors.

two food service providers in our case studies also reinforce the distinction by genderizing the dining space and experience.

CONCLUSION

Gender is not a biologically fixed category (Butler 2004). Rather, it is performed and socially constructed through everyday enactments (Varman, Goswani, and Vijay 2018, 934). This chapter analyzed the market-constructed gendered differences through the lens of Lefebvrian spatiality and interpretations of a few feminist scholars in the context of food consumption. The spatial trio we presented enables researchers to critically examine the construction of gendered space through its discourses (representation of space), physical construction and expression (representational space), and spatial practices. Korean foodways have experienced dramatic changes over the past two decades. With the popularity of *Hallyu* and the ever-growing K-pop economy, Koreans are now exposed to a diversity of choices in the food marketspace. The two cases presented in this chapter illustrate the gendered differences in food consumption preferences and behavior. To some extent, our chapter reported that the market agents continue to reinforce the "men earn the living, and women take care of the house and children" ideology (Sorenson 2020) even though Paris Baguette has also attempted to empower young women. This echoes a critique made by Rose (1993) that traditional spatial structures produce and reproduce masculinist societies and the "social map" of patriarchy continues to translate into "ground rules" of spatial behavior.

The contribution of this chapter is threefold. First, our comparative case studies provide new angles to explore the intersection of gender, food, and space in contemporary Korean society. Second, the connection between

Westernized and traditional food consumption preferences among women and men also presents an interesting angle to explore the reversal of cultural heritage between two genders. Last but not least, our study on K-Food presents the role of the market in reconfiguring the gender and food culture in Korea. Future study could further explore how the transformation of K-Food influences nonlocal consumers' perception of Korean foodways. Cross-cultural comparison would also allow researchers to further understand how the cultural context influences gender and food interactions. In conclusion, we hope that this chapter can spearhead further inquiries into the gendered foodways in contemporary East Asia. Our study on K-Food sheds light for academic researchers regarding the role of the market in shaping and reshaping representations of gender and the representations of places based on Lefebvre's theory of space.

NOTE

1. Séance means "meeting" in French (Kim 2015).

REFERENCES

Ardener, S. 1981. "Ground Rules and Spatial Maps for Women: An Introduction." In *Women and Space: Ground Rules and Social Maps*, edited by S. Ardener, 11–34. London: Croom Helm.

Arsel, Z., K. Eraranta, and J. Moisander. 2015. "Introduction: Theorising Gender and Gendering Theory in Marketing and Consumer Research." *Journal of Marketing Management* 31 (15–16): 1553–1558.

Belk, R. W., and J. A. Costa. 1998. "The Mountain Man Myth: A Contemporary Consuming Fantasy." *Journal of Consumer Research* 25(3): 218–240.

Bourdieu, P. 1977. *Outline of a Theory of Practice*. Cambridge: Cambridge University Press.

———. 1984. *Distinction: A Social Critique of the Judgement of Taste*. Cambridge, MA: Harvard University Press.

Bruno, A. L. 2017. "Italian Food Suits Korean Women." *Cultural International Journal of Philosophy of Culture and Axiology* 14 (1): 111–119.

Butler, J. 1990. *Gender Trouble: Feminism and the Subversion of Identity*. New York: Routledge.

———. 2004. *Undoing Gender*. New York: Routledge.

———. 2011. "Judith Butler: Your Behavior Creates Your Gender | Big Think." https://bigthink.com/videos/your-behavior-creates-your-gender.

Castilhos, R. B., P.-Y. Dolbec, and E. Veresiu. 2017. "Introducing a Spatial Perspective to Analyze Market Dynamics." *Marketing Theory* 17 (1): 9–29.

Chung, H.-K., H. Y. Yang, D. Shin, and K. R. Chung. 2016. "Aesthetics of Korean Foods: The Symbol of Korean Culture." *Journal of Ethnic Foods* 3 (3): 178–188.

Duncan, N. (Ed.) 1996. *Bodyspace: Destabilizing Geographies of Gender and Sexuality*. London: Routledge.

Gregory, D. 1986. "Spatial Structure." In *The Dictionary of Human Geography*, edited by R. J. Johnston et al., 451. Oxford: Blackwell.

Hwang, J., S. Kim, J. Y. Choe, and C.-H. Chung. 2018. "Exploration of the Successful Glocalization of Ethnic Food: A Case of Korean Food." *International Journal of Contemporary Hospitality Management* 30 (12): 3656–3676.

Jessop, B., N. Brenner, and M. Jones. 2008. "Theorizing Sociospatial Relations." *Environment and Planning D: Society and Space* 26 (3): 389–401.

Karababa, E., and Ger, G. 2011. "Early Modern Ottoman Coffeehouse Culture and the Formation of the Consumer Subject." *Journal of Consumer Research* 37 (5): 737–760.

Kim, H. 2019. "P.1.17 Working Time, Smoking, and Caffeine Intake by Working Type of Taxi Drivers in Korea." *Occupational and Environmental Medicine* 76 (Suppl 1): A81–A82.

Kim, H.-W. 2019. "Paris Baguette, '1587 Billion Won' Overwhelmingly Topped by Card Payment for Pastry and Bakery in March" (P'ari baget'ŭ, 3wŏl Chekwajeppang k'ad ŭ kyŏlje aptojŏk 1 wi '1587 ŏk'). *Updown News*, April 16. http://www.updownnews.co.kr/news/articleView.html?idxno=201889.

Kim, K. 2015. "What Made a Bakery Franchise No. 1 in Korea? The Story of Paris Baguette and its Success Factors." *Journal of Marketing Thought* 2 (1): 14–26.

Kim, V. 2020. "Eat Where Seoul's Cab Drivers Eat. It's Where the Real Lives and Flavors Are." *Los Angeles Times*, August 31. https://www.latimes.com/world-nation/story/2020-08-31/eat-where-seouls-cab-drivers-eat-its-where-the-real-lives-and-flavors-are.

Korea Herald 2016. "Gukbap, a Warm Pot of Consolation for the Weary." *Korea Herald*, September 2. http://www.koreaherald.com/view.php?ud=20160901000994.

Korean Overseas Information Services (KOIS). 2020. *Women's Role in Contemporary Korea*. New York: Center for Global Education. https://asiasociety.org/education/womens-role-contemporary-korea.

Kozinets, R. V. 2002. "Can Consumers Escape the Market? Emancipatory Illuminations from Burning Man." *Journal of Consumer Research* 29 (1): 20–38.

Kozinets, R. V., J. F. Sherry, D. Storm, A. Duhachek, K. Nuttavuthisit, and B. DeBerry-Spence. 2004. "Ludic Agency and Retail Spectacle." *Journal of Consumer Research* 31 (3): 658–672.

Kwon, D. Y. 2015. "What Is Ethnic Food?" *Journal of Ethnic Foods* 2: 91.

Kwon, D. Y., and K. R. Chung. 2018. "Korean Diets and Their Tastes." In *Korean Functional Foods: Composition, Processing and Health Benefits*, edited by K.-Y. Park, D. Y. Kwon, K. W. Lee, and S. Park, 23–42. Boca Raton, FL: CRC Press.

Lee, C. H. 1995. "Changes in the Dietary Patterns, Health, and Nutritional Status of Koreans during the Last Century." *Korean and Korean American Studies Bulletin* 6: 32–47.

———. 2018. "Korean Foods—History, Culture, and Characteristics." In *Korean Functional Foods: Composition, Processing and Health Benefits*, edited by K.-Y. Park, D. Y. Kwon, K. W. Lee, and S. Park, 1–21. Boca Raton, FL: CRC Press.

Lee, C. H., and T. W. Kwon. 2005. "History of Soybean Utilization." In *Soybean*, edited by Soy-world Museum Construction Committee, 3–44. Seoul: Korea University Press.

Lee, C. H., H. P. Moon, and Y. T. Kim. 2015. *Korean Unification and Food Security*. Seoul: Sikanyeon Publishing.

Lee, E. J., and K.-R. Lee. 2018. "Comparison of Solo Eating Perception and Dietary Behaviors According to Gender in the Seoul and Gyonggi-do Regions." *Journal of Korean Society and Food Culture* 33 (6): 531–542.

Lee, M.-O. 2018. "A Study on the Effects of K-Wave, K-Drama, K-Pop and K-Friend Preference on Korean Food Preference, Satisfaction and Repurchase Intention of International Students in Korea—Focusing on Busan Area." *Journal of Korean Society and Food Culture* 33 (6): 501–511.

Lee, S. 2018. "The Relationship between Coping Style for Stress and Emotional Eating Behavior by Gender Difference." *Journal of Korean Society and Food Culture* 33 (1): 11–17.

Lefebvre, H. 1991. *The Production of Space*. Oxford: Blackwell.

Li, E. P. H., H. J. Min, and S. Lee. 2021. "Soft Power and Nation Rebranding: The Transformation of Korean National Identity through Cosmetic Surgery Tourism." *International Marketing Review* 38 (1): 141–162.

Loveman, M. 2005. "The Modern State and the Primitive Accumulation of Symbolic Power." *American Journal of Sociology* 110 (6): 1651–1683.

Messerlin, P. A., and W. Shin. 2017. "The Success of K-pop." *Asian Journal of Social Science* 45 (4–5): 409–439.

Oldenburg, R. 1989. *The Great Good Place: Cafés, Coffee Shops, Community Centers, Beauty Parlors, General Stores, Bars, Hangouts, and How They Get You through the Day*, 1st ed. New York: Paragon House.

———. 2001. *Celebrating the Third Place: Inspiring Stories about the "Great Good Places" at the Heart of our Communities*. New York: Marlowe & Co.

Peñaloza, L. 2000. "The Commodification of the American West: Marketers' Production of Cultural Meanings at the Trade Show." *Journal of Marketing* 64 (4): 82–109.

———. 2001. "Consuming the American West: Animating Cultural Meaning and Memory at a Stock Show and Rodeo." *Journal of Consumer Research* 28 (3): 369–398.

Rhee, J. 2019. "Gender Politics in Food Escape: Korean Masculinity in TV Cooking Shows in South Korea." *Journal of Popular Film and Television* 47 (1): 56–64.

Rhee, J., and N. Otmazgin. 2016. "Expanding Transnational Dialogue in Asia through Hallyu." *The Asia-Pacific Journal—Japan Focus* 14 (7): 1–6.

Rose, G. 1993. *Feminism and Geography—The Limits of Geographical Knowledge*. Cambridge: Polity Press.

Schmid, C. 2008. "Henri Lefebvre's Theory of the Production of Space: Towards a Three-Dimensional Dialectic." In *Space, Difference, Everyday Life: Reading Henri*

Lefebvre, edited by K. Goonewardena, S. Kipfer, R. Milgram, and C. Schmid, 27–45. New York: Routledge.

Soja, E. 1999. "Thirdspace: Expanding the Scope of the Geographical Imagination." In *Human Geography Today*, edited by D. Massey, J. Allen, and P. Sarre, 260–278. Cambridge: Polity Press.

Sorenson, C. W. 2020. *The Value and Meaning of the Korean Family*. New York: Center for Global Education. https://asiasociety.org/education/value-and-meaning-korean-family.

Sredl, K. C. 2018. "Gendered Market Subjectivity: Autonomy, Privilege, and Emotional Subjectivity in Normalizing Post-socialist Neoliberal Ideology." *Consumption Markets & Culture* 21 (6): 532–553.

Stalker, N. K. 2016. "Gourmet Samurai." *Gastronomica* 16 (4): 78–90.

Varman, R., P. Goswani, and D. Vijay. 2018. "The Precarity of Respectable Consumption: Normalising Sexual Violence against Women." *Journal of Marketing Management* 34 (11–12): 932–964.

Waldeck, Y. 2020. "South Korea's Music Industry—Statistics & Facts." *Statista*, August 31. https://www.statista.com/topics/5098/music-industry-in-south-korea.

Yin, R. K. 2003. *Case Study Research: Design and Methods*, 3rd ed. Thousand Oaks, CA: Sage Publications.

Yoon, K. 2019. "Transnational Fandom in the Making: K-pop Fans in Vancouver." *The International Communication Gazette* 81 (2): 176–192.

Chapter 12

Grace Chu

Chinese Cooking at the Crossroad of Ethnicization and Emplacement

Violetta Ravagnoli

ABSTRACT

This chapter analyzes the life of Grace Zia Chu, a renowned Chinese American chef and teacher. Grace Chu's life evolved at the intersection between a modernizing China, a globalizing world, and a new life in America. Madame Chu was a teacher of physical education in the early stages of her career and of Chinese cooking later in life. An exploration of her mobile life and a perusal of her two cookbooks will exhibit the powerful role of this translocal woman who moved from Shanghai to Boston, from D.C. to New York City, while also traveling all over the world. By following Grace's life from her school years to her retirement, this chapter demonstrates how Grace capitalized on the craft of food-making in the United States to survive, to consciously build her identity as a Chinese diasporic woman, and to thrive as a representative of Chinese culture by means of her culinary teaching skills.

INTRODUCTION

"Chinese cooking was invented in 1920 in Wellesley, Massachusetts. I know, because I invented it," declared Grace Zia Chu in a 1983 interview for the *Alumnae Magazine* of her alma mater, Wellesley College. Of course, that was far from the truth as Chinese cuisine is regarded among the most ancient and sophisticated in the world. Why, then, did Madame Chu make such a bold declaration?

Grace is most known for her cookbook, *The Pleasure of Chinese Cooking*, first published in 1962 by Simon and Schuster, but her achievements go well beyond food preparation. Starting in the 1950s, Madame Chu worked as a teacher of Chinese cooking at the Cooking Institute of America in New York City, among other venues. She used to tell her students, "I have a missionary spirit about Chinese cooking," as "I want you to become thoroughly absorbed with Chinese culture, history, and philosophy as it relates to food." Hence, she positioned herself as a cultural mediator and a pioneer of Chinese cookery in America.

This chapter is divided into five sections, each chronicling different moments of Grace's life in relation to food, identity, home, and the adopted land. By following Grace's life from her school years to her retirement, this chapter wishes to emphasize Grace's agency in shaping her diasporic identity. She capitalized on the craft of food-making in the United States to survive, and she thrived as a representative of Chinese culture through her culinary teaching skills.

Grace's Life: First Act

Grace was born on April 23, 1899, and grew up during the tumultuous years that witnessed the fall of the Qing empire in 1911 and the birth of the Republic of China. She was the first of nine siblings from a wealthy family of urbanites, employed as educators and editors in the intellectually stimulating years of the early twentieth century. Her family highly valued education; therefore, despite the traditional restrictions to women's schooling, Grace was sent to Shanghai to join the student body of the McTyeire School, an all-girl Christian private institution. Her parents died when she was still in high school, and when she was offered the possibility to study in America, she welcomed it with open arms. Therefore, in 1920, at the age of twenty-one, Grace departed for Massachusetts to start her undergraduate degree at Wellesley College, leaving behind a country in the midst of political, social, and ideological turmoil.

These years were shaped by the spirit of the May Fourth Movement,[1] which animated discussions among educated youth about democracy and women's liberation, nationalism, and socialism; critiqued the traditional ways of the empire; and inspired an enthusiastic cohort of students to urge the creation of new institutions, especially modern hospitals and schools, modeled on the Western ones. Weili Ye, in her study of late Qing female students living abroad (*nü liuxueshen* 女留学生), created three groups. The first was made of women linked to missionary schools who went abroad before the end of the nineteenth century to study medicine; their numbers were not conspicuous. The second group journeyed abroad as a consequence of the government's adoption of the Japanese concept of *ryōsai kenbo*, or "good wife, wise mother," translated in Chinese with the ideal of *xianqi liangmu* (贤妻良母): "good mother/virtuous wife" (Ye 2001). These two groups, Ye argued, "internalized the anxiety of the male-dominated Chinese society about the potential threats posed by women's education" (Ye 2001, 115), and they remained wary about maintaining femininity as an essential feature of women. They asserted themselves mainly by entering the field of teaching. They also promoted new concepts of home life, helping to bring "modernity" to the urban domestic sphere. The last group was made of the post–May Fourth generation and was the largest. Women of this group were the most influenced by American secular ideas and were the principal advocates for women's independence and emancipation to contribute to a strong nation.[2]

Actually, Grace encapsulated all three waves of Chinese students abroad, and her life choices can be read as a reflection of the debates developing in her motherland and an adaptation and reformulation of them within the transnational environment she experienced.[3] Textbooks for women written at this time linked physical education to the ability to give birth to physically strong citizens, making it a highly desirable subject for "modern women" to study. In the textbook titled *Newest Ethics Textbook for Girls and Women*, the section "Women Are Mothers of Citizens" stated: "The superiority or inferiority of their physical health is thus linked to the strength or weakness of the citizenry" (Judge 2008, 120). As a matter of fact, at Wellesley Grace majored in physical education, incorporating the nationalistic discourse of the need of strong women for a stronger nation, and after graduation, when she returned to China, she became a teacher of physical education, a career promoted by Liang Qichao as a timely occupation for women who wanted to "protect the nation" (Liu, Karl, and Ko 2013, 195).

Grace's Life in America

Grace set foot in Boston when the Chinese Exclusion Act of 1882 had not yet been repealed. This law was created to forbid the entrance of Chinese laborers to the United States for ten years. According to the law, laborers were banned, but people from specific upper classes were not. Therefore, rich merchants, diplomats, and students continued to reach America. In 1892 the act was prolonged for ten more years and was then declared permanent in 1902. Political discourses used by Congress to pass the Chinese Exclusion Act employed a rhetoric that depicted Chinese people as unassimilable, filthy, and heathens. The provisions of the legal system reverberated in popular articles like Clarice Howard's description of her trip to Chinatown with a group of friends after a basketball game, which appeared on April 30, 1910, in the *Boston Globe*. She wrote that besides one boy who liked chop suey, for the rest it was "such a mixture!" and she commented: "I could not eat more than two spoonful's [*sic*] of it"; hence, "we all solemnly declared never again to visit Chinatown," that "horrid, dark place" where she "looked behind every tree expecting to see a Chinaman ready to kill us."[4] This was the America where Grace arrived, full of hope for a modern, just, and open society. Common Americans were not acquainted with the social and political revolutions happening in China; therefore, popular perceptions were shaped by a general distrust toward the "celestials"[5] fed by a generalized fear of unskilled laborers flooding America.

Grace spent five years in Boston, from 1920 to 1925. The political changes in China, which had become a republic, rendered Chinese culture, customs, and cuisine a more accepted object of curiosity. In 1929, one of the *Boston Globe*'s sections named "Man's Daily Story" described Chinatown as "improving" in respect to the past—however, with a condescending attitude. The writer specified that Chinese residents are now capable of speaking English, but the author puts the word "English" in quotation marks. Why? The allusion was to an imperfect language, far from the norm, and the article concluded with a joke on the culinary rendering of broken English, which encapsulated a long-lasting prejudice about the perverted eating habits of the "celestials." In fact, the article quoted a paradoxical conversation between a Chinese waiter and a customer, in which the server proposed a dessert of "Lice pudding and bluebelly pie," which only after being "Englished" could become acceptable items to order.[6]

A more structured analysis of articles published in the *Boston Globe* between the 1880s and the 1950s revealed a disconnect between the appreciation of the millenarian civilization of China and the perceptions, often biased, regarding Chinese migrants living in America. Interestingly, the only article published before the approval of the Chinese Exclusion Act reported a very accurate description of a funeral ceremony for the death of a rich merchant. The descriptions of the rites, the processions, the different meats served, the music, the women's reverence to the deceased tell of a curious eye interested in cross-cultural explorations.[7] The article did end, though, with the image of the remains of the merchant being sent back to China as a confirmation that the "celestials" were guests in America and ultimately belonged to a different place.

In all other articles published after 1882, there were interesting descriptions of practices and traditions, but disparaging denominations like "chinks" appeared. More than ten out of the fifty articles were news about how many "Chinamen" had been arrested for gambling, violence, drinking, and drug usage; how many had been deported; how many were not admitted to the United States; or stories of American girls abducted by Chinese. Over time, the articles showed a clear division between stories of upper-class, well-educated Chinese and descriptions of the misconduct and dubious morals of the

"Chinamen" of the lower classes. This division reflected the mandates of the exclusion laws—unskilled laborers were not allowed to enter anymore, while members of the upper classes were. The abrupt interruption of the migration flow of the lower classes left the early communities of bachelors without women until 1943, when the Magnuson Act allowed for family reunifications.

Meanwhile, Grace Zia had arrived in Massachusetts. In China she was used to a comfortable life shared among family and friends. Thus, at Wellesley, she often felt lonely and craved the noisiness of her family's dinner table as well as the flavors of the simple Chinese delicacies that meant home for her. The monotony of boiled cod and mashed potatoes from the college cafeteria frustrated Grace to the point of feeling sometimes demoralized. Yet, she did not allow herself to be overwhelmed by melancholy; she instead reacted by trying to engineer ways to reproduce home away from the family table.

Young Grace was determined not to let a pathetic and bland white fish sadden her experience abroad. Therefore, even if in China Grace was used to having cooks and servants, she bravely stepped into the kitchen. The memories of smells and flavors from home were vivid in her mind; she knew how dishes could and should taste; therefore, from her early years in the United States, she invested in culinary knowledge and relied on personal craftiness to find ingredients and tools. Ultimately, she found the strength to make her melancholy become her pièce de résistance.

Her Wellesley years were also filled with fun and action. Grace's circles were made up of the elites of the Chinese modernizing nation—scholars at Harvard, MIT, and other distinguished institutions of the area. Inspired by the sweeping changes in the motherland, students abroad founded journals and magazines, and they became journalists, editors, and hosts of formal or less formal events. In the "Student World" section of the *Chinese Student's Monthly*, we can see that Grace Zia was happily involved in mundane celebrations. One such ceremony was the thirteenth Double Ten Anniversary (the Republic of China was founded on October 10), which was celebrated in Boston on the evening of October 9, 1924. The guest of honor was the poet Wan-yin Hsieh. The article demonstrates the tight links Chinese students, both male and female, kept with the destiny of their land. In the article we read a report on the poet's speech that is particularly telling of the environment Grace lived in:

> Miss Wan-yin Hsieh, the celebrated poet and leader of new literary movement with admirable eloquence delivered the first speech of the evening. Under the theme "non-leadership," Miss Hsieh assailed the prevailing notion that Chinese students by virtue of their being in the country are the undisputable leaders of China. It is chance, Miss Hsieh unerringly observed, that has brought us to America. Merely stepping on the American soil does not transform us into

> leaders. It is therefore lamentable to see those poisoning their own mind and obstructing the road to progress by self-styling the all-important personages of the young Republic. Miss Hsieh concluded with that idea the true leadership is built on the sound foundation of humbleness and willingness to start from the bottom, and it is this kind of leadership or non-leadership that can truly serve our beloved country.[8]

Such politically involved discussions were commonplace among students abroad. Students entertained themselves also by taking part in artistic and theatrical representations every year and during ceremonies with professors, Chinese visitors, and businessmen. Skilled students organized performances and recitals, and Grace became known for her voice and her ability as a soloist singer. She was very well-liked by her peers, to the point that in 1924 she won the "Most Popular Girl" award in the Annual Popularity Contest, organized by *The Conference Daily*. Besides leisure activities, Grace was also involved with the more politically conscientious Chinese Students Alliance. Grace worked in the Social Committee and became first the secretary treasurer and then the vice president of the organization. During these years Grace met many other students, but one particular boy, Shih-ming Chu, made a long-lasting impression on her. He was studying engineering at MIT and soon became her fiancé.

Grace's Cosmopolitan Life

After graduation, Grace and Shih-ming moved back to China, and in 1928 they got married. Grace's husband pursued a military career and became affiliated with the Nationalist Party (Guo Min Dan, or GMD). Shih-ming had a brilliant career and soon started working as an aide-de-camp for Chiang Kai-shek. He then became lieutenant general and in 1943 was part of the entourage of Madame Chiang during her famous trip around the United States. After the war Grace's husband became the commanding general of the Japanese Theater and was sent to Japan during the Reconstruction years. During those years Grace went back to China where she became a teacher. Madame Chu taught at the Ginling College for Women in Nanjing, at the old high school, and worked also as a physical trainer for the government's directors.

During her college years in China Grace was involved with student movements and organizations. She was indeed the product of the modernizing China that demanded all its partakers to be zealous promoters of change, especially if graced with the possibility of learning. Grace found in her role as a teacher the right balance between *nei* (private sphere) and *wai* (public sphere)[9] and the fulfillment of the mission of the modern woman. With her experience as vice president of the Chinese Students Association while studying abroad, Grace was entrusted with important roles in the Young Women's Christian Association (YWCA) between 1935 and 1947. In 1942, she became the international vice president of the YWCA, and for the next five years she traveled internationally, advocating for the YWCA's mission to aid and educate working women.

After one year of marriage Grace gave birth to her first son, Samuel, and childbearing did not stop her career; in fact, Grace kept working and traveling while pregnant with her second son, Daniel, in 1933. As the wife of a military diplomat, Grace managed to travel extensively, seeing many interesting places and meeting many powerful people. For instance, Grace and her husband lived in Moscow for a short while, and there they met and dined with such political figures as Stalin and other prominent Russian politicians. Those were the prime years of the young couple and also of the young Chinese nation. Grace became a well-known coach, to the point that she was assigned to accompany a woman track star to the Berlin Olympic Games of 1936.[10] The Chus traveled to Germany and experienced first-hand the world's fear and fascination with the Führer. Hitler was determined to show the world the magnificence of Germany. The Berlin games were the first to be recorded and broadcasted on television. Hitler could not let this occasion pass without leaving a mark in the minds of all the participating nations and forever engrave the world's perceptions with the magnificence of the Third Reich. Among the social events organized in relation to the tournaments, Grace participated in one diplomatic reception where she met the Führer himself. She described him as "very animated, very talkative, very different from Stalin."[11] Grace's premium years brought her to break bread with many other notable political figures. Among them, we have records of encounters with President Roosevelt and Winston Churchill at the White House. In addition, Grace and her husband were guests at a dinner at General George Marshall's residence, and they also participated in a small party with lieutenant colonel, later to become president, Eisenhower and his wife. Naturally, among her illustrious acquaintances the most stable relationship was with Chiang Kai-shek. When, in 1937, Grace's husband was appointed as an aide to Chinese Nationalist leader Chiang Kai-shek, Madame Chu also became an active member of the Women's Advisory Committee in Chongqing, the capital of the Republic of China, and worked closely with Madame Chiang.

Grace's story adds normalcy to the imagery of highbrow international interactions and cultural encounters. Grace explained in several interviews that in all her travels she always managed to use food to find common ground. When she later moved permanently to the United States and decided to become a teacher of the "pleasures of Chinese cooking," she stated that she started this career because her friends from diplomatic circles always exhorted her to do so. Grace finally embraced cooking in America as her ambassadorial power while trying to establish herself in her new country, where she was no longer just a visitor. She did not hold diplomatic status anymore; she was a regular citizen.

Grace's Life in America: Second Act

On the eve of the Communist revolution and right before the nationalist government fled to Taiwan, Grace and Shih-ming and their two sons, Samuel and Daniel, moved back to the United States. Grace's husband was stationed in Japan during the years of the American occupation and passed away while there. Grace then decided to stay in the United States and moved to New York City, where she lived until she was in her seventies. After she became a naturalized citizen in 1955, she declared that she wanted to keep busy. This time she believed she could not go back to teach physical education as she felt she was too old for that; therefore, she found her new mission. She stated in an interview: "I had become an American citizen, but I wanted to contribute to America something of my heritage."[12]

Teaching was a typical career path for Chinese "mothers of citizens" schooled in the early twentieth century. Grace had practiced the profession in China after studying abroad; hence, when she found herself alone in the States with two children to maintain she reinvented herself by changing the subject of her classes. The switch to teaching Chinese cooking came about after years of following her husband around the globe and constantly finding herself teaching women from different backgrounds how to cook Chinese dishes. Grace Chu's first students were in fact the wives of high-ranking generals and diplomats she encountered wherever she went. These women motivated Grace to share her knowledge and passion outside the diplomatic circles until she consciously transformed her interest into her livelihood. She would later confess, "I am the first to admit I am not the best cook of any Chinese dish, but I know more than anyone about its background."[13] Teaching about food became Grace's new vocation. Over the years, Grace successfully demonstrated that by using food she was able to place herself in the American culinary scene and to communicate her cultural identity to her adopted land.

Her classes were very popular because Grace taught with authority and vigor and, at the same time, kindness and serenity. She explained that in China, "more often than not, the student chef is apt to find his teacher singularly uncooperative. The apprentice is never permitted to ask questions. Nor will an established chef volunteer any information. Whatever the apprentice chef learns, he learns by watching his teacher at work" (Chu 1962, 13–14). Instead, she welcomed her students' comments and questions.[14] Madame Chu distanced herself from traditional practices and openly challenged such customs as the notion that only men belonged in the kitchen. Therefore, Grace became a cooking master, even if only after settling in the United States. Her work represented the observant phase of the apprenticeship, followed, however, by the conscious realization and well-informed externalization that a lively dialogue among all members at a table is the key to a well-organized dinner party and a successful learning paradigm. Also, Grace never forgot where her lessons were taking place, usually in an American metropolis, demonstrating a remarkable ability to negotiate between tradition and modernity and to navigate with exceptional dexterity the culinary and cultural interstices between authenticity and adaptation, which is at the heart of diasporic identities.

During the late 1950s and 1960s, Grace worked in NYC with the Mandarin House School of Cooking, the Riverside Church, the Cooking Institute of America, and later she also taught in her own apartment in Manhattan. In class Grace maintained a meticulous organization—from general introductions to Chinese culture to an especially selected series of menus to prepare, cook, and share with her students. She always started off by describing the main tools and ingredients to cook Chinese food such as chopsticks, the wok, and the cleaver, and portrayed the differences between Western and Chinese customs. For instance, she explained the lack of entrées in Chinese cuisine as representing the intrinsic sociality of a Chinese dinner, made not of individual plates, but rather of a combination of dishes for everyone to share. Another key component of her teaching routines was the focus on cooking techniques; she stated that the secret of success of a well-executed recipe is in the planning and the preparation time. As a Chinese chef, Grace Chu confidently declared that Chinese cooking was actually easier in the United States than in China, in terms of availability of ingredients for substitutions and for the lack of need of "wood chopping, coal digging, and twig picking."[15] The late Qing infatuation with modernity is reflected in Grace's emphasis on modern American kitchens, with gas stoves and other cutting-edge gadgets that facilitated the overall cooking process.

Madame Chu was a forward-looking woman, educated at a time when women's voices were raising their volume globally. Grace never shouted her views or imposed her ideas but used instead the experiential learning of making and sharing food to engage in cultural exchange. Ingesting and digesting a meal requires functions like opening a mouth, activating senses, taking apart and absorbing nutriments, and ultimately tolerating food and ideally cultures and traditions with it; therefore, Grace's teaching style and content represented a revolutionary turn in the culinary world. Grace, a woman, overturned the rigid Chinese understanding of gender roles and was able to introduce the flavors of China to American households and, ultimately, transform and enrich the American palate.

Already, by 1963, when the Brooklyn Union Gas Company produced a short documentary based on Grace's first cookbook, *The Pleasure of Chinese Cooking*, she had come a long way since the bleak cod of the college cafeteria. The setting, the music, the curious objects used in the scenes of the short film like the abacus, and Mrs. Chu's calm and reassuring voice, the Chinatown store, the food, the elegantly set table, the clothes, all contributed to confer an aura of peaceful harmony to the art of exotic cooking coming from the still mostly unknown Far East. American society as well had experienced profound change vis-à-vis different cultures and ethnicities. After President Johnson signed the Immigration and Nationality Act in 1965,[16] a growing number of migrants from Asia reached American shores. The restaurant and catering businesses became one of the economic niches Chinese migrants exploited to make do in America. This sector rendered the daily encounters between mainstream America and the Chinese communities an ongoing cultural, social, and economic negotiation.

Grace's greatest ability lay in the fact that she was able to present and adapt a culinary millennial tradition to the taste, food practices, and shopping habits of twentieth-century American society. One especially interesting result of her diplomatic culinary efforts was to have succeeded in placing Chinatowns on the map. In both the cookbooks and the film Grace was deliberate in disclosing Chinatowns to the wider public. In the book she reserved a whole section for addresses and contacts of the main Chinese grocery stores of Chinatowns around America. As noted in section two, Chinatowns were perceived as foreign and dangerous localities in the early twentieth century; however, Grace charged them with the notion of being convenient and hospitable places. Grace built in the post-1960s a refreshed curiosity of Americans toward different cultures and applied a pragmatic approach to crossing physical and ethnic boundaries. In the short movie, she showed that when exchanging goods, groceries, and ideas, it was possible to create newly shared cultural contents.

Toward the end of her outstanding career, in 1983, Grace was honored at the New York Association of Cooking Teachers (NYATC) with a banquet and the prize for best cooking teacher. There, she was credited for having made Chinese cooking a reality in the homes of her American students. Even during this occasion when she was the guest of honor, Grace took the time to point out that all items on the menu, especially the most refined dishes such as stuffed crab claws, beef, scallops in bird nests made of fried taro, shark's fin soup, Peking duck, and homemade noodles, were made with ingredients easily available from stores in Chinatown.[17]

Cookbooks

Since the early twentieth century, publications of Chinese cookbooks have proliferated in America and elsewhere. Yong Chen reported that more than

300 books were published in the United States alone before 1985 (Chen 2017). Most of them were written by Asian Americans, with goals similar to Grace's—namely, to use food-making to express pride in Chinese history and cultural identity (Chen 2017). I analyze here Grace's two cookbooks and compare them with the work of another female author, Zhao Bu-wei Yang, who published a cookbook titled *How to Cook and Eat in Chinese* about twenty years before Grace. These two women encapsulate the essence, each in her own way, of a changing China and are symbols of the resilience and adaptability of Chinese translocal women living at the junction of two countries and two centuries. In chronological order we have first Zhao Bu-wei Yang's book, published in 1945, then Grace's first cookbook *The Pleasure of Chinese Cooking*, published in 1962, and lastly, Grace's *Madame Chu's Chinese Cooking School*, published in 1975.

These books and their writers have many similarities and represent two products of modern Chinese women's diasporic consciousness. However, there is also a striking difference between them; that is, Madame Zhao wrote *How to Cook and Eat in Chinese* with an openly uncompromising attitude. She wrote the book to offer glimpses of Chinese culture through food to those Americans who were willing to learn. She declared right up front that "I speak little English and write less. So I cooked my dishes in Chinese" (Chao 2013, xii). This often resulted in odd literal translations of dishes and their preparations, outcomes that Bu-wei proudly embraced as a mark of her Chineseness. She did assign the translations of the book to her daughter Rulan, a native English speaker, but she ultimately settled for eccentric translations of dishes. For instance, she translated "Shrimps Fried with Mushroom" with the literal "Mushrooms Stir Shrimps" and justified the choice with the sophistic argument, attributed to her husband, that if "Mr. Smith can Go to Town in a movie, why can't Mushrooms Stir Shrimps in a dish?" (Chao 2013, xii). Madame Zhao's book reads like a lecture, a culinary and cultural overview, delivered with erudite, sagacious, and clever inclinations. Grace as well placed herself in a teaching position, but she was never distant from her students; she rather maintained an open and conversant attitude in person and in her writing. Grace worked her entire life to transcend social limits and ethnic barriers, and her cookbooks are testaments to her diplomatic attitude of hospitality through conviviality.

Madame Zhao

Madame Zhao was born in 1889 into a wealthy family in Nanjing. She described herself as "a typical Chinese woman. [. . .] A woman with an unusual experience [. . .]," and then she added: "I like to move; I like to act. [. . .] But above all, I am myself and not somebody else" (Chao 2013, 56).

In 1905, as a young girl, Bu-wei went to the newly opened Lüning School for girls in Nanjing. The chapter of her autobiography in which she recounts her school years is titled "My First Modern School," which shows how the recurrent topic of modernity was internalized by her generation. Her entrance examination was a composition based on "the importance of education for women"[18] and yet, Bu-wei regretted how, in the name of modernity, she had paid so little attention to the study of the traditional art of calligraphy. When she realized that her exam was not going to receive an outstanding grade, she described with mockery the words she had opened her essay with—"such eternal truths as 'the women of today are the mothers of the future people of the country'" (Zhao 1947, 100). Bu-wei published her autobiography in 1947, and at that time she seemed to criticize the banality of her argument. However, in the early twentieth century, when she took the exam, the idea of modernity had permeated society at every level, and wealthy and progressive families and the schools they populated were especially influenced by it. When the esteemed principal of the Lüning School was transferred and the institute transformed into a training school for teachers, Bu-wei moved to the McTyeire School in Shanghai because she wanted to be a doctor, and afterward she transferred to Japan to study medicine. Later she followed her husband, a respected linguist who taught at Harvard and Berkeley, to America.

It is during her time in Massachusetts that she wrote and published her cookbook, which is quite entertaining. We gather that she is smart, witty, and self-confidently humble, as the very first few words of the cookbook demonstrate: "I am ashamed to have written this book [. . .] because I am a doctor and ought to be practicing instead of cooking" (Chao 2013, xii). Her father described her as being "as tenacious as a boy."[19] However, Bu-wei, as did Grace, crossed the predetermined gender boundaries over and over again with courage and confidence. With her adventurous spirit and her thirst for knowledge shaped by her New Learning (*xinxue*),[20] which crossed disciplines and countries, Bu-wei positively stated in the preface of her book: "How did I learn to cook so many things? My answer is: with an open mind and an open mouth" (Chao 2013, xii).

Bu-wei declared that her English was not good, and so she needed to rely on her daughter for translations. Nevertheless, she was so resolute about the rendering of her dishes in English that she described the continuous quarreling with Rulan, which almost strained their relationship. Bu-wei believed that her literal and amusing expressions maintained more of the Chinese essence she was trying to convey and defend. She was "a typical Chinese woman" of the time; her identity was inherently diasporic but spoke of her country and its culinary traditions from the perspective of a well-educated woman, anchored in the present abroad, but rooted in the land of her ancestors. As the title of her cookbook also reveals, she was promoting a translated version of her food ("How to cook and eat in Chinese" as if speaking a culinary language); she understood adaptation, but not at the expense of the Chinese spirit and values. Bu-wei kept her stance throughout the book. She wrote it in America, but she intentionally never mentioned "chop-suey," the dish believed in the United States to be quintessentially Chinese. From her standpoint, "chop-suey" belittled the essence of her Chinese culture and identity and was not worthy of a single mention. However, "chop-suey" was a reality espoused by many Chinese migrants who wished to survive in America. Bu-wei, as part of the upper class, did not experience directly the struggles of laborers and kept her professorial standpoint. Therefore, in her book she rather employed pages explaining and urging Westerners to learn typical Chinese cooking techniques for the sake of everyone's stomachs. To her determination can be credited the coinage of a new term: "stir-fry," which is today associated with anything regarding Chinese food and Chinese cooking, and it has also influenced the cooking practices of the entire globe.

Madame Chu

Grace as well belonged to the class of educated people admitted in America despite the exclusion laws; therefore, with her culinary art she purposedly embraced her role as an overseer and a negotiator of her culture overseas. She traveled and interacted with people of many different backgrounds, while probably engaging only rarely with Chinese laborers living in America. However, as a form of respect for her compatriots abroad, Grace did discuss "chop-suey" in her book. In fact, the main goal of *The Pleasure of Chinese Cooking* can be summarized with diplomatic conciliation. Grace dedicated much space to interactions with foreigners since it was in such exchanges that her diasporic consciousness developed and could be communicated. She was determined to make Chinese food and Chinese culture enter the homes of Americans everywhere; thus, she wrote: "I have taught Chinese cooking for many years, both in my home and at the China Institute in America. These experiences have given me some insight as to the Chinese foods that Americans are most likely to enjoy. The availability of Chinese materials and ingredients in the United States has been kept in mind in planning the recipes in this book" (Chu 1962, 14).

Grace wrote in simple language, easily understandable, and added many realistic drawings to make her words come alive. Throughout the book she paid attention to the right balance between adjustments and authenticity; for this reason, she also wrote a section titled "Menus Using Ingredients from American Markets" (Chu 1962, 71). Grace adapted many dishes, allowed for substitutions in her recipes, and included tips for replacing ingredients in her recipes, which was something that Chinese cooks would never do. In an interview regarding her teaching and cooking methods, she declared: "It shouldn't surprise you that I recommend canned Chinese products. [. . .] The Chinese are very practical people. [. . .] I don't throw tantrums in the kitchen, just because the fresh vegetables are not available. The end product, the beautiful dinner I am going to serve my guests is what I concentrate on."[21] Thus, Grace defied conventions, demonstrating how she was willingly, and successfully, trespassing on imposed cultural and physical boundaries.

After her husband died, Grace did not have a motherland to go back to. The Communist revolution had wiped out the Shanghai she used to live in and the world as she had known it. The nationalist government, led by Grace's friend Chiang Kai-shek, had been established in Taiwan, but Grace was more familiar with America than with Taiwan at that point. She needed to resettle and reinvent herself. In the process of living between cultures, with her children growing up in a place different from the familiar places of her youth, she opted to stay in the United States and embrace dialogue, flexibility, and ultimately to serve as an "ingredient" to happiness for those around her.

At this point of her career, Grace had internalized her translocal position; she acted as an impartial moderator, symbolized the in-betweenness of migrants' lives, and with her visibility she tried to demonstrate the richness of nuances and the benefits of negotiated views and readapted dishes. The last chapter of *The Pleasure of Chinese Cooking*, titled "Regional Chinese Cooking," marked Grace's timid attempt at introducing Chinese diversity. It was a two-and-a-half-page addendum in which she mentioned few regional traditions to delineate the vastness of the Chinese territory. This section tried to simplify the complexities of her motherland for an American audience, and there she acknowledged that most Chinese restaurants in America were run by Cantonese people. Probably inspired by still fashionable, yet unresolved, nationalistic ideals among Chinese in the diaspora, Grace's final picture was still of a single China. She glossed over complicated cultural variances but ultimately underlined the unifying power of the Chinese written language, even if it was often unknown to the common laborer. As a displaced person interacting with her new reality, she was trying to make translocal ends meet.

The most symbolic example of her role as a cultural mediator can be found after an accurate analysis of her second culinary publication, *Madame Chu's Cooking School*, released in 1975. The first book had opened with a description of what "We Chinese like to think of cooking", that is, cooking as "a distinctive art form—and a very practical one at that" (Chu 1962, 13). In her second manual, Grace abandoned the inclusivity of the *pluralis maiestatis* of the "We Chinese" for a more general "The Chinese," positioning herself in a new light—an intermediary between "here" and "there."

Finally, Grace's deliberate choices of negotiation and openness toward food-making, as well as in cultural production and identity reproduction, are best represented in the section of her second cookbook titled "Questions and Answers." There she included the many questions her students had asked her during her long tenure as a teacher of Chinese cookery. The section was an open statement on the importance of dialogue and a clear resistance against Chinese chefs' conventional practices. Only through personal exchanges was Grace able to live in peace, accept others, and thrive in her endeavors. Grace's teaching philosophy reflected the very Confucian notion that a good teacher is one who never stops learning because "when I walk along with two others, they may serve me as my teachers."[22]

CONCLUSION

This chapter showed how Grace's "consumption" of food, cookbooks, and culture spoke of her agency as a woman, a teacher, a mother, a business enthusiast, and a translocal actor. It analyzed the world that first shaped Grace's psyche, which she left behind when studying abroad. Then, it examined the foreign contexts that Grace engaged in during her adult life. Too often these two contexts are studied separately by scholars of different specializations. By following Grace's life, we peeked at her story of migration, adaptation, and agency from a "two shores" perspective (Choy 2003). Grace's translocal narratives make her a trendsetter for Chinese women's identities at home and abroad, be they imagined or experienced.

Madame Chu was no ordinary woman. Educated both in China and in the United States and later married to a Chinese diplomat, Madame Grace Zia Chu was culturally stimulated from an early age. Empowered by her studies, her travels, her hardships, and her overcoming, Grace became a symbol of strength and sensitivity. Grace explored the world from a privileged position, and a careful analysis of her life hopefully adds significant global substance to the entangled history of China and America, enriching the depiction of the incredible power of women living at the crossroads of cultures and nations.

Grace acted as a cultural ambassador of Chinese heritage and Chinese civilization in a globalizing context. Her mobile life speaks of connections across cultural, ethnic, and gender boundaries. She owned her role with flexibility, her womanhood with authority, and her life with fortitude. Her passion is clear, and it is opportune to conclude with Grace's own simple words: "I love to share, and I love people. It is probably this more than anything else that makes me enjoy my work and my students enjoy their classes. [. . .] And even more I enjoy the opportunity to develop teachers, for in this way my work of spreading Chinese culture through its cuisine will go much farther than I could ever have taken it alone."[23]

NOTES

1. The movement was an insurgency that erupted after the signing of the Treaty of Versailles in 1919, marking the end of World War I. Before the treaty, the Chinese government hoped to see the province of Shandong returned to China after being occupied by the Germans. The Chinese government had sent its men to Europe to help French and British armies and to add man power to their factories, hoping to receive something in exchange. Instead, the control of the northern province was assigned to the Japanese. In a sign of protest, enraged college and high school students flooded in the streets of big cities requesting the Chinese government to abandon the oppressive and backward past and fight back with all the mighty force of China, or Zhong Guo (中国), the Central State. China needed to stand up to international injustices.

2. The Meiji government created the notion of women as "good wives and wise mothers"—a motto that encapsulated the role attributed to modern women; that is, to be the backbone of the renewed state. Similarly in China, Liang Qichao argued that women needed to be more involved in society because they were the "mothers of citizens" and had the power to shape the nation. Nevertheless, the scope of this movement advocating for women's education remained imprecise and contradictory in its application. Liang Qichao still views women as a synonym of lack of progress; even women that were educated in the classics, the "talented women" (*cainü* 才女) of the upper classes, were considered useless. In fact, Liang's statements have been criticized for utilizing women within a very male-oriented national framework. Nanxiu Qian's (2003, 2015) study of women's journals of the late Qing era proves instead women's involvement in the reconceptualization of their position vis-à-vis the nation-state (*guo* 国); women did not simply accept Liang Qichao's nationalist ideology of "mothers of citizens," but contributed with many nuanced options. One of those was the belief that women needed to be as strong as men, so they proposed drastic changes in women's school curriculum, namely, "All women should take rigorous education equally with men, focusing specifically on soccer, wrestling, boxing, and all sorts of gymnastics. They should compete with one another." As we shall see, Grace went to America to pursue a degree in physical education, showing how these debates in the motherland contributed to shaping Grace's mentality.

3. For an interesting description of women's chronotypes, see Judge (2008).

4. Clarice Howard, "My Trip to Chinatown," *Boston Daily Globe*, April 30, 1910.

5. One of the many names used in newspapers to discuss Chinese people living in the United States.

6. "The Globe Man's Daily Story," *Boston Daily Globe*, September 11, 1929.

7. "Funeral Meats. The Notable Obsequies of a Rich Chinaman—a Peculiar Observation," *Boston Daily Globe*, February 22, 1880.

8. Rebecca Wong, "Student World," *Chinese Student's Monthly*, October 9, 1924.

9. In the *Book of Rites*, one of the classics of Confucian doctrine, women's role was solely associated with the inner chamber, while men existed and acted upon the

outer world (man should not speak of the domestic affairs, women should not speak of public affairs; *nan buyan nei, nü buyan wai* 男不言内，女不言外). Therefore, women had historically been forbidden from participating in the official education system, in the civil service examinations, and all activities related to official learning.

10. "Mme. Chu Shih-ming to Address Women's Group at Foundry," *Daily Tribune*, in World YMCA collection (1941–1952) of the Papers of Grace Zia Chu at the Schlesinger Library, Harvard University.

11. Joan McDonnell, "General's Widow Teaches Cooking," in the collection of the Papers of Grace Zia Chu at the Schlesinger Library, Harvard University.

12. Joan McDonnell, "General's Widow Teaches Cooking," in the collection of the Papers of Grace Zia Chu at the Schlesinger Library, Harvard University.

13. Joan McDonnell, "General's Widow Teaches Cooking," in the collection of the Papers of Grace Zia Chu at the Schlesinger Library, Harvard University.

14. See next section on cookbooks for a highlight of the outcomes of Grace's teaching strategy.

15. "Cooking Shown, Chinese Way," *King Feature Syndicate*, June 6, 1963, in the collection of the Papers of Grace Zia Chu at the Schlesinger Library, Harvard University.

16. The Act abolished the national-origins quotas and removed all references to race as a selection principle to enter the United States.

17. Irene Sax, "11-course salute to famous NY cooking teacher," in the "Awards, 1969–1986" folder of the collection of the Papers of Grace Zia Chu at the Schlesinger Library, Harvard University.

18. The prompt was a reference to the important document titled "On the Education of Women," published in 1897 by Liang Qichao, a prominent reformer and journalist, where he discussed the pros and cons of formally educating women.

19. All-China Women Federation, "Yang Bu-wei: Early-20th Century Feminist Pioneer," http://www.womenofchina.cn/womenofchina/html1/history/1609/3167-1.htm. Accessed January 2021.

20. A new way of learning inspired by Western knowledge.

21. Joan McDonnell, "General's Widow Teaches Cooking," in the collection of the Papers of Grace Zia Chu at the Schlesinger Library, Harvard University.

22. Confucius, *Analects*, Book VII, Chapter XXI (Project Gutenberg), 85.

23. Judith Bell, *Guide to US Cooking Schools*, in the collection of the Papers of Grace Zia Chu at the Schlesinger Library, Harvard University.

REFERENCES

Chao Pu-wei Yang. 2013. *How to Cook and Eat in Chinese*. Reprint. New York: The John Day Company.

Chen, Yong. 2017. "The Rise of Chinese Food in the United States." Oxford Research Encyclopedia of American History. https://doi.org/10.1093/acrefore/9780199329175.013.273.

Choy, C. C. 2003. *Empire of Care. Nursing and Migration in Filipino American History*. Durham: Duke University Press.

Chu, Grace. 1962. *The Pleasure of Chinese Cooking*. New York: Simon and Schuster.

———. 1975. *Madame Chu's Chinese Cooking School*. New York: Simon and Schuster.

Judge, Joan. 2008. *The Precious Raft of History. The Past, the West and the Women Question in China*. Stanford: Stanford University Press.

Liu, L., Rebecca Karl, and Dorothy Ko. 2013. *The Birth of Chinese Feminism. Essential Texts in Transnational Theory*. New York: Columbia University Press.

Qian, Nanxiu. 2003. "Revitalizing the Xianyuan (Worthy Ladies) Tradition: Women in the 1898 Reforms." *Modern China* 29 (4): 399–454.

———. 2015. *Politics, Poetics and Gender in Late Qing China. Xue Shaohui and the Era of Reform*. Stanford: Stanford University Press.

Ye, Weili. 1994. "'Nü Liuxuesheng': The Story of American-Educated Chinese Women, 1880s–1920s." *Modern China* 20 (3): 315–346.

———. 2001. *Seeking Modernity in China's Name. Chinese Students in the United States, 1900–1927*. Stanford: Stanford University Press.

Zhao, Buwei Yang. 1947. *Autobiography of a Chinese Woman*. Kindle: Camphor Press.

Chapter 13

Social Change and Gendered Gift-Giving Rituals

A Historical Analysis of Valentine's Day in Japan

Yuko Minowa, Olga Khomenko, and Russell Belk

ABSTRACT

Valentine's Day is a culturally hybridized and popularly celebrated consumption ritual in Japan.[1] We examine its historical transformation based on a visual and textual analysis of advertisements in print media over fifty years. Changes in the meanings, functions, and structure of gift-giving rituals correspond to changes in the national economy, social values, consumer ideology, and gender roles and power relationships in Japanese society. There are five major findings: one, the importance of food—chocolate—in the creolization process of the consumer ritual; two, the persistent gender-asymmetric nature of the Valentine's consumer holiday; three, the ritual's structural aspects and changes over time; four, the importance of confession in the ritual process; and five, the transformation of its role from a simple instrument of love and a way to elevate a relationship to a rite to reconfirm gender identity. This study supplements the very limited literature on Japanese gift-giving rituals.

SOCIAL CHANGE AND GENDERED GIFT-GIVING RITUALS: A HISTORICAL ANALYSIS OF VALENTINE'S DAY IN JAPAN

Gender and gift-giving rituals occupy a unique place in Japan's history. The genesis of the nation is recounted in the mythology as involving a gift from a woman. According to *Kojiki*, or *The Record of Ancient Matters*, written in 712, the sun goddess Amaterasu, supreme Shinto deity in its mythology, gave her grandson Ninigi-no-mikoto three items of imperial regalia: Yasuka curved beads, a mirror, and the Kusanagi sword. Thus, the rule of the state was authenticated (Kōnoshi 2000). The tale also involves cultural borrowing. Although the mythology says the regalia originated in Japan, this set of three artifacts—mirror, sword, and jewel—initially came from China, were adopted and reproduced by the Japanese, and were used by powerful regional clans as a symbol of power (Tsude 1989). The popularity of these hybridized Chinese treasures reflects Japan's forte in her subsequent history: kneading and molding foreign culture into favorite local shapes. Gifts from women to men, and from culture to culture, thus both have powerful symbolic roots in Japan's mythological history.

In contemporary Japan, gift-giving occasions are abundant, their social significance profound, and their economic consequences enormous (Rupp 2003). Aside from semiannual quasi-obligatory *chugen* and *seibo* gifts and numerous rites of passage and progression, there are *miyage* gifts from holiday trips, gifts for casual visits to a friend's home, for moving to a new neighborhood, or in meeting a new business partner. Expressions of gratitude, apology, friendship, respect, and romantic feelings all involve giving, *and* repayment, of gifts. The plethora of traditional occasions is further compounded by creolized Western holidays, such as Christmas and Valentine's Day, both of which exist outside of their original religious contexts and are celebrated by consumers in the secular, postmodern marketplace (Creighton 1993; Moeran and Skov 1993; Kimura 2001; Kimura and Belk 2004, 2005).

Valentine's Day in Japan, in particular, constitutes a culturally hybridized holiday ritual, from its definition to its ritual protocol. It is a commercially constructed consumer holiday where, according to Japanese cultural norms, women give men chocolates and other gifts, and not vice versa. The holiday was originally introduced by Morozoff Ltd. in 1936 targeted at resident foreigners in the Kobe area (Rupp 2003). When it was reintroduced to the mass market in the late 1950s, the initial consumer acceptance was poor. Only after the holiday was strategically reintroduced by the confectioners as the day for women to convey their romantic feelings to men, was the Valentine's gift-giving practice accepted by female consumers and subsequently adopted by Japanese society (Creighton 1993). To compensate for the asymmetry of the gendered gift-giving, White Day was formally set one month later in 1980, as a time when men give reciprocal (and generally larger) gifts to the women from whom they have received Valentine's gifts (Rupp 2003).

In the fifty years since its introduction in Japan, the Valentine's Day holiday has metamorphosed in its meaning as a reflection of changes in social values, the national economy, and consumer ideology. During the bubble economy of the late 1980s to the early 1990s in particular, the variety of gifts, their prices, and the process of gift exchange became diverse and extravagant, which augmented the multiplicity of the meanings that such gifts convey. At the same time, revulsion against the wasteful, commercially-driven gift giving has caused anti-Valentine sentiments and consumer resistance. Notably, however, this resistance does not stem from fear of cultural or religious erosion as has been the case in recent opposition in countries like India and Russia (Stinson and Ochetova 2008).

The purpose of the present study is to investigate the historical transformation of the Valentine's Day consumer holiday in Japan. Changes in the meanings, functions, and structure of the gendered gift-giving ritual are examined. These changes echo changes in social values, consumer ideology, gender roles, and power relationships in Japanese society over the past fifty years. In the present study we examine this historical transformation based on a visual analysis of advertisements in print media, supplement the extant literature on Japanese gift-giving rituals, and build a periodized understanding of the Valentine's Day holiday. This paper is novel as there has been a void of study involving a periodized analysis of this holiday ritual in Japan. The study is significant not merely because of its novelty but because of its contribution to consumer culture theory. By exploring cultural differences and addressing gender role dynamics in the sociohistorical analysis of gift-giving rituals in Japan, this study lays the ground for further theory developments on gendered gift giving.

LITERATURE REVIEW

Gift giving is multifaceted and a subject of multidisciplinary investigation. In anthropology, gift exchange is considered a "total social phenomenon," embodying economic, juridical, moral, aesthetic, religious, and mythological meanings (Mauss 1954; Hyde 1983), that goes beyond the Malinowskian assumption of dyadic transactions between self-interested individuals (Carrier 1991). Consumer researchers have investigated the subject by integrating theories from anthropology, sociology, and psychology (e.g., Belk 1979; Sherry 1983). Gift giving can vary from individuals' spontaneous acts to such formal rituals as rites of passage and progression (Rook 1985), as well as from utility-driven economic exchange to postmodern symbolic consumer behavior (Otnes and Beltramini 1996). Motivations for these rituals vary depending on situations, contexts, and perceived relationships. In the cycle of giving and receiving, consumers formulate, reformulate, and strengthen or weaken their relationships (Ruth, Otnes, and Brunel 1999) while they may use monadic giving, or self-gifts, for reward and therapeutic purposes (Mick and Demoss 1990). Gender plays a crucial role in gift-giving rituals as they are largely carried out by women and are often construed as women's work (Fischer and Arnold 1990).

Gift giving and receiving experiences among couples and those of the same or different genders have been studied in various contexts (e.g., Areni, Kiecker, and Palan 1998; Gould and Weil 1991; Newman and Nelson 1996; Rynning 1989). Belk and Coon (1993) divide gift giving among couples into three models of giving: (1) economic exchange, (2) social exchange, and (3) agapic (romantic) love. Their study broadened the realm of gift-giving research by adding selfless romantic giving to the exchange paradigm. Belk (1996) further examined "the perfect gift" as an expression of the selfless, altruistic love of the giver. Such a gift defines gift-giving and receiving ideals among couples. In the specific context of Valentine's Day gifts, Otnes, Ruth, and Milbourne (1994) investigated male consumers' ambivalent feelings about the occasion. Western Valentine's gifts provide an opportunity to show caring and affection to significant others, despite the pressure to participate. Rugimbana, Donahay, Neal, and Polonsky (2003) examined Western male consumers' motives for Valentine's gift-giving and found that, aside from self-interest, obligations, and altruism, perceived social power in exchange between genders is a latent motivational factor. Unlike heterosexual couples, their homosexual counterparts may use the holiday as an opportunity for self-affirmation and resistance against social oppression (Newman and Nelson 1996). While commercialization of the gift-giving rituals of Valentine's Day has been criticized, the consumer's negative attitude has not proven to necessarily result in avoiding or boycotting the holiday (Mortelmans and Damen 2001; Santino 1996; Schmidt 1995).

Studies of Japanese gift-giving have evolved primarily in anthropology. This culturally framed value-system approach has focused mainly on its traditional, reciprocal gift-exchange practices (e.g., Befu 1968; Benedict 1946; Hendry 1993; Rupp 2003). While ritual obligatory gift-exchange is termed *zōtoh*, the expression of affective feeling is called *purezento*, the Japanese way of pronouncing the English word present. In this regard, Minami (1997) discussed symbolic consumption and reciprocation of traditional and personal gift-giving rituals in the context of year-end *seibo* and bridal rituals. Minowa and Gould (1999) explored differences in giving and receiving experiences between Japanese women and men. Using the history of the Christmas cake in Japan as a focus for analysis and applying social constructionism as the theoretical approach, Kimura (2001) discussed gift giving as part of the adapted holiday ritual.

METHOD

Periodization is defined as "the process of dividing the chronological narrative into separately labeled sequential time periods with fairly distinct beginning and ending points" (Witkowski and Jones 2006, 77). Our primary method specifically involves context-driven periodization with a semiotic analysis of Valentine's Day editorials and advertisements in Japanese print media over a fifty-year period from 1958 to 2007. Using semiotics as an analytical scheme is considered not only useful in consumer research (Mick 1986; Mick and Oswald 2006) and historical analysis (Zhao and Belk 2008), but also appropriate in our case because Japan, or the *Empire of Signs* (Barthes 1982), is a "very visual country" saturated with imagery that does not reflect reality as much as it *is* the reality (Clammer 1995a).

By examining the historical written and visual data that appeared in Japanese newspapers and magazines, we detected five periods of the history of Valentine's Day gift-giving rituals in Japan. We initially collected 276 ads and texts from the nationally circulated newspaper and 82 articles and 39 ads from women's magazines. These newspaper ads and texts were collected exhaustively from 1958 to 2007 except for the following four years: 1963, 1974, 1980, and 2004. They were available on microfilm and in print in libraries. Magazine ads and texts were obtained mostly at a library in Tokyo which specialized in the collection of women's magazines. Our data source consisted of fourteen magazines that were targeted to varying segments of audiences in terms of their age and related demographic factors as well as their lifestyles.

By judgment, we selected twenty-six images for analysis. These images in advertisements were rich in symbolism and content and they were considered representative of the period. Six of these advertisements are discussed into detail in this paper. In determining the five periods, we first observed patterns in the data and tried to let the data speak for itself, instead of using decades or other fixed time intervals as a period ex ante. This contrasts with others who have applied quantitative measures and content analyses (e.g., Matsui 2009). Instead, we considered the events and economic conditions that appeared as turning points and helped us to establish these periods. Periodization using such turning points has been suggested as the most logical method for historical analysis (Hollander et al. 2005). The following five periods emerged from this approach: (1) chaos and polyvalence (1958–1969), (2) formation and ambivalence (1970–1979), (3) growth and outgrowth (1980–1991), (4) contraction and compunction (1992–2002), and (5) recovery and diversification (2003–2007). These periods are closely related to economic cycles (i.e., booms vs. recessions) since consumer spending on Valentine rituals depends on the availability of discretionary income and confidence in the future.

FIFTY YEARS OF VALENTINE'S DAY GIFT GIVING IN JAPAN

Phase 1: Chaos and Polyvalence (1958–1969)

In Japan's economy, this period was a combination of three economic cycles that included two of the longest booms: the Iwato and the Izanagi booms (Shinohara 1996). This was the period of prosperity and rapid economic development. In 1958, the term *shōhi kakumei*, or consumption revolution, appeared in a white paper for the first time (Amano and Sakurai 1992). The diffusion of television around the time of Tokyo Olympics (1964) exposed the audience to lifestyles and consumer goods available in the United States. In the late 1960s, the proportion of those who married for love (*ren'ai kekkon*) exceeded that of arranged marriages (*miai kekkon*) for the first time, indicating a shift in social values (National Institute of Population and Social Security Research 2002).

Although the initial introduction of Valentine's Day took place in 1936, it was targeted only at resident aliens in the Kobe area (Rupp 2003). In 1958, Mary Chocolate Co., Ltd. attempted to sell chocolates on Valentine's Day. Only a few chocolate bars were sold in the store. The earlier data show that the holiday did not necessarily involve a box of chocolates as a gift item. The gift could have been anything, including stocks and apparel. An advertisement by Nomura Securities in 1958 attempted to suggest that stocks were a proper gift item as it would fruitfully multiply and contribute to the wealth of the gift recipient. Some ads from this period claimed that sending something with a greeting card and a heart-shaped attachment was also considered appropriate as a holiday gift item.

The majority of Valentine's Day advertisements and articles show that the holiday was not necessarily a day for a woman to confess her love to a man. It was rather a day to express mutual affection to important others regardless their gender. Many ads are egalitarian: they encouraged men and women to exchange gift items. Valentine's Day was combined with other holiday occasions, such as the Doll's Day on 3/3 (the third day of the third month), to motivate giving to the beloved. Since Valentine's Day was generally defined as the day of love, but was not well defined during this period, the holiday was also used by department stores to motivate consumers to spend for a variety of sale items, even as self-gifts. In general, department stores have played a crucial role and have been instrumental in promoting various gift-giving occasions in modern Japan (Creighton 1992).

Women in ads of this period are generally portrayed as demure. Their gaze hardly meets their male counterparts. When a woman is depicted alone, she would be portrayed as carefree and active, as if she is free from men's gaze in the fictitious world of advertisements. Women's narratives (or men's narratives through the mouths of women in ads) demonstrate the undisguised gender relationship as much as the consumer culture of the period. In an ad by a major pharmaceutical company in 1965, the model says, "To you who like smoking, I am giving a gift of [vitamin drink]. A sweet sour taste of lemon. Each bottle contains 500cc of Vitamin C. . . . For you, who work so hard, Vitamin C is more useful than a woman." This ad signifies the masculine domination and patriarchal social system. Through the mouth of the female model, it indoctrinates female readers about gender role expectations. The model in the ad puts herself down. She is not as worthy as a vitamin drink. According to the copy, she is concerned about the remains of acne and the sunburn on her skin. She is happy with his compliment on the beauty of her skin. As if to indicate her preoccupation with the vitamin product and Valentine's gift giving, the visual in the ad shows an overwhelmingly large, conspicuously ornamented (with ribbons) vitamin product that dominates the multiple images of the model. Without the presence of a male model, this ad effectively reinforces the traditional social values and gender roles through consumption.

Phase II: Formation and Ambivalence (1970–1979)

This was a period characterized by slow economic growth and social problems caused by the rapid growth of the preceding period. The period included environmental pollution and degradation, the first demonstration for woman's liberation in 1970, and other social and economic turmoil. The prevalence of mass media successfully promoted an American casual style of consumption during this period. For example, the first McDonald's opened in the Ginza in 1971 (Watson 2006) and consumers enjoyed eating hamburgers on the street during the *hokōsha tengoku* (pedestrian heaven—Sunday afternoons when the street is closed to vehicles).

This period also generated ambivalence in social values: the total number of marriages continued to decrease; the proportion of *ren'ai* marriage steadily increased; and the proportion of marriages ending in divorce doubled between 1963 and 1983 (Fuess 2004). Becoming a full-time wife, a norm popularized only after World War I with the emergence of a new white-collar middle class, raised questions for this segment of women during the women's liberation movement. During the United Nations Decade for Women, in 1977, the Japanese government announced a series of plans to eliminate inequities and to improve women's position in society. From the mid-1970s, the proportion of females in the labor force started to increase while the national economy experienced a series of recessions. However, women in the labor force suffered from marginalization: they were treated as cheap, disposable workers (Ueno 1990). During this period, Japanese women seemed to realize that life was a competition, even to obtain a promising husband.

The media quickly started to mirror the social and political changes. In 1970, the women's magazine *an-an* started, and in 1971, *non-no*. These new magazines targeted the college-age and young OL (Office Lady) audience segments, called the *an-non* tribe, and taught them new ways of life, fashions, and "how to" spend leisure time. Starting in 1970, newspaper articles on Valentine's Day began to appear. An article in the February 9, 1970 issue, for instance, discusses the holiday as a day that women are allowed to confess their love to men and that those who lack courage may use jokingly in order to gauge men's feelings and avoid being hurt by possible rejection. The same article also encourages married women to give a clever gift to her husband and add an accent to their long, monotonous married life.

As if to reflect the women's movement and activists' demonstrations in 1970, some women were depicted in advertisements as looking at each other in solidarity and affinity. Alternatively, they were depicted as attempting to diverge from conventional social norms. For instance, the 1973 advertisement of Keisei department store in Tokyo titled "How is it? My kimono outfit" indicates the coexistence of multiple disparate values in consumer culture. The ad is dominated by the promotion for the kimono, the most traditional Japanese clothing. But the way the models pose in the ad does not follow the traditional ideal canon for illustrating a woman in kimono, such as *mikaeri-bijin* (a beauty looking over her shoulder) by seventeenth-century artist Moronobu. Here women's postures appear bold with wide-stretched arms as if to struggle for freedom from the social convention symbolized by the traditional clothes. On the right bottom corner is an illustration of the very traditional kimono vendor, wearing a *tasuki* sash across his shoulders. On the left margin, there is a list of promotional messages about the Valentine sales and promotions, such as the giveaway present of 10,000 "*mini-choko*" (miniature chocolates) on the pedestrian heaven on Sunday. So, the traditional Japanese (kimono) and the Western (chocolate) products, the old tradition (*goza-no-ichi*), and new customs (Valentine's commercial holiday) appear in disarray in this advertisement, symbolizing female consumer ambivalence toward self and others.

From the middle to late 1970s, ads and articles for Valentine's Day began to emphasize "strategy" in their headlines. The advertisement by Shinjuku Station Building for its shopping arcades loudly states in the headline, "The Grand Valentine Strategy. Another two days until February 14. Your rival might have already sent it." They started to instruct women "how to" beat rivals and win the man. Men became commoditized as the targets of such strategies. They were segmented for women based on such variables as personality types, astrological signs, and blood types. They were to be targeted with the right gift under the right conditions, a protocol prescribed in the magazines. The advertisement by Parco Co., Ltd. published in 1977 shows such segmentation. The ad is titled "Parco Valentine Sale. Men, their hearts are *doki doki*." *Doki doki* is an onomatopoeia of the heartbeat. It divides male markets into four types: the dandy, the active, the romantics, and the hobbyist. Western in her countenance, the woman illustrated in the center of the ad evokes a fortune teller or a cardsharp. Is the fortune she holds in her hand hers or his, or both?

Western models are often used to promote what is not Japanese. They are used to signal quality and sophistication for certain product categories. Alternatively, they are used to imply a stronger sexuality than Japanese (Clammer 1995b). Their body is considered an ideal standard of physical beauty (Barnes and Yamamoto 2008). Their popularity could be attributed to a manifestation of the nation's thirst and fascination for things Western, the fetishized other who symbolizes modernization and high status (Belk and Pollay 1985; Mueller 1992).

The comparison of this 1977 ad, combined with two prior advertisements by Parco in 1974 and 1976, reveals swift changes in gender role expectations during this period. In the 1974 ad a woman in profile appears to be introspective and in the dreamworld of her imagination. The headline of the ad says, "Now, be brave for your love." To encourage an indecisive woman to take action, the copy at the top says, "We write a love letter for you." The tone of the copy in the 1976 ad changes. In the ad titled "Parco. Valentine. From a beloved woman to you who love," the model directly looks at the reader. The woman no longer appears hesitant. As the copy indicates, she is not a passive anonymous "woman." She is brave enough to disclose herself. Nor, does she need help to write a love letter. When the women from the three advertisements are compared, we notice that the exposure of bare skin increased as time went by. In 1976, the brave woman shows her shoulder. In 1977, the woman strips her clothes; she is in her lingerie, exposing her cleavage and flat hips. Taking off her clothes, she gives the audience an impression that she is desperate to show her hand rather than keeping her strategic moves concealed. Despite the emergence of the women's liberation movement at the beginning of the decade and its reexamination of sexual mores, women continued to desire to please men with or without a gift, partly because of cultural conditioning (Tanaka 1995).

Throughout the 1960s and 1970s, advertisements encouraged the audience to popularize Valentine's Day gift giving and to stabilize it as a regular gift-giving custom. Toward the end of the 1970s, celebrating the Valentine's Day holiday seems to have become the prevalent custom. A newspaper article published on February 4, 1978, "Chocolates and children, the 14th is approaching," indicates that in 1972 (six years prior to the publication of the article), having brandy and chocolates were somewhat ordinary activities but not for the special Valentine's occasion for a married couple. Six years later, it became a popular custom and a topic of conversation among family members including adolescent children.

Phase III: Growth and Outgrowth (1980–1991)

In 1980, White Day was initiated by the National Candy Industry Cooperative Association. March 14, a month after Valentine's Day, was selected as the proper consumer holiday since it was the day that a couple who were saved by the martyred saint had sworn their eternal love. Also, the duration of one month was considered the longest appropriate for a return gift to be given as reciprocation according to social norms. By 1987, the beginning of the bubble economy, the suggested return gift was no longer limited to candies. Giving an item of underwear became popular from the late 1980s to the early 1990s as a return gift for *giri-choko* (obligatory chocolates). As the bubble economy continued, a wide variety of gift items, such as accessories and clothes, were promoted for the White Day return gifts (Minowa, Belk, and Matsui 2019).

This period included the high-tech boom that preceded the bubble economy between 1986 and 1991. The term *otaku* was coined to describe a person who was obsessed and absorbed with the subculture of anime, games, and computers ("nerd" might be a comparable term in English). The *rori-kon*, short for Lolita complex, became popular and it also became a fascination of the otaku subculture. Women in their late twenties who were stout, vigorous, active, and vital as men were called *Oyaji gyaru*, or Dad-like women, and they were perceived as rich. The new term *obatarian* became popular for describing middle-aged women who were blatant, shameless, and self-efficacious. *Madonna giin*, or female members of the congress, were regarded as the epitome of the *obatarian*. Young people were called *shin-jinrui*, or new breeds, and were considered to possess a new, individualistic value system and distinctive sensibilities (Anderson and Wadkins 1991). The emergence of such female descriptors as *asshī-kun* (driver of convenience) and *mitsugu-kun* (devotee of material gifts) signified the changing positions of men and women in society. Moreover, retired husbands were called *nure ochiba*, or wet falling leaves, as they did not stop sticking to their wives who were active in the community.

The 1980s were called the "women's era." At the end of the tenth year of United Nations Decade for Women, the Japanese government had to ratify the treaty and to start administering its laws. As a result, in 1986 the Equal Employment Opportunity Law and others passed to eliminate gender discrimination went into effect (Edwards 1988; Kano 1989). Takako Doi was elected to be the chair of the Socialist Party of Japan in 1986. Being the first female leader of any political party in Japan, she caused "Doi fever" in public. She became the chairperson of the House of Representatives in 1993. However, most of the women who sought advancement in their careers encountered dual exploitations: in the workplace and at home. As in the past, Japanese women were expected to play the role of housewife and mother. Thus, their advancement in the workplace did not mean the improvement of women's position in society but merely doubled their burdens (Ueno 2002). Women during this period were depicted in various ways: inarticulate decision makers, motherly caregivers, and strong power holders in society.

In an ad titled "I am waiting for a kiss" by Parco Co., Ltd. (1986), a young man in glasses poses in a sports jacket and a polka-dot tie over a button-down shirt. He seems to be flushed. Is it because we, the readers, are looking at him? His gaze does not meet that of the reader as if he is shying away. His attire and facial features hint at his place in society. He seems to be perhaps in his early thirties, the right age for a serious relationship and marriage. The copy of the ad is supposedly a letter written by this man, addressed to women. It says:

> It may be strange to say by myself but I am very shai (shy). My heart becomes my word and action, and it cannot make a stride forward. Well, I'm, what people may call, a *moji moji* [onomatopoeic for acting hesitant], a pampered-child-type, nice man. "That tickles my maternal instinct . . . ," frequently I am told something like that. So, in contrast, I like women who can talk directly. Especially, I like those women who aggressively come forward on the coming February 14th. There is something remarkable about the effort made by women today who advance to men's world and pressure us, "I love you, Marry me," with the power of a gift. I like such manly women. On Valentine's, men, who are not good at witty talk, are waiting. Who is going to give to me? I wish it would be that girl. Representing voices of voiceless that are heard everywhere these days, I decided to take a pen.

This ad was published in the year that the Equal Employment Opportunity Law was enforced. Women's position in society was expected to improve. Thus the ad is a reflection of the change in the social system and, accordingly, the change in gender role expectations for women: from a care-receiver to a care-giver. While this seems to be a confirmation of the positive social value, this ad can be interpreted as a loophole for men. Parts of the copy support the contention by Ueno (2002) that women were expected to play a role of mother, by suggesting that men long for women who feel a maternal instinct toward them and encouraging women to continue having such instincts even if they advance in the society and begin to obtain equal or higher positions than men.

The proliferation of consumer holidays was manifested on one hand in the magnitude of extravaganzas and on the other hand in the proliferation of product offerings. For instance, the 24k gold with 99.999 percent purity by Mitsubishi Materials instead of regular 99.99 exemplifies the time for the "Heisei gold rush." As the Dutch diamond company DeBeers not only successfully popularized diamonds in Europe but also made them the symbol of love, "a change in the language of love" was similarly explored and executed by commercial entities in Japan during this time (Creighton 1993). Escalation in the kind of product offerings developed during the bubble period can be observed in the newspaper article entitled, "Valentine unlimited commercial spirit," published on February 9, 1990. It reports a wide variety of industries trying to take advantage of the commercialized gift-giving holiday. According to the article, gift items were included not only for humans, such as Japanese confectionary, sake liquors, and heart-shaped beefsteaks, but also items for pet animals, such as decaffeinated chocolates and noodles for dogs (*wan-men*) and for cats (*nyan-men*). Gift items for humans were not limited to food, and included a telephone card that could store the giver's phone number in its memory, and a voice card that could record the sender's vocal message of up to ten seconds.

Phase IV: Contraction and Compunction (1992–2002)

In 1992, the bubble burst and the Heisei recessions began. The lost decade of the Heisei recessions might have reminded Japanese consumers of the familiar opening paragraph of *The Tale of the Heike*: that the prosperous must decline; the proud do not endure; and the mighty ultimately fall. This period was characterized by a series of natural and social catastrophes, such as the Tokyo sarin gas attack by Aum Shinrikyo, the Hanshin Awaji Great Earthquake, and the Kobe serial killer, stirring *fin-de-siècle* anxiety and self-doubt in the mind of consumers. The recession, together with deflation, bankruptcy, and a restructuring of organizations, compounded anxiety in society in general.

Leaving behind the glaring mammonism and undisguised materialism of the preceding period, this era was also characterized by the nation's quest for a simple lifestyle and genteel poverty, although apparent ersatz fineries were appealing to some. Increases in the number of *parasaito shinguru*, or parasite singles, who continued to live with their parents after schooling and of *hikikomori*, or young recluses who stayed home and avoided others to a pathological extent, both became concerns for society. By the millennium, *iyashi-kei*, or something "healing," became a buzzword in promoting various products such as music, as if to mirror the nation's fatigue from unending socioeconomic problems. The stagnant economy, aging society, and declining birthrate led the government to set up the Office for Gender Equality in 1994. It also passed the Basic Law for a Gender-equal Society in 1999, set up the Minister of State for Gender Equally, and founded the Council for Gender Equality in 2001 (Atoh and Tsuya 2007; Ōsawa 2003). In order to encourage women to marry and bear children while staying in the labor force, men's greater contributions to family affairs were promoted in the press.

Reflecting the deep economic recession, the consumption practices, including Valentine's rituals, of middle-class consumers seemed to be struggling. Advertisements from this period show that their lives seemed to be driven by "a rhetoric of despair" (Bourdieu 1984 and Baudrillard 1981, cited in Tobin 1992, 20). There was a sense of decay and hopelessness in consumer esprit manifested in their empty pursuit of fortune after decadence during the bubble. Salad days were over. Ersatz finery and apparently cheap stuff demonstrated consumers' relentless pretensions and fear against guilt and regret from spending.

Under the declining national fortunes, greeting cards become meaningless. Instead, the public lottery serves as a love letter, an expression of desire, which waits for an answer (Barthes 1978). From the burst of the bubble in 1992, being economical and getting rich by gambling (the public lottery) were emphasized. One of the advertisements by Japan Lottery Association, for instance, suggested giving a public lottery ticket with a Valentine's gift in order to also give hope and nourish dreams of the recipient. The copy on the right side says: "How would you like to give a public lottery [ticket] with Valentine chocolates this year? Love and dream, please send doubled sincerity this year." In the center of the ad, two models, the winners of 1992 Miss Public Lottery, also known as Goddesses of Fortune, smile with boxes of gifts in their arms. The one on the right seems to have a halo on top of her head. Inside the oval-shaped halo, the copy of the commercial scripture announces, "Gift of public lottery for Valentine." Other ads by the Public Lottery with such titles as "Make a fortune at one love on Valentine" and "Public lottery is the right gift of Heisei gals," also cater to the consumers' lack of confidence in economic recovery and the use of gift-giving occasions to give hope to each other.

After the bubble burst, exhibiting economical spending was also an appealing proposition. An ad by the Seiyu department store in 1993, for instance, openly discloses the *hon'ne* or true feeling of the woman who can please her male workers as well as herself with five chocolates for 1000 yen. The magazine advertisement published in 1998 titled "Valentine's coming. I want to mass produce *giri-choko* with a frying pan and pot" stresses the same unique selling proposition. The special report has instructions on how to save time and money by making *giri-choko* at home. On the other hand, the advertisement by Kodansha publishing company in 1996 shows a shifting of the target market for Valentine's gifts to children while diversifying the product items and reconceptualizing the holiday as a day of promoting communications. At the same time, the use of Snoopy and other cartoon characters from *Peanuts* in the visual component of the ad hints at the parents' inclination toward nostalgia, or a sentimentalized past, as the result of disparity between the reality and the bygone good-old-days of the bubble economy.

Phase V: Recovery and Diversification (2003–2007)

This period was characterized by temporary economic recovery and a fundamental structural change of society reflecting Japan's aging population and the disparity of wealth distribution in the nation. NEET—an acronym for the young unemployed who are not in school, employment, or vocational training —gained attention as a social problem around 2003 (Shinozaki 2008). The disparity between rich and poor, especially working poor, had widened, replacing the 100-million-all-middle-class society with *kakusa-shakai*, or a society of disparity (Gotō 2007; Watanabe 2007). The disparity of income, employment opportunities, and education produced successive generations of elite families. The nation was becoming dichotomized between winners and losers.

In this period, a declining trend in new marriages and an increasing number of single men and women as well as hikikomori (social withdrawal) were observed, especially in the cities. In Japanese a new word was even coined: *rich singles*. At the same time, studies have shown a rising degree of satisfaction with life among Japanese women, compared to Japanese men (Taga 2006). Women, who had received new rights and freedoms in the previous ten to fifteen years as a result of the enforcement of the Equal Employment Opportunity Law, acquired a taste for a freer lifestyle. These women do not want to part from their newfound freedom. They usually think that "to either marry someone or not marry is fine." They are more prone to spend money on themselves than on someone else.

Furthermore, under the influence of internal factors (e.g., economic changes, population aging, low birthrates, and a determination to stay on the same level as the rest of the world) and external factors (e.g., globalization and information technologies development), certain behavioral stereotypes in Japanese society have undergone some changes. These changes are expressed in mass media images as well as advertising. Such media have long been indicators of social changes. They suggest that Japan has become more tolerant and has stopped emphasizing the appropriateness or inappropriateness of particular behaviors as was the case during the forty years following World War II (Khomenko 2008). As a result, magazines have started showing different lifestyles and behavioral models, for example, married, unmarried, with or without children.

During the first five years of the twenty-first century, two new phrases, *tomo-choko* and *gohōbi-choko*, became popular, along with the tradition to present chocolates and gifts to men on Valentine's Day. *Tomo-choko* means a present from a woman to her girlfriends, and *gohōbi-choko*, a present from the woman to herself. *Jibun no gohōbi* implies a special present or good experience given by a woman to herself as a reward. *Jibun no gohōbi* can include not only chocolate, but other gifts, for example, expensive jewelry or trips, including *onsen* (spa) trips. For example, one of the *onsen* in the hot springs area of Hakone offers its visitors an extremely extravagant service—a chocolate bath (Tsuno 2009). Most recently, *gyaku-choko* has appeared in the market. *Gyaku* means opposite or reverse and now some men also give chocolates to women on Valentine's Day. Therefore, we can claim that since 2002 there has been another change in the meaning of Valentine's Day in Japan. The general concept of this holiday has changed. Women continue giving gifts to men, but devote much more attention and spending money not only on men, but also on other women and themselves. To sum up, the current-day Valentine's Day gift-giving norms are multimodal: Women may give gifts to men—to their "true love" and to their male coworkers—as well as to the self and to other women who may give reciprocal gifts on the same day. Male recipients may or may not reciprocate on White Day a month later. In addition, some men now give gifts to women on Valentine's Day.

The ad titled "With me. Tender luxury, at moments when I am alone. Carré de chocolat." by Morinaga & Co., Ltd. in 2007 exemplifies this case. The copy on the upper right says, "Chocolates for adult women," and on the lower bottom, "*gohōbi* chocolate for time alone." This advertisement is polysemous. The most interesting part is its lack of a simple story line. The cropped shot that hides the model's face creates both intrigue and puzzlement while it opens the text to a greater plurality of readings. A ring on her third finger equivocally hints at her marital status. The textured cashmere sweater hints at her wealth and taste. Her faceless torso incites the audience's imagination. Her anonymity symbolizes emancipation; she is free from convention, the truth about her aging, the disclosure of private feelings, and being the target of others' immediate gratification. Her privacy is assured. A cup of black coffee and the Venezuela Bitter brand chocolate on the table serve as signifiers of Latino-like masculinity while her reticent independence is signified. Two antipodal characters—the Japanese as cold, detached, and controlled and the Latino as expressive, passionate, and sensual—seem to be conflated. The visual as a whole suggests the magical power of chocolate: the possible coexistence of the self and the Exotic Other through the consumption (Savigliano 1992). At the same time, the multivocality of this advertisement seems to be a reflection of the time period: diversification of the meanings of Valentine's gift giving in the society.

DISCUSSION

The current research has examined the historical transformation of the Valentine's Day consumer holiday in Japan. By periodizing the fifty years of this commercial holiday, we investigated the historical transformation based on a visual and textual analysis of advertisements in print media. We aimed to supplement the very limited literature on Japanese gift-giving rituals. Changes in the meanings, functions, and structure of the gendered gift-giving ritual were all examined. These changes correspond with changes in the national economy, social values, consumer ideology, and gender roles and power relationships in Japanese society. The historical events, market characteristics, and gift characteristics in each of the five periods are summarized in table 13.1. While our study provides rich qualitative analysis that is linked to the consumption behavior of the Japanese and offers interpretations of Valentine's Day as a commercial holiday, the method is at the same time a limitation of our study as it leaves room for subjectivity. Future studies should include analysis of media targeted to male consumers and be more reflexive: Women's knowledge of Valentine's Day is constructed partly by their perception and knowledge of the expectations of their male counterparts.

There are five major findings. One is the importance of food in the creolization process of the consumer ritual. Chocolate has played the central, mediating role for fluid, symbolic meaning transfers between the East and the West, local and global, and consumer ideology and praxis in the historical transformation of the Valentine's Day ritual. This is somewhat analogous to the role Christmas cake played for the creolization of Christmas celebration in Japan (Kimura 2001). Started as cake, chocolate was introduced to the Japanese palate in the late nineteenth century, and its candies were commercialized in the early twentieth century. However, chocolate in the postwar Japan under the GHQ occupation became a symbol of America, the nation that was synonymous with the entire West to many. At the beginning of the 1950s, Japanese children were still asking American GIs for chocolates, following their transport vehicles on the street and shouting, "Give me chocolate" (Hashimoto 2007). These children became about the first generation of Valentine's Day holiday celebrants ten years later. Collectively imagined, fictitious "America" as a model to emulate has been a classless social paradise that is an infeasible alternative to the hierarchical Japanese society (Ohnuki-Tierney 2006). Because the local construction of American culture had a significant impact on how consumption goods from the West were perceived, chocolate and the Valentine's Day holiday seemed to partly represent the enviable, romanticized Other to emulate in its early stage in Japan. Conversely, the emergence and prevalence of handmade chocolate in subsequent years, desacralized by the touch of local hands, symbolized the localization of the global and the conflation of Self with imagined Other. The coexistence of plural, alternative types of chocolate, from luxury to handmade, today seems to demonstrate the ubiquitous existence of different levels of hybridization of the ritual, reflecting the multiplicity of consumer segments, in terms of demographics and lifestyles, who participate in this consumer holiday ritual.

Another finding is the persistent gender-asymmetric nature of the Valentine's consumer holiday. While Bailey (1988) contends that courtship conventions including consumption are *produced*, Erikson (1982) postulates all ritual behavior is deep-seated in the human psyche, and rituals with affiliative themes such as gift giving between genders originate in young adults' psychosocial crises of intimacy and isolation. Media in the marketplace legitimatize and normalize gendered gift-giving rituals such as Valentine's Day in Japan to generate opportunities and pressures to potentially resolve young adult consumers' identity crises. Thus, while the meanings of the Valentine's Day holiday have evolved and diversified over time, its initial gender-asymmetric nature remains the central motif of the ritual. To compensate for this asymmetry, on White Day exactly one month later, men give reciprocal (and generally larger) gifts to the women from whom they have received Valentine's gifts.

Three, structural aspects of ritual varied over the period of time. By structure, we do not refer to "structure" theorized by Lévi-Strauss: logical classifications and the form of the relations between them. Rather, we follow Turner (1969) to signify "structure" defined by the ritual process and the social structure comprised of mutually dependent institutions and actors they imply. In the early stage of the Valentine's Day holiday ritual, the gift-giving process was rather straightforward: A tripartite structure consisting of gestation, presentation, and reformulation stages of the gift-giving process (Sherry 1983). And artifacts and the protocol that define the ritual were loosely structured and were agents of commercial promotions. The structural change followed by the social change was the introduction of "confession" in the process, augmenting liminality to the protocol of the presentation stage and elaborating its importance. Another structural change occurred in the 1980s by the introduction of White Day. The gift-giving ritual process then became complete by the rite of reciprocation which was explicitly separated from the reformulation stage. The introduction of *giri-choko*, or obligation chocolate, around the same time, led to another structural change: It created dual ritual processes, one for an individual gift-giving ritual that was supposed to be an expression of love emulating the West, and another for an institutionalized rite that became another obligatory seasonal Japanese gift-giving ritual in organizations. More recently, alteration of structure (e.g., *gohōbi choko* for self-gift without the reformulation stage) and anti-structure (e.g., *gyaku choko*

Table 13.1 Fifty Years of Valentine's Day Gift-Giving in Japan

Phases	*Historical Events*	*Market Characteristics*	*Gift Characteristics*
1. Chaos and Polyvalence (1958–1969)	Iwato-Izanagi booms; high economic growth	Morozoff (1936) targeted to alien residents	Heart-shaped ornament attached to cards
	Consumption Revolution; Western influence through TV	St. Mary (1958) targets mass market	Diverse gift items, e.g., securities and apparel
	Tokyo Olympic	Bundle holidays and occasion to express affection	
	Space Shuttle Apollo	Women often depicted demure in ads	
2. Formation and Ambivalence (1970–1979)	Slow economic growth and environmental degradation	Becomes a day for confession	A tool to measure men's feelings
	Woman's Liberation and increase in labor force	Women are comrades for politics and foes in love affairs	A stimulant for married couple's communication
	UN Women's Decade	Strategy themes becomes popular	Promotional give away items
	Decrease in marriage	Segmentation based on blood types, personality traits, astrological signs	Valentines services, e.g., writing love letters
	An-non-zoku emerges	Occasion to gauge men's feeling; family event	
3. Growth and Outgrowth (1980–1992)	Bubble economy	White Day is founded	Giri [obligation] choko starts
	Shin-jinrui (new anthrop) emerges among youth	Ads encourage women aggressive move with gifts	Gift no longer limited to candies, e.g., underwear
	Equal Opportunity Employment Law into effect	Women are care-giver as well as care-receiver	Heisei gold rush; extravaganza with expensive jewelry
	Otaku subculture; Rori-kon (Lolita complex)		Valentine unlimited commercial spirit; a variety of items
			Gift for pets

4. Contraction and Compunction (1992–2002)	Heisei recession; Bankruptcy; Risutora	Rational decision-making encouraged	Popularity of the public lottery as a gift
	Tokyo sarin gas attack	Economy emphasized	Homemade, mass-produced giri choko
	The Hanshin Awaji Great Earthquake	Women are provider of hope and dreams with gifts	Chocolates bought with price deals are welcome
	Kobe serial killer	Shifting of target market to children	Gift to promote human communications
5. Recovery and Diversification (2002 to present)	Aging society; Decline in new marriages	Women are happier than men	Proliferation of new terms, e.g., tomo-choko, gohobi-choko
	globalization; IT development	Day to reconfirm and manifest the female gender	New luxury, e.g., jewelry and onsen trip for chocolate bath
	Rich singles and parasite singles	Day for self-expression for younger adults	Emphasis on self-gift and indulgence in luxury
	Diverse lifestyles	Shift of target market to tweens	Indulgence in luxury

or reverse chocolate, a sign of resistance to the existing norm, which altered the ritual protocol) emerged. Their coexistence in society implies mutually permissible consumer norms and value systems in today's consumer market in Japan.

Another finding involves the importance of confession in the Valentine's ritual process. In this "ritual of reversal" where women are liberated from the traditional gender role restrictions (Creighton 1993), the confession of romantic feeling in particular encompasses a cultural idiosyncrasy in the gendered ritual protocol. The confession is supposed to be an inexorable and exhaustive expression of the woman's secrets. According to Foucault (1988, 61), confession is "a ritual that unfolds within a power relationship," since the man to whom the confession is made is the one who requires the confession, judges it, and determines its consequences. In the context of Valentine's Day ritual, the confession entails women's demonstration of *kawaisa*, or cuteness. At the same time, confession is a moment of liberation for women while, in an aggregate sense, Valentine's Day was considered a "liberator of women," a facet of Western influences and ideology that resulted in women's movement (Creighton 1993). In terms of the gendered ritual process, this is a moment of threshold, or a liminal point, that alters the status of the woman. As a performance, playing the role of being cute acts as a transitional moment in gender power negotiations with male counterparts. Women have a serious intent of expressing affection or liking, although they appear playful, as is apt for the social drama of the Valentine's Day holiday ritual.

Lastly, Valentine's Day has been transformed from a simple instrument of love and a way to elevate a relationship to a different level, into a unique opportunity to manifest the female gender (not only giving men gifts, but also girlfriends, as in the case of *tomo-choko*, or the women themselves). Valentine's Day has become a rite to reconfirm the gender identity. In this regard, the holiday mirrors the influence of social changes on gender identity, since in the early 1990s Valentine's Day was still considered to "reaffirm traditional gender ideals and women's lower status vis-à-vis men" (Creighton 1993, 2). The holiday also is becoming a tool for self-expression with an emphasis on their own individuality and uniqueness (not just giving simple presents to themselves, but an extremely expensive present or experience, as in the case of the chocolate bath). In other words, Valentine's Day in the present period can be called not only a holiday, but among other meanings, it now is being transformed into another tool for manifesting identity in the process of searching for a new self for some Japanese women. Finally, the fact that this change started occurring since 2002, when Japan entered a new period of economic growth (and before the subsequent recession), may be also a sign of a gender shift in power in Japanese society, involving a feminization and strengthening of the animus in the society.

CONCLUSION

"In the beginning, woman was the sun." Hiratsuka Raicho, the founder of Seitōsha (Blue Stocking Society), wrote this in her manifesto in the first issue of *Seitō*, the key feminist magazine in Japan, in 1911. Whether it referred to the position of the women in the ancient matrilineal communal society or to liberated women in Raicho's mystic imagination is not clear. But it powerfully evokes the sun goddess Amaterasu. Unlike those who fought for liberty in radical movements, the role of the goddess was not to emphasize the power of females. Rather, she ensured the birth and the continuity of the society by giving the gift of the three sacred treasures to men.

But even mythologically, this was a different era. Gifts were important for their symbolism and their role in society, not for their economic worth. Today's Valentine's and White Day gifts still have symbolic significance, but their economic worth has become increasingly important, not least with the help of promotions by luxury goods marketers. Although Vaughan (1997) argues that women participate in a gift economy, while men think more in terms of the market economy, the advertisements and editorials analyzed here suggest that gifts have become both more strategic and more a matter of economic concern for women. While Valentine's Day, like Christmas, is less obligatory and mandatory than *seibo* and *chugen*, it appears to becoming more so. It still plays an important societal role, and it is in many ways empowering for women. But by making the male reciprocal occasion of White Day a month later, Japan has also reduced the male anxiety that would exist to a greater degree with a simultaneous gift-giving occasion like Valentine's Day is in the West.

NOTE

1. This chapter is a slightly edited version of the paper by Minowa, Khomenko, and Belk (2011).

REFERENCES

Amano, Masako, and Atsushi Sakurai. 1992. *Mono to on'na" no sengoshi—shintaisei, kateisei, shakaisei wo jiku ni* [Postwar history of material things and women—based on corporeality, familiarity, and sociality]. Tokyo: Yuushino.

Anderson, Laurel, and Marsha Wadkins. 1991. "Japan—A Culture of Consumption?" In *Advances in Consumer Research*, vol. 18, edited by Rebecca H. Holman and Michael R. Solomon, 129–134. Provo, UT: Association for Consumer Research.

Areni, Charles S., Pamela Kiecker, and Kay M. Palan. 1998. "Is It Better to Give than to Receive? Exploring Gender Differences in the Meaning of Memorable Gifts." *Psychology and Marketing* 15 (January): 81–109.

Atoh, Makoto, and Noriko Tsuya. 2007. *Jinkō genshō jidai no nihon shakai* [Japanese society in the age of population decline]. Tokyo: Harashobō.

Bailey, Beth L. 1988. *From Front Porch to Back Seat.* Baltimore, MD: The Johns Hopkins University Press.

Barnes, Bradley, and Maki Yamamoto. 2008. "Exploring International Cosmetics Advertising in Japan." *Journal of Marketing Management* 24 (3/4): 299–316.

Barthes, Roland. 1978. *A Lover's Discourse: Fragments.* Translated by Richard Howard. New York: Hill and Wang.

———. 1982. *Empire of Signs.* Translated by Richard Howard. New York: Hill and Wang.

Baudrillard, Jean. 1981. *For a Critique of the Political Economy of the Sign.* Translated by Charles Levin. St. Louis: Telos.

Befu, Harumi. 1968. "Gift-giving in a Modernizing Japan." *Monumenta Nipponica* 23 (3–4): 445–456.

Belk, Russell W. 1979. "Gift-giving Behavior." In *Research in Marketing*, vol. 2, edited by Jagdish Sheth, 95–126. Greenwich, CT: JAI Press.

———. 1996. "The Perfect Gift." In *Gift Giving: A Research Anthology,* edited by Cele Otnes and Richard F. Beltramini, 59–84. Bowling Green, OH: Bowling Green State University Popular Press.

Belk, Russell W., and Gregory Coon. 1993. "Gift Giving as Agapic Love: An Alternative to the Exchange Paradigm Based on Dating Experiences." *Journal of Consumer Research* 20 (December): 393–417.

Belk, Russell W., and Richard W. Pollay. 1985. "Materialism and Status Appeals in Japanese and U.S. Print Advertising." *International Marketing Review* 2 (4): 38–47.

Benedict, Ruth. 1946. *The Chrysanthemum and the Sword: Patterns of Japanese Culture.* Boston, MA: Houghton Mifflin Company.

Bourdieu, Pierre. 1984. *Distinction: A Social Critique of the Judgment of Taste.* Translated by Richard Nice. Cambridge, MA: Harvard University Press.

Carrier, James G. 1991. "Gifts, Commodities, and Social Relations: A Maussian View of Exchange." *Sociological Forum* 6 (1): 119–136.

Clammer, John. 1995a. *Difference and Modernity: Social Theory and Contemporary Japanese Society.* New York: Kegan Paul International.

———. 1995b. "Consuming Bodies: Constructing and Representing the Female Body in Contemporary Japanese Print Media." In *Women, Media and Consumption in Japan*, edited by Lise Skov and Brian Moeran, 197–219. Honolulu: University of Hawaii Press.

Creighton, Mille R. 1992. "The Depāto: Merchandising the West While Selling Japaneseness." In *Re-Made in Japan: Everyday Life and Consumer Taste in a Changing Society*, edited by Joseph J. Tobin, 42–57. New Haven: Yale University Press.

———. 1993. "'Sweet Love' and Women's Place: Valentine's Day, Japan Style." *Journal of Popular Culture* 27 (3): 1–19.

Edwards, Linda. 1988. "Equal Employment Opportunity in Japan: A View from the West." *Industrial & Labor Relations Review* 41 (January): 240–250.

Erikson, Erik H. 1982. *The Life Cycle Completed.* New York: W.W. Norton & Company.

Fischer, Eileen, and Stephen J. Arnold. 1990. "More than a Labor of Love: Gender Roles and Christmas Gift Shopping." *Journal of Consumer Research* 17 (December): 333–345.

Foucault, Michel. 1988. *The History of Sexuality, Volume I: An Introduction.* New York: Vintage Books.

Fuess, Harald. 2004. *Divorce in Japan: Family, Gender, and the State, 1600–2000.* Stanford, CA: Stanford University Press.

Gotō, Michio. 2007. "Kakusa shakai no jittai to haikei" [The status quo and background of the society with disparity]. In *Kakusa shakai to tatakau: "Doryoku, chansu, jiritsu" ron hihan* [Fighting against the society with disparity: Criticism on "effort, chance, independence" theory], edited by Michio Gotō, Shōji Yoshizaki, Akirō Takeuchi, Shintarō Nakanishi, and Norimasa Watanabe, 11–66. Tokyo: Aoki shoten.

Gould, Stephen J., and Claudia E. Weil. 1991. "Gift-giving Roles and Gender Self-concepts." *Sex Roles* 24 (9/10): 617–637.

Hashimoto, Katsuhiko. 2007. *Dankai no shōzō: warera no sengoshi* [A portrait of the baby boom generation: Our postwar history]. Tokyo: Nihon Hōsō Shuppan Kyōkai.

Hendry, Joy. 1993. *Wrapping Culture: Politeness, Presentation, and Power in Japan and Other Societies.* Oxford: Oxford University Press.

Hollander, Stanley C., Kathleen M. Rassuli, D. G. Brian Jones, and Laura Farlow Dix. 2005. "Periodization in Marketing." *Journal of Macromarketing* 25 (1): 32–41.

Hyde, Lewis. 1983. *The Gift: Imagination and the Erotic Life of Property.* London: Vintage Books.

Kano, Masanao. 1989. *Fujin, josei, onna: Josei-shi no toi* [Lady, woman, female: Questions about the history of women]. Tokyo: Iwanami shoten.

Khomenko, Olga. 2008. "Sengo no shōhin kōkoku to josei aidentiti keisei: 'mono' to 'shiawase' no kankei" [Postwar advertising of commercial goods and the formation of female gender identity: the relationship between "material things" and "happiness"]. *Nikkei kōkoku kenkyūjo hō* [Bulletin of Nikkei Advertising Research Institute] 238 (April): 15–21.

Kimura, Junko. 2001. *Kōchikushugi no shōhiron: kurisumasu shōhi wo tōshita purosesu bunseki* [Consumption theory based on Constructionism: Analysis of process through the Christmas consumption]. Tokyo: Chikura shobō.

Kimura, Junko, and Russell W. Belk. 2004. "Shōhi bunka no juyō katei no saikentō: Nihon no kurisumasu shōhi ni miru bunka no saiseisan" [The reexamination of the demand-process of consumption culture: The reproduction of culture observed in the Christmas consumption in Japan]. *Ryōtsū Kenkyū* [Journal of Marketing and Distribution] 7 (2): 39–55.

———. 2005. "Christmas in Japan: Globalization versus Localization." *Consumption, Markets and Culture* 8 (September): 325–338.

Kōnoshi, Takamitsu. 2000. "Constructing Imperial Mythology: Kojiki and nihon shoki." In *Inventing the Classics: Modernity, National Identity, and Japanese Literature*, edited by Haruo Shirane and Tomi Suzuki, 51–67. Stanford, CA: Stanford University Press.

Matsui, Takeshi. 2009. "The Social Construction of Consumer Needs: A Case Analysis of the 'Healing Boom' in Japan." In *Advances in Consumer Research,* vol. 36, edited by Ann L. McGill and Sharon Shavitt, 581. Duluth, MN: Association for Consumer Research.

Mauss, Marcel. 1954. *The Gift: Forms and Functions of Exchange in Archaic Societies*. Translated by Ian Cunnison. London: Cohen and West.

Mick, David G. 1986. "Consumer Research and Semiotics: Exploring the Morphology of Signs, Symbols, and Significance." *Journal of Consumer Research* 13 (September): 196–213.

Mick, David G., and Michelle Demoss. 1990. "Self-Gifts: Phenomenological Insights from Four Contexts." *Journal of Consumer Research* 17 (December): 322–332.

Mick, David G., and Laura R. Oswald. 2006. "The Semiotic Paradigm on Meaning in the Marketplace." In *Handbook of Qualitative Research Methods in Marketing*, edited by Russell W. Belk, 31–45. Cheltenham: Elgar.

Minami, Chieko. 1997. *Gifuto māketingu* [Gift Marketing]. Tokyo: Chikura shobō.

Minowa, Yuko, and Stephen J. Gould. 1999. "Love My Gift, Love Me or Is It Love Me, Love My Gift: A Study of the Cultural Construction of Romantic Gift Giving among Japanese Couples." In *Advances in Consumer Research*, vol. 26, edited by Eric J. Arnould and Linda M. Scott, 119–124. Provo, UT: Association for Consumer Research.

Minowa, Yuko, Olga Khomenko, and Russell W. Belk. 2011. "Social Change and Gendered Gift-Giving Rituals: A Historical Analysis of Valentine's Day in Japan." *Journal of Macromarketing* 31 (1): 44–56.

Minowa, Yuko, Russell W. Belk, and Takeshi Matsui. 2019. "Practicing Masculinity and Reciprocation in Gendered Gift-Giving Rituals: White Day in Japan, 1980–2009." In *Gifts, Romance, and Consumer Culture*, edited by Yuko Minowa and Russell W. Belk, 101–125. New York: Routledge.

Moeran, Brian, and Lise Skov. 1993. "Cinderella Christmas: Kitsch, Consumerism, and Youth Culture in Japan." In *Unwrapping Christmas*, edited by Daniel Miller, 105–133. Oxford: Oxford University Press.

Mortelmans, Dimitry, and Sofie Damen. 2001. "Attitudes on Commercialisation and Anti-commercial Reactions on Gift-Giving Occasions in Belgium." *Journal of Consumer Behaviour* 1 (2): 156–173.

Mueller, Barbara. 1992. "Standardization vs. Specialization: An Examination of Westernization in Japanese Advertising." *Journal of Advertising Research* (Jan/Feb): 15–24.

National Candy Industry Cooperative Association. 2003. White Day Official Website by the White Day Committee. http://www.candy.or.jp/whiteday/index.html.

National Institute of Population and Social Security Research. 2002. Kekkon nenji betsu ni mita miai kekkon ren'ai kekkon kōsei no suii [Changes in the composition of love and arranged marriages based on the year of marriage]. In *Dai jūnikai shussei dōkō kihon chōsa* [The twelfth basic research on birth trend]. www.ipss.go.jp/ps-doukou/j/doukou12/chapter2.html#22b.

Newman, Peter J., Jr., and Michelle R. Nelson. 1996. "Mainstream Legitimization of Homosexual Men through Valentine's Day Gift-giving and Consumption Rituals." *Journal of Homosexuality* 31 (1/2): 57–69.

Ohnuki-Tierney, Emiko. 2006. "McDonald's in Japan: Changing Manners and Etiquette." In *Golden Arches East: McDonald's in East Asia*, edited by James L. Watson, 161–182. Stanford, CA: Stanford University Press.

Ōsawa, Mari. 2003. "Japanese Government Approaches to Gender Equality Since the Mid-1990s." In *Challenges for Japan: Democracy, Finance, International Relations, Gender*, edited by Gil Latz and Izumi Koide, 111–126. Tokyo: The International House of Japan.

Otnes, Cele, and Richard Beltramini. 1996. "Gift Giving and *Gift Giving*: An Overview." In *Gift Giving: A Research Anthology*, edited by Cele Otnes and Richard Beltramini, 3–15. Bowling Green, OH: Bowling Green State University Popular Press.

Otnes, Cele, Julie A. Ruth, and Constance C. Milbourne. 1994. "The Pleasure and Pain of Being Close: Men's Mixed Feelings about Participation in Valentine's Day Gift Exchange." In *Advances in Consumer Research*, vol. 21, edited by Chris T. Allen and Deborah Roedder John, 159–164. Provo, UT: Association for Consumer Research.

Rook, Dennis W. 1985. "The Ritual Dimension of Consumer Behavior." *Journal of Consumer Research* 12 (December): 251–264.

Rugimbana, Robert, Brett Donahay, Christopher Neal, and Michael Jay Polonsky. 2003. "The Role of Social Power Relations in Gift Giving in Valentine's Day." *Journal of Consumer Behaviour* 3 (September): 63–73.

Rupp, Katherine. 2003. *Gift-Giving in Japan: Cash, Connections, Cosmologies*. Stanford, CA: Stanford University Press.

Ruth, Julie A., Cele C. Otnes, and Frederic F. Brunel. 1999. "Gift Receipt and the Reformulation of Interpersonal Relationships." *Journal of Consumer Research* 25 (March): 385–402.

Rynning, M. 1989. "Reciprocity in a Gift-Giving Situation." *The Journal of Social Psychology* 129 (6): 769–778.

Santino, Jack. 1996. *New Old Fashioned Ways: Holidays and Popular Culture*. Knoxville, TN: University of Tennessee Press.

Savigliano, Marta E. 1992. "Tango in Japan and the World Economy of Passion." In *Re-Made in Japan: Everyday Life and Consumer Taste in a Changing Society*, edited by Joseph J. Tobin, 235–252. New Haven: Yale University Press.

Schmidt, Leigh Eric. 1995. *Consumer Rites: The Buying and Selling of American Holidays*. Princeton, NJ: Princeton University Press.

Sherry, John F. 1983. "Gift Giving in Anthropological Perspective." *Journal of Consumer Research* 10 (September): 157–168.

Shinohara, Miyohei. 1996. "Cyclical Dynamics of the 50 Years of Postwar Japan: Interplay among Different Cycles." *Japanese Economic Review* 47 (1): 62–78.

Shinozaki, Takehisa. 2008. "Hizaigaku, hishūgyō, hikyūshokuchū no jakunen mugyōsha (niito) no tokuchō" [The characteristics of the young unemployed who are not in education, employment, or training (NEET)]. In *Nihonjin no ishiki to kōdō: Nihon-ban sōgōteki shakai chōsa JGSS ni yoru bunseki* [Values and behavioral patterns in Japan: An analysis based on Japanese General Social Surveys, 2000 to 2003], edited by Ichirō Tanioka, Michio Nitta, and Noriko Iwai, 163–178. Tokyo: University of Tokyo Press.

Stinson, Jeffrey, and Yulia Ochetova. 2008. "Russia Targets Halloween, Valentine's Day: Lawmakers Propose Measure to Ban Western Celebrations." *USA Today*, September 19, 13A.

Taga, Futoshi. 2006. *Otokorashisa no Shakaigaku* [Sociology of manhood]. Kyoto: Sekai shisōsha.

Tanaka, Yukiko. 1995. *Contemporary Portraits of Japanese Women*. Westport, CT: Praeger Publishers.

Tobin, Joseph J. 1992. "Introduction: Domesticating the West." In *Re-Made in Japan: Everyday Life and Consumer Taste in a Changing Society*, edited by Joseph J. Tobin, 1–41. New Haven: Yale University Press.

Tsude, Hiroshi.1989. *Kofun jidai no ō to minshū* [Emperors and the people during the tumulus period]. Tokyo: Kodansha.

Tsuno, Yoshikazu. 2009. "Barentain ni chinami chokorēto buro, Hakone Kowakien" [Chocolate bath for Valentine's Day, Hakone Kowakien]. AFP BB News. www.afpbb.com/article/life-culture/life/2569335/3766907.

Turner, Victor W. 1969. *The Ritual Process: Structure and Anti-structure*. Chicago: Aldine Publishing Company.

Ueno, Chizuko. 1990. "Henbō suru shihonsei to kafuchōsei: 'josei no shokuba shinshutsu' no shinwa to genjitsu" [Transforming capitalism and patriarchy: The myth and truth about "women's participation in the workplace"]. In *Josei to kazoku no henyō* [Transfiguration of women and family], edited by Noriko Mizuta, 17–29. Tokyo: Gakuyō Shobō.

———. 2002. *Sai no seijigaku* [Political science of disparity]. Tokyo: Iwanami Shoten.

Vaughan, Genevieve. 1997. *For-Giving: A Feminist Criticism of Exchange*. Austin, TX: Plain View Press.

Watanabe, Norimasa. 2007. "Kakusa shakai ron wo yominaosu" [Revisit the theory on society with disparity]. In *Kakusa shakai to tatakau: "Doryoku, chansu, jiritsu" ron hihan* [Fighting against the society with disparity: Criticism on "effort, chance, independence" theory], edited by Michio Gotō, Shoji Yoshizaki, Akirō Takeuchi, Shintarō Nakanishi, and Norimasa Watanabe, 11–66. Tokyo: Aoki shoten.

Watson, James L., ed. 2006. *Golden Arches East: McDonald's in East Asia*. Stanford, CA: Stanford University Press.

Witkowski, Terrence H., and D. G. Brian Jones. 2006. "Qualitative Historical Research in Marketing." In *Handbook of Qualitative Research Methods in Marketing*, edited by Russell W. Belk, 70–82. Northampton, MA: Edward Elgar Publishing, Inc.

Zhao, Xin, and Russell W. Belk. 2008. "Politicizing Consumer Culture: Advertising's Appropriation of Political Ideology in China's Social Transition." *Journal of Consumer Research* 35 (August): 231–244.

Index

About the Editors and Contributors

EDITORS

Jooyeon Rhee is assistant professor of Asian studies and comparative literature at Pennsylvania State University, University Park, and a former visiting scholar at the Research Center for Korean Studies of Kyushu University. She has published a monograph, *The Novel in Transition: Gender and Literature in Early Colonial Korea* (Cornell University Press, 2019), and has edited five special issues for peer-reviewed journals on diasporic art, socially engaged art, and popular culture. She has also published peer-reviewed journal articles and book chapters on Korean literature and film and Japanese film. Currently, she is writing a monograph on Korean and Japanese detective fiction and has initiated another research project on food literature and film in Global Korea.

Chikako Nagayama is associate professor at G30 Linguistics and Cultural Studies Program, Graduate School of Humanities, Nagoya University. Her research critically examines gender and racial relations in film, media, and society in Japan and Canada. She has taught undergraduate and graduate courses in gender studies, cultural studies, and sociology in Canadian and Japanese universities. She has also assisted Japanese-English translations of documentary films featuring Asia-Pacific War atrocity survivors and witnesses.

Eric Ping Hung Li is currently an associate professor at the Faculty of Management of the University of British Columbia—Okanagan campus. He is also the principal's research chair (Tier 2) in Social Innovation for Health Equity and Food Security and the colead, Rural Health Equity Eminence Research Cluster at the University of British Columbia—Okanagan campus.

His research includes social enterprise and social innovation, not-for-profit marketing, pro-social behavior, multicultural marketing and consumption, consumer well-being, health promotion, consumer privacy, food economy and market system, fashion and popular culture, and digital marketing and social media marketing. His work has been published and presented in a number of academic journals and conferences.[1]

CONTRIBUTORS

Russell Belk is a York University Distinguished Research Professor, Royal Society of Canada Fellow, and Kraft Foods Canada Chair in Marketing at the Schulich School of Business in York University. His research involves the extended self, meanings of possessions, collecting, gift-giving, sharing, digital consumption, and materialism. He has received a number of research and teaching awards and has over 700 publications. His work is primarily qualitative and is often conceptual, visual, and cultural. He has had visiting positions at many universities around the world and has spent a year or more in Romania, Zimbabwe, the United States, and Hong Kong with shorter visiting stints of one to three months in India, Brazil, New Zealand, Australia, Sweden, the United Kingdom, France, and Italy.

Shelley W. Chan is professor of Chinese language and cultural studies at Wittenberg University. She received her PhD from University of Colorado-Boulder, her MA from University of Wisconsin-Madison, and her BA from Hong Kong Baptist University. She is the author of *A Subversive Voice in China: The Fictional World of Mo Yan* (New York: Cambria Press, 2011) and the editor of *Mo Yan—Year 2000 Series: Close Readings on China* (Hong Kong: Ming Pao, 1999). She has published articles, translations, and book/film reviews on Chinese literature and culture in the United States, France, Germany, Australia, Sweden, China, Hong Kong, and Taiwan. Before joining Wittenberg University, she taught at Stanford University, Kalamazoo College, and Beloit College.

Su Young Choi is assistant professor of communication and media studies at Stetson University. Her research interests include digital media, environmental communication, and energy and food activism in the context of contemporary South Korea. She is currently engaging a research project about the producers of Korean vegan media and their food activism. Her work has appeared in such journals as *Media, Culture & Society*, *Environmental*

Politics, *Korean Studies*, and *Javnost—the Public: Journal of the European Institute for Communication and Culture*.

Jonathan Deschênes is associate professor of marketing at HEC Montréal. Jonathan is cofounder of the IDEOS Social Innovation Hub at HEC Montréal. He is a member of the CRISES research group on social innovation. He also cofounded a mindfulness meditation initiative at HEC Montréal and is cofounder of a mindfulness in organizations research group. His research revolves around topics related to mindfulness, responsible brands, pro-social behavior, vulnerable consumers, donation, and nonprofit organizations from a *Consumer Culture Theory* perspective. His current and past work has led him to collect data in Canada, Europe, and China, where he spent on average a month each year over the past decade.

Dandan Fang is currently a lecturer in marketing and a PhD candidate in marketing at John Molson School of Business, Concordia University, Quebec, Canada. Her research mainly focuses on consumer behavior, personality, emotion, luxury, and choice. She is also interested in topics such as gender, food, and culture. Before pursuing her doctoral degree in Canada, her educational background in linguistics and translation enabled her to contribute to three published translation of books in China. With great passion for academic research, she is recently working on her thesis and several other research projects.

Guojun (Sawyer) He is assistant professor in marketing at SKEMA Business School, Lille, France. Prior to his move to France, Sawyer started his PhD program in England and earned his doctoral degree from HEC Montréal, Quebec, Canada. Sawyer held multiple teaching/research positions at University of Bath, HEC Montréal, and Bishop's University. His research focuses on consumer culture theory, branding, material culture studies, and politics of consumption. Sawyer has dozens of peer-reviewed publications, which honor him to serve as a frequent reviewer for the *Journal of Business Research*, and for various conferences organized by the American Marketing Association, Association for Consumer Research, Consumer Culture Theory Consortium, and Administrative Sciences Association of Canada. Sawyer holds several coauthorships of research projects funded by the Social Sciences and Humanities Research Council, Canada, and is currently working on several manuscripts for other peer-reviewed journals and books.

Nathan Hopson is associate professor of Japanese history and language in the School of Foreign Languages, University of Bergen, Norway. He is currently completing a manuscript on the social history of nutrition science in modern Japan as a technology of nation building, focusing on school feeding (*gakkō kyūshoku*) and government-led nutritional activism as its central case studies. Publications on this topic include "Nutrition as National Defense: Japan's Imperial Government Institute for Nutrition, 1920-1940" (*Journal of Japanese Studies* 2019), "Ingrained Habits: The 'Kitchen Cars' and the Transformation of Postwar Japanese Diet and Identity" (*Food, Culture & Society* 2020), and "Nutritionists in Japan as a Professional Elite, 1914–1964" (*Professional Elites of Modern Japan*, forthcoming). His previous research on the social and intellectual meanings of the Tōhoku region in modern Japan includes "Takahashi Tomio's Phoenix: Recuperating Hiraizumi, 1950-71" (*Journal of Japanese Studies* 2014) and *Ennobling Japan's Savage Northeast, Tōhoku as Postwar Thought, 1945-2011* (2017).

Matt M. Husain is a postdoctoral fellow at the Faculty of Management at UBC Okanagan. His interdisciplinary research includes broad thematic areas of poverty, health inequities, transnational migration, social justice, and governance, seeking to create bridges across research, practice, and pedagogy. Dr. Husain's work is featured in a range of journal articles, book chapters, and edited volumes, as well as press coverage in *The Times Higher Education*.

Amélie Keyser-Verreault is a postdoctoral fellow affiliated with the Simone de Beauvoir Institute (Concordia University) and the Global Asia Research Center (National Taiwan University). She holds a doctoral degree in socio-cultural anthropology (Laval University) and research body politics and gender with a focus on beauty practices, maternity, aging, and resistance in East Asia. Her work has been published in academic journals such as *Feminism & Psychology*, *Taiwan Journal of Women's and Gender Studies* (女學學誌), *Taiwan Journal of Anthropology* (台灣人類學刊), *International Journal of Taiwan Studies*, and *Anthropologica*. Her research has been acknowledged by the Social Sciences and Humanities Research Council, the Fonds de recherche du Québec—Société et culture, and the MOFA, among others. She is currently working on an ethnography of the fat-activism movement in Taiwan.

Olga Khomenko is associate professor at Kyiv School of Economics. She holds a PhD in Area Studies, specifically on the history of Japan, from the University of Tokyo (2005), and an MBA from the Kyiv School of Economics (2017). Previously, she was a Fulbright visiting scholar at the Ukrainian Research Institute, Harvard University, Japan Society for Promotion of Science visiting scholar, and a Hakuho Foundation international fellow. Her research interests include the history of postwar Japan, the history of Japanese business and consumption culture, and the history of Ukraine-Japan relations with a focus on Ukrainians in the Far East and Manchuria under Japanese occupation. Khomenko wrote a book of essays on the history of Ukraine titled *From Ukraine with Love* (Gunzosha, 2014), and is the co-translator of *Modern Anthology of Ukrainian Literature* (Gunzosha, 2005), both published in Japanese.

Somin Lee is a research assistant and an undergraduate student at the University of British Columbia—Okanagan campus. She has published the manuscript "Soft Power and Nation Rebranding: The Transformation of Korean National Identity through Cosmetic Surgery Tourism" in the *International Marketing Review*. Her interests in research include marketing, Korean culture, and psychology.

Yuko Minowa is professor of marketing at the Brooklyn Campus of Long Island University, and a former visiting scholar at the Jerome A. Chazen Institute for Global Business/Graduate Business School of Columbia University. She earned her PhD from the Rutgers, the State University of New Jersey. Her research involves theoretical study of consumption phenomena and consumer behavior with a focus on consumption rituals, interpretive research methods, semiotic analysis of cultural media, and historical research in marketing and consumer behavior. Her research is published in the *Marketing Theory*, *Journal of Business Research*, *Journal of Macromarketing*, and *Consumption, Markets & Culture*, among others. She is the coeditor of *Gifts, Romance, and Consumer Culture* (with Russell Belk).

Maria Osetrova is associate professor at Moscow State Linguistic University and also a researcher at the Center for Korean Studies (Institute of Far Eastern Studies, Russian Academy of Sciences). She received her PhD in Korean Studies from Yonsei University in 2016 with a dissertation entitled "National Food and Gastronationalism in Contemporary Korea." Her main research interests include contemporary Korean culture and society (both North and South), cultural politics, food anthropology, and past and present of Russian-Korean cultural relations.

Chien-wei Pan received his PhD from the University of Edinburgh in 2020. He is interested in food writing, material culture, cross-cultural studies, gender studies, and ecocriticism. His doctoral dissertation examines different intimate relationships in Taiwanese food literature/culture and their significance in reconstructing a new Taiwanese identity. His other publications can be seen in *Routledge Companion to Literature and Food* and *Archiv orientální*.

Violetta Ravagnoli is assistant professor of East Asian history at Emmanuel College in Boston. Her research work focuses on Chinese migration and diasporas. She is responsible for the minor in Migration Studies shared among the Colleges of the Fenway. She is currently working on a comparative history of Chinese and Italian migrations to Boston since the late nineteenth century with a focus on women and foodways.

Gabriel F. Y. Tsang is assistant professor at Hong Kong Baptist University. He completed his PhD and MA degrees in Comparative Literature at King's College London and the University of Hong Kong respectively, with experiences of serving the British Postgraduate Network for Chinese Studies as president and researching at Stanford University, the National University of Singapore, and Sun Yat-sen University. His research outcomes have been widely published by peer-reviewed academic journals, such as *Journal of Narrative Theory*, *Sungkyun Journal of East Asian Studies*, *Asian Studies*, *International Journal of China Studies*, and *The Language and Semiotic Studies*.

NOTE

1. https://management.ok.ubc.ca/faculty/eli/.

Ingram Content Group UK Ltd.
Milton Keynes UK
UKHW021258100523
421523UK00009B/130

9 781793 623546